Monsters

A BEDFORD SPOTLIGHT READER

Monsters

SECOND EDITION

A BEDFORD SPOTLIGHT READER

Andrew J. Hoffman
San Diego Mesa College

bedford/st.martin's
Macmillan Learning
Boston | New York

For Bedford/St. Martin's
Vice President, Editorial, Macmillan Learning Humanities: Edwin Hill
Executive Program Director for English: Leasa Burton
Senior Program Manager: John E. Sullivan III
Executive Marketing Manager: Joy Fisher Williams
Director of Content Development, Humanities: Jane Knetzger
Executive Development Manager: Maura Shea
Editorial Assistant: William Hwang
Content Project Manager: Louis C. Bruno Jr.
Senior Workflow Project Manager: Lisa McDowell
Production Supervisor: Robin Besofsky
Media Project Manager: Rand Thomas
Manager of Publishing Services: Andrea Cava
Project Management: Lumina Datamatics, Inc.
Composition: Lumina Datamatics, Inc.
Text Permissions Manager: Kalina Ingham
Text Permissions Researcher: Mark Schaefer/Lumina Datamatics, Inc.
Photo Permissions Editor: Angela Boehler
Photo Researcher: Allison Ziebka
Director of Design, Content Management: Diana Blume
Text Design: Castle Design; Janis Owens, Books By Design, Inc.;
    Claire Seng-Niemoeller
Cover Design: William Boardman
Cover Image: Dragon Bridge, Ljubljana, Slovenia, East Europe.
    © Marco Bottigelli/Getty Images
Printing and Binding: LSC Communications

Copyright © 2020, 2016 by Bedford/St. Martin's

Manufactured in the United States of America.

5   6   24   23   22

For information, write: Bedford/St. Martin's, 75 Arlington Street, Boston,
    MA 02116

ISBN 978-1-319-05633-9

Acknowledgments
*Text acknowledgments and copyrights appear at the back of the book on pages
325–27, which constitute an extension of the copyright page. Art acknowledgments and copyrights appear on the same page as the art selections they cover.*

About The Bedford Spotlight Reader Series

The Bedford Spotlight Reader Series is a growing line of single-theme readers, each featuring Bedford's trademark care and quality. The readers in the series collect thoughtfully chosen readings sufficient for an entire writing course—about thirty-five selections—to allow instructors to provide carefully developed, high-quality instruction at an affordable price. Bedford Spotlight Readers are designed to help students make inquiries from multiple perspectives, opening up topics such as borders, food, gender, happiness, humor, money, monsters, and sustainability to critical analysis. An editorial board of a dozen compositionists whose programs focus on specific themes have assisted in the development of the series.

Bedford Spotlight Readers offer plenty of material for a composition course while keeping the price low. Each volume in the series offers multiple perspectives on the topic and its effects on individuals and society. Chapters are built around central questions such as "How Do Monsters Reflect Their Times?" and "What Is the Power of the Monster?" and so offer numerous entry points for inquiry and discussion. High-interest readings, chosen for their suitability in the classroom, represent a mix of genres and disciplines as well as a choice of accessible and challenging selections to allow instructors to tailor their approach. Each chapter thus brings to light related—even surprising—questions and ideas.

A rich editorial apparatus provides a sound pedagogical foundation. A general introduction, chapter introductions, and headnotes provide context. Following each selection, writing prompts provide avenues of inquiry tuned to different levels of engagement, from reading comprehension ("Understanding the Text"), to critical analysis ("Reflection and Response"), to the kind of integrative analysis appropriate to the research paper ("Making Connections"). An appendix, "Sentence Guides for Academic Writers," helps students with the most basic academic scenario: having to understand and respond to the ideas of others. This is a practical module that helps students develop an academic writing voice by giving them sentence guides, or templates, to follow in a variety of rhetorical situations and types of research conversations. A website for the series offers support for teaching, with a sample syllabus, additional readings, video links, and more; visit **macmillanlearning.com/spotlight**.

Preface for Instructors

Monsters seem to be everywhere, and it's easy to see why: they're fun. Young and old pile into movie theaters to watch the latest releases from Hollywood featuring both the scary and the attractive: carnivorous zombies, love-struck vampires, bloodthirsty werewolves, and even methodical serial killers. Some of the best-selling books of recent years have been those that feature monsters and murderers. Television series now use monsters not as enemies to be combated, but as protagonists saving humans from even worse evils. Pop culture analysis has become a serious focus in many college classrooms. In this setting, such monsters can be seen as manifestations of our cultural fears and desires and so can provide excellent material for deep critical analysis. In the very being of these monsters lies a sense of what we do not comprehend and yet should be familiar with: the Other, who may be another embodiment of ourselves. Could that love-struck vampire represent a longing for eternity, perhaps a love that lasts literally forever? Does that werewolf connect to primordial fears of the forest and our own animalistic past? Zombies might indeed be all around us each and every day in the form of struggles and crises that never seem to end. We fight them off valiantly for fear of succumbing to them. And Dr. Frankenstein's monster might be a repository for fears that science is running too far ahead of human ethics. Monsters therefore tie in with many of the concerns, anxieties, and desires that our students bring to class daily. By providing students with an analytical framework, *Monsters: A Bedford Spotlight Reader* helps channel that energy into productive activity, conversation, and writing.

The notion of monsters has deep roots in human history, going back as far as writing records the human imagination. Through time and across cultures, the shapes and types of monsters have varied, but monsters have always existed. In *The Epic of Gilgamesh*, which dates to 2700 BCE, the character of Enkidu is introduced as a hairy man-beast, a human who has been raised among animals.[1] His friendship with Gilgamesh elevates him to a more human status, a key distinction. Mary Shelley's *Frankenstein*, first published in 1818 with a human-like creature that sprang from Shelley's imagination, continues to be popular today because we have so many of the same anxieties about science and "playing God" with nature

---

[1]The names and titles of monsters have been standardized and formatted for clarity. [Editor's note]

as people in the early nineteenth century did. Indeed, today's scientific advancements in the fields of cloning, genetically modified organisms, and artificial intelligence, have created new threats to express in monster form. Aliens from outer space arrived in H. G. Wells's novel *The War of the Worlds* (1897), adding to our anxiety, and we haven't let go of them since, whether they're monsters intent on conquering us or intelligent beings sent to save us from ourselves. The study of these more recent monsters is no less valuable than investigations into monsters with longer histories. Indeed, studying a wide range of imaginary monsters that embody our fears and desires might help us cope with the existence of real monsters, such as the German dictator Adolf Hitler and the serial killers John Wayne Gacy, Ted Bundy, and Jeffrey Dahmer—all ordinary-seeming people who performed extraordinarily evil deeds. Could the monster inside them also be inside us, in one guise or another?

The idea of using monsters as the theme for this reader came easily for two main reasons. First, monsters are universal. They appear throughout recorded human history in all parts of the globe. The topic of monsters enables students to explore something they are already familiar with but in all likelihood have never studied in a classroom before, and as a result, students may realize that there's much they never knew about monsters—and about the possibilities for academic inquiry. Second, teaching monsters provides an opportunity to introduce students to interdisciplinary learning. *Monsters* features viewpoints based in art, literature, science, history, philosophy, sociology, psychology, religion, and even criminal justice. There's something for everyone when it comes to monsters.

Monsters offers instructors important advantages in creating and teaching a course. The textbook provides flexibility in designing a syllabus. Instructors can focus on assigning just a few readings in each chapter or can explore one chapter in depth while skipping another. The types of sources are varied: some primary texts, some pop culture texts, and some scholarly works, which introduce first-year composition students to the nature of academic discourse. The sources span genres as well, including excerpts from monographs, poems, journal articles, magazine articles, biographies, scholarly books, and science fiction. To encourage critical inquiry, each reading has three levels of questions: the first set of questions focuses on reading comprehension, to help students understand the selection's core concepts; the second set calls for students to analyze important issues in the reading; and the third set requires students to make connections between the reading and another work—either another selection in the textbook or a work outside the textbook, leading the student to do research. The last two sets of questions can be used as prompts for compositions requiring argumentation or research. In addition, *Monsters* allows instructors to take a variety of approaches in the classroom. There are opportunities to discuss personal experiences, literature, film, pop culture, history, science, and more, making *Monsters* a resource that is adaptable to instructors' individual approaches in the classroom.

Ultimately, whether students decide to focus on scientific research surrounding monsters or respond to an instructor's creative writing prompt, studying monsters will raise their awareness of the variety of human experiences and human comprehension and encourage them to ask these fundamental questions: If the monster is the Other—the thing outside ourselves—when we look at it more closely, can we see ourselves within it? If so, do we like what we see?

New to the Second Edition

New and Diverse Reading Selections

Monsters are a universal phenomenon, and this second edition reflects this universality by expanding the nature of the readings. More than a third of the readings are new to this edition, and the number of works written by women and minority writers has increased. Many of the readings have been published in scholarly journals and university press books, reflecting the growing academic interest in monster studies. Consequently, students reading this textbook are invited to partake in substantive discourse on the topic of monsters. Notable new readings include Clarisse Loughrey's "Slender Man: A Myth of the Digital Age," Carol J. Clover's "Final Girl," and Judith Halberstam's "Bodies That Splatter: Queers and Chain Saws."

New Chapter 3 Examines How Gender Affects Monsters

Gender issues are prominent in scholarly discussions of our time, and monsters are part of that conversation, too. Whether considering the gender of the monster or the gender of the monster's victims, students and instructors will have new materials to prompt discussions and raise questions. Chapter 3 includes many works new to this edition as well as relevant works retained from the first edition. In addition to Clover's and Halberstam's pioneering works in both gender studies and queer theory, this chapter also features Amy Fuller's examination of a story of mother-as-monster in "The Evolving Legend of La Llorona." Other studies of gender include Sophia Kingshill's "Reclaiming the Mermaid" and, from the first edition, Karen Hollinger's "The Monster as Woman: Two

Generations of Cat People." Classic literary works provide two canonical stories in which gender is significant: the monstrous Sirens from *The Odyssey* by Homer and the character of Caeneus from Ovid's "The Battle of the Lapiths and Centaurs." Caeneus, a Greek hero born female but turned into a male, presents an example of a transgender character from ancient mythology—a potential tie-in with Halberstam's contemporary analysis of gender and the monster. This chapter provides many opportunities to examine the role that gender plays in the conception of monsters and in the cultures that create them.

New Chapter 4 Explores the Power of the Monster
Another new chapter explores the power that monsters have over us. That power is not simply an adversarial physical power but a psychological pull. We are attracted as we are repulsed, and, at times, we're unable to turn away because the monster goes where we'd like to go but, as humans, cannot. Chapter 4 starts with Jeffrey Jerome Cohen's "Fear of the Monster Is Really a Kind of Desire," taken from his longer work, *Monster Culture (7 Theses)*. Cohen argues that we envy the monster's transgressions. Two works representing two very different vampires follow: a selection from the classic *Dracula* by Bram Stoker and "(Un)safe Sex: Romancing the Vampire" by Karen Backstein, an examination of the modern vampire myth presented in Stephenie Meyer's *Twilight* series. Elizabeth Lawrence addresses the appeal of the werewolf by examining its historical past and its still powerful place as a monster that crosses the boundaries of nature and civilization. New to the second edition is a passage from Robert Louis Stevenson's *Dr. Jekyll and Mr. Hyde*, which forces the reader to recognize that the appeal of evil may be alive deep inside each of us. Also new is a work of criticism by Erica McCrystal, "Hyde as the Monster Villain." This chapter concludes with a new work, "The Lure of Horror" by Christian Jarrett, which argues that the true power of the monster may be, ironically, to prepare us for dangers in real life. The examination of how the monster exerts its powerful influence can lead to fascinating discussions of needs, values, actions, and consequences.

Expanded Attention to Technology as a Monster
Monsters are not just in the past. Accordingly, this second edition includes new works that focus on monsters of our own (supposedly) more rational, scientific times. One product of the internet era is a new monster, introduced to readers here in Clarisse Loughrey's "Slender Man: A Myth of the Digital Age." Other new works explore the dangers of artificial intelligence

and advanced robotics. Nick Bostrom's "Get Ready for the Dawn of Super-intelligence" and Isaac Asimov's tale "Robbie" provide substance for discussions of how scientists might well be on their way to creating real-life monsters that would make Godzilla or Frankenstein's creature look like playthings. As we advance in technological capabilities, are our morals and ethics advancing as well? Monster stories can test that question.

New Literary Sources of Monsters

Of course, one way to better understand monsters is to read the original stories themselves. This second edition retains several tales from the first edition, including selections from *Beowulf,* Mary Shelley's *Frankenstein,* Bram Stoker's *Dracula,* Homer's *The Odyssey,* and Ovid's "Battle of the Lapiths and Centaurs." Two new original texts have been added. The first is Gerald Vizenor's "Naanabozho and the Gambler," a tale from the Anishinaabe people of the Great Lakes region. The story tells of a young hero's encounter with an evil presence that threatens his people. Also new to this edition is a passage from Robert Louis Stevenson's nineteenth-century thriller, *Dr. Jekyll and Mr. Hyde.* Reading the original literary work that introduced people to a particular monster is an exciting way for students to achieve a more comprehensive understanding of the subject.

New Rhetorical Situation Questions

Also new to this second edition is an expansion of the reading comprehension questions that follow each work. In addition to updating selected questions throughout the text, a new question type has been added to each of the "Understanding the Text" sections. The final question in these sections now prompts students to consider the work's rhetorical approach to the topic. The questions encourage students to reflect on issues of language, structure, form, purpose, word choice, and other issues that writers face when constructing a written text. Instructors can teach valuable composition lessons by presenting the works as models of writing for students to analyze.

New Appendix, "Sentence Guides for Academic Writers"

Following the last chapter of the book, this new appendix helps with an essential skill: working with and responding to others' ideas in writing. This practical module helps students develop an academic writing voice by giving them sentence guides, or templates, to follow in a variety of composing situations.

Acknowledgments

I would like to acknowledge the many people who made the writing of *Monsters* possible. I wish to first thank Amy Shefferd, sales representative for Macmillan Learning, and Lauren Arrant, humanities specialist at the time. For years, Amy and Lauren showed up at my office at San Diego Mesa College and pushed me to write for Bedford/St. Martin's, and I can only hope that I have repaid their trust. The editors at Bedford/St. Martin's have been outstanding, including Edwin Hill, Vice President, Editorial, Macmillan Learning Humanities; Leasa Burton, Program Director for English; and John Sullivan, Senior Program Manager for Readers and Literature, who offered me this wonderful opportunity. Without their leadership and guidance, *Monsters* would never have been published. I am grateful for the help of Louis Bruno and Vanavan Jayaraman, who guided the book through production; Kathleen Lafferty for careful copyediting; William Boardman for the cover design; and Mark Schaefer and Allison Ziebka for obtaining permissions. An enormous thank-you goes to Leah Rang, developmental editor for the first edition, who went over my work with a fine-tooth comb, corrected my errors, tightened my use of language, and generally made *Monsters* a far better textbook than it would have been without her. My gratitude also goes out to Maura Shea, developmental editor for this second edition, who has been invaluable in updating the textbook, making it an even better work than it was. William Hwang provided vital assistance in creating the second edition, including creating new entries for the annotated contents.

As the poet John Donne wrote, "No man is an island," and he could have added, "textbook writers least of all." We depend on the advice and counsel of our colleagues throughout the writing process, and I want to thank those who reviewed this edition of the book: Debra Brown, Southeastern University; Patricia DiMond, University of South Dakota; Brenna Dixon, Iowa State University; Jeanene Elder, San Diego Mesa College; Roland Finger, Cuesta College; Matthew Fledderjohann, University of Wisconsin–Madison; Erin Herold, Modesto Junior College; Charlene Keeler, California State University, Fullerton; Steven Keeton, Baton Rouge Community College; Kristine Kotecki, Hawaii Community College; Tim Melnarik, Pasadena City College; Elizabeth Nollen, West Chester University of Pennsylvania; Lesia Miller Schnur, Kennesaw State University; and Mary Williams, San Jose State University. My colleagues at San Diego Mesa College, Chris Sullivan and Jeanene Elder, offered helpful suggestions for new source material. I also wish to thank Devin Milner, librarian at San Diego Mesa College, as well as Anna Kalina and Michael Boyd, librarians at the San Diego Central Library. A library is a valuable resource, and librarians are even more valuable.

Last, I would like to thank my wife, Cathy Hoffman. I am fortunate to be married to the best teacher I've ever known. Cathy teaches at San Diego State University in the Department of Rhetoric and Writing Studies, and with more than thirty years of classroom experience, she has a keen eye for what will work with students and what will not. She was the first reviewer of nearly every word I wrote, and she steered me clear of many bad decisions. She has been my biggest critic and biggest supporter throughout this process. Without her, *Monsters* could not have been written.

Andrew J. Hoffman

From day one, our goal has been simple: to provide inspiring resources that are grounded in best practices for teaching reading and writing. For more than thirty-five years, Bedford/St. Martin's has partnered with the field, listening to teachers, scholars, and students about the support writers need. We are committed to helping every writing instructor make the most of our resources.

How Can We Help *You*?

- Our editors can align our resources to your outcomes through correlation and transition guides for your syllabus. Just ask us.

- Our sales representatives specialize in helping you find the right materials to support your course goals.

- Our *Bits* blog on the Bedford/St. Martin's English Community (**community.macmillan.com**) publishes fresh teaching ideas weekly. You'll also find easily downloadable professional resources and links to author webinars on our community site.

Visit **macmillanlearning.com** or contact your Bedford/St. Martin's sales representative to learn more.

Print and Digital Options for *Monsters*

Choose the format that works best for your course, and ask about our packaging options that offer savings for students.

Print

- *Paperback.* To order the second edition, use ISBN 978-1-319-05633-9.

Digital

- *Innovative digital learning space.* Bedford/St. Martin's suite of digital tools makes it easy to get everyone on the same page by putting student writers at the center. For details, visit **macmillanlearning.com/englishdigital**.

- *Popular e-book formats.* For details about our e-book partners, visit **macmillanlearning.com/ebooks**.

- *Inclusive Access.* Enable every student to receive their course materials through your LMS on the first day of class. Macmillan Learning's Inclusive Access program is the easiest, most affordable way to ensure all students have access to quality educational resources. Find out more at **macmillanlearning.com/inclusiveaccess**.

Your Course, Your Way

No two writing programs or classrooms are exactly alike. Our Curriculum Solutions team works with you to design custom options that provide the resources your students need. (Options below require enrollment minimums.)

- *ForeWords for English.* Customize any print resource to fit the focus of your course or program by choosing from a range of prepared topics, such as Sentence Guides for Academic Writers.
- *Macmillan Author Program (MAP).* Add excerpts or package acclaimed works from Macmillan's trade imprints to connect students with prominent authors and public conversations. A list of popular examples or academic themes is available upon request.
- *Bedford Select.* Build your own print handbook or anthology from a database of more than 900 selections, and add your own materials to create your ideal text. Package with any Bedford/St. Martin's text for additional savings. Visit **macmillanlearning.com/bedfordselect**.

Instructor Resources

You have a lot to do in your course. We want to make it easy for you to find the support you need—and to get it quickly.

Instructor Resources for *Monsters,* Second Edition, are available as PDFs that can be downloaded from **macmillanlearning.com**. In addition to suggestions for books or media to supplement the reading selections, the instructor resources feature sample syllabi.

Contents

Chapter 1   Why Do We Create Monsters?   13

Stephen King, *Why We Crave Horror Movies*   16
One of the most popular horror writers of our time examines the attraction of horror: why do we want to be scared? King argues that we need a release for the negative, uncivilized emotions that swim around in the basement of our psyche like alligators looking for fresh meat.

Mary Shelley, from *Frankenstein: The Modern Prometheus*   20
On the basis of a challenge, a young woman created a story that has thrilled and horrified people for two centuries. In this excerpt, Victor Frankenstein wakes up to find, to his horror, that his efforts to control the laws of nature have been successful: out of dead matter, he has reanimated life—and created a monster.

Susan Tyler Hitchcock, *Conception*   23
A professional writer of biographical and literary histories tells the story of the summer of 1816, when the famous poets Lord Byron and Percy Bysshe Shelley; Shelley's young lover, Mary Godwin; and Byron's doctor, John Polidori, challenged themselves to write horror stories, leading to two of the most enduring monsters in literature: Dr. Frankenstein's creature and the vampire.

Guillermo del Toro and Chuck Hogan, *Why Vampires Never Die*   35
A popular filmmaker joins with a writer of vampire novels to describe why the myths of vampires are so prevalent across time and culture: because vampires, for good or bad, connect us to the idea of eternity.

Contents by Discipline

Literature and Writing

Philosophy and Religion

Sciences

Social Sciences

Contents by Theme

History and Politics

Identity

Literature

Society and Culture

Monsters

A BEDFORD SPOTLIGHT READER

Introduction for Students

In Maurice Sendak's *Where the Wild Things Are*, young Max, wearing a wolf costume, is sent to bed without any supper. Angry and still rebellious, he sails off to the land where the wild things are, where they "roared their terrible roars, gnashed their terrible teeth, rolled their terrible eyes and showed their terrible claws." How many young children have delighted in Sendak's words and images, wanting to be like Max, leading a wild rumpus filled with monstrous creatures? For young children, Max's journey echoes many childhood desires — to break free of dependence on parents, to dance and howl at the moon, to send monsters to bed without any supper.

Our childhood experiences with monsters might also go in a different direction, far less benign than in Sendak's tale. Some monsters may come from our own imaginations: the creature in the dark corner of the closet, the monster lurking under the bed, the beast outside the window whispering our name. The irrationality of the experience is unimportant in the mind of the child: what's real is the fear. A parent telling the child the monster is gone clearly misses the point, for the monster will come back as soon as Mom or Dad leaves.

Some of the monsters that stalk our imaginations we inherited from writers of the past — even the far past. In the nineteenth century, Mary Shelley dreamed of a monster and gave us the creature from *Frankenstein*, and Bram Stoker brought together centuries of vampire mythology in the character Count Dracula. Ancient cultures from around the world have left us with a variety of monsters, such as centaurs and Sirens, griffins and rocs, cannibals and witches. Explorers of new worlds expected to find strange and marvelous monsters, and their imaginations rose to the occasion, interpreting foreign creatures as mythical beasts and conceiving fantastical figures as a way to explain the unknown. And the modern world is still creating monsters — Godzilla and space aliens, zombies and robots — filling some sort of need we have to be terrorized and amused.

Monsters are creatures not only *from* but also *of* their times. Whereas today's teachers and parents might have grown up on Sendak's tale, today's college students may associate monsters with creatures on the Yu-Gi-Oh! or Pokémon cards they played with as children. An older generation may have experienced monsters most powerfully in black-and-white films featuring Lon Chaney or Bela Lugosi. Instead of the creepy and frightening vampires of the past, today's young audience may think of the model-quality good looks of Robert Pattinson playing Edward Cullen in the *Twilight* movies. Yesterday's villain is today's hero, and recognizing such shifts can enrich critical inquiry into the representations of monsters, opening up questions about good and evil, and about monsters' roles in a cultural moment.

Recognizing the evolution from villain to hero is not to say today's monsters are without teeth. There are plenty of evil vampires, rapacious werewolves, creepy zombies, and other creatures to keep us checking under the bed and behind the door, even in the twenty-first century. The need to express our fears, to make sense of a world that so often seems in chaos and confusion, has hardly disappeared. Into this need steps the monster as an embodiment of all that is unmanageable around us. We might call this repository of our fears the Other, and no matter what monstrous shape the Other assumes, it is not going away any more than the fear is going away. We are in an era in which genetically modified foods evoke the specter of Dr. Frankenstein working to give life to his creature; when the relentless buzz of everyday life threatens to turn us into zombies; when flesh-eating bacteria, Ebola, and AIDS — resisting the best efforts of modern medicine — duplicate the destruction of a vampire or werewolf; when advances in computer technology threaten to surpass our ability to understand or control the machines we create; and when horrific crimes evoke images and memories of the most terrible monsters of all, human beings. Monsters are arguably as much a part of our collective consciousness as ever.

Why Should I Study Monsters?

You may be tempted to dismiss the study of monsters in the college classroom if you approach monsters solely as a frivolous pop culture fad or the product of ignorant superstition. But monsters have long lived in the minds of humans, going back to the dawn of recorded civilization, and anything that is such an integral part of human culture deserves study. There must be, after all, a reason monsters have appeared across cultures and times. Stories of werewolves, for instance, can be traced to ancient Greece; stories of vampire-like creatures have been around for thousands of years all around the world. More recently, new monsters, such as Godzilla and space aliens (both friendly and hostile), have been created to give expression to newfound fears and anxieties. Monsters vary in many aspects but also have many qualities in common, which should only enhance our curiosity about the subject.

Monsters are not merely entertainment. The study of monsters is the study of what it means to be human in a world that provides much to fear and avoid. Since time immemorial, people have had to deal with fear: fear of the wild, fear of the unknown, even fear of each other. Monsters may be a repository for much that is negative in the human experience. In this way, monsters provide us with the opportunity to connect to important issues of psychology, science, medicine, gender, culture, art, and religion. Indeed, much of the research about monsters is published in the scholarly journals of those fields. There are also a growing number of peer-reviewed scholarly journals that focus on monsters exclusively, such as the *Journal of Dracula Studies*, *Golem: Journal of Religion and Monsters*, *Monsters and the Monstrous*, and the *Irish Journal of Gothic and Horror Studies*, to name a few. In addition, there are many scholarly books written about monsters, as well as more general audience-oriented books, websites, blogs, and magazines. It's rather hard to escape the reach of monsters!

Many times in composition courses, the instructor will teach several themes in a term, often from a textbook that contains many different topics to choose from. Other times, there may be no theme at all, as the instructor wants the students to come up with their own writing topics. So why focus on a single theme? First and foremost, having a single theme allows you to explore the topic in much greater detail than if you worked on multiple themes. There is a sustained involvement in the topic — in this case, monsters. Rather than picking up only a superficial impression of the theme — which is often quite complex — you can acquire a deeper, more

Max and the Wild Things from Maurice Sendak's classic children's book, *Where the Wild Things Are* (1963).
Photofest

substantial understanding of the topic. When you do that, you are able to write more serious, sophisticated papers, which can be more informative and interesting for any reader. Such assignments allow you to practice and hone your critical reading, thinking, and writing skills. You might ask, then, "Why monsters? Why not something else?" Good question.

Monsters Are Relevant Figures in Society, History, and Culture

Monsters appear in virtually every culture and time in the world. The particular details of monsters may be different — how they were created, what they look like, what they do — but there are always monsters. That alone makes the topic important and worthy of investigation. The psychology behind the creation of monsters and monster myths is important as well. What do the monsters tell us about ourselves? When we examine monsters, we're really examining human nature and experience.

Monsters Are a Diverse, Multicultural Phenomenon

Throughout many times and places, monsters have made their appearance. From the centaurs and Sirens of the classical Western world, to the giant roc of the Middle Eastern tales of Sinbad the Sailor, to the stories of mermaids and mermen that have appeared all around the world, monsters have an extensive global history. They can be as interesting in their diversity as the cultures that spawn them. Even the same type of monster might take on different characteristics to reflect different times. The history of vampire myths alone shows an evolution, as vampires have progressed from lurid cannibals arising from the grave to feed on humans to glamorous heroes who save people.

Monsters Are Extremely Personal

Even though every culture has its own variations of monsters, each individual has his or her unique relationship to them. This may often be connected to childhood experiences, perhaps through comic books, video games, television shows, websites, movies, or Halloween costumes — even the antics of an older brother or sister who took a certain sadistic delight in donning a werewolf mask and leaping out of the closet. Some monsters may be deeply personal and unique — an unnamed, unshaped Thing that haunts the darkness. Others may be so popular as to spawn their own fan clubs. One monster may be particularly loathsome or frightening to one person, but it may hardly strike a chord in another. As an adult, you might have put aside the fear of monsters long ago — at least of the jumping-out-of-the-closet kind — only to discover new monsters that might go unnamed though not unfelt.

The Study of Monsters Is an Interdisciplinary Pursuit

An entire cottage industry has been created around the study of monsters. Indeed, the advent of the discipline of monster studies — and the associated scholarly publications in which research on monsters is published — no doubt springs from the recognition that monsters are complex and important phenomena. After all, if monsters are reflections of us — and humans are notoriously complex already — the monsters we create and fill with meaning are complex, too. What we fear, what we avoid, and what we don't know how to assimilate in our lives can all give rise to monsters. Monsters are discussed in many different areas of study — from art, literature, and history to psychology and science. This interdisciplinary approach to studying monsters may help you see possibilities for further study in your own field.

For instance, an art history major could explore the representations of monsters in classical paintings and sculpture, or a psychology major might examine the emotional human dynamic reflected in certain monsters. A gender studies student might focus on why the genre of the horror film frequently uses the woman as victim or how sexual orientation is presented and manipulated in monster stories. A science student might examine how and why certain physical or biological phenomena could lead people to think they have witnessed the actions of a monster. You may not wish to pursue further study of monsters after your composition course is over, but you will have gained some valuable insight into and experience with processes of inquiry, research, and critical thinking that will be useful in any course of study.

The In-Depth Study of Monsters Will Give You Discourse Knowledge
All intellectual endeavors involve participation in an ongoing conversation called a *discourse*. It is not the same type of conversation you might have with a roommate or a group of friends. Rather, it is the type of conversation that takes place among many people over many years using various methods of expression, including books, essays, articles, speeches, and more. All college students are expected to develop the skills to absorb, assimilate, and synthesize information gathered from many different sources within a variety of discourses and to find their own voice within them. That is a basic pattern in the production of knowledge. This book offers a range of interrelated readings focusing on the discourse about monsters. Learning how to evaluate and analyze that discourse and how to shape your own voice and perspective within it is an important part of your college education.

How Is This Book Organized?

Monsters is organized as a progression of topics, starting with the creation of monster myths; moving on to an examination of the different aspects of monsters, including their form, history, and power; and concluding with the human monsters that prey on us in real life. The chapters feature primary texts (the stories that first gave us some popular monsters), general-interest articles from books and magazines, and scholarly research from peer-reviewed journals. The variety in types of sources offers different levels of analysis from various perspectives. The selections represent a span of nearly three thousand years — from a passage from Homer's *The Odyssey* to more contemporary discussions of vampires in Hollywood blockbusters like the *Twilight* movies — which makes the text relevant, easy to use, informative, and fun.

Chapter 1: Why Do We Create Monsters?

Monsters are not self-made, but are instead human creations, developed at specific times in specific places. Chapter 1 introduces you to the origins of monsters: why we create them and what that says about us and our cultural moment. For instance, Mary Shelley created her monster in the midst of exciting and disturbing scientific experimentation to highlight the potential dangers of scientific knowledge and of "playing God." Although of a different era, Godzilla also represents the dangers of modern science: the monster arose from the radioactive ashes of post–World War II Japan to embody the devastation, both physical and psychological, experienced by that nation as a result of two atomic blasts. Other monsters have been resurrected, invented, and reinvented — such as vampires, werewolves, zombies, and new creatures like Slender Man — to provide a catharsis or to give form to a shared, lived experience. Learning about the creation of monsters may lead you to ask further questions — for instance, why certain monsters, such as the vampire or the creature in *Frankenstein*, have had such strong staying power in our imaginations, but others, such as the Chimera and centaur, no longer resonate today.

Chapter 2: How Do Monsters Reflect Their Times?

To explore a monster is to explore the time and place that created it. If the monster can embody our fears, it can tell us what those fears are — whether it is fear of the unknown, fear of the different, or fear of the confusing. For much of human history, much of the world was unknown. When Aztecs witnessed Spaniards on horseback, bands of Vikings sailed in Scandinavian waters, or Puritan colonists settled in remote villages in the New World, they encountered many things they had never seen before. They described unusual animals they saw as monstrous and labeled people who didn't fit their mold as half-human demons or even witches. Their accounts may seem like tall tales to us today, but their monster stories tell us about the times in which they lived. Monsters in many ways represent their times and, indeed, our own time. Although we might not fear a man on horseback, a robot operating with superintelligence may represent a new fear of our own creation.

Chapter 3: How Does Gender Affect the Monster?

Gender — its roles, its expectations, even its physical nature — has been brought into question in today's world, and monsters reflect that, too. Gender affects the monster in terms of both the monster and its victim. Chapter 3 begins with the story of a woman who failed to fulfill a traditional gender role for females: being a self-sacrificing mother. Instead, La Llorona, the Wailing Woman, killed her own children because of a lover, and now she wanders the earth, futilely searching for them. Another traditional gender role, the woman as temptress, is seen in monster figures such as Sirens and mermaids, who lure men to their doom. The gender of the victim can be important, too. For example, in typical slasher film narratives, women are the targets of the monster, but that dynamic can be flipped on its head when the woman becomes the aggressor. Queer theory investigates how the physical body becomes part of the monster narrative, forcing the reader to examine his or her own assumptions about monsters, victims, sexuality, and gender itself.

Chapter 4: What Is the Power of the Monster?

Despite the inherent danger in monsters, they have an allure. We are drawn to them because they have something that we lack: complete and utter freedom from the rules, laws, and concepts of sin and shame that govern our own behavior. This freedom is what fuels the monster's power and allows it to push the boundaries of what is possible. As humans, how often might we succumb to the temptation of wanting to be more than we are? Sometimes we just want to ignore the "Thou Shalt Not" commands that have existed in some form in all human societies across time. Monsters do not recognize or acknowledge limits. Analyzing how we desire to be like these dangerous figures can reveal our own values and ambitions.

Chapter 5: Is the Monster within Us?

Sometimes *we* are the monsters. How can we account for the actions of human monsters such as serial killers, murderous autocrats, cannibals, and others who do things that go far beyond the realm of what is typically termed "human"? With these examples, we find the Other — that unknown, fearsome presence — in ourselves. No longer can the monster be seen as a perverse product of nature or even a result of science gone terribly wrong. The monster is in us, and there's something about that awareness that is likely to be more disturbing than any thoughts we might have about werewolves or zombies.

What Do We Mean by Critical Reading, Thinking, and Writing?

You have already attained a strong level of competence in the ability to read, or you wouldn't be taking this course. However, you can develop and hone your skills further. At the college level, when instructors talk about reading, they're actually talking about a much more proactive approach to reading than what you might do casually on your own. The term frequently used is *critical reading*. The word *critical* does not simply mean "fault-finding" as it often does in everyday conversation. A better sense of the word is that we are questioning what we read. Critical reading is not only about comprehension — that's just a first step. Many times texts have some vocabulary words you don't know. *Monsters* includes definitions of some unusual, difficult, or technical terms, but if you encounter others that you don't know, look them up in a dictionary. Similarly, you may find allusions to works, writers, characters, cultures, or monsters that you have never heard of before. Do some research on your own so that you are able to understand more fully what the author is trying to communicate. Most texts will reveal more if you give them a second or third reading. Only then will you be truly ready to ask questions.

One of the features of this textbook is that there are three sets of questions with each selection. The first group is called "Understanding the Text." You may use these questions to make sure you understand the selection and can recognize the key ideas in it. Your instructor may also have additional reading comprehension questions.

When you read a text critically, you will be asking questions of the text as well as responding to it. Depending on the text itself, you may question its form and the author's use of language. Why is the text written the way it is and not in other ways? Why did the author choose a particular word and not another? You also might ask questions about the attitude present in the text. Is the author biased in favor of or against an issue? Is the author neutral? How is that position revealed? Whenever you have a question or make a particular observation, record your comments in the margins of your textbook, on note cards, on paper, or in a computer file. Your composition instructor may have additional ideas on how to read critically, but a common theme is that a critical reader is an *active* reader. Do not see yourself as a passive consumer of the text; instead, get actively involved in what you're reading — exploring, pushing, and questioning as you go.

Critical thinking is a term that is frequently used in college classrooms. When you read critically, you're thinking critically about a particular text and using reading strategies such as annotation to help you work with the text. But critical thinking can involve much more. When you think critically, you may ask questions that involve your own reactions to the text, or you may extend your inquiry further and ask questions of the text and its relationship to other selections you've read in this book. Even more, you may respond to the text by doing research beyond this book and then asking additional questions. For example, after reading one of the selections here, you might ask a question such as "What does this reading reveal about our cultural attitudes toward this type of monster?" or "How does the author's argument about the significance of this monster compare to the origin story of the monster from a classical text or a Hollywood movie interpretation of it?" Then, to answer your questions and support your own ideas about the topic, you might log on to your campus library's website to research other discussions of the monster or other representations of it.

So, along with the "Understanding the Text" questions, there are two sets of writing questions that may be used as prompts for writing assignments. The "Reflection and Response" questions focus on the issues present in the text. They require critical reading skills and analytical thinking. The "Making Connections" questions require not only critical reading and analytical thinking but also that you engage multiple texts. Sometimes the other texts are from this book or refer to stories or films you may have read or seen on your own, but other times the questions require you to do library research. Your instructor may assign only one type of question or both types, depending on his or her preference. However, even if the questions are not assigned, reading them can provide useful ways for you to approach and think through the selection.

Writing in college is different from writing that you may do elsewhere. When you write in college, you're creating what can be called *academic writing*. Academic writing is an opportunity to engage with an idea, develop an argument, examine an idea from all sides, present a new approach that will change a reader's perspective, fit into a conversation, and fully learn and understand the material and its context. Whether expository or persuasive, academic writing is typically more formal in tone and style than other writing, addresses serious topics, and is usually less personal. You are expected to develop your ideas and the ideas of others to a level where they can be taken seriously by any reader. That doesn't necessarily mean your opinions won't be present in your writing, but you will be required to support your ideas with evidence. In terms of types of support, instructors vary in how much importance or value they place on personal experience: some may encourage you to bring your own life experiences into a composition; others may require that you use only the text and library research. Generally, though, academic writing demands a high level of competence in the use of language. Grammar errors, misspellings, and awkward sentences negatively affect the quality of your compositions. All instructors have certain expectations about the structure of each composition and its development. The particulars will vary from instructor to instructor, but in many cases, academic writing is marked by the use of logic and reason and by ideas presented in a clear and orderly fashion.

All the questions following each reading ask you to write academically — to use a tone and style that follow the conventions of academic discourse, to use logic and reason to present and support your arguments, and to synthesize ideas from texts and your own understanding of them to offer an interesting or unique perspective on a topic. Some questions may be answered in a few short sentences, but other questions will require longer compositions that could even be adapted into multimedia presentations with visuals, film clips, and more. Studying the questions provided after each reading might even inspire you to ask and answer your own questions about the selections and monsters in general.

My ultimate goal is that you enjoy your experience with this book as you explore the worlds of vampires, zombies, werewolves, mermaids, centaurs, and many others. Learning to write compositions can sometimes seem an arduous task, and often in college, students read texts they are not interested in at all. With *Monsters* as your guide, I hope neither of these occurs, and I hope you find that the subject of monsters can be fun and educational at the same time. Happy studies!

Andrew J. Hoffman
San Diego Mesa College

P.S. Don't be afraid to use a night-light.

Marco Bottigelli/Getty Images

1 | Why Do We Create Monsters?

With our current culture's emphasis on reason and science, the notion of a monster seems quaint, possibly romantic — harking back to a time when people believed more readily in fantastic phenomena. Yet the allure of monsters today is still strong. Whether it is the vampire, the zombie, the werewolf, Frankenstein's creature, or some other being of a mystical but threatening character, the twenty-first century does not seem to lack for monsters. Perhaps, as many psychologists, historians, social critics, and others have suggested, we need monsters to symbolize our fears. If so, we need to investigate how monsters encapsulate those fears and what those fears suggest about us and the values of our time. Vampires are as popular today as ever, yet the vampire stories told by Stephenie Meyer are a far cry from the one written by Bram Stoker in the nineteenth century. The zombie enjoys wide popularity these days, but its close cousin, the mummy, no longer resonates within the popular imagination. Why is the brain-eating zombie an appropriate monster for today's fears but a suffocating mummy is not?

Monsters reflect the anxieties of the cultures that create them. In analyzing these monsters, we can learn something about the people of those periods. Stephen King, perhaps the most famous and prolific horror writer today, explains the attraction we have to being frightened. We cannot always be calm and rational because inside all of us is the inner lunatic who needs to be let out once in a while to race about and howl at the moon. Mary Shelley anticipated the great upheavals that science and industry would bring to the nineteenth century. She tells the story of Dr. Victor Frankenstein, who builds a monster from the various parts of dead people. Reanimated by the power of electricity, the creature's awakening horrifies even its own creator. As Shelley would later explain, her creative inspiration came not out of a void, but out of chaos: the chaos of her time. Susan Tyler Hitchcock describes the political, social, scientific, personal, and even environmental anxieties of the particular time in which Shelley wrote

photo: Marco Bottigelli/Getty Images

Frankenstein. A pair of contemporary filmmakers, Guillermo del Toro and Chuck Hogan, examine the enduring popularity of the vampire myth, which goes back to ancient times and is arguably as strong in modern imaginations as ever. They point out that the vampire connects us to the concept of eternity. Chuck Klosterman examines the zombie phenomenon and argues that the zombie is a suitable metaphor for the obstacles we must conquer just to get through our daily lives. Peter H. Brothers examines the influences behind the making of the movie *Godzilla* in post–World War II Japan. Director Ishirô Honda created a monster that seemed to encapsulate the fears of a nation that experienced the trauma of atomic warfare and the humiliation of defeat. The monster, with its destructive potential, serves as a symbol of science — and human ambition — run amok. Clarisse Loughrey discusses how the internet and other new digital technologies have given rise to a new monster — Slender Man — a character whose roots are in older tales but who comes with disturbing new twists. Examining threats at a national level, Stephen T. Asma argues that events such as the terrorist attacks of September 11, 2001, and the Great Recession drive our need for monsters. The promise is that if we can control the monster, we can control our lives.

The monster is a response to the world around us, and since the world never stops bringing crises, threats, and uncertainties, our need for monsters doesn't end either. Sometimes we modify a long-standing monster such as the vampire to fit the psychological needs of our times; other times we construct a new monster, as Mary Shelley did in the nineteenth century or internet users have done today. Whatever the case, these monsters are sure to both frighten and, ironically, reassure us that there may be a good reason for our fears after all.

Read for Fri.

Why We Crave Horror Movies

Stephen King

Stephen King is one of the most popular and prolific horror writers of our time. His works include *Carrie* (1974), *The Shining* (1977), *The Dead Zone* (1979), and *Misery* (1987), all of which have been made into popular movies. A native of Maine, King began writing for his college newspaper at the University of Maine. Later, he wrote short stories for men's magazines and received his first big break when he published *Carrie* in 1974. The following essay, which initially appeared in *Playboy* magazine in January 1981, is an excerpt from King's book *Danse Macabre* (1981). King argues that the horror movie performs a helpful task, taking on feelings, urges, and impulses that don't fit neatly into the rational, reasonable, and sane parts of our lives. Indeed, King proposes that the horror movie gives "psychic relief" because in most parts of our lives, "simplicity, irrationality and even outright madness" are so rarely allowed. As such, the horror film functions like a pressure-release valve for the inner monster we must typically repress.

I think that we're all mentally ill; those of us outside the asylums only hide it a little better — and maybe not all that much better, after all. We've all known people who talk to themselves, people who sometimes squinch their faces into horrible grimaces when they believe no one is watching, people who have some hysterical fear — of snakes, the dark, the tight place, the long drop . . . and, of course, those final worms and grubs that are waiting so patiently underground.

When we pay our four or five bucks and seat ourselves at tenth-row center in a theater showing a horror movie, we are daring the nightmare.

Why? Some of the reasons are simple and obvious. To show that we can, that we are not afraid, that we can ride this roller coaster. Which is not to say that a really good horror movie may not surprise a scream out of us at some point, the way we may scream when the roller coaster twists through a complete 360 or plows through a lake at the bottom of the drop. And horror movies, like roller coasters, have always been the special province of the young; by the time one turns 40 or 50, one's appetite for double twists or 360-degree loops may be considerably depleted.

We also go to re-establish our feelings of essential normality; the horror movie is innately conservative, even reactionary. Freda Jackson as the horrible melting woman in *Die, Monster, Die!* confirms for us that no matter how far we may be removed from the beauty of a Robert Redford or a Diana Ross, we are still light-years from true ugliness.

And we go to have fun. 5

Ah, but this is where the ground starts to slope away, isn't it? Because this is a very peculiar sort of fun, indeed. The fun comes from seeing others menaced—sometimes killed. One critic has suggested that if pro football has become the voyeur's version of combat, then the horror film has become the modern version of the public lynching.

It is true that the mythic "fairy-tale" horror film intends to take away the shades of gray. . . . It urges us to put away our more civilized and adult penchant for analysis and to become children again, seeing things in pure blacks and whites. It may be that horror movies provide psychic relief on this level because this invitation to lapse into simplicity, irrationality and even outright madness is extended so rarely. We are told we may allow our emotions a free rein . . . or no rein at all.

If we are all insane, then sanity becomes a matter of degree. If your insanity leads you to carve up women like Jack the Ripper or the Cleveland Torso Murderer, we clap you away in the funny farm (but neither of those two amateur-night surgeons was ever caught, heh-heh-heh); if, on the other hand, your insanity leads you only to talk to yourself when you're under stress or to pick your nose on your morning bus, then you are left alone to go about your business . . . though it is doubtful that you will ever be invited to the best parties.

The potential lyncher is in almost all of us (excluding saints, past and present; but then, most saints have been crazy in their own ways), and every now and then, he has to be let loose to scream and roll around in the grass. Our emotions and our fears form their own body, and we recognize that it demands its own exercise to maintain proper muscle tone. Certain of these emotional muscles are accepted—even exalted—in civilized society; they are, of course, the emotions that tend to maintain the status quo of civilization itself. Love, friendship, loyalty, kindness—these are all the emotions that we applaud, emotions that have been immortalized in the couplets of Hallmark cards and in the verses (I don't dare call it poetry) of Leonard Nimoy.°

When we exhibit these emotions, society showers us with positive 10 reinforcement; we learn this even before we get out of diapers. When, as children, we hug our rotten little puke of a sister and give her a kiss, all the aunts and uncles smile and twit and cry, "Isn't he the sweetest little thing?" Such coveted treats as chocolate-covered graham crackers often follow. But if we deliberately slam the rotten little puke of a sister's fingers

Leonard Nimoy (1931–2015): American actor best known for playing Spock in the original *Star Trek* television series. He later turned to poetry, music, and other artistic pursuits.

in the door, sanctions follow—angry remonstrance from parents, aunts and uncles; instead of a chocolate-covered graham cracker, a spanking.

But anticivilization emotions don't go away, and they demand periodic exercise. We have such "sick" jokes as, "What's the difference between a truckload of bowling balls and a truckload of dead babies?" (You can't unload a truckload of bowling balls with a pitchfork . . . a joke, by the way, that I heard originally from a ten-year-old.) Such a joke may surprise a laugh or a grin out of us even as we recoil, a possibility that confirms the thesis: If we share a brotherhood of man, then we also share an insanity of man. None of which is intended as a defense of either the sick joke or insanity but merely as an explanation of why the best horror films, like the best fairy tales, manage to be reactionary, anarchistic, and revolutionary all at the same time.

> "The mythic horror movie . . . deliberately appeals to all that is worst in us."

The mythic horror movie, like the sick joke, has a dirty job to do. It deliberately appeals to all that is worst in us. It is morbidity unchained, our most base instincts let free, our nastiest fantasies realized . . . and it all happens, fittingly enough, in the dark. For those reasons, good liberals often shy away from horror films. For myself, I like to see the most aggressive of them—*Dawn of the Dead*, for instance—as lifting a trap door in the civilized forebrain and throwing a basket of raw meat to the hungry alligators swimming around in that subterranean river beneath.

Why bother? Because it keeps them from getting out, man. It keeps them down there and me up here. It was Lennon and McCartney who said that all you need is love, and I would agree with that.

As long as you keep the gators fed.

Understanding the Text

1. King states that when we see a horror film, we are "daring the nightmare" (par. 2). What does he mean by that?

2. King uses the metaphor of "emotional muscles" that need exercise (par. 9). Some of these emotions are seen as positive in that they maintain civilization. What are some of the emotions that don't maintain the social status quo, and why do they still need to be exercised?

3. King relies heavily on metaphors and allusions to create a humorous tone while making his argument. What is the advantage of approaching the topic of horror in this way?

4. How would you describe the tone King uses in this article? What advantage does this give him in addressing his subject matter? In what ways might the tone limit what King does?

Reflection and Response

5. Consider your own experience with horror films. Are you a fan of horror or not? If so, what about horror attracts you, and if not, what repels you? Now consider your response in light of King's statement "We also go [to horror films] to re-establish our feelings of essential normality" (par. 4). Does your response to horror connect to your feelings of normality? If so, how?

6. King argues that we have some emotions that are affirming of civilization and its norms and others that are not — or, "anticivilization emotions," as he terms them (par. 11). Identify and analyze how these negative emotions are "exercised" (to use King's metaphor, par. 9) in your own life experiences beyond watching horror films.

Making Connections

7. Compare King's essay with Chuck Klosterman's "My Zombie, Myself: Why Modern Life Feels Rather Undead" (p. 39). How does Klosterman differ from King in his analysis of the need for horror in people's lives? In what ways are the two in agreement? Explain your responses using specific textual support from both essays.

8. King reports that one critic said, "the horror film has become the modern version of the public lynching" (par. 6). King continues the metaphor when he claims, "The potential lyncher is in almost all of us" (par. 9). Do some research on the history of lynching in the United States. After your research, argue whether the comparison between public lynching and horror films is either fair and accurate or overdone and exaggerated. Defend your response.

From Frankenstein: The Modern Prometheus

Mary Shelley

Mary Wollstonecraft Godwin was born in 1797 to celebrated radical thinkers William Godwin and Mary Wollstonecraft, the pioneering feminist writer who died just days after Mary was born. Godwin recognized his daughter's intellect and gave her a rich education, raising her to follow his liberal political ideals and become a writer. However, he withdrew his support when sixteen-year-old Mary became attached to the twenty-one-year-old poet Percy Bysshe Shelley, who was already famous and married to another woman. In 1816, Mary traveled with Shelley to Geneva, where she answered a writing challenge with one of the most enduring works and characters of Western literature. Her creation, *Frankenstein*, was first published in 1818 and has lived on in the popular imagination ever since. In this passage, after almost two years of hard work in his laboratory, Victor Frankenstein beholds his own creation, only to react with horror at what he has done.

It was on a dreary night of November that I beheld the accomplishment of my toils. With an anxiety that almost amounted to agony, I collected the instruments of life around me, that I might infuse a spark of being into the lifeless thing that lay at my feet. It was already one in the morning; the rain pattered dismally against the panes, and my candle was nearly burnt out, when, by the glimmer of the half-extinguished light, I saw the dull yellow eye of the creature open; it breathed hard, and a convulsive motion agitated its limbs.

How can I describe my emotions at this catastrophe, or how delineate the wretch whom with such infinite pains and care I had endeavored to form? His limbs were in proportion, and I had selected his features as beautiful. Beautiful! Great God! His yellow skin scarcely covered the work of muscles and arteries beneath; his hair was of a lustrous black, and flowing; his teeth of a pearly whiteness; but these luxuriances only formed a more horrid contrast with his watery eyes, that seemed almost of the same color as the dun-white sockets in which they were set, his shriveled complexion and straight black lips.

The different accidents of life are not so changeable as the feelings of human nature. I had worked hard for nearly two years, for the sole purpose of infusing life into an inanimate body. For this I had deprived myself of rest and health. I had desired it with an ardor that far exceeded moderation; but now that I had finished, the beauty of the dream vanished, and breathless horror and disgust filled my heart. Unable to endure the aspect of the being I had created, I rushed out of the room and continued a long time traversing my bed-chamber, unable to compose my mind to sleep. At length lassitude succeeded to the tumult I had before endured, and I threw myself on the bed in my clothes, endeavoring to seek a few moments of forgetfulness. But it was in vain; I slept, indeed, but I was disturbed by the wildest dreams. I thought I saw Elizabeth, in the bloom of health, walking in the streets of Ingolstadt.° Delighted and surprised, I embraced her, but as I imprinted the first kiss on her lips, they became livid with the hue of death; her features appeared to change, and I thought that I held the corpse of my dead mother in my arms; a shroud enveloped her form, and I saw the grave-worms crawling in the folds of the flannel. I started from my sleep with horror; a cold dew covered my forehead, my teeth chattered, and every limb became convulsed; when, by the dim and yellow light of the moon, as it forced its way through the window shutters, I beheld the wretch — the miserable monster whom I had created. He held up the curtain of the bed; and his eyes, if eyes they may be called, were fixed on me. His jaws opened, and he muttered some inarticulate sounds, while a grin wrinkled his cheeks. He might have spoken, but I did not hear; one hand was stretched out, seemingly to detain me, but I escaped and rushed downstairs. I took refuge in the courtyard belonging to the house which I inhabited, where I remained during the rest of the night, walking up and down in the greatest agitation, listening attentively, catching and fearing each sound as if it were to announce the approach of the demoniacal corpse to which I had so miserably given life.

> "By the dim and yellow light of the moon, as it forced its way through the window shutters, I beheld the wretch — the miserable monster whom I had created."

Oh! No mortal could support the horror of that countenance. A mummy again endued with animation could not be so hideous as that wretch. I had gazed on him while unfinished; he was ugly then, but when those muscles and joints were rendered capable of motion, it became a thing such as even Dante could not have conceived.

Ingolstadt: a city in Germany along the Danube River.

Understanding the Text

1. Immediately after he animates the creature, Frankenstein calls the act a "catastrophe" (par. 2). Why? Examine the details of Frankenstein's description of the creature to support your answer.

2. Frankenstein awakens from a bad dream only to confront the reality of his creation. What effect does Shelley create by juxtaposing the dream with the curious monster's invasion of Frankenstein's bedchamber?

3. Why does Frankenstein call his own creation a "demoniacal corpse" (par. 3)? If his creation is a demon, what does that say about Frankenstein as a creator?

4. Sometimes authors will use allusions — references to other creative works, events, or people — to advance an idea. This passage concludes with Dr. Frankenstein referencing "Dante" (par. 4). Who was Dante, and how does this allusion further develop the horror of Dr. Frankenstein's observations?

Reflection and Response

5. Analyze Frankenstein's immediate repulsion toward his creation. What is the basis of his repulsion? Note that Frankenstein claims he had "selected [the creature's] features as beautiful" (par. 2). What is the relationship between beauty and horror? Cite specific passages from the text to support your position.

6. Frankenstein's nightmare begins with a healthy Elizabeth (his love interest), who then turns into the corpse of his dead mother in his arms. How does this dream sequence relate to Frankenstein's actions in giving life to the creature?

7. How does the creature act? Does the lack of aggression surprise you, given the typical popular culture depictions of Frankenstein's monster? Describe the action in this passage from the point of view of the monster.

Making Connections

8. In his essay "Monsters and the Moral Imagination" (p. 59), Stephen T. Asma argues that there are cultural uses for monsters — that they somehow reflect the anxieties of their time. Investigate the culture and time in which Mary Shelley was writing (1816) and argue how time and place came to influence the story of Frankenstein.

9. Compare the passage of the creature's awakening with film depictions of the same. Some choices include the classic movie *Frankenstein* (1931), an updated version of *Frankenstein* (1994), and an even more recent take on the story, *I, Frankenstein* (2014). What differences do you see from the original story by Shelley, and what is the significance of those differences?

Conception

Susan Tyler Hitchcock

Susan Tyler Hitchcock is a book editor for the National Geographic Society and an author of numerous books. In this excerpt from *Frankenstein: A Cultural History* (2007), Hitchcock describes two of the leading literary figures of their day — Lord Byron and Percy Bysshe Shelley — and the challenge they took part in during the summer of 1816. The two men — accompanied by Byron's physician, John Polidori; Shelley's young lover, Mary Wollstonecraft Godwin, and their newborn son; and Mary's stepsister Claire Clairmont — had settled in Geneva that summer. The weather was unusually cold and rainy, probably the result of a volcanic eruption in far-off Indonesia. But the time, place, climate, and personal relationships of the companions made possible the creation of not one but two famous monster stories, neither by the famous poets: *Frankenstein* by Mary Godwin (later Mary Shelley) and *The Vampyre* by John Polidori.

> Archetypes make their way into the conscious part of the mind seemingly from the outside and of their own accord. They are autonomous, sometimes forcing themselves in overpoweringly. They have a numinous quality; that is, they have an aura of divinity which is mysterious or terrifying. They are from the unknown.
>
> — WILSON M. HUDSON, *Folklorist*

> It would have been naive to think it was possible to have prevented this.
>
> — IAN WILMUT, *Embryologist Responsible for Dolly, the Cloned Sheep*

The weather was strange all summer long in 1816. Twice in April the year before, Indonesia's Mount Tamboro had erupted—the largest volcanic eruption in history—spewing masses of dust into the atmosphere, which lingered and dimmed the sun's rays throughout the northern latitudes. Temperatures stayed at record lows. In New England killing frosts occurred all summer. In Europe crops—deprived of light and bogged down with too much rain—did not ripen. Grain prices doubled. In India food shortages triggered a famine, which very likely led to the cholera epidemic that spread west during the next two decades, infecting thousands in Europe and North America. Fierce storms of hail, thunder, and lightning swept through many regions. It was a dreary season indeed.

"An almost perpetual rain confines us principally to the house," wrote eighteen-year-old Mary Godwin to her half sister Fanny. "The thunder storms that visit us are grander and more terrific than I have ever seen before." She wrote from a house on the eastern bank of Lake Geneva, into which she had just moved with three fellow travelers: Percy Bysshe Shelley, her twenty-three-year-old lover; Claire Clairmont, her stepsister, also eighteen; and little William, the infant son born to her and Shelley in January. Nearly five months old, the baby—"Willmouse," as they called him—would have been smiling and reaching out to grasp a finger offered to him. One calm evening when they had first arrived, just the three of them—father, mother, child—had gone out on the lake in a little skiff at twilight. They skimmed noiselessly across the lake's glassy surface, watching the sun sink behind the dark frown of the Jura Mountains. Since then, though, storms had moved in. They did at least provide entertainment. "We watch them as they approach," Mary wrote Fanny,

observing the lightning play among the clouds in various parts of the heavens. . . . One night we enjoyed a finer storm than I had ever before beheld. The lake was lit up—the pines on Jura made visible, and all the scene illuminated for an instant, when a pitchy blackness succeeded, and the thunder came in frightful bursts over our heads amid the darkness.

Beyond the weather there was an excitement simply in being in Geneva, the intellectual birthplace of the French and American Revolutions. Mary described in her letter to Fanny the obelisk just outside the city, built in honor of Jean-Jacques Rousseau, once banished from his city but now recognized as an intellectual hero. Rousseau had declared that the imperfections and suffering in human life arose not from nature but from society. Human beings had only to free themselves from social oppression and prejudice in order to regain their native joy and liberty. A shared commitment to that idea had bonded her mother and father in an all-too-brief partnership; had drawn the young poet Percy Bysshe Shelley to her father, William Godwin, the radical philosopher he most revered; and had flamed the passion between herself and Shelley from the moment they met.

That first meeting had taken place in 1814, when she was sixteen and he was twenty-one. Now, two years later, they were making a household together. She could find pleasure simply in that: In those two years they had been such wanderers. First this odd threesome, she and Shelley and Claire, had sneaked out of London on a dark night in July 1814 and trekked through France and Germany on barely any money. Three months later they returned to London and found themselves roundly shunned. Shelley was, after all, married to another and father to a child. That November, Harriet Shelley had given birth to a second child. Now, in the summer of 1816, the legal Mrs. Shelley was raising

Ianthe and Charles—a girl aged three, a boy eighteen months—on her own. Shelley rationalized his behavior with a philosophy of free love. "Love," he would write, "differs from gold and clay: / That to divide is not to take away." His passions—Mary, liberty, poetry, atheism—meant more to him than his responsibility for an estranged and earthly family.

Life with Mary, however, soon developed its own earthly obliga- 5 tions. She had become pregnant during the 1814 escapade and stayed wretchedly sick through it all. In those times, and especially in Mary's own experience, birth and death mingled inextricably. Her own mother, Mary Wollstonecraft, had never risen from bed after giving birth to her. An infection developed, the fever never ceased, and Wollstonecraft died ten days after childbirth. Fear certainly exacerbated young Mary Godwin's condition. On February 22, 1815, a daughter was born prematurely, "unexpectedly alive, but still not expected to live," as Shelley wrote in a journal. One week later parents, baby, and Claire moved from one end of London to the other, from Pimlico to Hans Place. "A bustle of moving," Mary wrote in her journal on March 2. Four days later she wrote: "find my baby dead ———— . . . a miserable day." She managed to write a letter to a friend: "It was perfectly well when I went to bed—I awoke in the night to give it suck[. I]t appeared to be *sleeping* so quietly that I would not awake it—it was dead then but we did not find *that* out till morning—from its appearance it evedently [sic] died of convulsions." The child was never given a name.

Meanwhile Harriet Shelley pleaded for help for her two children from the fathers of both her husband and his runaway lover. Timothy Shelley, a baronet of ample means, felt fury over family shame more than anything else and clamped down viciously on his son's access to any inheritance. William Godwin, now remarried, no longer enjoyed popularity as a radical author. He and his wife barely made ends meet by running a bookshop and publishing books for children. They shared the baronet's parental outrage, however, and Godwin turned Shelley's kidnapping, as he termed it, of his daughter and stepdaughter into an opportunity for a gentlemanly sort of blackmail. By the summer of 1816, to meet the demands of Harriet Shelley and William Godwin, not to mention his own household obligations, Percy Bysshe Shelley was negotiating with moneylenders and solicitors for post-obit bonds—loans against his future estate.

Mary, Percy, and Claire moved restlessly, often hiding from creditors, Shelley all the while corresponding frantically with William Godwin about money. On January 25, 1816, though, at the end of a letter full of logistics concerning loans and payments, Shelley wrote: "Mrs. Godwin will probably be glad to hear that Mary has safely recovered from a very favorable confinement, & that her child is well." Mary Godwin and Percy Bysshe Shelley, unmarried, welcomed a son into the world. In a decision rife with contradictions, they named him William, after her father.

As if that weren't enough, now, in the cold and rainy summer of 1816, there was a new secret to keep from the Godwins.

Claire Clairmont — Mary's stepsister, the daughter of the second Mrs. Godwin — had been the one who selected Geneva as the destination of their upstart band. She was chasing after the outlandish yet irresistibly popular poet George Gordon, Lord Byron. Some speculate that early on Claire, as well as Mary, had had her eyes on Percy Bysshe Shelley. But by 1816 she was feeling like the odd woman out and, presented with the opportunity to meet the notoriously libertine Byron, Claire Clairmont had plotted — and pounced. Exploiting a tenuous personal connection, she approached Lord Byron. "An utter stranger takes the liberty of addressing you," her first letter to him began. It grew more presumptuous with every paragraph: "It may seem a strange assertion, but it is not the less true that I place my happiness in your hands." Rebuffed, Claire wrote again, explaining that she had drafted a play and sought Byron's advice on her composition. "You think it impertinent that I intrude on you," she wrote. "Remember that I have confided to you the most important secrets. I have withheld nothing." Slyly she implied submission even before he pursued her.

Claire was an annoying distraction during a troubled period of Byron's 10 life. He had married Annabella Milbanke in January 1815, but the marriage swiftly self-destructed, despite the birth of a daughter, Ada. The new wife and mother could not ignore Byron's fascination with his half sister, Augusta, and she had heard rumors of his sexual relations with men. She hired a doctor to investigate his mental condition. Byron was diagnosed sane. If he wasn't insane, he was immoral and dangerous, Annabella reasoned, and presented him with separation papers. Evidences of his incest and sodomy were whispered, even published, throughout Britain. "He is completely lost in the opinion of the world," wrote one London socialite. Byron decided to leave England. He would travel to Switzerland, birthplace of the Enlightenment, tolerant of iconoclasts like Rousseau — and himself.

So when Claire's letters began appearing, Byron was not in a particularly amorous mood. Sometime in late April, though, Claire's plot achieved consummation. As Byron wrote a friend some months later, "A man is a man, and if a girl of eighteen comes prancing to you at all hours there is but one way." It was a heartless fling, Byron said later: "I never loved nor pretended to love her." He probably thought he would shake her loose once he departed from England, but Claire Clairmont did not let go. Learning where Byron was going, she persuaded her friends to head for Geneva, too.

Diodati Escapades

According to Byron's physician and traveling companion, John William Polidori, the Shelley party first encountered Lord Byron on May 27, 1816. "Getting out [of a boat]," wrote Polidori in his diary, "L.B. met M. Wollstonecraft Godwin, her sister, and Percy Shelley." Byron's fame made the younger poet somewhat diffident, yet Byron hosted Shelley for dinner that very night. Polidori described him as "bashful, shy, consumptive, twenty-six: separated from his wife; keeps the two daughters of Godwin, who practise his theories; one L.B.'s." He got Shelley's age wrong by two years but immediately grasped the dynamics between Claire and Byron.

The scene was set for the momentous summer of 1816. Byron rented the Villa Diodati, an elegant estate house above Lake Geneva. John Milton himself, the author of *Paradise Lost*, had stayed in the house in 1638, while visiting the uncle of his dear friend Charles Diodati. Byron must have enjoyed communing with such an eminent forebear. Shelley, Mary, and Claire rented a humbler house down the hill, closer to the lake's edge, and visited Villa Diodati often. One wonders whether Mary ever brought her baby with her into that environment, electric with testosterone and nerves. She hired a Swiss nursemaid, but she still must have felt torn between her duties as a mother and her fascination with her poet friends. Sometimes fierce lightning storms broke open the skies above Villa Diodati. Together with the storms, sharp wit and intellectual sparring may have kept her at the villa longer than she planned.

They spoke of literature, debating the virtues of the writers of the time. Robert Southey, then Britain's poet laureate, had published *Thalaba the Destroyer* and *The Curse of Kehama*, passionate epics set in mysterious Eastern realms and peopled by unknown deities. Shelley so respected these poems that he used them as models, but Byron mocked them for their pageantry and melodrama. William Wordsworth presented an entirely different aesthetic, finding poetry in the language of the common folk—shepherds, idiots, children. Samuel Taylor Coleridge's poems evoked powers unseen and unnamed. Meanwhile Walter Scott, already revered for poems that sang of his native Scotland, was suspected of being the author of *Waverley*. What a shock if it were true—that a popular poet would descend to write a novel, a new and not altogether respected literary form.

No poet of any renown would write a novel; no elevated per- 15
son would stoop to read one. Yet in the wee hours of the night, their
tongues unleashed by sherry or other elixirs, those present at the Villa
Diodati might admit a fascination with an occasional Gothic romance,
Mrs. Radcliffe's *Mysteries of Udolpho* or Matthew Gregory Lewis's *The
Monk*, perhaps. Set in a dimly imagined past, these popular books of the
time pitted established strictures against native human desire, raising the
very questions that radical philosophers had been asking about convention and society. Ghosts and spirits haunted the churchyards, vaults, and
abbeys; gore, horror, lust, and crime oozed onto the printed page. There
was something in the human imagination that made such stories irresistibly fascinating.

Electrifying Science

Poetry was much on the minds of those gathered at the Villa Diodati,
but science charged the conversation as well. Polidori, after all, had
been trained in medicine, and Shelley had intended to become a doctor
when he entered Oxford in 1810. A friend described his college quarters
as cluttered with chemistry flasks and retorts.° Early-nineteenth-century
advances in science opened up realms of thought as fantastic as any coming from the imagination of a poet. In fact, to some, philosophy, poetry,
and science converged to promise revolutionary changes in human
knowledge and worldview.

Erasmus Darwin, for example, grandfather to Charles, had proffered
an early theory of evolution. "Organic life beneath the shoreless waves /
Was born and nurs'd in ocean's pearly caves," he wrote in his epic poem
The Temple of Nature; or, the Origin of Society, published in 1803. As Darwin
described it, life forms "new powers acquire, and larger limbs assume /
Whence countless groups of vegetation spring, / And breathing realms of
fin, and feet, and wing." Notions of evolving life forms led logically back
to questions about the origin of life itself. Joseph Priestley, discoverer of
oxygen, used mold on vegetables to demonstrate the spontaneous generation of life. Darwin saw similar things going on in aging wheat-flour
slurry: "In paste composed of flour and water, which has been suffered to
become acescent [to sour], the animalcules called eels, vibrio anguillula,
are seen in great abundance." The eggs of such creatures could not possibly "float in the atmosphere, and pass through the sealed glass phial,"

---

retorts: a vessel, commonly a glass bulb with a long neck bent downward, used for
distilling or decomposing substances by heat.

Darwin reasoned, so they must come into being "by a spontaneous vital process." Evolution and spontaneous generation may be concepts difficult to accept, Darwin granted, but "all new discoveries, as of the magnetic needle, and coated electric jar, and Galvanic pile" seemed just as incredible.

Once Benjamin Franklin and others had managed to harness naturally occurring electricity, experimenters went to work on devices to collect, control, and generate electrical power. The galvanic pile, as Darwin called it—precursor of the electric battery—was named for the Italian scientist Luigi Galvani, whose famous experiments of the 1790s tested the effect of electrical current on the bodies of animals. When a charged metal rod caused disembodied frog leg muscles to move, Galvani glimpsed that electricity motivated living nerve and muscle. His work advanced understanding of what was called "animal electricity," soon renamed "galvanism." By 1802 the *Journal of Natural Philosophy* announced that "the production of the galvanic fluid, or electricity, by the direct or independent energy of life in animals, can no longer be doubted." Galvani's nephew, Luigi Aldini, toured Europe during the first years of the nineteenth century, demonstrating how electrical charges could move not only the legs of frogs but also the eyes and tongues of severed ox heads as well.

In a famous presentation to the president of the Royal College of Surgeons, Aldini demonstrated galvanism with the body of a recently executed murderer. Aldini connected wires from a massive battery of copper and zinc to the corpse's head and anus. As an eyewitness described it:

On the first application of the process to the face, the jaw of the deceased criminal began to quiver, the adjoining muscles were horribly contorted, and one eye was actually opened. In the subsequent part of the process, the right hand was raised and clenched, and the legs and thighs were set in motion. It appeared to the uninformed part of the by-standers as if the wretched man was on the eve of being restored to life.

London newspapers reported the phenomenon, and Aldini mounted shows for the public. Even the Prince Regent attended one. It did not seem farfetched to consider this newly entrapped natural force, electricity, the quintessential force of life. "Galvanism had given token of such things," Mary Godwin wrote as she later recalled how discussions at Villa Diodati of these scientific marvels had filled her with ideas. "Perhaps the component parts of a creature might be manufactured, brought together, and endued [sic] with vital warmth."

The Challenge

Poetry and science, Gothic horror and reanimation—those topics tingled 20
in the Geneva air that summer of 1816. Somebody pulled out a collection
of tales of the supernatural, *Phantasmagoriana*, which became one evening's entertainment. The book had been translated from German into
French in 1812 and subtitled *Recueil d'histoires d'apparitions, de spectres,
revenans, fantomes, &c. traduit de l'allemande, par un amateur*—"a collection of stories about apparitions, specters, dreams, phantoms, etc., translated from the German by an amateur." The book must have enjoyed
popularity at the time, because an English edition came into print in
1813, with the simple title *Tales of the Dead*. The group at Villa Diodati
read the stories to one another from the French edition.

"Poetry and science, Gothic horror and reanimation — those topics tingled in the Geneva air that summer of 1816."

"There was the History of the Incon-
stant Lover," Mary later recalled—its
French title "La Morte Fiancée"—which
told of an Italian courtier in love with a
woman whose identical twin had died
mysteriously the year before. "There
was the tale of the sinful founder of
his race," as she called "Les Portraits de
Famille," in which ancient portraits hanging on cold stone walls assumed
supernatural powers. "I have not seen these stories since then," she wrote
in 1831, "but their incidents are as fresh in my mind as if I had read
them yesterday."

After listening to a few of these tales, chilling yet clumsily written,
Byron challenged his companions. Any one of them could do better.
" 'We will each write a ghost story,' said Lord Byron; and his proposition
was acceded to," Mary Shelley recounted in 1831. "There were four of
us," she begins, although there were five. The one she left out was Claire
Clairmont—maybe Claire was not present, or she simply chose not to
write, or maybe Mary was deliberately ignoring her stepsister. Byron
only started a story, "a fragment of which he printed at the end of his
poem of Mazeppa," Mary reported—a two-thousand-word passage that
introduces two Englishmen in a Greek landscape: Augustus Darvell, celebrated, mysterious, and haunted by "some peculiar circumstances in his
private history"; and the story's narrator, younger, ingenuous, and mesmerized by Darvell. "This is the end of my journey," Darvell whispers.
He has led his young friend into an old Muslim cemetery, full of fallen
turban-topped tombstones. He hands him a ring engraved with Arabic
characters, with strict instructions to fling it into Eleusinian springs after
he dies. A stork alights on a nearby tombstone, a snake writhing in her

beak. As she flies away, Darvell breathes his last. The narrator buries him in an ancient grave. "Between astonishment and grief, I was tearless," he says—and at that, Byron abandoned the story.

Percy Shelley appears not to have composed even a fragment in response to the challenge. His wife's explanation, written after his death, was that storytelling was just not his style. Spirits did seem to haunt him—in 1813 he had fled a Welsh cottage, convinced that a ghost had fired a gun at him—but grotesques were not the stuff of his poetry in 1816. Shelley, she wrote, was "more apt to embody ideas and sentiments in the radiance of brilliant imagery, and in the music of the most melodious verse that adorns our language, than to invent the machinery of a story." Ironically, therefore, Byron and Shelley—the two poets destined for the highest echelons of English Romantic literature—fizzled out in response to the ghost-story challenge, but their two companions wrote pieces that would evolve into the two greatest horror stories of modern times.

John Polidori was inspired to write two works, both published three years later. One was a short novel, *Ernestus Berchtold*, little known by anyone but professors of English today. The other, he freely admitted, began with Byron's unfinished story. "A noble author having determined to descend from his lofty range, gave up a few hours to a tale of terror, and wrote the fragment published at the end of Mazeppa," Polidori explained. "Upon this foundation I built the Vampyre," as he titled his story. "In the course of three mornings, I produced that tale."

Like Byron's fragment, Polidori's *Vampyre* tells the tale of two 25 Englishmen—Aubrey, a young gentleman, orphaned and innocent, and Lord Strongmore, a shadowy nobleman "more remarkable for his singularities, than for his rank." Strongmore suggests, much to Aubrey's amazement, that the two tour the Continent together. Repelled by Strongmore's appetite for sex and gambling, Aubrey takes off on his own and falls in love with Ianthe, a Greek country maid, who soon turns up dead, her throat pierced with "marks of teeth having opened the vein of the neck." "A Vampyre! a Vampyre!" the villagers all cry. The assailant turns out to be Lord Strongmore, who next sets his sights on Aubrey's own sister. Aubrey warns his family and mysteriously dies at midnight, leaving others to discover that "Lord Strongmore had disappeared, and Aubrey's sister had glutted the thirst of a VAMPYRE!" The story, borrowed from a poet and written by a man of little talent, would in a few years burst back on the literary scene and then proliferate through the nineteenth century, influencing Bram Stoker as he wrote *Dracula*, the vampire classic, in 1897. Thus on the same night in Geneva in 1816 were born the world's two most famous monsters.

While vampires populated Polidori's imagination, Mary Godwin worried that hers seemed so vacant. "I busied myself *to think of a story,*—a story to rival those which had excited us to this task," she wrote fifteen years later. Conscious exertion seemed to get her nowhere. "I felt that blank incapability of invention which is the greatest misery of authorship, when dull Nothing replies to our anxious invocations. *Have you thought of a story?* I was asked each morning, and each morning I was forced to reply with a mortifying negative." Her mind remained as if a blank slate, and discussions between Byron and Shelley concerning "various philosophical doctrines" including "the nature of the principle of life" made impressions on it. They cited examples; they speculated as to extremes—sometimes the discussion was detailed and technical, sometimes visionary. Details of Aldini's galvanic demonstrations may have mingled with descriptions of gruesome phantasms or translucent° fairies.

With such ideas swirling in her head, Mary Godwin went to bed. "I did not sleep, nor could I be said to think," she recalled. A story presented itself, as she described it, the life force less in her than in the visions appearing to her.

My imagination, unbidden, possessed and guided me, gifting the successive images that arose in my mind with a vividness far beyond the usual bounds of reverie. I saw—with shut eyes, but acute mental vision,—I saw the pale student of unhallowed arts kneeling beside the thing he had put together. I saw the hideous phantasm of a man stretched out, and then, on the working of some powerful engine, show signs of life, and stir with an uneasy, half vital motion.

To enter the original moment of the creation of Frankenstein's monster, strip away all the modern imagery created to portray it. No more white lab coat, no more electrical coils and transformers, not even a dank stone tower. The author herself gives us very little: a "pale student," "kneeling" on the floor; beside him, "the thing he had put together"—a "hideous phantasm," "some powerful engine" whose force only made him "stir."

Granted, these few words are themselves just garments wrapped by the author around wordless moments of inspiration. It is as if she, one with her character, had gazed for the first time upon "the horrid thing" standing at the bedside, staring at her with its "yellow, watery, but speculative eyes"—for, at the moment that she glimpsed this kernel of her story, she opened her own eyes "with terror," seeking the comfort of the outside world.

translucent: clear, transparent.

The idea so possessed my mind, that a thrill of fear ran through me, and I wished to exchange the ghastly image of my fancy for the realities around. I see them still; the very room, the dark parquet, the closed shutters, with the moonlight struggling through, and the sense I had that the glassy lake and white high Alps were beyond. I could not so easily get rid of my hideous phantom; still it haunted me. I must try to think of something else. I recurred to my ghost story,—my tiresome unlucky ghost story! O! if I could only contrive one which would frighten my reader as I myself had been frightened that night!

Soon the two thoughts merged into one: her waking dream *was* her ghost story. "On the morrow I announced that I had *thought of a story*," Mary later recalled. "I began that day with the words, *It was on a dreary night of November*, making only a transcript of the grim terrors of my waking dream."

Mary Godwin Shelley's account of the genesis of her novel, written for its 1831 edition, may contain a few fabrications, a few exaggerations, a few skewed memories. But it is still the most reliable rendition we have of how the story of Frankenstein began, and therefore a good starting point.

Understanding the Text

1. This article begins with two quotations. What is the significance of the quotations to the text and to each other?

2. How is the relationship between Percy Bysshe Shelley and Mary Godwin complicated by issues on both sides?

3. Identify some of the details of Lord Byron's history as detailed in this passage. In what ways did he come to embody the Romantic hero?

4. Hitchcock's article can be best described as a history of the creation of two great horror figures. How does knowing this background enhance your understanding of Frankenstein's creature and the modern vampire?

Reflection and Response

5. Hitchcock writes, "No poet of any renown would write a novel; no elevated person would stoop to read one" (par. 15). In what ways are certain styles or genres of art connected with class consciousness? What specific styles or genres of art today are affected by awareness of social class, and how is such art restricted or liberated by that?

6. Hitchcock takes some time to document the lives and celebrity of Lord Byron and Percy Bysshe Shelley. In particular, both Byron and Shelley were notorious for their lifestyles, rejecting social conventions and morality, living only for their art. To what extent does the lack of social conventions allow

and inspire artists to be more creative? Consider this question given that in the challenge, Shelley and Byron were not successful, but Mary Godwin and John Polidori were.

Making Connections

7. Mary Godwin Shelley later wrote about how difficult it was *"to think of a story"* (par. 26). Instead, the idea of *Frankenstein* came to her in a dream. What kinds of connections are there between dreaming and the creative imagination? Reread the excerpt from Shelley's *Frankenstein* that describes the creation of the monster (p. 20) and argue whether the scene has dreamlike qualities or not.

8. Hitchcock cites the work of Luigi Galvani, who sent electric charges through the bodies of dead frogs to watch their muscles move. How did scientific experiments and advances shape the environment in which Mary Godwin Shelley created the story *Frankenstein*? How do current developments, such as the creation of genetically modified organisms or other advances in medical technology, create the conditions in which scientists or doctors act like God? Are developments in medical technology as threatening today as they were in Shelley's time? Why or why not?

Why Vampires Never Die

Guillermo del Toro and Chuck Hogan

Why are vampires as popular now as ever? The stories of vampires — found in different languages, cultures, and times dating back to prehistory — have a strength and power that suggest not only an archetypal origin connected to cannibalism but also a contemporary need. According to Guillermo del Toro and Chuck Hogan in this *New York Times* column, the essential qualities of the modern vampire — combining lust and death — still speak to deep desires and fears. Fascination with the vampire is driven by the desire to move beyond the mortal to the immortal and, in a way, regain the sense of wonder that the modern world often removes. Del Toro is a writer and director of films such as *Pan's Labyrinth* (2006), *The Shape of Water* (2017), and the Hellboy series. Hogan is the author of such novels as *Prince of Thieves* (2004) and *Devils in Exile* (2010). Together, del Toro and Hogan wrote *The Strain* vampire trilogy, which was adapted into an FX television series.

Tonight, you or someone you love will likely be visited by a vampire — on cable television or the big screen, or in the bookstore. Our own novel describes a modern-day epidemic that spreads across New York City.

It all started nearly 200 years ago. It was the "Year without a Summer" of 1816, when ash from volcanic eruptions lowered temperatures around the globe, giving rise to widespread famine. A few friends gathered at the Villa Diodati on Lake Geneva and decided to engage in a small competition to see who could come up with the most terrifying tale — and the two great monsters of the modern age were born.

One was created by Mary Godwin, soon to become Mary Shelley, whose Dr. Frankenstein gave life to a desolate creature. The other monster was less created than fused. John William Polidori stitched together folklore, personal resentment, and erotic anxieties into *The Vampyre*, a story that is the basis for vampires as they are understood today.

With *The Vampyre*, Polidori gave birth to the two main branches of vampiric fiction: the vampire as romantic hero, and the vampire as undead monster. This ambivalence may reflect Polidori's own, as it is widely accepted that Lord Ruthven, the titular creature, was based upon Lord Byron — literary superstar of the era and another resident of the lakeside villa that fateful summer. Polidori tended to Byron day and night, both as his doctor and most devoted groupie. But Polidori resented him as well: Byron was dashing and brilliant, while the poor doctor had a rather drab talent and unremarkable physique.

But this was just a new twist to a very old idea. The myth, established 5 well before the invention of the word "vampire," seems to cross every culture, language and era. The Indian Baital, the Ch'ing Shih in China, and the Romanian Strigoi are but a few of its names. The creature seems to be as old as Babylonia and Sumer. Or even older.

The vampire may originate from a repressed memory we had as primates. Perhaps at some point we were—out of necessity—cannibalistic. As soon as we became sedentary, agricultural tribes with social boundaries, one seminal° myth might have featured our ancestors as primitive beasts who slept in the cold loam of the earth and fed off the salty blood of the living.

Monsters, like angels, are invoked by our individual and collective needs. Today, much as during that gloomy summer in 1816, we feel the need to seek their cold embrace.

Herein lies an important clue: in contrast to timeless creatures like the dragon, the vampire does not seek to obliterate us, but instead offers a peculiar brand of blood alchemy.° For as his contagion bestows its nocturnal gift, the vampire transforms our vile, mortal selves into the gold of eternal youth, and instills in us something that every social construct seeks to quash: primal lust. If youth is desire married with unending possibility, then vampire lust creates within us a delicious void, one we long to fulfill.

In other words, whereas other monsters emphasize what is mortal in us, the vampire emphasizes the eternal in us. Through the panacea° of its blood it turns the lead of our toxic flesh into golden matter.

In a society that moves as fast as ours, where every week a new "block- 10 buster" must be enthroned at the box office, or where idols are fabricated by consensus every new television season, the promise of something everlasting, something truly eternal, holds a special allure. As a seductive figure, the vampire is as flexible and polyvalent° as ever. Witness its slow mutation from the pansexual, decadent Anne Rice creatures to the current permutations—promising anything from chaste eternal love to wild nocturnal escapades—and there you will find the true essence of immortality: adaptability.

Vampires find their niche and mutate at an accelerated rate now—in the past one would see, for decades, the same variety of fiend, repeated

seminal: creative, original; containing the seeds of later development.
alchemy: the process of transforming something ordinary into something special.
panacea: a cure-all; a remedy for all illnesses or difficulties.
polyvalent: having multiple powers of attraction.

in multiple storylines. Now, vampires simultaneously occur in all forms and tap into our every need: soap opera storylines, sexual liberation, noir detective fiction, etc. The myth seems to be twittering promiscuously to serve all avenues of life, from cereal boxes to romantic fiction. The fast pace of technology accelerates its viral dispersion in our culture.

But if Polidori remains the roots in the genealogy of our creature, the most widely known vampire was birthed by Bram Stoker in 1897.

Part of the reason for the great success of his *Dracula* is generally acknowledged to be its appearance at a time of great technological revolution. The narrative is full of new gadgets (telegraphs, typing machines), various forms of communication (diaries, ship logs), and cutting-edge science (blood transfusions) — a mash-up of ancient myth in conflict with the world of the present.

Today as well, we stand at the rich uncertain dawn of a new level of scientific innovation. The wireless technology we carry in our pockets today was the stuff of the science fiction in our youth. Our technological arrogance mirrors more and more the Wellsian° dystopia of dissatisfaction, while allowing us to feel safe and connected at all times. We can call, see or hear almost anything and anyone no matter where we are. For most people then, the only remote place remains within. "Know thyself" we do not.

Despite our obsessive harnessing of information, we are still ultimately 15 vulnerable to our fates and our nightmares. We enthrone the deadly virus in the very same way that *Dracula* allowed the British public to believe in monsters: through science. Science becomes the modern man's superstition. It allows him to experience fear and awe again, and to believe in the things he cannot see.

> "Despite our obsessive harnessing of information, we are still ultimately vulnerable to our fates and our nightmares."

And through awe, we once again regain spiritual humility. The current vampire pandemic serves to remind us that we have no true jurisdiction over our bodies, our climate or our very souls. Monsters will always provide the possibility of mystery in our mundane "reality show" lives, hinting at a larger spiritual world; for if there are demons in our midst, there surely must be angels lurking nearby as well. In the vampire we find Eros and Thanatos fused together in archetypal embrace, spiraling through the ages, undying.

Forever.

Wellsian: H. G. Wells (1866–1946); British writer best known for his science fiction.

Understanding the Text

1. What are the two main branches of vampire lore that John Polidori fused in his story *The Vampyre*? How does this relate to what the authors call his "ambivalence" about Lord Byron (par. 4)?

2. How do vampires relate to practices of cannibalism? If cannibalism is far in our past, why do vampires still have such popularity today?

3. According to the authors, "As a seductive figure, the vampire is as flexible and polyvalent as ever" (par. 10). What do they mean by that? Explain, citing specific examples.

4. This article originally was published in the *New York Times*. As is common in newspaper writing, the paragraphs are short — many are only two or three sentences long. Compare the paragraphs to those in Hitchcock (p. 23), which are longer and more developed. What are the effects of shorter and longer paragraphs in writing? How does the original publication form (e.g., newspaper or book) affect how a work is written? Why?

Reflection and Response

5. Del Toro and Hogan state that Bram Stoker's *Dracula* welded together the old vampire mythology with the technological revolutions going on in Stoker's time. What about today's technological advances can be looked at as modern instances of the "new gadgets" (par. 13) of Stoker's time, and how do they influence more current renditions of the vampire myth?

6. The authors argue that "we are still ultimately vulnerable to our fates and our nightmares" (par. 15). Have science and technology taken away our sense of "fear and awe"? If so, how does the vampire myth help return that to us? If not, has science become "the modern man's superstition" (par. 15), as argued by the authors? Use examples to develop your response.

Making Connections

7. The authors state that the vampire combines lust and death. Read the selection from Bram Stoker's *Dracula* (p. 190) and use specific details to argue how that passage combines both of these elements. How do our current cultural attitudes toward lust and death influence more recent vampire stories?

8. Using a current vampire myth, such as the *Twilight* series by Stephenie Meyer, the Anne Rice books, or even Guillermo del Toro and Chuck Hogan's *Strain* trilogy, show how it helps us, as the authors say, "regain spiritual humility" (par. 16). Consider also the assumption in the same statement that spiritual humility has been lost and that we now believe we have "true jurisdiction over our bodies." Is this belief a result of our advances in medicine or technology? How does the vampire myth you have chosen serve to help us regain that humility? Support your argument with specific examples.

9. Research the human history of cannibalism and the history of vampires in older cultures and myths. (Del Toro and Hogan have named several that will give you a good starting point.) Analyze how the practice of cannibalism, whether from the prehistoric past or more recent times, relates to the stories of vampires.

10. Research past medical practices, such as the widespread use of leeches, and argue how vampires can be seen as connected with disease.

My Zombie, Myself: Why Modern Life Feels Rather Undead

Chuck Klosterman

The zombie is a relatively recent monster, a creation that is not alive, is not particularly intelligent, and simply seeks to eat the brains of humans. It can also reproduce itself. In this article that originally appeared in the *New York Times*, Chuck Klosterman argues that the zombie is a metaphor for our modern, task-filled world in which the problems we face seem to multiply faster than we can solve them. Thus, zombies neatly encapsulate our fears and anxieties about modern life. Klosterman is a popular writer of nonfiction, including *Sex, Drugs, and Cocoa Puffs* (2003) and *I Wear the Black Hat* (2013). He has also written two novels, *Downtown Owl* (2008) and *The Visible Man* (2011).

Zombies are a value stock. They are wordless and oozing and brain dead, but they're an ever-expanding market with no glass ceiling. Zombies are a target-rich environment, literally and figuratively. The more you fill them with bullets, the more interesting they become. Roughly 5.3 million people watched the first episode of *The Walking Dead* on AMC, a stunning 83 percent more than the 2.9 million who watched the Season 4 premiere of *Mad Men*. This means there are at least 2.4 million cable-ready Americans who might prefer watching Christina Hendricks if she were an animated corpse.

Statistically and aesthetically that dissonance° seems perverse. But it probably shouldn't. Mainstream interest in zombies has steadily risen over the past 40 years. Zombies are a commodity that has advanced slowly and without major evolution, much like the staggering creatures George Romero popularized in the 1968 film *Night of the Living Dead*. What makes that measured amplification curious is the inherent limitations of the zombie itself: You can't add much depth to a creature who can't talk, doesn't think and whose only motive is the consumption of flesh. You can't humanize a zombie, unless you make it less zombie-esque. There are slow zombies, and there are fast zombies—that's pretty much the spectrum of zombie diversity. It's not that zombies are changing to fit the world's condition; it's that the condition of the world seems more like a zombie offensive. Something about zombies is becoming more intriguing to us. And I think I know what that something is.

dissonance: inconsistency between the beliefs one holds and one's actions.

Zombies are just so easy to kill.

When we think critically about monsters, we tend to classify them as personifications of what we fear. Frankenstein's monster illustrated our trepidation about untethered science; Godzilla was spawned from the fear of the atomic age; werewolves feed into an instinctual panic over predation and man's detachment from nature. Vampires and zombies share an imbedded anxiety about disease. It's easy to project a symbolic relationship between vampirism and AIDS (or vampirism and the loss of purity). From a creative standpoint these fear projections are narrative linchpins; they turn creatures into ideas, and that's the point.

But what if the audience infers an entirely different metaphor? 5

What if contemporary people are less interested in seeing depictions of their unconscious fears and more attracted to allegories of how their day-to-day existence feels? That would explain why so many people watched the first episode of *The Walking Dead*: They knew they would be able to relate to it.

A lot of modern life is exactly like slaughtering zombies.

If there's one thing we all understand about zombie killing, it's that the act is uncomplicated: you blast one in the brain from point-blank range (preferably with a shotgun). That's Step 1. Step 2 is doing the same thing to the next zombie that takes its place. Step 3 is identical to Step 2, and Step 4 isn't any different from Step 3. Repeat this process until (a) you perish, or (b) you run out of zombies. That's really the only viable strategy.

"The principal downside to any zombie attack is that the zombies will never stop coming; the principal downside to life is that you will never be finished with whatever it is you do."

Every zombie war is a war of attrition. It's always a numbers game. And it's more repetitive than complex. In other words, zombie killing is philosophically similar to reading and deleting 400 work e-mails on a Monday morning or filling out paperwork that only generates more paperwork, or following Twitter gossip out of obligation, or performing tedious tasks in which the only true risk is being consumed by avalanche. The principal downside to any zombie attack is that the zombies will never stop coming; the principal downside to life is that you will never be finished with whatever it is you do.

The Internet reminds us of this every day. 10

Here's a passage from a youngish writer named Alice Gregory, taken from a recent essay on Gary Shteyngart's dystopic novel *Super Sad True Love Story* in the literary journal *n + 1*: "It's hard not to think 'death drive' every time I go on the Internet," she writes. "Opening Safari is

Andrew Lincoln as Rick Grimes in the zombie television series *The Walking Dead*.
AMC/Photofest

an actively destructive decision. I am asking that consciousness be taken away from me."

Ms. Gregory's self-directed fear is thematically similar to how the zombie brain is described by Max Brooks, author of the fictional oral history *World War Z* and its accompanying self-help manual, *The Zombie Survival Guide*: "Imagine a computer programmed to execute one function. This function cannot be paused, modified or erased. No new data can be stored. No new commands can be installed. This computer will perform that one function, over and over, until its power source eventually shuts down."

This is our collective fear projection: that we will be consumed. Zombies are like the Internet and the media and every conversation we don't want to have. All of it comes at us endlessly (and thoughtlessly), and—if we surrender—we will be overtaken and absorbed. Yet this war is manageable, if not necessarily winnable. As long as we keep deleting whatever's directly in front of us, we survive. We live to eliminate the zombies of tomorrow. We are able to remain human, at least for the time being. Our enemy is relentless and colossal, but also uncreative and stupid.

Battling zombies is like battling anything . . . or everything.

Because of the Twilight series it's easy to manufacture an argument in which zombies are merely replacing vampires as the monster of the

15

moment, a designation that is supposed to matter for metaphorical, non-monstrous reasons. But that kind of thinking is deceptive. The recent five-year spike in vampire interest is only about the multiplatform success of Twilight, a brand that isn't about vampirism anyway. It's mostly about nostalgia for teenage chastity, the attractiveness of its film cast and the fact that contemporary fiction consumers tend to prefer long serialized novels that can be read rapidly. But this has still created a domino effect. The 2008 Swedish vampire film *Let the Right One In* was fantastic, but it probably wouldn't have been remade in the United States if Twilight had never existed. *The Gates* was an overt attempt by ABC to tap into the housebound, preteen Twilight audience; HBO's *True Blood* is a camp reaction to Robert Pattinson's flat earnestness.

The difference with zombies, of course, is that it's possible to like a specific vampire temporarily, which isn't really an option with the undead. Characters like Mr. Pattison's Edward Cullen in Twilight and Anne Rice's Lestat de Lioncourt, and even boring old Count Dracula can be multidimensional and erotic; it's possible to learn why they are and who they once were. Vampire love can be singular. Zombie love, however, is always communal. If you dig zombies, you dig the entire zombie concept. It's never personal. You're interested in what zombies signify, you like the way they move, and you understand what's required to stop them. And this is a reassuring attraction, because those aspects don't really shift. They've become shared archetypal knowledge.

A few days before Halloween I was in upstate New York with three other people, and we somehow ended up at the Barn of Terror, outside a town called Lake Katrine. Entering the barn was mildly disturbing, although probably not as scary as going into an actual abandoned barn that didn't charge $20 and doesn't own its own domain name. Regardless, the best part was when we exited the terror barn and were promptly herded onto a school bus, which took us to a cornfield about a quarter of a mile away. The field was filled with amateur actors, some playing military personnel and others that they called the infected. We were told to run through the moonlit corn maze if we wanted to live; as we ran, armed soldiers yelled contradictory instructions while hissing zombies emerged from the corny darkness. It was designed to be fun, and it was. But just before we immersed ourselves in the corn, one of my companions sardonically critiqued the reality of our predicament.

"I know this is supposed to be scary," he said. "But I'm pretty confident about my ability to deal with a zombie apocalypse. I feel strangely informed about what to do in this kind of scenario."

I could not disagree. At this point who isn't? We all know how this goes: If you awake from a coma, and you don't immediately see a member of the hospital staff, assume a zombie takeover has transpired during your incapacitation. Don't travel at night and keep your drapes closed. Don't let zombies spit on you. If you knock a zombie down, direct a second bullet into its brain stem. But above all, do not assume that the war is over, because it never is. The zombies you kill today will merely be replaced by the zombies of tomorrow. But you can do this, my friend. It's disenchanting, but it's not difficult. Keep your finger on the trigger. Continue the termination. Don't stop believing. Don't stop deleting. Return your voice mails and nod your agreements. This is the zombies' world, and we just live in it. But we can live better.

Understanding the Text

1. What are the inherent limitations of zombies, according to Klosterman? In what way do those limitations make zombies different from other monsters, such as vampires?

2. Klosterman writes, "When we think critically about monsters, we tend to classify them as personifications of what we fear" (par. 4). What are those fears, and how does Klosterman connect them to specific monsters?

3. Klosterman quotes Alice Gregory as stating, "Opening Safari is an actively destructive decision. I am asking that consciousness be taken away from me" (par. 11). What is Safari, and what does she mean by this?

4. Klosterman makes use of the personal "I" in this article to prove his point. However, some writing instructors frown on the use of the first-person point of view. What is the advantage for Klosterman of his use of the personal "I"? What are the disadvantages?

Reflection and Response

5. Analyze the difference between the zombie as a monster and the vampire. What different fears do they represent, and how are those fears to be combated? What does the presence of the zombie in popular imagination say about people's anxieties about modern life?

6. One metaphor that Klosterman uses is the computer, and in particular the internet. Examine how zombies can be seen as a metaphor for the internet. Based on your experience with the internet, do you think this is an apt metaphor? Explain, using specific types of websites or other internet functions to illustrate and support your answer.

7. Klosterman poses a key question in paragraph 6: "What if contemporary people are less interested in seeing depictions of their unconscious fears and more attracted to allegories of how their day-to-day existence feels?" If we are attracted to the zombie as an allegory for a boring daily existence filled with repetitive, seemingly meaningless tasks, do these tasks prove more persistent and resilient than zombies? After all, Klosterman argues, "Zombies are just so easy to kill" (par. 3), but real-life tasks often are not. Give examples from everyday life to support your position.

Making Connections

8. Read Matt Kaplan's "Cursed by a Bite" (p. 91). Pay particular attention to Kaplan's argument about the origin of the myth of zombies. How does the argument that zombies may have existed on plantations in the Caribbean connect to contemporary society? Cite both Klosterman's and Kaplan's articles in your response.

9. Klosterman references several movie and television versions of the zombie myth: *Night of the Living Dead* (1968), *World War Z* (2013), and *The Walking Dead* (AMC). View at least one of these and argue whether his metaphor of zombies as incarnations of our daily challenges (e.g., "reading and deleting 400 work e-mails," par. 9) seems correct or not. Develop your response with specific examples from both Klosterman's essay and the movie or television version of the zombie myth you viewed.

Japan's Nuclear Nightmare: How the Bomb Became a Beast Called Godzilla

Peter H. Brothers

One of the most popular monster films of all time is *Godzilla* (1954), made in Japan less than a decade after atomic bombs devastated the cities of Hiroshima and Nagasaki. Still reeling from the trauma of atomic annihilation and the subsequent effects of radioactive poisoning, a team of Japanese filmmakers created a monster that embodied the fears and anxieties in Japan resulting from nuclear warfare. Originally conceived as a response to other film beasts, especially *King Kong* (1933), Godzilla in many ways surpassed them: the reptilian monster (and the film) stands as an enduring symbol of what happens when people tamper with science in such a way that the consequences extend beyond the imagination. Peter H. Brothers is an actor, director, lecturer, and author of several books, including *Mushroom Clouds and Mushroom Men: The Fantastic Cinema of Ishiro Honda* (2009), *Devil Bat Diary: The Journal of Johnny Layton* (2011), and *Terror in Tinseltown: The Sequel to "Devil Bat Diary"* (2012). This article was first published in 2011 in *Cineaste*, a magazine that covers the art and politics of film.

In 1954, while barely recovering from a devastating defeat in the Second World War and a humiliating seven-year-long American occupation, the Japanese were once again reminded of their unwilling participation in the Atomic Age, which began with the bombings of Hiroshima and Nagasaki. In March of that year a Japanese tuna trawler named *The Lucky Dragon No. 5* returned to port after finding itself covered in radioactive ash following the detonation of the first underwater nuclear explosion from the American "Operation Crossroads" atomic-bomb tests, which brought home to the Japanese the recurring and haunting images of the death, destruction, and demoralization befalling them at the end of WWII. It also gave Toho Studios producer Tomoyuki Tanaka a way to save face, following an aborted coproduction film project with Indonesia, by initiating a Japanese production unprecedented in that nation's history.

Inspired by the success of *The Beast from 20,000 Fathoms* (1953) and influenced by *King Kong* (1933), the film that resulted is singularly Japanese. *Godzilla* (*Gojira*) is a film less about a giant dinosaur running amuck and more about the psychological recovery of a people trying to

45

rebuild their cities, their culture, and their lives threatened by radioactive fallout. Just as those individuals who were once a part of America's "Greatest Generation" are rapidly fading from the scene, so too are those Japanese for whom the possibility of a nuclear catastrophe was never far away. Caught—if not in the cross hairs then decidedly in the line of fire—between two feuding superpowers, Japan's island nation had every reason to believe that their time could come again in dealing with the terrifying consequences of the Atomic (soon Nuclear) Age.

Tanaka saw a way to make a monster movie and cash in on a current craze while special-effects master Eiji Tsuburaya saw it as an opportunity to make his personal tribute to *King Kong*, the film that had motivated him to go into effects work in the first place. But for forty-year-old journeyman director Ishirô Honda, who was handed the assignment after the original director Senkichi Taniguchi turned it down, he resolved to use the monster as a metaphor for the growing fears of a nation living in the shadow of doomsday. As Honda said years later, "I wanted to make radiation visible." As a result, the Bomb became the Beast.

Honda knew firsthand the horrors of war. With over seven years of duty as an infantryman in China behind him, he had not only experienced combat but while on leave had also witnessed some of the fire raids on Japanese cities. After the surrender he spent six months as a POW, and after being repatriated he walked through the rubble of what was once the city of Hiroshima. As a result of these events, this film (and it is every inch his film) is a somber testimony of those experiences, continually reinforcing the feeling that nothing can be settled by armed conflicts and that potential destruction still looms over a Japanese populace helpless to prevent it.

In later years Honda stated that a direct reference to the real-life *Lucky Dragon* incident was intentionally avoided so as to not make an obvious connection and thereby upset and dismay the moviegoing public. He wanted to make a film that was entertaining yet not preachy, to dramatize and not traumatize. Yet this intention is difficult to accept in light of the film's opening scene:

Japanese sailors are relaxing in the hot summer sun when suddenly a bright flash of light appears that justifiably gets their attention. While getting a closer look they are blinded for their efforts, and those staggering to get away are awash in atomic fire, which will melt the flesh off their bones as the radio operator sends a fervent, final, and futile message before he dies.

The bright light the sailors saw was a representation of a phenomenon known to the survivors of Hiroshima and Nagasaki as the *"pikadon"* or "flash-boom" caused by the explosion of the atomic bombs, and the sinking of the ship calls to mind the destruction of the Japanese Merchant

Marine by U.S. submarines during the war. The fact that we witness the death of the radio operator is not a coincidence, for it was Aikichi Kuboyama—the real-life radio operator of *The Lucky Dragon*—who died of radiation poisoning from that fatal encounter just one month before the film was released. If that weren't enough, the life raft visible on the ship's railing in the film reads *Eiko-Maru No. 5*. A more direct parallel is difficult to imagine.

Godzilla is in fact a virtual re-creation of the Japanese military and civilian experience during the final months of WWII, even to Godzilla itself, as Honda insisted that the monster's roar sound like an air-raid siren while its footsteps should sound like exploding bombs. Numerous other WWII analogies in *Godzilla* (the WWII events are in bold and the movie scenes are italicized) can be cited.

On the night of March 9, 1945, American B-29s laid down tons of incendiaries on the city of Tokyo, destroying 250,000 homes, burning out ten square miles of the city, leaving one million homeless and 100,000 dead.

The "sea of fire" engulfing Tokyo during Godzilla's rampage.   10

The Japanese Home Defense mobilizes to fight the invasion of the Japanese mainland from the sea in what was known to the Americans as "Operation Olympic."

The Japanese Home Defense gets ready to repel Godzilla's second attack, which is an invasion from the sea.

In the last months of the war the Japanese military is overwhelmed by superior enemy technology and sheer weight of numbers.

The Japanese military is helpless in their attempts to stop Godzilla.

Japan will face America alone, Germany and Italy having already surrendered.   15

Japan faces Godzilla alone with no other country giving or offering aid.

Radio bulletins warn of impending evening American air raids as searchlights are employed and sirens alert residents to seek shelter.

Reports come over the radio notifying the citizens of Tokyo that the monster is approaching, as searchlights slice through the sky and sirens wail.

The Kamikaze (Divine Wind) unit flyers wore *hachimaki* headbands, usually anointed with religious symbols and inspirational words, in a desperate last-ditch attempt to defeat the Allied powers.

Ogata and Serizawa prepare to fight Godzilla with an unconventional   20
weapon (the "Oxygen Destroyer") as they don their headbands.

Japanese cities are reduced to rubble by means of conventional bombings, fire raids, and the atomic bombings.

After Godzilla's final assault on Tokyo, the camera pans over a devastated landscape of broken buildings and burning rubble.

Hospitals in Japan are overflowing with victims, known as the "*gembakusha*," of the two atomic-bomb attacks.

After Godzilla's second attack Japanese hospitals are filled with patients suffering from terrible radiation burns.

Ironically, when the film was released in America two years later (as 25 *Godzilla; King of the Monsters!*), *Boston Traveler* critic Alta Maloney stated of the hospital scenes: "They look suspiciously like actual films taken after the dropping of the atom bombs in Japan. They are uncomfortable views." This backhanded compliment is typical of the condescending attitude most Western critics had towards Japanese cinema at large, yet Honda's "uncomfortable views" were not pilfered from American-occupation footage but were solely the work of Honda and his chief cameraman Masao Tamai.

As it happens, these scenes are far less shocking and graphic than the real thing and the reason for this was simple. Honda was a man of extreme good taste and decency and did not want to disturb or horrify his audience; it was for this same reason that the scars on the scientist Serizawa's face were toned down considerably in the film from their original conception seen in production photos. Honda wanted his public to concentrate on the suffering within the individuals and not be sickened or distracted by their physical deformities.

Godzilla is a film that deserves to be taken seriously, but to accept what the movie is saying on its own terms one must understand its subtle anti-American tone and dissertation of destruction, which has been difficult for American critics to acknowledge, for to do so is to admit the guilt belonging solely to the society that had dropped the bombs in the first place (in America the Bomb is viewed as a necessary evil; in Japan the Bomb is evil, period).

To view this film objectively is to come face to face with the burden of responsibility for having laid waste to entire Japanese cities with fire and radiation. While it has been argued that there never would have been a Hiroshima had there never been a Pearl Harbor, what is also true is that without Hiroshima there would never have been a *Godzilla*. The relevancy of Honda's intention, however, has now faded with time. With the end of the Cold War, and the beginning of Strategic Arms Limitation Talks and test-ban treaties, and with some (but not all) of the nations of the world slowly dismantling their nuclear arsenals, the Black Shadow of Death that was the original conception of *Godzilla* has become merely camp to some and corny to others. What they fail to see is the deeper meaning of the film, but because of the efforts of those involved with its creation, *Godzilla* remains a superbly-crafted and engaging motion picture with more conviction, drama, and mood than any other so-called

A movie poster for the 1956 American adaptation of *Godzilla*, starring Raymond Burr.
World History Archive/Alamy

"monster movie" before or since. *King Kong* may be considered the greater film, but *Godzilla* is better.

While technically brilliant from an effects standpoint, *Kong* is a stylized melodrama suffering from dated dialog, stagy machismo overtones, and graphically-shocking images, whereas *Godzilla* is a subdued and contemporary film dealing with an issue that is pertinent and real, one that hangs over our heads today as did the mushroom clouds over Japan in 1945. *Kong* is pure fantasy told in storybook style meant to entertain, *Godzilla* is a window to an alternate reality meant to enlighten. *Kong* is a film about a giant gorilla, *Godzilla* is a film about men. There is a difference.

> *"[King] Kong is a film about a giant gorilla, Godzilla is a film about men. There is a difference."*

Godzilla is also a far more emotionally powerful viewing experience. In *King Kong*, as the giant ape shakes screaming sailors off a tree trunk into a deep chasm, we witness their deaths from a distance, thus maintaining an objective viewpoint and are not particularly appalled or saddened. Japanese commuters in *Godzilla* are killed riding on their train into Tokyo and Honda pulls his camera in close on the reactions of female onlookers, and as a result we are much more involved, intimately experiencing their shock and horror. *Kong* is an exaggeration of an ape representing the summation of the fears and frustrations of a time long since passed, the Great Depression of the early 1930s, whereas *Godzilla* is a metaphor of man's tampering with science, as relevant a message today as it was over fifty years ago.

• • •

In America the film was altered substantially (to tone down, intentionally or not, the Atomic Bomb connection), incorporating new scenes with the American actor Raymond Burr so as to make the film more acceptable for Western viewers (the distributor, Embassy Pictures, felt there was no way Americans would attend an all-Japanese production just fifteen years after Pearl Harbor). Even then director/editor Terry Morse handled the film with extraordinary care, retaining the spirit, if not the letter, of the original (happily all of Ifukube's brilliant score was retained, which was not always the case, as his films were usually mutilated for their American release).

The differences between the two versions is worthy of an article in itself, but essentially the original ninety-eight-minute version was cut to only eighty minutes (which included the insertion of twenty minutes of

Americanized footage). Lost on the cutting-room floor were scenes focusing on the "love triangle" relationship between Emiko (engaged to Serizawa) and her lover Ogata, and the tension they feel in having to inform Serizawa of their relationship, as well as the adoption of the Odo Island native boy Shinkichi by Dr. Yamane after the boy's parents have been killed by Godzilla.

Also eliminated were important dialog scenes, which were substituted with new scenes of Burr — posing as newspaper reporter Steve Martin — interacting with characters not in Honda's film informing him of what is happening; in some instances Burr simply narrates over the source material. Burr also has "conversations" with the actors in Honda's film, thanks to intercutting between close-ups of the new and original footage, with Burr often seen chatting with extras with their backs to the camera clothed in wardrobes similar to the original actors!

The biggest alteration involves the distillation of the atomic bomb connection, such as the deletion of a scene where train commuters complain about Nagasaki and once again having to seek refuge in bomb shelters, as well as Yamane's crucial soliloquy at the end of the film in which he warns the audience of the dangers of atomic experimentation. Also deleted was an argument between Ogata and Yamane where the younger man mentions the "atomic cloud that still haunts us Japanese." The American "A-Bomb" becomes the Russian "H-Bomb" and the word "radiation" — used consistently in Honda's film — is never heard in the new footage, with the scars the survivors are experiencing now referred to as "strange burns" (for those interested in comparing the two versions, they are available on the *Gojira/Godzilla* DVD "Collector's Edition" from Classic Media).

Sadly, the film's desperately serious message was disavowed by critics 35 both in Japan and in America, largely because they considered *Godzilla* as a monster movie not worthy of serious consideration, whereas many able to see beneath the surface discovered the film's moral. Strangely, the fact that *Godzilla* was a great commercial success may have worked against it, spawning as it has over two dozen sequels of inferior quality that have tended to cheapen the original film's intent by simply attempting to cash in on a major merchandising enterprise.

For his part, Honda felt most moviegoers missed the point by getting caught up in the visuals, often musing that the kids would eventually get it once they reached adulthood. He was right, yet Honda wanted it both ways: by not making a direct statement and discreetly avoiding the real issue, he nevertheless made a picture so stunning that it succeeds as entertainment, thereby distracting many viewers from its moral compass. Whether or not he ultimately succeeded depends on the interpretation gleaned by the individual viewer; some understand the "hidden" meaning while others are simply captivated by the intriguing story, or just enjoy watching the fantasy elements. In his later years, Honda acknowledged his naive hope that the film would persuade the nations of the world to cease and desist their nuclear development. He did live long enough to see the end of the Cold War, nuclear tests, and the beginning of nuclear disarmament treaties, but his hope for a world without nuclear energy never came to pass.

● ● ●

There are a number of reasons to appreciate *Godzilla*'s role in film history, one of which was its enormous impact on the Japanese film industry. *Godzilla* was not only the first Japanese film to be made under a security lid and the first to be storyboarded, it was also the studio's most expensive and daring production up to that time. More important still is that before *Godzilla* all movies produced in Japan were indigenous products: domestic stories made only for their domestic audiences and where stories involving monsters were not to be taken seriously as authentic living creatures. The resultant production that premiered on November 3, 1954, was not only the first film in the longest running movie series originating from a single studio and the birth of a still-popular genre, but has also become the greatest international success in the history of Japanese filmmaking. It remains to this day the most famous Japanese film ever made.

It was also a gamble without precedent as no such film had ever been made in Japan before and there was no guarantee that Tsuburaya could pull off the heretofore untried special effects; nor was there any way of knowing how Japanese audiences would react to a thinly-disguised version of the horrific events that befell them during the war.

As it happened, *Godzilla* drew in nearly ten million Japanese viewers who were now able to deal with images that were indelibly integrated into their national psyche. Indeed the cathartic effect° the film apparently had was quite possibly the main reason for *Godzilla*'s success; the horrific sufferings of the past could be addressed and soothed by the most horrific fiction of the present.

The film was a supreme collaborative effort created by individuals 40 whose lives were forever changed by the specter of the mushroom cloud, many of whom were either directly involved or profoundly affected by

cathartic effect: the release of strong emotions, such as pity or fear, especially through an interaction with art.

the traumatic events of those times, including special-effects photographer Sadamasa Arikawa, who told a crowd at a screening of the film in 2003 that "*Godzilla* was very much a picture of its time." Just as the explosions over Hiroshima and Nagasaki were watershed moments in the archives of the twentieth century, representing an initial gaze into a frightening new world of terror, *Godzilla* will forever remain a portal to a past many Americans would prefer to forget and that the Japanese can never forget. It is now recognized as not only the cinema's first antinuclear film but also the finest re-creation of the mood and desperation of a civilian population devastated by the worst weapon ever used.

Moreover it stands as the greatest achievement of a team that would collaborate on many more fantasy films, including the producer who needed a last-minute replacement for an aborted coproduction, a special-effects maverick and an iconoclastic musician, and, ultimately, a sensitive and thoughtful director named Ishirô Honda, who made more films seen by more people around the world than any other Japanese filmmaker.

The terrible irony in all of this is that if *Godzilla* is indeed the representation of the dangers of man's tampering with atomic and nuclear power, it has more recently surfaced in such places as Three Mile Island, Chernobyl, and now in Fukushima, where at the time of this writing a possible nuclear-reactor meltdown threatens consequences beyond even the imagination of the men who brought such a terrible fiction to life (a recent e-mail sent by one of the workers at the plant desperately trying to avert catastrophe reads like dialog from *Godzilla*: "If we're in hell now, all we can do is to crawl up towards heaven. Who could stand this reality?").

Regarded by many today as merely "pop culture," at its time the movie *Godzilla* was a warning about a newly-christened crisis, one which has yet to be fully appreciated, and a legacy which should never be forgotten.

Understanding the Text

1. What is important about the movie's opening scene with the Japanese sailors? How does it create a context for the film?

2. Brothers details a number of parallels between the events at the end of World War II and scenes in the movie. What connections does he point out between the real events and the film?

3. Why did Ishirô Honda deliberately make the physical injuries and scarring to victims "far less shocking and graphic than the real thing" (par. 26)? What is the ultimate effect?

4. What are the principal differences between the original Japanese version of *Godzilla* and the first remake for American audiences, starring Raymond Burr? What were the reasons for those differences?

5. Brothers argues that the important issues in *Godzilla* were not taken seriously by its audience (par. 35). What is it about the monster/horror genre in general that may prevent audiences from considering issues seriously?

Reflection and Response

6. Brothers asserts that *Godzilla* is more about people than a monster. In what ways is that true? How does Godzilla the monster function as a representation of the very real fear of atomic destruction as well as the trauma of humiliating defeat in war?

7. Why has *Godzilla* had such staying power in people's imaginations? Consider that there are more than two dozen feature-length remakes or sequels to the film, not to mention two separate American television series and a large number of video games that feature Godzilla.

Making Connections

8. Brothers states that "*Godzilla* is a metaphor of man's tampering with science, as relevant a message today as it was over fifty years ago" (par. 30). Compare and contrast *Godzilla* and Mary Shelley's *Frankenstein* (p. 20), another story that springs from anxieties about meddling with science. What similarities are there in the creatures from *Frankenstein* and *Godzilla*, and how does the fact that Honda's Godzilla is a distinctly nonhuman monster create differences between it and Shelley's invention?

9. View the original Japanese version of *Godzilla* and compare it with a later version, either the one with Raymond Burr, presented as *Godzilla, King of the Monsters!* (1956), or a more contemporary version, such as *Godzilla* (1998) or *Godzilla* (2014). How do they differ, and what is the significance of the differences? Support your response with details from both films.

10. *Godzilla* was partially inspired by *King Kong* (1933). View the original *King Kong* and research the background of that film and its era. Then compare and contrast *Godzilla* and *King Kong*. How was *King Kong* an expression of the fears and anxieties of its time, and how were those fears different from the ones expressed in *Godzilla*? What in society has changed over time that makes *King Kong* less popular than *Godzilla* today?

Slender Man: A Myth of the Digital Age

Clarisse Loughrey

Not surprisingly, the internet has spawned its own monster, Slender Man. In the same way that the Frankenstein story originated as a response to a challenge to write a ghost story, Slender Man's origins can be traced to an online Photoshop challenge to edit a normal photograph through a paranormal lens. Slender Man sprang from the creative response of Eric Knudsen. However, much like Mary Shelley's creature in *Frankenstein*, Knudsen's Slender Man has developed far beyond its origins. Clarisse Loughrey, writing for the *Independent*, a British publication, examines the evolution of the Slender Man myth, the monster's various manifestations and victims, and its surge in popularity, moving from the online universe into the mainstream world of cinema and beyond. Loughrey, the culture reporter for the *Independent*, also runs a weekly movie review channel on YouTube, *That Darn Movie Show*, and has written extensively as a freelance writer in both print and online formats. This article appeared in the *Independent* on August 26, 2018.

It's inevitable that the modern-day boogeyman would live on the internet. As birthed by forums, fan art, and shaky YouTube footage, the Slender Man is a startling example of modern-day mythmaking. His form is deep-rooted in tradition and folklore: a spirit of the woods, he's largely characterized as a claimer of young souls.

He appears as a tall figure with overstretched limbs and dressed in a black suit, faceless. He has no motivation. He cannot be placated. And to witness him often brings its own death sentence.

When any phenomenon arises, of course, Hollywood is keen to cash in. With the myth first materializing in 2009, it's a little surprising to see that it's taken until now, and Sony's *Slender Man*, for it to finally skulk onto the big screen.

It's a story primed for the medium, especially in the context of its popularity within the world of "copypasta": small, easily digestible stories whose viral appeal is reliant on shock twists and intriguing hooks.

These are stories, also, that have the potential to be endlessly manip- 5 ulated and reimagined—a key ingredient in mythmaking, although the peculiarity of Slender Man is that, thanks to the nature of the internet, each of these retellings have been preserved; creating a digital trail that can trace the myth straight back to its originator. And to a single author: Eric Knudsen.

Slender Man watches children at play in a still from the 2018 Sony Pictures film, *Slender Man.*
Sony Pictures/Photofest

Under his username "Victor Surge," Knudsen created the Slender Man in 2009 as part of a Photoshop challenge on the "Something Awful" forum, in which users were asked to manipulate real photos to give them a paranormal edge. Knudsen submitted two examples, both black-and-white shots of children with a haunting, spectral figure in its background.

One caption read: " 'We didn't want to go, we didn't want to kill them, but its persistent silence and outstretched arms horrified and comforted us at the same time . . . ' — 1983, photographer unknown, presumed dead."

The other read: " 'One of two recovered photographs from the Stirling City Library blaze. Notable for being taken the day which fourteen children vanished and for what is referred to as 'The Slender Man.' Deformities cited as film defects by officials. Fire at library occurred one week later. Actual photograph confiscated as evidence.' — 1986, photographer: Mary Thomas, missing since June 13, 1986."

Knudsen's creation was immediately arresting, a perfect combination of Stephen King's flair for mystery (his direct inspiration was "That Insidious Beast" from *The Mist*) and H. P. Lovecraft's Gothic sensibility.

Knudsen's initial post was built on, as more details of the Slender Man's 10 nature and history were created by fellow users. From there, it exploded into a massive process of collective storytelling.

The Slender Man had become a viral sensation. There are infinite variations of the myth (*Wired* alone estimated the digital art-hosting site DeviantArt holds more than 113,000 sketches of Slender Man), with several major conflicting attributes: sometimes he has tentacles, sometimes not.

At times his victims are solely children, becoming more reminiscent of traditional folkloric beasts and faeries, at other times he stalks teenagers in true urban legend style.

However, there have been two major forces (possibly three, if the *Slender Man* film makes enough of a mark) that have significantly helped to shape the Slender Man myth. The first is a freeware survival horror titled *Slender: The Eight Pages*, released in 2012, which drops players into the middle of a dense forest with only a flashlight to defend themselves with.

The objective, should you dare, is to collect all eight pages spread across the map without locking eyes with the Slender Man himself, who has a tendency to suddenly appear at the most inconvenient of times. It was downloaded over 2 million times in its first month of availability. A sequel titled *The Arrival* was released in 2013.

The second greatest influence on the Slender Man myth is Troy Wagner and Joseph DeLage's YouTube series *Marble Hornets*. The channel's 87 episodes have amassed over 96 million views.

Told through found footage, its story concerns itself with a young man who investigates the mysterious circumstances surrounding an unfinished student film, only to become a target for a figure known as "The Operator"—who appears as a clear iteration of the Slender Man.

A film adaptation, titled *Always Watching: A Marble Hornets Story*, was released in 2015, with *The Shape of Water*'s Doug Jones in the role of "The Operator."

In 2014, the Slender Man broke out of internet culture, and into the wider consciousness, but only under the most tragic of circumstances. In Waukesha, Wisconsin, two 12-year-old girls stabbed their friend 19 times, later telling police it was under the orders of Slender Man.

They were picked up by law enforcement as they attempted to trek to the Nicolet national forest, convinced they would find his home there. Both girls were sentenced to mental institutions, with one eventually diagnosed with early-onset schizophrenia.

Since then, the Slender Man's legacy has been a complex one. It's an example both of the most wondrous and most destructive parts of our digital age: of how digital mythmaking has created a whole new collective force of imagination and ingenuity, while further blurring the line between fact and fiction, as has always been the danger of the myth's hazy origins.

> "Digital mythmaking has created a whole new collective force of imagination and ingenuity."

Understanding the Text

1. Loughrey states, "It's inevitable that the modern-day boogeyman would live on the internet" (par. 1). What does she mean by the "boogeyman"? Why is its presence on the internet inevitable?

2. What makes the myth of Slender Man modern? In what other ways does the myth draw from older tales?

3. What are the two forces that have worked to shape the Slender Man myth? Why are they important?

4. Loughrey finishes her article by retelling the story from 2014 of two girls who lured a third girl into a forest and stabbed her multiple times. What impression is conveyed by this story? How does it connect to the myth of Slender Man and its place in today's collection of monsters?

Reflection and Response

5. Examine the influences on the character of Slender Man. You may trace several that Loughrey cites in her article as well as additional ones you find on your own. How do these influences echo Mary Shelley's *Frankenstein* (p. 20) or John Polidori's "The Vampyre" — not just in the sense of the challenge, but in the external influences that work their way into the stories?

6. Loughrey makes much of the role of technology in the Slender Man myth: the Photoshop challenge, video gaming, online forums, and eventually the traditional cinema. Discuss how technology helped create, promulgate, and even invent variations of the central myth.

7. The Slender Man usually victimizes young children or teenagers, depending on the version of the myth. How does this myth relate to real-life stories of missing children and the fear all parents experience for the safety of their children? In your response, consider also the role of audience: is Slender Man a myth addressed to parents, or is it addressed to younger people? How might the answer to that question complicate your understanding of the fear created by Slender Man?

Making Connections

8. Consider other monster stories that have benefited from digital technology. A good starting point might be *The Blair Witch Project* (1999), which was one of the first popular movies to use the digital environment to create a whole new horror movie experience. Argue how the online world is one in which new monster stories can be invented — and flourish. Cite multiple examples.

9. Loughrey cites the works of Stephen King and H. P. Lovecraft as predecessors to the Slender Man myth. Examine how some monster stories influence other later works. Focus on one monster myth and trace its influences as far back as you can. How do those influences form new myths?

Monsters and the Moral Imagination

Stephen T. Asma

In this article, Stephen T. Asma, a professor of philosophy at Columbia College Chicago, argues that monsters have a purpose — not merely to express our fears but also to test our sense of morality. Although the likelihood of a real-life zombie attack seems negligible, other crises and traumas can and do occur. In fact, in our post-9/11 world, monsters have seen a sort of resurgence. Perhaps, as Asma argues, we create monsters as a reaction to the fears we experience and our inability to control the world around us. This article first appeared in the *Chronicle of Higher Education* in October 2009.

Monsters are on the rise. People can't seem to get enough of vampires lately, and zombies have a new lease on life. This year and next we have the release of the usual horror films like *Saw VI* and *Halloween II*; the campy mayhem of *Zombieland*; more-pensive forays like *9* (produced by Tim Burton and Timur Bekmambetov), *The Wolfman*, and *The Twilight Saga: New Moon*; and, more playfully, *Where the Wild Things Are* (a Dave Eggers rewrite of the Maurice Sendak classic).

The reasons for this increased monster culture are hard to pin down. Maybe it's social anxiety in the post-9/11 decade, or the conflict in Iraq — some think there's an uptick in such fare during wartime. Perhaps it's the economic downturn. The monster proliferation can be explained, in part, by exploring the meaning of monsters. Popular culture is re-enchanted with meaningful monsters, and even the eggheads are stroking their chins — last month saw the seventh global conference on Monsters and the Monstrous at the University of Oxford.

The uses of monsters vary widely. In our liberal culture, we dramatize the rage of the monstrous creature and Frankenstein's is a good example — then scold ourselves and our "intolerant society" for alienating the outcast in the first place. The liberal lesson of monsters is one of tolerance: We must overcome our innate scapegoating, our xenophobic° tendencies. Of course, this is by no means the only interpretation of monster stories. The medieval mind saw giants and mythical creatures as God's punishments for the sin of pride. For the Greeks and Romans, monsters were prodigies — warnings of impending calamity.

After Freud, monster stories were considered cathartic journeys into our unconscious; everybody contains a Mr. Hyde, and these stories give

---

xenophobic: relating to the fear of outsiders or foreigners.

us a chance to "walk on the wild side." But in the denouement° of most stories, the monster is killed and the psyche restored to civilized order. We can have our fun with the "torture porn" of Leatherface and Freddy Krueger or the erotic vampires, but this "vacation" to where the wild things are ultimately helps us return to our lives of quiet repression.

Any careful reading of Bram Stoker's *Dracula*, for example, will reveal 5 not only a highly sexualized description of blood drinking, but an erotic characterization of the count himself. Even John Polidori's original 1819 vampire tale *The Vampyre* describes the monster as a sexually attractive force. According to the critic Christopher Craft, [the] Gothic monster tales *Frankenstein, The Strange Case of Dr. Jekyll and Mr. Hyde, Dracula,* [and] Anne Rice's *Vampire Chronicles* rehearse a similar story structure. "Each of these texts first invites or admits a monster, then entertains and is entertained by monstrosity for some extended duration, until in its closing pages it expels or repudiates the monster and all the disruption that he/she/it brings," he writes.

● ● ●

A crucial but often-ignored aspect of monsterology is the role those beasties play in our moral imaginations. Recent experimental moral psychology has given us useful tools for looking at the way people actually do their moral thinking. Brain imaging, together with hypothetical ethical dilemmas about runaway trolley cars, can teach us a lot about our real value systems and actions. But another way to get at this subterranean territory is by looking at our imaginative lives.

Monsters can stand as symbols of human vulnerability and crisis, and as such they play imaginative foils for thinking about our own responses to menace. Part of our fascination with serial-killer monsters is that we (and our loved ones) are potentially vulnerable to sadistic violence—never mind that statistical probability renders such an attack almost laughable. Irrational fears are decidedly unfunny. We are vulnerable to both the inner and the outer forces. Monster stories and films only draw us in when we identify with the persons who are being chased, and we tacitly ask ourselves: Would I board up the windows to keep the zombies out or seek the open water? Would I go down to the basement after I hear the thump, and if so, would I bring the butcher knife or the fireplace poker? What will I do when I am vulnerable?

---

denouement: the ending of a story; the climax and resolution, when everything is explained and made clear.

The comedy writer Max Brooks understands that dimension of monster stories very well. In books like *The Zombie Survival Guide* and *World War Z*, Brooks gives us painstaking, haunting, and hilarious advice about how best to meet our undead foes. For its April Fools' edition, the otherwise serious journal *Archaeology* interviewed Brooks, asking him (tongue firmly in cheek): "Does the archaeological record hold any zombie-related lessons for us today? What can our ancestors teach us about meeting and, ultimately, defeating the undead menace?" Brooks replied: "The greatest lesson our ancestors have to teach us is to remain both vigilant and unafraid. We must endeavor to emulate the ancient Romans; calm, efficient, treating zombies as just one more item on a rather mundane checklist. Panic is the undead's greatest ally, doing far more damage, in some cases, than the creatures themselves. The goal is to be prepared, not scared, to use our heads, and cut off theirs."

Brooks is unparalleled in parodying a well-worn monster tradition, but he wouldn't be so funny if we weren't already using monster stories to imagine strategies for facing enemies. The monster is a virtual sparring partner for our imagination. How will I avoid, assuage, or defeat my enemy? Will I have grace under pressure? Will I help others who are injured? Or will I be that guy who selfishly goes it alone and usually meets an especially painful demise?

In a significant sense, monsters are a part of our attempt to envision the 10 good life or at least the secure life. Our ethical convictions do not spring fully grown from our heads but must be developed in the context of real and imagined challenges. In order to discover our values, we have to face trials and tribulation, and monsters help us imaginatively rehearse. Imagining how we will face an unstoppable, powerful, and inhuman threat is an illuminating exercise in hypothetical reasoning and hypothetical feeling.

You can't know for sure how you will face a headless zombie, an alien face-hugger, an approaching sea monster, or a chainsaw-wielding psycho. Fortunately, you're unlikely to be put to the test. But you might face similarly terrifying trials. You might be assaulted, be put on the front lines of some war, or be robbed, raped, or otherwise harassed and assailed. We may be lucky enough to have had no real acquaintance with such horrors, but we have all nonetheless played them out in our mind's eye. And though we can't know for sure how we'll face an enemy soldier or a rapist, it doesn't stop us from imaginatively formulating responses. We use the imagination in order to establish our own agency in chaotic and uncontrollable situations.

People frequently underestimate the role of art and imagery in their own moral convictions. Through art (e.g., Shelley's *Frankenstein*, Hitchcock's *Psycho*, King's and Kubrick's *The Shining*), artists convey moral visions. Audiences can reflect on them, reject or embrace them, take inspiration from them, and otherwise be enriched beyond the entertainment aspect. Good monster stories can transmit moral truths to us by showing us examples of dignity and depravity without preaching or proselytizing.

"Good monster stories can transmit moral truths to us by showing us examples of dignity and depravity without preaching or proselytizing."

But imagining monsters is not just the stuff of fiction. Picture yourself in the following scenario. On the evening of August 7, 1994, Bruce Shapiro entered a coffee bar in New Haven, Conn. Shapiro and his friends had entered the cafe and were relaxing at a table near the front door. Approximately 15 other people were scattered around the bar, enjoying the evening. One of Shapiro's friends went up to the bar to get drinks. "Suddenly there was chaos," Shapiro explained in the *Nation* the next year, "as if a mortar shell had landed." He looked up to see a flash of metal and people leaping away from a thin, bearded man with a ponytail. Chairs and tables were knocked over, and Shapiro protected one of his friends by pulling her to the ground.

In a matter of minutes, the thin man, Daniel Silva, had managed to stab and seriously injure seven people in the coffee shop. Using a six-inch hunting knife, Silva jumped around the room and attacked with lightning speed. Two of Shapiro's friends were stabbed. After helping some others, Shapiro finally escaped the cafe. "I had gone no more than a few steps," he recalled, "when I felt a hard punch in my back followed instantly by the unforgettable sensation of skin and muscle tissue parting. Silva had stabbed me about six inches above my waist, just beneath my rib cage."

Shapiro fell to the pavement and cried out, "Why are you doing this?" 15 Standing over him, Silva plunged the knife into Shapiro's chest, beneath his left shoulder. "You killed my mother" was the incoherent response that Silva offered his victim. Silva then pulled the knife out of Shapiro and rode off on a bicycle. He was soon apprehended and jailed.

Was Silva a monster? Not exactly. He was a mentally ill man who snapped and seemed to think that his mother had been wronged and felt some obscure need to avenge her. (She was, in fact, in a nearby hospital at the time, being treated for diabetes.) But from the perspective of raw experience, this horrifying event shares many qualities with the imagined monster attack. Shapiro and his unfortunate company were suddenly presented with a deadly, irrational, powerful force that sent them reeling for mere survival. And yet the victims demonstrated an impressive ability to reach out and help each other. While the victims were leaping away from Silva's angry knife blade, I suspect that he was for them, practically speaking, a true monster. I would never presume to correct them on that account. In such circumstances, many of us are sympathetic to the use of the monster epithet.

One of the fascinating aspects of Shapiro's experience is how people responded to his story after the fact. I have been suggesting that monster stones are encapsulations of the human feeling of vulnerability—the monster stories offer us the "disease" of vulnerability and its possible "cures" (in the form of heroes and coping strategies). Few monster stories remain indefinitely in the "threat phase." When fear is at a fever pitch, they always move on to the hero phase. Hercules slays the Hydra, George slays the dragon, medicine slays the alien virus, the stake and crucifix slay the vampire. Life and art mutually seek to conquer vulnerability. "Being a victim is a hard idea to accept," Shapiro explained, "even while lying in a hospital bed with tubes in veins, chest, penis, and abdomen. The spirit rebels against the idea of oneself as fundamentally powerless."

This natural rebellion may have prompted the most repeated question facing Shapiro when he got out of the hospital. When people learned of Daniel Silva's attack on seven victims, they asked, "Why didn't anyone try to stop him?" Shapiro always tried to explain how fast and confusing the attack was, but people failed to accept this. Shapiro, who was offended by the question, says, "The question carries not empathy but an implicit burden of blame; it really asks 'Why didn't you stop him?' It is asked because no one likes to imagine oneself a victim." We like to see ourselves as victors against every threat, but of course that's not reality.

• • •

Believers in human progress, from the Enlightenment to the present, think that monsters are disappearing. Rationality will pour its light into the dark corners and reveal the monsters to be merely chimeric.° A familiar upshot of the liberal interpretation of monsters is to suggest that when we properly embrace difference, the monsters will vanish. According to this view, the monster concept is no longer useful in the modern world. If it hangs on, it does so like an appendix—useful once but hazardous now.

I disagree. The monster concept is still extremely useful, and it's a per- 20 manent player in the moral imagination because human vulnerability is permanent. The monster is a beneficial foe, helping us to virtually represent the obstacles that real life will surely send our way. As long as there

chimeric: mythical, illusory, or imaginary.

are real enemies in the world, there will be useful dramatic versions of them in our heads.

In 2006, four armed men in Kandahar, Afghanistan, broke into the home of an Afghan headmaster and teacher named Malim Abdul Habib. The four men held Habib as they gathered his wife and children together, forcing them to watch as they stabbed Habib eight times and then decapitated him. Habib was the headmaster at Shaikh Mathi Baba high school, where he educated girls along with boys. The Taliban militants of the region, who are suspected in the beheading, see the education of girls as a violation of Islam (a view that is obviously not shared by the vast majority of Muslims). My point is simply this: If you can gather a man's family together at gunpoint and force them to watch as you cut off his head, then you are a monster. You don't just seem like one; you are one.

A relativist might counter by pointing out that American soldiers at Abu Ghraib tortured some innocent people, too. That, I agree, is true and astoundingly shameful, but it doesn't prove there are no real monsters. It only widens the category and recognizes monsters on both sides of an issue. Two sides calling each other monsters doesn't prove that monsters don't exist. In the case of the American torturer at Abu Ghraib and the Taliban beheader in Afghanistan, both epithets sound entirely accurate.

My own view is that the concept of monster cannot be erased from our language and thinking. It cannot be replaced by other more polite terms and concepts, because it still refers to something that has no satisfactory semantic° substitute or refinement. The term's imprecision, within parameters, is part of its usefulness. Terms like "monster" and "evil" have a lot of metaphysical residue on them, left over from the Western traditions. But even if we neuter the term from obscure theological questions about Cain, or metaphysical questions about demons, the language still successfully expresses a radical frustration over the inhumanity of some enemy. The meaning of "monster" is found in its context, in its use.

So this Halloween season, let us, by all means, enjoy our fright fest, but let's not forget to take monsters seriously, too. I'll be checking under my bed, as usual. But remember, things don't strike fear in our hearts unless our hearts are already seriously committed to something (e.g., life, limb, children, ideologies, whatever). Ironically then, inhuman threats are great reminders of our own humanity. And for that we can all thank our zombies.

---

semantic: relating to the study of meanings.

Understanding the Text

1. What are the different interpretations of monster stories that Asma cites, including those of the ancient Greeks and Romans, the medieval era, and Sigmund Freud?

2. Asma connects monsters with the "moral imagination." What does he mean by this term? Cite specific examples from the article.

3. What is the point Asma makes with the story of Bruce Shapiro? How does it connect to the idea of monsters? How does it relate to Shapiro's statement that "no one likes to imagine oneself a victim" (par. 18)?

4. What is the effect of juxtaposing monster stories with real-life incidents of crime and war? What benefit does that give Asma toward advancing his own argument? What is that final argument?

Reflection and Response

5. Asma speaks of learning from scientific "brain imaging" about people presented with "hypothetical ethical dilemmas" (par. 6). Do you find him convincing when he goes from real-life situations to situations regarding monsters? Why or why not?

6. According to Asma, "The monster concept is still extremely useful, and it's a permanent player in the moral imagination because human vulnerability is permanent" (par. 20). Apply this statement to a monster of your choice and argue how that particular monster concept can be useful.

Making Connections

7. Is Asma's thesis in "Monsters and the Moral Imagination" compatible with other explanations of monsters in this book? Consider, for example, the explanations given by Guillermo del Toro and Chuck Hogan for the popularity of vampires (p. 35), Chuck Klosterman's discussion about zombies (p. 39), or Sophia Kingshill's discussion of mermaids (p. 139). Do these ideas dovetail with Asma's, or do they contradict his assertions?

8. Asma makes the connection between imaginary monsters and serial killers or other real-life monsters. Investigate the impact of serial killers in Chapter 5 of this book or in other sources. Do real-life monsters have the same impact on the moral imagination as fictional creatures, or are there substantial differences? Defend your answer.

2 How Do Monsters Reflect Their Times?

Records of monsters date back to the earliest traces of the human experience, when people sparred with nature and the unknown just to stay alive. Monsters have never left our consciousness, although the characteristics of monsters have often changed. Certain monsters seem tied to particular times: the sphinx, for instance, belongs to the classical world, and it seems lost in today's monster landscape. By contrast, aliens from other planets have a prominent role in our imaginations today. Examining monsters and the times from which they come can open pathways of analysis and investigation of specific cultural values, practices, attitudes, and historical events.

Sometimes it's easy to laugh at other people's fear and confusion: we can look at descriptions of various monsters and know they could not possibly exist. However, as Ted Genoways recalls, many Americans were terrified by Orson Welles's radio broadcast *The War of the Worlds* in 1938. For many listeners, already nervous about an approaching war in Europe, an alien invasion from the sky seemed all too believable. Daniel Cohen examines the connection between culture and monsters in his look at centaurs, griffins, and rocs, as well as more exotic creatures such as the Persian *senmurv* and the *garuda* of India. Cohen reveals that earlier humans may have had better reasons for believing these creatures existed than modern observers are willing to admit. In the centuries after the fall of Rome, the fearsome forests of northern Europe brought rise to the creature Grendel, who slaughters those trying to build a new civilization as told in the epic poem *Beowulf*. Gerald Vizenor presents a traditional Native American tale in which a young hero, Naanabozho, challenges a monster, the great gambler. The tale features traits common to other hero/monster stories, but with interesting twists in the nature of both the hero and monster. Supporting the idea that monsters are derived from logical combinations of the cultures, values, and knowledge of the times, Matt Kaplan uses scientific and historical facts to show how people have been enticed to believe in vampires and zombies. W. Scott Poole shifts the focus to the monsters of the New World. Early explorers and settlers found plenty to be afraid of there, so they created monsters to accommodate their religious beliefs and their experiences of the natural world. For instance, the Puritans, struggling to bring control and order to their surroundings, felt that the devil, in all his disguises, was among them. The Salem witch trials were only one result of this mentality, which found monsters in those who were poor, elderly, or different. Nick Bostrom addresses an issue that threatens to overtake us in the future: Artificial Intelligence (AI). Bostrom asks the question: even though AI is our own creation, will it surpass us and potentially replace us? The chapter finishes with an excerpt from Isaac Asimov's classic science fiction work, *I, Robot.* The short tale "Robbie" forces us to examine the definition of life itself as robots become increasingly similar to humans.

If monsters are truly our own creations, paying attention to them can tell us a lot about ourselves, our past, and our present. Witches, aliens, women with serpent hair — all can be symbols for much more. Rational, scientific analysis can offer explanations for why a certain creature may appear to have the qualities that it does, but the monster remains monstrous. The values of a society and a culture are revealed in what it approves of and in what it rejects.

Here Be Monsters

Ted Genoways

Ted Genoways, former editor of the prestigious *Virginia Quarterly Review*, explores the connections between the monsters of the past and those of the present in an editorial introduction. In the early days of exploration, the unknown regions were thought to be populated with strange and dangerous creatures. To reflect that thinking, maps included the warning "Here Be Monsters." Today, although we've charted the planet, we still find monsters. Sometimes the monster is of our own creation, such as the threat of the nuclear age. Other times the monster is a real enemy, such as Adolf Hitler or Al Qaeda. How we react to the monster, real or imagined, says a lot about who we are. Genoways is the author of *The Chain: Farm, Factory, and the Fate of Our Food* (2014) and is currently editor-at-large for *onEarth*, an online publication of the Natural Resources Defense Council. He received a Guggenheim Fellowship in the Humanities in 2010.

On old nautical maps, cartographers inscribed uncharted regions with the legend "Here Be Monsters." Sometimes they would draw pictures of these fanciful beasts rising from the waters, and occasionally would even show them devouring wayward ships. This fear of the unknown, of that future that lies just past the horizon, has been with us always. To contain and put a face to it, our imagination has conjured everything from leviathans of the deep to beasts part-human and part-animal to a woman with snakes for hair and a gaze that turns men to stone. Imagining what we cannot truly imagine, we brace ourselves for the worst.

> "This fear of the unknown, of that future that lies just past the horizon, has been with us always."

In the pages of this magazine in 1939, as the United States teetered on the brink of entering World War II, Eleanor Roosevelt reflected on this very subject. By then, however, we had monsters of a different sort: space aliens. Discussing the public panic that occurred after Orson Welles's famous broadcast of *War of the Worlds*, Roosevelt wrote:

> [T]hese invaders were supernatural beings from another planet who straddled the skyway and dealt in death rays. . . . A sane people, living in an atmosphere of fearlessness, does not suddenly become hysterical at the threat of invasion, even from more credible sources, let alone by the Martians from another planet, but we have allowed ourselves to be fed on propaganda which has created a fear complex.

A monster threatens to devour a ship in *The Arrival of the Englishmen in Virginia* (1588) by Theodor de Bry.

Even after we defeated the Nazis and the Axis powers, the new technology that ended the war also brought new anxieties.

At the dawn of the nuclear age and the space age, we grappled with these fears — similar in many ways to our old ones, but arriving now from more infinite shores. Splitting the atom awoke the public to a universe almost too small for comprehension and aroused the fear that tampering with such elemental forces of nature might stir unknown monsters or, through the horrors of radiation, transform us into monsters ourselves. Likewise, propelling astronauts beyond the reaches of our own atmosphere seemed to heighten the possibility of alien encounters. And whenever we imagined the motives of these alien visitors, we again pictured the worst. They wanted earth women for breeding or men as slaves. Or, worse yet, they just wanted us for food.

. . . George Garrett reflects on his loopy and ill-fated role in writing one of these pictures. (In *Frankenstein Meets the Space Monster* [1965] the aliens aren't just after earth women; they're singling out go-go dancers!) These movies feel like high camp to us today, a kind of kitsch° that seems trapped in time, but what held thousands of viewers at drive-ins

5

kitsch: something that appeals to popular, lowbrow tastes.

across America in thrall? Surely, it didn't feel safe and distant then. It must have something to do with deep-seated anxieties about the future of our own planet, about our place in an uncompromising universe. Or even new parts of the world we thought we knew. Steve Ryfle, in his essay on *Godzilla*, reveals that the original 1954 Japanese version of the film—before the bad overdubbing and the cheeseball scenes with Raymond Burr inserted—was an overt commentary on the dangers we pose to ourselves in the nuclear age. The film's central figure, a scientist, has developed a weapon more terrible than the bomb and faces the dilemma of whether or not to use it against the monster awoken from the ocean floor by an atomic test. If we unleash this weapon, won't it only lead to another? Won't every new unknown be more horrific than the last?

Today we must grapple with the reality of these problems more than ever before. The unknown evil, in this case, will not turn out to be a stuntman in a rubber suit. In this one way, we can all agree: those who mean to do us harm are real and they are among us. Now the President of the United States must decide how to defend us without purveying fear and its conjoined twin, hatred. The evil intentions of Al Qaeda are not in doubt, any more than the evil intended—and carried out—by the Nazis was evident. And yet, it is not a simple matter of out-muscling a weaker foe. As Eleanor Roosevelt concluded:

It is not only physical courage which we need, the kind of physical courage which in the face of danger can at least control the outward evidences of fear. It is moral courage as well, the courage which can make up its mind whether it thinks something is right or wrong, make a material or personal sacrifice if necessary, and take the consequences which may come.

If we do not hew to this standard, if we give in to our fear, we face the real possibility of the permanent loss of liberty.

In the wake of the tragic school massacre in Beslan [in 2004], Russian President Vladimir Putin unveiled sweeping governmental reforms in the name of increased security. Stephen Boykewich, a Fulbright scholar in Moscow, writes . . . about the aftermath and impact. Succumbing to their fear, most Russians have chosen to allow Putin whatever control he desires. When [Secretary of State] Colin Powell expressed concern over these changes and suggested that Putin should instead seek a peaceful resolution with the Chechen separatists, Putin angrily replied, "Why don't you meet Osama Bin Laden, invite him to Brussels or to the White House and engage in talks, ask him what he wants and give it to him so he leaves you in peace?"

Obviously, this is impossible; nevertheless, we must resolve to find new ways to reach out to the world community, to be seen as a strong and benevolent power again, not simply a lion with a thorn in its foot. If we cannot right ourselves, regain our focus, and steady our nerves, we will be forever jumping at shadows and strong-arming those who we perceive as threats. We will retreat further from our fellow travelers on this lonely planet and everywhere we look, we will see monsters.

Understanding the Text

1. What does Eleanor Roosevelt suggest was the cause of the fears sparked by Orson Welles's *War of the Worlds* broadcast?

2. What does Genoways mean when he says that at the dawn of the nuclear age, our fears were "arriving now from more infinite shores" (par. 3)? Why should this be so if by that time the earth itself was completely charted? What does that suggest about how people's fears had changed?

3. What is the main conflict, according to Steven Ryfle, in the original *Godzilla* movie? How does it reflect the time period in which it was made?

4. In his closing paragraph, Genoways refers to a lion with a thorn in its foot. Research this reference if it is not familiar to you. What is it about? Why did Genoways choose this allusion to conclude his article?

Reflection and Response

5. Genoways lists a variety of monsters of different times, from the monsters that appeared on ancient maps in places that were uncharted, to the space aliens who threatened the United States prior to World War II, to Godzilla in the postwar world. What are the prominent monsters today, and how do they reflect our current fears and anxieties?

6. When Genoways says that the president of the United States must respond to threats "without purveying fear and its conjoined twin, hatred" (par. 5), what attitude does this reflect toward the real-life monsters that threaten us? Is such an attitude realistic? Support your response with specific examples and reasons.

Making Connections

7. Genoways writes that in the post-9/11 world, our responses toward those who mean us harm will in many ways determine who we are: "If we give in to our fear, we face the real possibility of the permanent loss of liberty" (par. 5). Do some research on legal changes in the United States in regard to freedom, privacy rights, laws pertaining to search and seizure, and other areas. Have we become a nation that sees monsters all around us and so have given up liberty for security? Or have we avoided the trap that Genoways warns us about? Explain your answer.

8. Pick an era in America's past and research the monsters that figured prominently in the culture at that time, whether in literature, film, television, or another medium. Analyze how the culture is reflected in those monsters.

The Birth of Monsters

Daniel Cohen

How do monsters such as centaurs, griffins, and rocs come into the human imagination? Daniel Cohen explores how people encountering strange beasts, or unfamiliar combinations such as a man on horseback, could be confused. He circles the globe to find examples of animal combinations, such as the Persian *senmurv* and the *garuda* of India. Some of these creatures are seen as good, but most are dangerous monsters. Cohen wrote more than one hundred books, many directed to children, such as *Southern Fried Rat and Other Gruesome Tales* (1989) and *Railway Ghosts and Highway Horrors* (1991). This selection comes from a more serious, adult-oriented book, *A Modern Look at Monsters* (1970).

When Hernán Cortés invaded Mexico he had fifteen cavalry men under his command. This handful of mounted men had an effect far exceeding their limited number. The Aztecs, who had never seen a horse before, much less a man on horseback, were terrified. They thought that man and horse were one.

The Incas of Peru reacted even more violently to Pizarro's horsemen. When one of the riders fell from his horse, the Inca warriors fled in panic, thinking that somehow the monster had broken in two.

William Prescott, who wrote the classic history of the conquest of Latin America, drew the analogy between the first impressions of the Aztecs and Incas upon seeing a man on horseback and the centaur, the half-man, half-horse monster of Greek mythology. Unlike the Indians, the early Europeans knew horses or at least horselike creatures. Early civilizations had used horse-drawn wagons, and somewhat later the horse-drawn war chariot became a standard part of the equipment of armies throughout the Middle East and North Africa. But riding was a comparatively late introduction in the civilized world.

The first riders that civilized peoples of the Middle East saw were probably nomadic tribesmen who swept out of the Eurasian steppe° as robbers and invaders. Riding almost certainly developed on the steppe, and the nomads were traditionally superb horsemen. Even later invaders like the Huns continued to inspire an almost supernatural terror among the peoples of the Roman world. Roman writers mentioned again and again how Hunnish rider and horse seemed to be one. It is not hard to imagine

steppe: a vast, treeless tract of land in southeastern Europe or Asia.

74

that those civilized city dwellers who faced the first invasion of mounted men reacted exactly the same way that the Aztecs and Incas had: they believed that horse and rider were one. And thus began the legend of the centaur. In Greek mythology centaurs were described as fierce, wild, and tribal—words which could well apply to the nomadic horsemen.

It is comforting to begin a search for the origins of ancient monster legends with this story of the centaur. If only one could speak with such easy assurance about the origins of the other monsters. A search for the beginning of the stories of the griffin (or gryphon), that fearsome half lion, half eagle, is typically tangled. Most of us probably became acquainted with the griffin through *Alice in Wonderland*: "They very soon came upon a Gryphon, lying asleep in the sun. (If you don't know what a Gryphon is, look at the picture.) . . . Alice did not quite like the look of the creature. . . ." As it turned out Lewis Carroll's griffin was a harmless even vapid° creature. This, however, was far from typical of griffins. A medieval bestiary warns men to stay away from the griffin "because it feasts upon them at any opportunity." The warning continues: "It is also extremely fond of eating horses."

Some people have suggested that, despite its frequent mention in literature, the griffin was never seriously believed to be a real animal. The griffin, they say, owes its origin to a heraldic practice called dimidiation. When two noble families were joined in marriage the elements that had dominated the coat of arms of each side were combined into a new design. Thus, the family of the eagle might at some point have married into the family of the lion, and the result was a hybrid, the griffin, which adorned the new coat of arms. The griffin was a common creature of heraldry.

This solution, though theoretical, is attractive but for one small detail—the griffin is far older than the practice of heraldry. One medieval bestiary speaks of the griffin as living mostly in "high mountains or in Hyperborean lands" —that is somewhere to the far north. The Romans had heard rumors of griffins in Central Asia. The depredations of these wild creatures were cited by refugees who came to Rome from the East as one of the major reasons for the mass movement of barbarian peoples which ultimately brought down the Roman Empire. The griffin was also a common element in the art of the nomadic Scythians of the steppe, and it seems likely that they picked it up from peoples to the north and east.

But the griffin was not associated solely with the northland. Pliny wrote of "the Gryphon in the country of the Moors." Pliny, you will recall, did not believe that such a monster existed.

5

---

vapid: dull, lacking liveliness.

Throughout the Middle Ages, objects reputed to be "griffin's claws" were brought to the markets of Europe. Those that came from the north were usually the tusks of extinct mammoths or the horns of the equally extinct woolly rhinoceros. Those "griffin's claws" from the southern regions were most often the horns of antelopes.

The griffin is not unique in the animal mythology of the world. A variety of fierce mammal-birds play an important role in the legends of many parts of the Middle East and India. The Persian *senmurv* or *sinamru* (perhaps "dog-bird"), while terrible in appearance and power, was thought to be a protector of mankind. The *garuda* of India is also benevolent. This deity is part bird and part man and closely associated with the god Vishnu. In Japan there was the troublesome *tengu*, a part-bird, part-man creature. In China the *T'ien Kou* or Heaven Dog was more terrifying than troublesome. It was an omen of evil often associated with comets and other frightening meteorological phenomena.

Are these various Oriental mammal-birds ancestral to the griffin? It is hard to say, for the family tree is not at all clear, but it seems reasonable to suspect that all of these various mythological conceptions developed in response to the same sort of creature in the natural world—the eagle or some other large bird of prey. The eagle might indeed seem fierce as a lion when compared with the other birds. Perhaps thousands of years ago men described the eagle or hawk as a "lionlike bird" or even a "lion bird." What began as a descriptive phrase might have been transformed by the artist into a hybrid which combined features of both eagle and lion. Ultimately the origins of this hybrid would be lost and the griffin, half lion and half eagle, would be enshrined in medieval bestiaries as a real animal that lived in a distant land. This myth would be reinforced by the occasional appearance of griffin's claws on the market. In addition there were doubtless tales told by travelers who said they had actually seen the monster firsthand, or had at least talked to people who had seen it firsthand.

While on the subject of bird monsters, we might have a look at the origins of that giant among fabulous birds, the roc. The roc is best known to us from the tales of the voyages of Es-Sindibad, or Sindbad the Sailor. Sindbad's adventures were related in *A Thousand and One Nights*, a collection of ancient tales from the Middle East.

The size of the roc is expressed in nothing but superlatives. When Sindbad first saw the roc's egg he thought it was the dome of a great building. Then the sky darkened and Sindbad saw "a bird of enormous size, bulky body, and wide wings, flying in the air; and this it was that concealed the body of the sun, and veiled it from view." The roc, says the story, fed

"The roc, says the story, fed elephants to its young."

elephants to its young. When Sindbad angered a roc, the giant bird took its revenge by dropping stones on his ships and sinking one.

If ever there was a purely imaginary monster, the roc sounds like it. Yet there are hints that the roc was more than a legend. Marco Polo mentions the roc, and says that the Great Khan of Cathay asked for evidence of the creature. An envoy brought back to the khan a gigantic feather from the island that was supposed to be the roc's home. The khan was impressed.

Marco indicates that the island home of the roc was Madagascar, and Madagascar was the home of a really gigantic bird. The bird is called *Aepyornis maximus*, or the elephant bird. It looked like a big ostrich and may have been the largest bird that ever lived. But more impressive than the size of the bird itself was the size of its eggs. They had the capacity of six ostrich eggs or 148 chicken eggs.

While *Aepyornis maximus* is definitely no longer with us, the time of its extinction is not known with any certainty. The elephant bird may very well have survived into the sixteenth century, and its extinction was probably brought about by hunters who preyed both on the huge birds and on their eggs. The trip from Madagascar to Baghdad, the city of *A Thousand and One Nights*, is a long one, but medieval Arabs were great sailors and traders. They conducted a thriving trade along the east coast of Africa, before the trade was disrupted by the Portuguese in the fifteenth and sixteenth centuries. Arab traders undoubtedly visited Madagascar, and they might have seen living specimens of *Aepyornis maximus*. Large numbers of broken eggshells of the giant bird have been found along the coast, and this has given rise to the theory that the Arab sailors themselves helped kill off the birds by stealing eggs for food and for use as convenient cups for holding liquid. Such monstrous eggshells would also have been valuable trade items and curious souvenirs to bring back to show the family and friends.

These same Arab merchants traveled as far as China and carried the tale of the roc with them to the court of the Great Khan. The "feather" shown at the khan's court could have been the frond of *sagus ruffia*, a palm tree that grows on Madagascar. This particular palm has enormous fronds. The general similarity of shape of the palm frond and a feather would not have escaped the notice of canny merchants anxious to impress the rich khan with the wonders of the Africa trade.

But the roc cannot be explained so simply, for our roc is really the *rukh*, a huge bird that figured prominently in ancient Indian mythology. Perhaps it would be more accurate to say that *A Thousand and One Nights* is really based on traditional tales of the Middle East and India, some of which date back to the third or fourth millennium BC. Therefore the legend of the roc was around a long time before anyone in the Middle East

15

could have gotten to Madagascar to catch sight of *Aepyornis maximus*. And there are other problems with this identification. The roc is definitely a flying bird, yet *Aepyornis maximus*, like the ostrich, was flightless. Its size might well have inspired legends of giants, but not flying giants.

For the origins of the roc-rukh legends we must again turn to the eagle or other large birds of prey. These creatures seem to have played an extremely important part in the mythology of the Middle East from earliest times. Eagle-like figures pop up in the art of the Sumerians, the earliest-known civilization. After centuries of retelling, one branch of the legendary cycle that surrounded the eagle must have grown into the legends of the huge rukh. When Arab traders returned from Madagascar with tales of enormous eggs, or with the eggshells themselves, this doubtless strengthened the legend of the rukh. People could no longer doubt its existence simply because they had never seen it. With their own eyes they beheld the shells of eggs that could not have been laid by any ordinary bird. Naturally the eggs were nowhere near the size of the one described in the Sindbad tales, but those stories were avowedly fiction, and the storyteller's exaggeration was taken for granted.

Few had seen the roc alive because these monstrous birds lived in   20
a distant island that was very hard to get to. No doubt more than one latter-day Sindbad spiced up his reminiscences of past voyages with descriptions of the roc that he was supposed to have seen. Who could dispute such a story? All of these—traditions, misinterpretations, misleading evidence, and deliberate falsehoods—converged to make the tale of the monster bird, the roc.

I suspect that most monster legends grew in a manner similar to those of the griffin and the roc. They started with observations of a real creature. These observations then became exaggerated and twisted through constant retelling, until the animal with which they had originally been associated was forgotten completely. The next step was to place this legendary animal in some distant or otherwise hard-to-reach place to explain why it was not seen more frequently. Bits of evidence like the griffin's claws or the roc's eggs were brought back to support the legend, and so it continued to flourish. Travelers' tales added an additional flavor of authenticity to the story.

Understanding the Text

1. After a discussion of centaurs, Cohen states: "It is comforting to begin a search for the origins of ancient monster legends with this story of the centaur. If only one could speak with such easy assurance about the origins of the other monsters" (par. 5). What does he mean by this statement? What other monsters does he discuss whose origins are not as easy to find?

2. Why does Cohen think that the heraldic explanation — that the griffin was created as a combination of symbols on coats of arms — is not convincing?

3. What other hybrid monsters does Cohen examine from around the world? What, if any, qualities do they have in common?

4. Cohen ends this selection with a discussion of a roc. What is a roc, and how is it different from the other monsters he examines?

5. How do physical artifacts figure into the creation stories of monsters, according to Cohen?

Reflection and Response

6. What is it about the griffin (part-lion, part-eagle) that seems to make it a particularly powerful symbol? Are the human values attached to the griffin an accurate reflection of how we see each part (lion and eagle), or is it more than the sum of its parts? Take note of the various regions of the world where the griffin is alleged to have lived. How might the belief that the griffin originated in far-distant lands affect the attitudes people have toward the griffin?

7. Cohen is best known for his children's books. Is there a connection between children's books and mythological creatures? If so, what is it? Cite examples in your answer.

8. The roc is the only monster in this selection that is not a hybrid; it is simply a vastly oversize bird. Do you think the roc qualifies as a monster? Explain your reasoning.

Making Connections

9. How do the stories of the Aztecs' and the Incas' first encounters with humans on horseback relate to our contemporary experience with technology that threatens to outstrip our own understanding and control, as described in Nick Bostrom's "Get Ready for the Dawn of Superintelligence" (p. 114)?

10. Cohen lists four specific mammal-birds: the *senmurv* or *sinamru* of Persia, the *garuda* of India, the *tengu* of Japan, and the *T'ien Kou* of China. Research more about these monsters. What aspects of these mammal-bird combinations led people to regard them with terror and fear or in a more positive light?

From Beowulf

Anonymous

The epic poem *Beowulf* is one of the few surviving texts originally written in Old English. The characters in the poem, however, are not English. Rather, they are from Germanic tribes that inhabited areas in what are now Denmark, Sweden, and other surrounding countries. This selection from the poem records the initial assault on Heort, a mead hall that is more than just a place to eat and drink: the hall is an attempt to bring civilization to a wild, unknown world. Angered by hearing sounds of feasting and songs of praise to God, the monster Grendel invades the hall at night, slaughtering the men inside. He does so night after night, with no man able to kill him and avenge the deaths. The original text is from about 1000 CE, but the story may have originated as much as four hundred years earlier. This translation is by Stanley B. Greenfield (1922–1987), who was a literary critic, prolific scholar and translator of Old English, and professor of English at the University of Oregon. [Editor's note: line numbers follow the Greenfield translation.]

The Building of Heort, and Grendel's Attacks

Then good luck in war was Hrothgar's lot:
glory in battle came and kinsmen   65
gladly obeyed him, a band of youths
swelled soon to a mighty host. His mind
conceived a great hall: he commanded
such a mead-hall be built as would be
ever held by men in memory;   70
therein determined to distribute
to young and old all gifts God gave him,
except public land and people's lives.
Then I heard that many tribes on earth
from far and wide were ordered to work   75
to make that building beautiful; soon
it was finished, finest of great halls,
in a short time. He whose very word
was widely held as law called it Heort.
He made good his vow: he gave out rings,   80
treasure at the feast. The hall towered
high, wide-gabled, awaited the hostile
surge of flame in battle, though the feud
of father- and son-in-law still lay
in distant time for dire hate to rouse   85

Then that powerful demon, he who dwelt
in darkness' impatiently endured
a time of torment, hearing daily
loud joy in the hall, the harp's music,
the bard's clear song. He said, who could best   90
tell of man's ancient origin,
how the Almighty Lord made the earth,
this wondrous land circled by Water;
how He set in triumph sun and moon
as lights for those living on the land,   95
and adorned all corners of the earth
with leaves and branches; how He breathed life
into all kinds of moving creatures.
So that lordly band lived joyfully,
happily, until a hellish fiend   100
inflicted painful crimes upon them:
that gruesome demon was called Grendel;
he haunted the waste borderland, held
in fief the moors and fens° and fastness.
The miserable man dwelt with monsters   105
all the while, proscribed by the Creator
among the kin of Cain, whose killing
Abel the Eternal Lord avenged:
Cain reaped no joy from that crime, for God
exiled him far from mankind for it.   110
Thence all wicked progeny awoke:
ogres and elves and the walking dead,
and those giants who strove against God
a long time: the Lord requited that.

When night descended, Grendel set out   115
to seek the towering hall, to see
how the Ring-Danes fared after drinking.
There within he found a troop of thenes°
asleep after the feast, unaware
of human care. That evil creature,
furious and greedy, grim and fierce,
at once was ready, and from their rests

fens: lowlands covered wholly or partially by water.
thenes: thanes; retainers or close warriors of the war-lord Hrothgar.

ripped thirty thanes, and thence departed
homeward bound exulting in booty,
sought his lair with his feast of the slain.   125
Then in the dawn of advancing day,
Grendel's ravage was revealed' to men; then
after feasting there was weeping, loud
morning wailing. The illustrious
prince, deserving good, sat dejected,   130
the mighty lord mourned the loss of thanes,
when they saw clearly the loathsome spoor°
of the damned spirit: here was strong strife,
hateful and long-lasting! In no less
than one night he once again performed   135
more atrocious and murderous acts,
unrepenting of his evil ways.
It was not hard then to find the thane
who sought a more distant sleeping place
elsewhere in softer chambers when he   140
had such evidence of enmity
from *this* hall-thane: he who escaped
that foe kept farther off, more secure.
Thus he ruled and fought unrightfully
one against all, till that best of halls   145
stood desolate. A long time things stood
thus: twelve years the Scyldings'° lord endured
such woe, more painful each passing one,
suffered dreadfully; and by sad songs
it became no secret to the sons   150
Of men that for a great while Grendel
waged hateful war against King Hrothgar,
season after season persisted
on his sinful path, would make no peace
with any man among the   155
    Danish host
or cease from crime, pay
    compensation:
no counselor had any cause for hope
of settlement from that slayer's
    hands!

"But the dreadful foe, death's
dark shadow, kept on killing
both the old and young, lurked
near and waylaid them, night
after night"

---

spoor: tracks of an animal that is being hunted.
Scyldings': another name for Hrothgar's warriors.

But the dreadful foe, death's dark shadow,
kept on killing both the old and young,   160
lurked near and waylaid them, night after night
roamed the misty moors: a mystery
to men, the twists and turns of demons.

So mankind's foe committed crimes,
the gruesome exile took grievous toll;   165
he dwelt in Heort in the dark of night,
making the hall, bright with treasure, his,
though God kept him from the throne where gifts
were shared, and showed him no affection.
Great anguish of mind and heartfelt grief   170
distressed the Scyldings' lord. Strong men
often sat in council, considering
how warriors who had courage might best cope
with his terrible and swift attacks.
At times in heathen temples they made   175
offerings, prayed to the soul-slayer for
aid against the great and endless calamity.
Such was their custom, the hope of
heathens: it was hell that
governed in their thoughts, not knowing God,   180
judge of deeds and true Lord, nor justly
how to praise Heaven's Protector,
the King of glory. Unkind the fate
of him who through cruel need must thrust
his sinning soul into the fire's embrace,   185
have no hope for change! Happy the fate
of him who after his death-day seeks
bountiful peace in the Lord's embrace!

Beowulf rips off the arm of the monster, Grendel.

Chronicle/Alamy Stock Photo

Understanding the Text

1. Why is Grendel upset by songs of praise to God? Consider his lineage, as a descendant of Cain. How is it fitting that Grendel is part of that lineage?

2. How long does Grendel rule over the hall? At what time of day does he rule? Why is he not able to approach the throne?

3. Because the characters in the story are not Christianized, the poet says that "it was hell that / governed in their thoughts, not knowing God, / judge of deeds and true Lord, nor justly / how to praise Heaven's Protector, / the King of glory" (ll. 179–83). What does the poet say is the result of their not knowing God?

4. How does the fact that *Beowulf* was written as a poem (and was likely sung) influence the presentation of the story? In your opinion, how might the work be different if it were written in prose form?

Reflection and Response

5. In your opinion, why does Grendel attack only the mead hall and not the surrounding huts and other lodgings? Why does he attack only at night? Consider what this means about the purpose of his attacks.

6. A key feature of the Germanic tribal culture of *Beowulf* is the concept of *wergild* in which one must seek revenge for the killing of a fellow member of the tribe. The revenge can be either another killing or receipt of a monetary payment — "pay compensation" (l. 156). Since the Danes are unable to kill the monster Grendel or induce him to pay for the deaths, how does he represent a threat not only to their lives but also to their cultural values?

7. Analyze the tension that exists between the Christian poet and the pagan characters of the poem. Examine particularly the criticism the poet launches against the characters who pray at pagan shrines for relief from Grendel. How might the poet use the monster to tell a moral tale?

Making Connections

8. Read more of *Beowulf* (many texts are available online as well as in libraries) to see how the hero Beowulf ultimately defeats Grendel. Then argue whether or not the modern world still sees the need for heroes who conquer monsters.

9. The popularity of *The Hobbit* and *The Lord of the Rings*, written by J. R. R. Tolkien, has led to the creation of an entire genre of its own: an early medieval fantasy world populated by knights, dragons, and numerous strange creatures in which good fights against evil. Not surprisingly, Tolkien himself was a scholar of Old English who knew the story of *Beowulf* well. Consider which kinds of actions are praised and admired, and which kinds are condemned, in *Beowulf* and in this new genre. How are the social values and actions of characters in *Beowulf* present, in one form or another, in one of Tolkien's stories or in another story in the same genre (e.g., the HBO series *Game of Thrones*)?

Naanabozho and the Gambler

Gerald Vizenor

Native American tribes have a rich history of storytelling. This tale is from the Anishinaabe people, who lived in what is now referred to as the Great Lakes region of the United States and Canada. In this tale, a young hero, Naanabozho, an orphaned child of a human mother and the god of the north wind, confronts a monster that threatens his tribe, a trickster figure known as the great gambler. This tale is part of a longer sequence that tells the story of Naanabozho, who was raised by his grandmother. Naanabozho has shape-shifting power that enables him to bring fire to his people; he also survives being swallowed by a whale before confronting the great gambler. The story is translated and edited by Gerald Vizenor, a member of the Minnesota Chippewa Tribe. Vizenor is a scholar, translator, and creative writer. He is a professor at the University of New Mexico and professor emeritus of the University of California, Berkeley. This excerpt is from *Summer in Spring: Anishinaabe Lyric Poems and Stories, New Edition* (1993).

Naanabozho and His Father

Naanabozho made extensive preparations to go on the war path. He painted himself as no *anishinaabe* ever was painted, and arming himself with a war club, he started for the fourth fold of the skies. The *manidoo*° saw his grandchild coming while he was yet in council and he became very much alarmed as *naanabozho* was invincible to the *manidoo* as well as the living, so it was hurriedly decided that he must endeavor to appease the anger of his grandchild by offering and granting him the full control of the earth, as sovereign lord and master. So when *naanabozho*, who was in the shape of a black cloud, came in sight several *manidoog* tried to persuade him in order to talk and reason with him so that he would not harm his father, but their appeals were of no avail. In blind frenzy *naanabozho* rushed at his father, who calmly stood, erect and firm with arms folded across his massive chest, and his snowy locks trailing to the ground.

When *naanabozho* came near, he raised one of his hands and motioned for him to stop. Then in a deep, full voice he spoke thus: *My beloved son, why do you seek to kill me. I did not kill your mother. I loved her too well to do that, but your dear mother died that you might live. You, whom I have guarded so fondly from infancy, and now you seek and would kill me.*

---

manidoo (plural manidoog): god, spirit.

Again *naanabozho* was obdurate and raising his war club on high would have struck his father down, but suddenly there appeared before him a beautiful vision, as of a young man with eyes that seemed over-flowing with mercy and kindness and who seemed to look through and through *naanabozho*. Then the vision spoke and said: *Listen my brother, let not your hand be raised against another. Seek not to take away or destroy that which you cannot give. Be reconciled, the earth is given you control, now peace be with you.*

Naanabozho knew that this was the *manidoo* of peace, his brother. So he allowed his father to go unmolested while he went about consulting the many *manidoog* as to the best course he should pursue in assuming charge and control of the earth. After he had learned what he desired to know, he returned to *nookomis*° and with the avowed purposed of making a tour of the earth.

After *naanabozho* had returned to *nookomis* and had refreshed himself 5 with the soothing comforts of sleep and food, he related to her the inci-dents attendant on his journey, and of the authority vested in him. He concluded by informing *nookomis* of his intention of making an extended tour of his realm, which would occupy about two years. When *nookomis* learned this, she was much grieved.

My grandchild, the land which you intend to visit is infested with majimani-doo, evil spirits, principally the followers of wiindigoo, the cannibal, who are very numerous, powerful and ferocious. And no one who has ever got within their power has ever been known to return. They first charm their victims by the sweetness of their songs, then they strangle and devour them. But your principal enemy will be the gichi nita ataaged, the great gambler, who has never been beaten and who lives beyond the realm of the niibaa giizis, dark-ness, and near the shores of the happy hunting-ground. I would beseech you, therefore, not to undertake so dangerous a journey.

With the increasing laurels of conquest, *naanabozho* felt that he was brave and as such, should know no fear. The warning words of *nookomis* were unheeded. After having made all necessary preparations he bid *noo-komis* goodbye and started on his journey. He followed the trail which led to the realms of *niibaa giizis* where all was shrouded in total darkness. Here he stopped and meditated as to what was best to be done. He con-sulted with the different birds and animals and friendly *manidoog*, and it was finally decided that *gookooko oo*, the owl, would lend him his eyes, and that *waawaatesi*, the firefly, should also accompany him to light the way. They were soon on their way through the realms of *niibaa giizis*. All

---

nookomis: grandmother.

around was darkness and *naanabozho*, in spite of his great owl eyes, could discern nothing for some time but the flitting of *waawaatesi*. For the first time in his life he experienced the chilly breath of fear, and wished that he had listened to the counsel of *nookomis*. But just then a voice whispered in his ear saying: *I am with you. You should never fear.* At this his fears were dispelled and he boldly walked on.

The path which *naanabozho* was traveling led him through swamps and over high mountains and by yawning chasms sometimes on the very verge of some awful precipice, and then again near the thundering roaring and maddening rush of some furious stream or cataract. From pit and chasm he saw the hideous stare of a thousand gleaming eyes. He heard the groans, the hisses and yells of countless fiends gloating over their many victims—the victims of sin and shame. Then *naanabozho* knew that this was the place where the *great gambler* consigned the spirits of his many victims and he vowed that if he ever destroyed the *gichi nita ataaged*, he would liberate the victims who were being tortured.

> "He heard the groans, the hisses and yells of countless fiends gloating over their many victims — the victims of sin and shame."

At last all noises gradually ceased, darkness disappeared, and it was again sunlight. *Naanabozho* put off his owl eyes and bid *waavaatesi* to return from whence he had come. He then proceeded to a high eminence where he looked about for the *wiigiwaam*° of the great gambler and he saw in the distance a large *wiigiwaam*. When he was very near the *wiigiwaam*, he saw that there were numerous trails coming from different directions but all leading towards the *wiigiwaam*. This *wiigiwaam* presented a ghastly and hideous appearance, it being completely covered with human scalps.

Naanabozho and the Gambler

Naanabozho approached the entrance of this ghastly abode and raising   10
the mat of scalps, which served for a door, found himself in the presence of the great gambler. He was a curious looking being and seemed almost round in shape and *naanabozho* thought he could not be a very dexterous gambler who would let himself be beaten by the being who was then grinning at him. Finally the great gambler spoke and said: *So, you too, have come to try* your *luck. And you think I am not a very expert gambler.* He grinned and chuckled—a horrible mingling of scorn and ridicule.

---

wiigiwaam: wigwam, lodge.

Reaching for his war club he continued: *All those hands you see hanging around this wiigiwaam are the hands of your relatives who came here to gamble. They thought as you are thinking. They played and lost and their life was the forfeit. I seek no one to come and gamble with me but they that would gamble. Seek me and whoever enters my lodge must gamble. Remember, there is but one forfeit I demand of those who gamble with me and lose, and that forfeit is life. I keep the scalps and ears and hands, the rest of the body I give to my friends the wiindigoo and their spirits I consign to niibaagiizis. I have spoken. Now we will play.*

At the conclusion of this speech, *naanabozho* laughed long and heartily. This was unusual for those who came there to gamble and the great gambler felt very uneasy at the stolid indifference of his guest.

Now, said the great gambler taking the *pagessewin—anishinaabe* dish game—*here are four figures—the four ages of man—which I will shake in the dish four times. If they assume a standing position each time, then I am the winner. Should they fall, then I am the loser.*

Again *naanabozho* laughed a merry laugh saying: *Very well, I will play, but it is customary for the party who is challenged to play any game to have the last play.* The great gambler consented to do this. Taking up the dish he struck it a sharp, quick blow on a spot prepared for the purpose on the ground. The figures immediately assumed a standing position. This was repeated three times, and each time the figures stood erect in the dish. But one chance remained, upon which depended the destiny of *naanabozho* and the salvation of the *anishinaabe* people.

He was not frightened, and when the great evil gambler prepared to   15
make the final shake, *naanabozho* drew near and when the dish came down on the ground he made a whistle on the wind, as in surprise, and the figures fell. *Naanabozho* then seized the dish saying: *It is now my turn, should I win, you must die.*

Understanding the Text

1. Naanabozho is capable of shape-shifting. What shape is he when he goes to confront his father, the god of the north wind, whom he believes has killed his mother? In your opinion, why does Naanabozho take that shape?

2. Where does the great gambler live? What dangers does that place present to Naanabozho? How does he deal with those dangers?

3. Describe the nature of the great gambler's game. Why does Naanabozho lack fear in the face of possibly losing his life?

4. This story was passed down for generations orally before being translated and printed in English. What are some of the problems inherent in understanding a story from an oral tradition, particularly one that originates in another language?

Reflection and Response

5. What is the role of *nookomis* in the story? What does it show about the role women played in Anishinaabe culture? How does it contrast with the role of men?

6. How would you describe the character of the great gambler? How is he a threat to Naanabozho's people? What might he symbolically represent?

Making Connections

7. How does the story of Naanabozho fit into the mold of other hero stories from different times and places? Research more about the myth of the hero across different cultures. You may wish to read more of Naanabozho's story as well as other mythical heroes. (Joseph Campbell's *A Hero with a Thousand Faces* is a good starting point for a discussion of mythic heroes.) Examine points of similarity and difference in your analysis.

8. Naanabozho confronts his father, the god of the north wind, at the start of this passage. How does Naanabozho's hostility to his father reflect other monster stories in which a character fights against his or her creator? What is the conflict about, and how is it resolved? How is this resolution different from what happens in other stories? Be specific.

Cursed by a Bite

Matt Kaplan

Investigating the origins of vampires and zombies, Matt Kaplan uses history and biochemistry to decipher how the myths about these creatures could have evolved from actual events. Vampires may be the logical repository for fears about death and disease — fears that could have been exacerbated by the appearance a human corpse has when exhumed. Zombies may have been the creation of plantation owners looking to enslave workers by poisoning them with a dangerous cocktail of anesthetics, muscle relaxants, and hallucinogens. Kaplan is a science journalist who regularly contributes to publications such as *National Geographic*, *Nature*, *New Scientist*, and the *Economist*. This excerpt comes from his book *Medusa's Gaze and Vampire's Bite: The Science of Monsters* (2012).

Slinking through the shadows of night, they come to feed on the innocent. Seemingly human in appearance, the threat that they pose becomes apparent only as needle-sharp fangs pierce the throat of their intended victim and blood is sucked away. When every last drop of this precious life essence is consumed, prey becomes predator, seeking out blood to fuel its own newly acquired supernatural hunger. Vampires are among the world's most celebrated and popular monsters, and they have an extremely complex history and biology surrounding them, supported by a long line of books and movies featuring them as both villains and heroes. Yet working out exactly which fears drove the rise of vampires is a tricky question to answer because they are such multifaceted monsters with no clear point of origin.

On the face of it, they are predators like lions and play upon the terror of being killed by a nocturnal hunter. With such a basic fear, one would expect vampires to be present during ancient times when fears of beasts lurking in the night were at their height, yet vampires as we know them today arrived on the scene only in the eighteenth century. Even so, earlier reports of creatures resembling these monsters do exist.

In the *Odyssey*, Odysseus is forced to travel to the land of the dead and confront the ghosts of people he once knew in order to gain information to aid him on his quest. The witch Circe advises that he must allow the ghosts to feed on blood freshly spilled from the body of an animal to gain their trust and knowledge. At first he is highly protective of the pool of blood that he spills on the ground, allowing only the ghost of the wise man, Teiresias, to feed and answer his questions. But then the ghost of Odysseus's mother appears and fails to recognize him as her own son. Odysseus turns to Teiresias for answers: "Tell me and tell me true, I see my poor mother's ghost close by us; she is sitting by the blood without saying a word, and though I am her own son she does not remember me and speak to me; tell me, Sir, how I can make her know me." Teiresias replies, "Any ghost that you let taste of the blood will talk with you like a reasonable being, but if you do not let them have any blood they will go away again." Odysseus then allows the ghost of his mother to feed on the blood, and her memories of him come flooding back.

For Homer, blood is clearly a link between the dead and the living, even if it has to be spilled from an animal's body onto the ground to have this effect. However, while the spirits in the *Odyssey* are a tantalizing ancestor to the modern vampire, they are still very different, and it is not until nearly two thousand years after Homer, during the late 1100s, that creatures more like the vampires of modern fiction appear in Europe. The person who documents these monsters is William of Newburgh, an English historian who is widely thought to have had a network of trustworthy informants who helped him report on historic events that took place between the days of William the Conqueror in 1066 and those of Richard the Lionheart in 1198.

• • •

William of Newburgh told many . . . stories of the dead rising from the grave, and he had much company. In 1591, in the town of Breslau (now the Polish city of Wrocław), a shoemaker who killed himself by putting a knife through his neck, came back to haunt those around him by pressing against their necks in the night. He was ultimately found in his grave with the wound in his neck just as fresh and red as it had been when he died. In 1746, the French abbot Augustin Calmet reported, "A new scene is offered to our eyes. People who have been dead for several years, or at least several months, have been seen to return, to talk, to walk, to infest the villages, to maltreat people and animals, to suck the blood of their close ones, making them become ill and eventually die."

"Terrified by these sights, people chopped off heads, drove stakes through hearts, and jammed bricks into decaying mouths to keep the monsters from biting anything more."

The solution to the undead threat that locals turned to was exactly what William of Newburgh described. They dug up the graves of the offending monsters to destroy them and found that recently buried corpses often had blood on their lips, bloated stomachs that looked as if they had just fed, blood still flowing inside their bodies, fresh-looking organs, clawlike fingernails, and elongated canine teeth. Terrified by these sights, people chopped off heads, drove stakes through hearts, and jammed bricks into decaying mouths to keep the monsters from biting anything more. It must have been dreadful business, but there are no reports of the monsters ever fighting back. They are always just corpses in graves taking a beating.

Finally, after hundreds of years of terrorizing Europe, all these walking corpses and ghosts earn the name "vampire" in the second edition of the *Oxford English Dictionary* in 1745. It was described as "a preternatural being of a malignant nature (in the original and usual form of the belief, a reanimated corpse), supposed to seek nourishment, or do harm, by sucking the blood of sleeping persons." People must have been scared out of their socks.

Mortifying Misunderstanding

With so many traits and behaviors being associated with these early vampires, it is likely there were several fears merging together to form these monsters. As such, it seems best to start with the most concrete details being described: Vampires had bloody mouths, bloated stomachs, fresh blood in their bodies, and, sometimes, claws and fangs.

The Europeans who were initially digging up corpses were probably not exaggerating. After people die, bacteria living within the body often continue to be productive and generate gases that collect inside. The gas production leads to an effect that morticians refer to as "postmortem bloat," and while it has nothing to do with diet or recent feeding, it can make the belly look swollen and lead people to conclude that the corpse has recently eaten.

In addition, gas buildup inside the body can cause blood to get pushed   10
up from the lungs, passed through the trachea, and out of the mouth so that it stains the teeth and lips. This likely created the illusion that the bloated stomach was not simply full, but full of blood that the corpse had recently consumed, logically leading to the idea that the monster fed on blood.

Furthering the idea of the animated corpse, under certain circumstances bacteria-created gases can move past the vocal cords and create sound. This often occurs when bodies are handled or meddled with after death, causing corpses to make noises as if they are groaning or, in rare cases, speaking.

As for elongated canines and clawlike fingernails, there is a medical explanation for this too. After death, tissues die and waste away; the skin begins to shrink, and this leads it to be pulled back along both the nail beds and the gum line. As a result, the nails and teeth become more prominently exposed than they were at the time of burial. Of course, this is an illusion, but to early vampire hunters who had worked themselves into a lather over the perceived plague of the undead, these were fangs and claws indicative of a vampiric transformation.

All of these natural processes can explain the descriptions of early vampires and can even account for why Homer, way back in ancient Greece, suggested that the dead liked to feed on blood. But one thing that is not immediately clear is why the belief of the dead leaving their graves to attack the living gained such popularity during the 1100s when William of Newburgh was writing but not during the days of Homer. One possibility worth considering is that people being buried during William's time were not actually dead.

Today there are a lot of tools available, like blood pressure cuffs, stethoscopes, and heart monitors, that help doctors determine whether someone is alive or dead. Yet even with these devices, patients with very weak or infrequent heartbeats can easily be declared dead by mistake. As an example, in Jan Bondeson's book *Buried Alive*, which goes into great detail on how accidental burials happened (and still do), the tale is told of a Frenchman named Angelo Hays who suffered a brutal motorcycle accident in 1937. At the hospital he was not breathing, had no detectable pulse, and had a serious head injury. The doctor, using a stethoscope, could not hear anything, and Hays was sent to the morgue. Three days later, as he was buried, an insurance company realized Hays had been covered by a policy for up to 200,000 francs and sent an inspector out to investigate the accident before paying up. The inspector ordered the body exhumed to look at the injuries and to confirm the cause of death. Remarkably, the doctor in charge found the corpse to still be warm. Hays returned to the land of the living and is thought to have survived his near-death ordeal by being buried in loose soil that allowed some flow of oxygen to the coffin and by needing very little oxygen in the first place as the result of his head injury reducing all metabolic activities in the body. Bondeson relates a few more similar stories and argues that if we see such cases now, they probably were taking place somewhat more often in the past when vital sign monitoring tools were not available. Could such events of still-living but "geologically challenged" patients have been feeding into undead mythology?

Rising from the Grave

In 1938, the author, folklorist, and anthropologist Zora Neale Hurston, 15 then a student of the noted anthropologist Franz Boas at Columbia University, proposed there might be some material basis for the stories told in Haiti of individuals being raised from their graves by voodoo masters. These raised people, or zombies, legends said, were robbed of their identities, enslaved, and forced to work indefinitely on plantations. Hurston was not believed. For decades, the wider research community ignored her suggestions and in some cases actively ridiculed her, but this attitude eventually changed.

In May 1962, a man spitting up blood and sick with fever and body aches sought help at the Albert Schweitzer Hospital, a facility operated in Haiti by an American charity. Two doctors, one of whom was an American, did their best to save him, but to no avail. The man's condition deteriorated and he was declared dead shortly after his arrival. At the time of his death, he was diagnosed as suffering from critically low blood pressure, hypothermia, respiratory failure, and numerous digestive problems. What exactly caused such systemwide problems remained a mystery. The man's sister was called in to identify his body and stamped her thumbprint to the death certificate to confirm he was her brother and that he was, indeed, dead. Eight hours later he was buried in a small cemetery near his village, and ten days later a large stone memorial slab was laid over his grave.

In 1981, the sister was approached by a man at her village market who introduced himself to her using the boyhood name of the dead brother. It was a name that only she and a handful of other family members knew, so he seemed real enough. The man explained that he had been made into a zombie and forced to work on a sugar plantation with many other zombies until their master died and the zombies were freed. The media went crazy with the story, particularly in Haiti, and Lamarck Douyon, the director of the Psychiatric Institute in Port-au-Prince, made up his mind to test whether this zombie tale could possibly be true.

Douyon knew that digging up the grave would prove nothing; if the man and his zombie story were fraudulent, it would have been easy for the deceivers to remove remains from a rural village cemetery. Instead, Douyon collaborated with the family to construct the ultimate identity test. He would ask the man a series of questions that only the brother would know all the answers to. The man passed the test, and later, when the sister's thumbprint and the thumbprint on the death certificate were confirmed by Scotland Yard to be identical, Douyon concluded the man's story was likely true. There had to be something real about the zombie mythology of the island.

All of the evidence pointed to the idea that some sort of a poison had been used to make the man appear dead after making him quite ill. Then, after he was buried, he had been exhumed by his poisoner so he could be enslaved. Realizing that this was a matter for a biochemist rather than a psychologist, Douyon and other doctors in Haiti asked the Harvard ethnobiologist Edmund Wade Davis to get involved.

Davis conducted several expeditions to Haiti and collected five zom 20 bie poison recipes from four different locations. All the poisons varied in the number of tarantulas, lizards, millipedes, and nonvenomous snakes added to the brew, but there were a handful of similarities that caught Davis's attention. All recipes contained a species of ocean-dwelling worm (*Hermodice carunculata*), a specific tree frog (*Osteopilus dominicensis*), a certain toad (*Bufo marinus*), and one of several puffer fish (also known as blowfish in some regions).

Since these organisms appeared in all the different zombie poisons, Davis focused his attention on them. He found that the worm had bristles on its body that could paralyze people, and the tree frog was closely related to a frog species that released toxins on its body that could cause blindness in those who touched it. Furthermore, the toad, he learned, was a chemical nightmare. Some of the compounds in its body functioned as anesthetics, some as muscle relaxants, and some as hallucinogens. He noted that earlier studies conducted with the toad compounds had discovered they induced a rage similar to the berserker rages found in Norse legends, and these studies suggested that compounds of closely related toads had once been consumed by ancient barbarians as they charged with reckless courage into battle and shrugged off all but the most lethal attacks. But by far the most interesting ingredients in the zombie poisons were the puffer fish.

Puffer fish, which are well known for their deadly nerve toxins, are said to be tasty. Eating them comes with the serious risk of being poisoned, but this doesn't put off the Japanese. Called fugu in Japan, puffer fish is something of a dining adventure that popularly leaves consumers with feelings of body warmth, euphoria, and mild numbness around the mouth. Of course, if the chef gets fugu preparation wrong, diners end up in the hospital. Because the fish is so popular, hospitalization occurs with relative frequency and, as a result, there is a lot of medical literature on what fugu poisoning looks like.

Common symptoms include malaise, dizziness, nausea, vomiting, very low blood pressure, headache, and initial numbness around the lips and mouth that spreads to the rest of the body and often becomes severe. Eyes become glassy, and patients who survive the experience say it felt as if their bodies were floating while they could not move. They remained fully aware of their surroundings and alert during the poisoning experience. In one dramatic account, a fourteen-year-old boy in Australia, who accidentally ate puffer fish while on a camping trip with his family, recalled his family talking in the car as he was taken to the hospital, the nurses wishing him good morning and good night, and the doctors speaking their medical mumblings all while entirely paralyzed and feeling "light."

Davis found this intriguing because when he interviewed the man who claimed to have been made a zombie, he learned that he had remained conscious the entire time, heard his sister weeping when she was told that he had died, and had the sensation of floating above the grave. These descriptions, in combination with the medical reports filed when the man had been in the hospital on the night of his "death," suggested that puffer fish poison had been at work.

Upon further investigation, Davis learned that zombie makers created their poisons and exposed victims to these toxins by releasing them in the air near where the person lived or by putting them in places where the person was likely to make contact, such as on door handles or window latches. Lacing food with the poison was never done, because zombie makers believed it would kill the victim too completely. 25

After burial, zombie makers had their assistants pull victims out of their graves and then beat them fiercely to drive their old spirit away. This was followed by binding the exhumed person to a cross, baptizing them with a new zombie name, and force-feeding them with a paste made from sweet potato, cane syrup, and *Datura stramonium*, one of the most hallucinogenic plants known.

Davis suggested in the *Journal of Ethnopharmacology* in 1983 that these ghastly experiences, combined with the potent initial poisoning, created a state of psychosis that literally transformed people into zombies who would do anything they were told by their masters. This, he argued, explained why voodoo magic was widely perceived as raising the dead and why Hurston was right. People literally were being buried alive and then dragged back to the living world as zombies.

Undead Plague

But what of vampires? The early stories about these monsters do not support the "buried alive" theory very strongly, and there are no indications of poisons or zombie makers being involved with vampire creation. The vampire historian Paul Barber points out in his book *Vampires, Burial, and Death* that none of the early vampiric accounts actually describe vampires digging themselves out of graves, a fact that William of Newburgh's stories support. The protovampires just tend to emerge from the grave. This hints that early proponents of the vampire myth might have been making up this element of vampire behavior to explain something they were seeing in the world around them.

Today, if a person in a family falls ill with a contagious and potentially lethal disease, doctors usually have the knowledge to identify it, prescribe treatment, and suggest quarantine measures if they are needed. In the days before modern medicine, when understanding of infectious disease transmission was rudimentary, people exposed to lethally contagious individuals had a good chance of following their friends to the grave. But they would not have done so immediately. Viruses and bacteria take time to spread through the body before having noticeable negative effects. This delay, which is known in the medical community as the incubation period, varies with the disease and can range from hours for some gut and respiratory infections to years for viruses like HIV. In most cases, though, incubation for diseases is a matter of days.

Imagine what people in those days saw after a loved one died from a highly lethal and contagious disease, like tuberculosis or a nasty strain of influenza. First, those who had lived with the diseased individual would fall ill upon the completion of the incubation period and run a high risk of dying. Then, those who had tended to these diseased individuals would also fall ill and transmit the disease before dying. One death would follow another in a dominolike progression. In a morbid sense, these patients were literally killing their friends and relatives, but from their deathbeds rather than from the hereafter. However, because of the incubation period, it wasn't clear to anyone how the disease was being passed along.

Driven into a panic by plagues of contagious diseases, people desperately sought an explanation. This search for answers even appears in William of Newburgh's story: The monster "filled every house with disease and death by its pestiferous breath." People were already somewhat aware of what was going on, but rather than pointing the finger at microscopic pathogens (which would have been impossible since microscopes were not even in use until the mid-1600s), they came up with the idea of the dead returning to kill off their friends and family. This led someone at some point to open up a grave and have a look. Shocked by the discovery of a bloody-mouthed corpse with a bloated belly, claws, and fangs, a connection was likely made between this horrific sight and the plague of death spreading throughout the community.

This seems logical, but it raises a question about timing. Why does the fear of vampires begin during the 1100s, when William of Newburgh was writing? Highly lethal and contagious diseases were hardly new things. In fact, Ian Barnes at Royal Holloway, University of London, published a study in the journal *Evolution* in 2011 revealing that infectious disease has played a key role in human evolution for centuries. Remarkably, this study found that humans who have been dwelling in places where population densities have been high for a long time carry genes that are particularly good at granting resistance to certain contagious diseases. This makes sense since places with higher population densities would have more humans available (and living in closer proximity) for diseases to infect and thus tend to be reservoirs where the infections could linger for long periods. People who carried genes that coded for immune systems strong enough for them to survive this pathogenic onslaught proliferated while those who did not, died out. The study specifically notes that people from Anatolia in Turkey, where dense settlements have been around for nearly eight thousand years, carry a gene granting an innate resistance to tuberculosis, a disease that wreaked havoc in ancient cities. In contrast, people with almost no history of dense urban living, like the Saami from northern Scandinavia and the Malawians in Africa, do not show similar genetic resistance.

So it seems unreasonable to argue that people started digging up graves and inventing vampires as monsters only to explain the spread of contagious disease. If this were the whole story, vampires would be expected to have emerged as monsters much earlier. There had to have been other factors associated with the rise of the modern vampire, and clues to what these might have been can be found in one of the stranger vampire traits.

The Sweet Smell of Garlic

According to some folktales, vampires are repelled by garlic, and for the most part this idea has remained tethered to the monsters for centuries. While modern enthusiasts of Gothic horror accept this trait as simply part of what vampires are, if you stop to think about it, being repelled by garlic is a rather bizarre quality to associate with a monster. The threat of sunlight makes the most sense. Evil things tend to be active in the dark and thus sunlight should naturally harm them. However, early vampire lore does not present sunlight as a threat. It is garlic that gets mentioned.

Garlic has a history of being used to protect the innocent from the 35 forces of evil. The Egyptians believed that it could repel ghosts, and in Asia, garlic has long been smeared on the bodies of people to prevent them from being targeted by the spells of witches and wizards. Is there logic to this?

Some studies have shown that garlic fights infection, reduces blood pressure, and lowers cholesterol. For this reason, you could argue that any monster conjured up to explain inexplicable diseases, including vampires, came to be viewed as "fended off" by garlic because it was helping to boost immune system function. However, there is a problem. The scientific community is nowhere near any sort of consensus on the powers of garlic because its effects are, at best, weak. So one has to wonder: If modern researchers testing garlic's potential in controlled laboratory settings are having trouble determining if it really grants sub-stantial benefits, were ancient people able to detect benefits at all? Or was there something else going on?

Foul odors created by corpses were often covered up by powerful smells like that produced by garlic, and there is some literature suggest-ing that, along with strong-smelling flowers, garlic was used at funerals where the corpse was getting a bit stinky. This may have been how it came to be connected with protecting people from the evil and the walk-ing dead. Yet a most intriguing explanation for garlic being associated with vampires stems from the field of neurology.

During the 1600s, many Romanians believed that rubbing garlic around the outside of the house could keep the undead away, that holy water would burn them like boiling oil, and that throwing a vampire's sock into a river would cause the menace to enter the water searching for the sock and be destroyed. Intriguingly, Juan Gómez-Alonso, a neu-rologist at the Hospital Xeral in Vigo, Spain, points out that these three things all have a connection to rabies.

In a report published in the journal *Neurology* in 1998, Gómez-Alonso explains that while the rabies virus can cause animals to become increas-ingly paralyzed as it spreads, in afflicted humans it can have a frighten-ing effect on the mind leading to a condition known among medical practitioners as furious rabies. As the virus attacks their nervous system, patients become restless; some leave their beds and wander the surround-ing area. They have trouble swallowing, frequently drool bloody saliva, become fiercely dehydrated and very thirsty. Worse, they often suffer from persistent feelings of terror and have a tendency to become angry and aggressive. Most important, furious rabies frequently attacks the sec-tion of the brain controlling how the body manages emergency respira-tory activities like coughing and gasping.

Nerve cells in the lining of the nose, throat, larynx, and windpipe 40 become extremely sensitive to noxious fumes and liquids. For this rea-son, patients with furious rabies suffer from spasms and extreme fear when they are forced to endure exposure to pungent odors (like that of garlic) or are presented with water (remember, they are desperately thirsty but cannot swallow). What do these spasms look like? When con-fronted, rabies patients tend to make hoarse gasping noises, clench their teeth, and retract their lips like animals.

Rabies has another connection to vampires based upon the way it is transmitted. Unlike, for example, influenza and tuberculosis, which are spread invisibly by particles in the air, rabies is primarily transmit-ted through bites. Most infections in people occur when a rabid animal breaks human flesh with its teeth and contaminates the wound with the infected saliva. The animals that most commonly spread rabies to humans in this way are dogs, wolves, and bats, all of which have a history in legends of being associated with vampires (bats are more recent than dogs and wolves, but all have been connected to the monsters for a while). Human-to-human transmission of rabies is all but unheard of today; however, historical accounts of people being bitten by rabid individuals do exist, and it seems likely that incidents of authorities or doctors being bitten while trying to subdue or capture rabid patients have taken place. In this case, the bite wound would heal as the rabies virus incubated inside the newly infected person's body. The individual who made the bite would die, but in time a new monster would be born.

Rabies is spread not only through bites. It can also be spread through sexual activity. Furious rabies can cause hypersexuality and leave people with powerful feelings of sexual excitement. Men with the condition can develop erections that last for several days, and one individual is documented as having had sexual intercourse thirty times in a twenty-four-hour period before the disease claimed him. With such powerful sexual stimulation at work and with patients so severely mentally compromised, it is hardly surprising the rabies literature reports violent rape attempts being common.

However, as tempting as it might seem to make a direct connection between rabies and vampires, rabies is very much a disease of the living and does not suggest that anything is returning from the grave. This does not disqualify rabies from being involved with the evolution of vampires. The virus probably did inspire the concept of vampirism spreading via bite and then merged with the perception that vampires were bloodsuckers. It is the undead element of vampires that rabies does not resolve, but, as mentioned earlier, there are many contagious diseases, like tuberculosis and influenza, that could explain how people came to believe that the dead were returning from the grave to claim their loved ones.

In the end, the fears that ultimately led to the rise of vampires as they are known today may have come from people trying to make sense of two disease epidemics that took place roughly simultaneously. Tuberculosis was at epidemic levels in Europe throughout much of the 1700s just as a major rabies epidemic struck the wild dogs and wolves of the region. In one case, in 1739, a rabid wolf in France bit seventy people, and in another case, in 1764, forty people were bitten. To what extent these bites led to cases of rabid people biting one another is unknown, but if such a situation did develop at the same time as a town was suffering a tuberculosis epidemic, fears from each medical condition could have become intertwined. Even so, the idea of a curse turning man into a monster appeared long before vampires.

Understanding the Text

1. What similarities are there between the story told by the likes of William of Newburgh and modern vampire myths? What is the naturalistic explanation for the physical features of the exhumed monsters?

2. According to some accounts, how were zombies made in Haiti? List the important ingredients.

3. What is different about today's understanding of disease transmission from the way diseases were understood in the time of William of Newburgh and even for centuries thereafter? How does that past understanding connect to the powers of monsters?

4. How is rabies connected to belief in vampires?

5. What techniques does Kaplan use to sway the reader? That is, what types of appeals does he use to convince the reader of his argument? Appeals to facts? Examples? Data? Emotion? Human nature? Psychology? How do his various appeals corroborate his thesis about the origins of these monsters?

Reflection and Response

6. Argue whether Kaplan's historical and biological explanations for the origins of the myths about either vampires or zombies are convincing or not. Does he explain all aspects of these myths, or are there elements he doesn't cover?

7. What connection does Kaplan make between the growth of population density and the rise of certain monster myths, such as those about vampires? Is his argument convincing? In what other ways has population growth caused cultural beliefs to shift?

8. What is the importance of blood in the origin myths of vampires? Examine its role as both a giver of life and a symptom of death.

Making Connections

9. Research the practice of voodoo in Haiti. Explore further its connection to zombies. You might also research the socioeconomic conditions of Haiti and how they could lead to belief in the supernatural more easily than conditions in more developed nations.

10. How are the monsters in this selection connected to their times? What about our present time has led to changes in the portrayals of these monsters, such as in the *Twilight* or *Harry Potter* series?

11. Kaplan offers biological, scientific, and historical evidence for the belief in vampires and zombies. Is this approach compatible with more philosophical and psychological arguments for the existence of these creatures? In answering the question, consider arguments presented elsewhere in *Monsters*, such as in Guillermo del Toro and Chuck Hogan's "Why Vampires Never Die" (p. 35) or Chuck Klosterman's "My Zombie, Myself: Why Modern Life Feels Rather Undead" (p. 39).

Monstrous Beginnings

W. Scott Poole

W. Scott Poole, a professor of history at the College of Charleston, is the author of eight books, including *Vampira: Dark Goddess of Horror* (2014), *Satan in America: The Devil We Know* (2009), and *Never Surrender: Confederate Memory and Conservatism in the South Carolina Upcountry* (2004). In this excerpt from *Monsters in America: Our Historical Obsession with the Hideous and the Haunting* (2011), Poole examines the attitudes of European settlers and explorers since Christopher Columbus toward the New World and its inhabitants. Although some saw these native inhabitants as savages in need of salvation, others saw them as monsters in league with Satan, unable to be redeemed. Poole narrows his focus to the experiences of the Puritans, English Dissenters who came to America in the early seventeenth century to escape persecution in England. The Puritans perceived Native Americans as violent, hypersexual monsters who needed to be removed. Once they had taken measures to do so, they found monsters among themselves, leading to the famous Salem witch trials.

Christopher Columbus came to the "New World" seeking gold, slaves, and monsters. Columbus reported both in his personal diary and correspondence that the native peoples he encountered in the Caribbean in 1492 and 1493 told him of "one eyed men and other men with dog heads who decapitated their victims and drank their blood." Michael Palencia-Roth notes that the Genoese explorer's private diary of the first voyage shows that finding the monsters of the New World "became an obsession for Columbus."

A long tradition of legend and theological speculation about monstrous creatures informed Columbus' beliefs about what he might find in the new world. Medieval mental maps of a world inhabited by monstrous races prepared Spanish and Portuguese explorers to encounter giants, dog-men, ape-men, and various creatures out of the medieval bestiary. Christian theological speculation about the work of the devil, combined with the ongoing geopolitical conflict with the Islamic powers of the Mediterranean world, encouraged European explorers to see these monstrous races as allied with the evil one, the enemies of God and of the church.

Some scholars argue that the first European conquerors in the New World did not think of the native people themselves as monsters. Contemporary historian Peter Burke, for example, contends that Europeans always saw the native peoples of Africa and the Americas as part of the human family, even as they categorized them as an uncivilized or even degraded branch of that family. Burke notes that, throughout the era of European expansion, a debate took place among churchly scholars over the ethnic origins of "the savages of America." The very fact that such a debate was held meant that Europeans assumed the humanity, if not the equality, of the native peoples. A monster has no ethnic origin. If Burke is correct, European explorers saw the people of the New World as vastly inferior cousins but not as monsters.

Contrary evidence, however, suggests that such an ambivalent view of the natives had very little traction among most early modern Europeans. The conquerors of the New World saw, not simply a savage version of humanity, but the monstrous races of their mythology. Even significant Enlightenment thinkers such as the French naturalist Buffon in his *Natural History* connected the creation of monstrosities with the etiology° of the "darker races." Monsters represented the progeny of these supposedly savage peoples, a concept that reappeared again and again throughout American history, with a lineage that stretches from Puritan minister Cotton Mather to the twentieth-century horror maestro H. P. Lovecraft.

New kinds of technology in the period of exploration contributed to   5 European monster mania. The print revolution of the fifteenth century, though normally seen as an important moment in the expansion of modernity, provided a way to spread the concept of the monster, locating it in the enemy other. Numerous Reformation tracts portrayed either Martin Luther or the Pope as monstrous beings empowered by the devil. In 1727 a popular Portuguese tract, *Emblema Vivente*, described a Turkish monster "fifteen palms high" with an eerie light emanating from its chest every time it breathed. Historians of early modern Europe Laura Lunger Knoppers and Joan B. Landes argue that this tract "blurs the boundaries of science and religion," in its description of the monster both as an oddity of nature and malformed beast. The monster incarnated fears of the religious other whose land it inhabited, the Ottoman Turk.

Emblema Vivente's blurring of conceptual boundaries is representative of the emerging Enlightenment view of the monster. While many eighteenth-century thinkers dismissed theological explanations for the birth of monsters, they did not reject the reality of monsters themselves. The natural scientist Buffon suggested a number of purely natural explanations for the monstrous peoples and creatures that walked the earth. In 1796 the Enlightenment Encylopedist Diderot speculated about the possible natural origins of monsters. The New World, with its strange

---

etiology: the causes of a disease or abnormal condition.

creatures and peoples, offered new opportunities for sightings of such creatures.

Europeans found the monsters they searched for. Not only did explorers and settlers readily believe wonder tales, they tended to ascribe morally monstrous qualities to the peoples they encountered. This process began with the early explorations of Africa and provided some of the earliest materials for the racist imagination of the modern West. Early European accounts of orangutans imagined a similarity between them and the native peoples of West Africa, the region that soon became the primary target for slave traders. Fabulous accounts written by European travelers dwelt on the monstrous appearance of the ape and on the monster's sexual proclivities. According to one account, the apes of India were "so venerous° that they will ravish their women," while an African baboon brought before a French monarch allegedly had a sexual organ "greater than might match the quantity of his other parts." These ideas had a calamitous effect on how the white mind encountered native African peoples.

Such imaginings became a familiar part of the racist folklore of the United States concerning African American men. An English naturalist, Edward Topsell, would write in 1607 of African men with "low and flat nostrils" who are "as libidinous as apes that attempt women and having thicke lips the upper hanging over the neather, they are deemed fools." Winthrop Jordan notes that these associations also drew on European folklore about the connection between apes and the devil. Contemporary demonological texts often made this connection explicit, seeing apes as incarnations of Satan or as the familiars of witches. Europeans encountering Africans in the context of the slave trade held in their minds these bizarre associations between monstrous apes, Satan, libidinous sexuality, and enormous sexual organs. They readily applied these folkloric images to the human beings they stuffed into the holds of their ships for a life of enslavement. Such poisonous associations would be reborn again and again in twentieth-century popular culture, most notably in *The Birth of a Nation* (1915) and *King Kong* (1933). They even played a role in the folklore that supported lynching, some of the most pathological violence ever to take place on American soil.

Europeans found monsters in the Americas as quickly as in Africa. Some of the earliest Spanish explorers of what would become the southeastern coast of the United States readily accepted Native American tales of monstrous peoples and saw the natives themselves as embodiments of

---

venerous: seeking gratification of sexual desires.

the marvelously monstrous. In the 1520s Spanish explorer Lucas Allyón hungrily devoured the stories of a local Native American Chicora° who spoke of all the lands north of Florida as being populated by "a race of men with tails for which they dug holes in the ground when they sat down." Chicora regaled Allyón, and later the Spanish court, with other stories of Native American tribes that stretched their children so that they became enormous giants.

Belief in the monsters of the New World influenced discussions about the moral justification for the enslavement and oppression of native peoples. These debates, with very few exceptions, assumed theological and cultural justifications for the economic exploitation of the New World. European explorers who willingly granted that the natives came from human stock often believed them to be a type of monstrous human, depraved beings whose moral leprosy had its source in the world of the demonic. Even the sixteenth-century friar Bartolomé de Las Casas, a strong proponent of the rights of Native Americans under Spanish law, saw the New World as firmly under Satan's domain. Friar Bartolomé saw the very air of the New World teeming with evil spirits who tempted and destroyed the unbaptized. 10

Such conceptions of the diabolism of native peoples led some Europeans to imagine the New World as a landscape of horror. Charges of perverse sexuality and inhuman appetites represent some of the most common descriptions of native peoples. Friar Tomas Ortiz described the natives of Terra Firme, colonial Panama, as flesh-eating monsters who had "no sense of love or shame. . . . [T]hey are bestial and they pride themselves in having abominable vices." Viewing them as "steeped in vices and bestialities," Friar Ortiz saw no reason their personal autonomy should be recognized. Monsters could be enslaved.

The New World itself often seemed a kind of monster to the early modern European imagination. One of the earliest allegorizations of America is Philippe Galle's 1580 *America*, in which we see a giantess with spear and bow that has cannibalized a man and triumphantly carries his severed head. Galle's own description of the image refers to America as an "ogress who devours men, who is rich in gold and who is skilled in the use of the spear and the bow." In 1595 Paolo Farinati painted an allegorical representation of the New World as a monstrous cannibal to decorate a villa in Verona, Italy. In Farinati's *America*, the artist imagines the New World as a giant roasting a human arm. A crucifix is shown on

Francisco de Chicora: a Native American who was kidnapped by Spanish explorers in 1521, was baptized and renamed as a Catholic, and accompanied the explorer Lucas Vásquez de Allyón to Spain, where he gave accounts of his homeland. In 1526, he returned to North America with another expedition and escaped.

his right, illustrating the hope that conversion to Christianity could tame the beast.

A sixteenth-century Dutch engraving in Hans Staden's *True History* best illustrates this very common representation of the Americas. Staden's work, a captivity narrative that allegedly describes his time among the natives of Brazil, tells a tale of cannibalism that rivals anything a modern master of horror could conjure. One of the more infamous images from that work shows a gory cannibal feast that zombie auteur George Romero might have filmed. A gaggle of cannibals roast human body parts over a fire. A dwarf gnaws on a human hand. Women, sketched according to the traditional European iconography of the witch, chomp on legs, arms, and unidentified bits of human detritus.

Images of a New World filled with monstrous races and the tendency to imagine the New World itself as a kind of cannibalistic beast grew out of the deep roots of European culture. Europeans who settled in the New World brought with them a head full of monsters and a well-practiced tendency to define the cultural and religious other in terms of monstrosity. A long history of military conflict with the Islamic world converged with early modern religious tensions and age-old legends of the world beyond the borders of Europe to convince most European explorers that they would encounter new lands crawling with monsters.

Numerous scholars have examined the European tendency to con- 15 struct the native peoples of North America as monstrous cannibals and demonic servants. Less attention has been paid to how supernatural beings and occurrences provided a way for white Americans in later historical periods to negotiate the meaning of the colonial period. Simplistic interpretations of folk belief in monsters have seen them as shorthand for death, sexuality, and metaphysical uncertainty. But the monster has, just as frequently, offered a way to ignore historical trauma and historical guilt, to remake the facts into a set of pleasing legends. The grotesquerie of the monster has offered relief from the gruesome facts of history.

* * *

Sex with the Devil

The Puritan settlements of New England have become representative symbols of early American settlement. Although not the first successful settlements in English North America (Jamestown dates to 1607), they occupy an integral place in the memory of the early American experience. There are many explanations for this importance, ranging from the dominance of New England historians and educational institutions in the writing of early American history, to the way the Puritans' own self-conceptions comport with Americans' tendency to view themselves as bearers of a special destiny.

The special place the Puritans have occupied in American memory made them multivalent° signifiers for national identity, appearing as everything from dour-faced party poopers to, ironically, the embodiment of the alleged American appreciation for the search for religious liberty. Their sermons and devotional tracts have provided the grammar of American understanding of sin, redemption, and national destiny, shaping both religious and political consciousness.

No aspect of Puritan experience lives more strongly in American memory than their fear of monsters, specifically their fear of witches that led to the trials of about 344 settlers during the course of the seventeenth century. The Salem witch trials, an outbreak of Puritan witch-hunting that ended in the executions of twenty people in 1692–1693, has become central to most Americans' perception of their early history. Salem historians Owen Davies and Jonathan Barry have noted the central role the event came to play in the teaching standards and curriculum of public schools, making knowledge of it integral to understanding the colonial era.

> "No aspect of Puritan experience lives more strongly in American memory than their fear of monsters."

For many contemporary people, Salem is read as a brief flirtation with an irrational past. At least some of the interest it garners comes from its portrayal as an anomaly, a strange bypath on the way to an unyielding national commitment to freedom and democracy. On the contrary, Salem was far from the first witch hunt in early New England. Nor did the American fascination with the witch disappear after 1693.

Puritans hunted monsters in the generation before Salem. In 1648 20 Margaret Jones of Charlestown, Massachusetts, became the first English settler accused of witchcraft, and later executed, in New England. The Massachusetts Bay Colony's first governor, John Winthrop, called Jones "a cunning woman," someone with the ability to make use of herbs and spells. Jones was further alleged to have had a "malignant touch" that caused her erstwhile patients to vomit and go deaf. Winthrop, after a bodily search of Jones by the women of Charlestown, claimed that she exhibited "witches teats in her secret parts," which was, by long

---

multivalent: having many values or meanings.

established superstition, the sign of a witch. The Puritan judiciary executed Jones in the summer of 1648. More trials and more executions followed.

The witch embodied all the assorted anxieties that early New England settlers felt about their new environment, their personal religious turmoil, and their fear of the creatures that lurked in the "howling wilderness." The Puritan movement in England grew out of the fear that the English Church retained too many elements of the "satanic" Roman Catholic Church. The Puritan conception of the spiritual life, embodied in John Bunyan's *The Pilgrim's Progress*, imagined the Christian experience as a war with monstrous beings inspired by the devil. This understanding of Christian experience as a struggle with the forces of darkness made its way to the New World. Not surprisingly, this new world became a geography of monsters in the minds of many of the Puritans.

Puritan clergyman Cotton Mather helped to construct a New World mythology that not only included the bones of antediluvian° giants but also the claim that native peoples in North America had a special relationship to Satan. In Mather's New World demonology, the Native Americans had been seduced by Satan to come to America as his special servants. This made them, in some literal sense, the "children of the Devil." Other Puritan leaders reinforced this view, seeing the Native Americans as a special trial designed for them by the devil. Frequently, Puritan leaders turned to Old Testament imagery of the Israelites destroying the people of Canaan for descriptions of their relationship with the New England tribes. The Puritans believed you could not live with or even convert monsters. You must destroy them.

The Puritans embodied the American desire to destroy monsters. At the same time, the Puritan tendency toward witch-hunting reveals the American tendency to desire the monster, indeed to be titillated by it. Contemporary literary scholar Edward Ingebretsen convincingly argues that the search for witches in the towns of New England should be read as popular entertainment as well as evidence of religious conflict and persecution. Ingebretsen shows that Mather makes use of the term "entertain" frequently when explaining his own efforts to create a narrative of the witch hunts. He uses the same term to describe the effect of the testimony of suspected witches on the Puritan courtrooms that heard them. Mather described the dark wonders that make up much of his writings as "the chiefe entertainments which my readers do expect and shall receive."

---

antediluvian: from the time before the biblical flood.

Mather obviously does not use the word "entertain" in the contemporary sense. And yet his conception of "entertainment" bears some relationship to the more modern usage of the term. Mather believed that his dark entertainments warned and admonished, but a delicious thrill accompanied them as well. Mather himself sounds like a carnival barker when he promises frightening spectacles that his readers "do expect and shall receive." Historian of Salem Marion Starkey, in *The Devil in Massachusetts*, notes that for all of Mather's righteous chest-thumping over the danger the New England colonies faced from the assaults of Satan, it is hard not to see him "unconsciously submerged in the thrill of being present as a spectator." He provided his readers the same thrill.

This thrill had clear erotic undertones, underscoring the close connection between horror and sexuality that became a persistent thread in American cultural history. The genealogy of the witch in western Europe already included many of the ideas that aroused, in every sense, the Puritan settlements. Folklore taught that any gathering of witches, known as the "witches sabbat," included orgiastic sex, even sex with Satan and his demons. European demonologists frequently connected the tendency to witchcraft with a propensity toward uncontrolled sexual desire. 25

Such ideas appeared again and again in the New England witch hunts. The trial of indentured servant Mary Johnson not only included accusations that she had used her relationship with Satan to get out of work for her master, but also the assertion that she had flirted, literally, with the devil. Cotton Mather wrote that she had "practiced uncleanness with men and devils." One of the first women accused of witchcraft in Salem village had a reputation for sexual promiscuity, while male testimony against women accused of witchcraft often included descriptions of them as succubi,° appearing at night dressed in flaming red bodices. The witch was not only one of the first monsters of English-speaking America. The witch also became America's first sexy monster and one who would be punished for her proclivities.

The end of the witch trials in 1693 came with numerous criticisms of how the cases had been handled. Petitions on behalf of the accused began to appear in the fall of 1692. In October of that year, Boston merchant Thomas Brattle, a well-traveled member of the scientific Royal Society with an interest in mathematics and astronomy, published an open letter criticizing the courts. He especially critiqued the Puritan judiciary for allowing "spectral evidence," evidence based on visions, revelations, and alleged apparitions. Significantly, Brattle did not challenge the idea that supernatural agency had been involved in the trials, only that it had

---

succubi: demons that assume female form to have sex with men in their sleep.

worked by different methods than the Puritan judiciary had supposed. Brattle wrote that the evidence of witches sabbats and apparitions put forward by those who accused (and by those who confessed) represented "the effect of their fancy, deluded and depraved by the Devil." In Brattle's mind, to accept such evidence would be tantamount to accepting the testimony of Satan himself. Like many skeptics during this period, Brattle challenged the courts on how they had used the belief in monsters, without questioning the reality of the existence of monsters.

Salem did not mark the end of the witch trials in America. Fear of that old black magic remained a crucial part of early American life. Marginalized women and enslaved Africans remained the most common target of the witch hunt. In 1705–1706, a Virginia couple, Luke and Elizabeth Hill, accused Grace Sherwood of witchcraft. Although the Virginia courts at first found little evidence for the charge, the time-honored search for the witch's teat soon revealed "two things like titts with Severall other Spotts." Sherwood next underwent the infamous "water test" in which the suspected witch was thrown into water to see if she floated or sank. Sherwood floated and faced reexamination by some "anciente women" who, this time, discovered clearly diabolical "titts on her private parts." She was subjected to another trial, although the record breaks off at this point, making her fate unclear.

Enslaved Africans faced accusations of a special kind of witchcraft known as "conjuration" or, more simply, "sorcery." The use of black magic against the white master class became a common charge against the instigators of slave rebellions. In 1779 a trial of slave rebels in the territory that would later become the state of Illinois ended with the execution of several slaves for the crimes of "conjure" and "necromancy."

The Puritans clearly had no monopoly on the belief in witchcraft. 30 Even in parts of colonial America without a strong tradition of witch trials, beliefs that supported such trials remained strong. An Anglican missionary in colonial Carolina, Francis Le Jau, complained in a 1707 journal entry that the colonial court had not severely punished "a notorious malefactor, evidently guilty of witchcraft." While the Puritans pursued their obsession with the most vehemence, the belief in dark powers inhabiting the American landscape remained common throughout the eighteenth century.

Puritans found more monsters in their new world than the witch. Although we tend to picture the dour Puritans in their equally dour meetinghouses, taking in Calvinist theology and morality in great drafts, the actual Puritans lived out at least part of their experience in what David D. Hall has termed "worlds of wonder." The work of Hall, and of colonial historian Richard Godbeer, has uncovered a variety of magical traditions, astrological beliefs, and conceptions of monstrosity among the Puritans that kept alive older European wonder-lore. Puritan conceptions of original sin, for example, contributed to their interest in abnormal births, often termed as "monstrous births," that functioned as signs and omens. Spectral, shapeshifting dogs haunted the edges of the Puritan settlements, as did demonic, giant black bears.

Predictably, much of the Puritan ministry saw any portents in nature as signs of the New Englanders' divine mission. The same clergymen, just as predictably, ascribed a diabolical character to any marvel or wonders that did not fit into their theological paradigm. For Puritan clergy, it came as no surprise to find the forests of New England populated with marvelous creatures. Their new world was surrounded by evil spirits of all kinds, as numerous as "the frogs of Egypt" according to Cotton Mather.

Reaction to an alleged sighting of a sea serpent early in the Puritan experiment showcases this attitude. Puritan observers claimed to have encountered sea serpents long before the nineteenth-century sightings in Gloucester harbor. They also more quickly ascribed dark religious meanings to the appearance of the creature off their shores. In 1638 New England settler John Josselyn reported that recent arrivals to the colonies had seen "a sea serpent or a snake." Nahant native Obadiah Turner described the same creature and worried that "the monster come out of the sea" might be "the old serpent spoken of in holy scripture . . . whose poison hath run down even unto us, so greatly to our discomfort and ruin." The monster could be a portent of divine providence or judgment. The only other possible explanation was that it was a creature of Satan.

Puritans were not alone in finding monsters on the American frontier. Sea serpents swam in many American waters, and strange beasts populated the wilderness that surrounded most new American settlements. But the American response to the monsters they met was not uniform and did not always share the Puritan desire to destroy the monster and cleanse the American landscape. Some even saw the monster as a strange partner in mastering the unruly frontier.

Understanding the Text

1. Why did past experiences make it so easy for early European settlers to believe in the existence of monsters in the New World?

2. According to the New World settlers and explorers, how were the native peoples they encountered connected to monsters — and thus to Satan?

3. During the Salem witch trials, what were the signs that a woman was a witch? What was the significance of Thomas Brattle's argument against the trials?

4. How does Poole make connections between religion, European history, and the demonization of native peoples by Europeans? Do you find his argument about these connections convincing, or has he left out other significant influences? Support your answer with specific details and examples.

Reflection and Response

5. What is your reaction to Poole's descriptions of the interactions between European settlers and native peoples and to the perceptions and treatment of the native peoples by the settlers?

6. Examine how the sexuality of native peoples became a weapon for European settlers to use against them. What role does sex play in justifying the perception that Native Americans were monsters? What were some of the consequences for the native peoples of the Europeans' perceptions about their sexuality?

Making Connections

7. Poole writes, "Europeans found the monsters they searched for. Not only did explorers and settlers readily believe wonder tales, they tended to ascribe morally monstrous qualities to the peoples they encountered" (par. 7). Research the social practices of Native Americans, including those regarding issues such as marriage and the family, sexual relations, warfare, and trade. Compare their practices with those of the Europeans of the time. Then argue whether the European perspective represents a misunderstanding of native cultures or not.

8. Conduct more research on the Salem witch trials. Investigate how and why accusations of sorcery were made, how they were supported during the trials, what was done to those who were convicted, and what brought the trials to an end. How did the Puritan preoccupation with evil, monsters, and Satan lubricate the process? What other "witch hunts" have caused such a frenzy or made such a mark on a culture or historical era?

Get Ready for the Dawn of Superintelligence

Nick Bostrom

Computer scientists across the world are hard at work trying to create and improve artificial intelligence (AI). This quest, however, brings with it the fear that we may produce computers so powerful that they will seek to replace us, a fear that has already entered the public imagination through movies such as *Terminator* and *The Matrix*. Nick Bostrom examines what seems to be inevitable: that at some point in the future, superintelligent machines will be a reality. How the human race fares then will depend on how we have designed these new machines. Bostrom is a professor of philosophy at the University of Oxford and the director of the Future of Humanity Institute. He has delivered his message in both academic and popular media outlets, with appearances on TED Talks and the publication of his book *Superintelligence: Paths, Dangers, Strategies* (2014). This article appeared in the July 2014 issue of *New Scientist*.

Humans have never encountered a more intelligent life form, but this will change if we create machines that greatly surpass our cognitive abilities. Then our fate will depend on the will of such a "superintelligence," much as the fate of gorillas today depends more on what we do than on gorillas themselves.

We therefore have reason to be curious about what these superintelligences will want. Is there a way to engineer their motivation systems so that their preferences will coincide with ours? And supposing a superintelligence starts out human-friendly, is there some way to guarantee that it will remain benevolent even as it creates ever more capable successor-versions of itself?

These questions—which are perhaps the most momentous that our species will ever confront—call for a new science of advanced artificial agents. Most of the work answering these questions remains to be done, yet over the last 10 years, a group of mathematicians, philosophers and computer scientists have begun to make progress. As I explain in my new book *Superintelligence: Paths, Dangers, Strategies*, the findings are at once disturbing and deeply fascinating. We can see, in outline, that preparation for the machine intelligence transition is the essential task of our time.

But let us take a step back and consider why machines with high levels of general intelligence would be such a big deal. By a superintelligence I mean any intellect that greatly exceeds the cognitive performance of humans in virtually all domains. Plainly, none of our current artificial intelligence (AI) programs meets this criterion. All compare unfavorably in most respects, even to a mouse.

So we are not talking about present or near-future systems. Nobody 5 knows how long it will take to develop machine intelligence that matches humans in general learning and reasoning ability. It seems plausible that it might take a number of decades. But once AIs do reach and then surpass this level, they may quickly soar to radically superintelligent levels.

After AI scientists become more capable than human scientists, research in artificial intelligence would be carried out by machines operating at digital timescales, and progress would be correspondingly rapid. There is thus the potential for an intelligence explosion, in which we go from there being no computer that exceeds human intelligence to machine superintelligence that enormously outperforms all biological intelligence.

The first AI system to undergo such an intelligence explosion could then become extremely powerful. It would be the only superintelligence in the world, capable of developing a host of other technologies very quickly, such as nanomolecular robotics, and using them to shape the future of life according to its preferences.

We can distinguish three forms of superintelligence. A speed superintelligence could do everything a human mind could do, but much faster. An intelligent system that runs 10,000 times faster than a human mind, it would be able to read a book in a few seconds and complete a PhD thesis in an afternoon. To such a fast mind, the external world would appear to run in slow motion.

A collective superintelligence is a system composed of a large number of human-level intellects organized so that the system's performance as a whole vastly outstrips that of any current cognitive system. A human-level mind running as software on a computer could easily be copied and run on multiple computers. If each copy was valuable enough to repay the cost of hardware and electricity, a massive population boom could result. In a world with trillions of these intelligences, technological progress may be much faster than it is today, since there could be thousands of times more scientists and inventors.

Finally, a quality superintelligence would be one that is at least as fast 10 as a human mind and vastly qualitatively smarter. This is a more difficult notion to comprehend. The idea is that there might be intellects that are cleverer than humans in the same sense that we are cleverer than other animals. In terms of raw computational power, a human brain may not be superior to, say, the brain of a sperm whale, possessor of the largest known brain, weighing in at 7.8 kilograms compared to 1.5 kg for an average human. And, of course, the non-human animal's brain is nicely suited to its ecological needs. Yet the human brain has a facility for abstract thinking, complex linguistic representations and long-range planning that enables us to do science, technology and engineering more successfully than other species. But there is no reason to suppose that ours are the smartest possible brains. Rather, we may be the stupidest possible biological species capable of starting a technological civilization. We filled that niche because we got there first—not because we are in any sense optimally adapted to it.

These different types of superintelligence may have different strengths and weaknesses. For example, a collective superintelligence would excel at problems that can be readily subdivided into independent subproblems, whereas a quality superintelligence may have an advantage on problems that require new conceptual insights or complexly coordinated deliberation.

The indirect reaches of these different kinds of superintelligence, however, are identical. Provided the first iteration is competent in scientific research, it is likely to quickly become a fully general superintelligence. That's because it would be able to complete the computer or cognitive science research and software engineering needed to build for itself any cognitive faculty it lacked at the outset. Once developed to this level, machine brains would have many fundamental advantages over biological brains, just as engines have advantages over biological muscles. When it comes to the hardware, these include vastly greater numbers of processing elements, faster frequency of operation of those elements, much faster internal communication and superior storage capacity.

Advantages in software are harder to quantify, but they may be equally important. Consider, for example, copyability. It is easy to make an exact copy of a piece of software, whereas "copying" a human is a slow process that fails to carry over to the offspring the skills and knowledge that its parents acquired during their lifetimes. It is also much easier to edit the code of a digital mind: this makes it possible to experiment and to develop improved mental architectures and algorithms. We are able to edit the details of the synaptic connections in our brains—this is what we call learning—but we cannot alter the general principles on which our neural networks operate.

"We cannot hope to compete with such machine brains. We can only hope to design them so that their goals coincide with ours."

We cannot hope to compete with such machine brains. We can only hope to design them so that their goals coincide with ours. Figuring out how to do that is a formidable problem. It is not clear whether we will succeed in solving that problem before somebody succeeds in building a superintelligence. But the fate of humanity may depend on solving these two problems in the correct order.

To a superintelligent entity, the world would appear to run in slow 15 motion.

Understanding the Text

1. What point does Bostrom make in his comparison of humans and gorillas (par. 1)? Why do you suppose he chose gorillas?

2. What are the risks involved in creating superintelligence, according to Bostrom?

3. Describe the three forms of superintelligence as Bostrom presents them.

4. Bostrom is a professor at the University of Oxford who is well versed in writing for other experts in academia. This work, however, is written for members of the general magazine-reading public who are interested in science. How does the issue of audience affect how Bostrom has written this article? Can you think of ways the article might have been changed if written for a more expert audience? How might it have been changed if written for a less educated audience?

Reflection and Response

5. In your opinion, are the dangers Bostrom describes of creating artificial intelligence (AI) sufficient to warrant fear? Support your answer with specific details.

6. Besides AI, what other research into technological advances being done today potentially poses a threat? Why? Be specific.

7. What attitude toward science and progress do you find in Bostrom's article? What contradictions, if any, do you find? Do you share that attitude? Why or why not?

Making Connections

8. Numerous movies, novels, and other creative works, such as *Terminator*, *The Matrix*, and *I, Robot*, explore the theme of AI run amok. Focus on one such creative work and argue how it develops its vision of the future in light of today's science and research. Consider whether the creators of this work place humankind in a position to save itself, and if so, how? Ultimately, do you find such fears convincing or not?

9. Fear of scientific advancement has a long history — consider Hitchcock's argument that experiments with electricity influenced Shelley's creation of the Frankenstein story, for example (p. 23). Research the facts about AI, the progress scientists have made in its development, its perceived uses, and its alleged dangers. Argue whether this area of scientific research poses a significant danger to humanity or not. Be specific.

Robbie

Isaac Asimov

Isaac Asimov was one of the most prolific and best-known science fiction writers of the twentieth century. He was a professor of biochemistry at Boston University, but he was best known for his novels and short stories that explored humanity in the future. "Robbie" appears in *I, Robot*, a collection of short stories originally published in 1950. In the story, an ordinary human family has — and then gets rid of — a household robot named Robbie. However, Gloria, the daughter of George and Grace Weston, still misses Robbie, whom she considers a friend. In an attempt to get Gloria to realize that robots are machines and not people, her parents take her to a factory where robots work, but an unforeseen event changes everything.

The Talking Robot was a *tour de force*, a thoroughly impractical device, possessing publicity value only. Once an hour, an escorted group stood before it and asked questions of the robot engineer in charge in careful whispers. Those the engineer decided were suitable for the robot's circuits were transmitted to the Talking Robot.

It was rather dull. It may be nice to know that the square of fourteen is one hundred ninety-six, that the temperature at the moment is 72 degrees Fahrenheit, and the air-pressure 30.02 inches of mercury, that the atomic weight of sodium is 23, but one doesn't really need a robot for that. One especially does not need an unwieldy, totally immobile mass of wires and coils spreading over twenty-five square yards.

Few people bothered to return for a second helping, but one girl in her middle teens sat quietly on a bench waiting for a third. She was the only one in the room when Gloria entered.

Gloria did not look at her. To her at the moment, another human being was but an inconsiderable item. She saved her attention for this large thing with the wheels. For a moment, she hesitated in dismay. It didn't look like any robot she had ever seen.

Cautiously and doubtfully she raised her treble voice, "Please, 5 Mr. Robot, sir, are you the Talking Robot, sir?" She wasn't sure, but it seemed to her that a robot that actually talked was worth a great deal of politeness.

(The girl in her mid-teens allowed a look of intense concentration to cross her thin, plain face. She whipped out a small notebook and began writing in rapid pot-hooks.)

There was an oily whir of gears and a mechanically-timbered voice boomed out in words that lacked accent and intonation, "I—am—the—robot—that—talks."

Gloria stared at it ruefully. It *did* talk, but the sound came from inside somewheres. There was no *face* to talk to. She said, "Can you help me, Mr. Robot, sir?"

The Talking Robot was designed to answer questions, and only such questions as it could answer had ever been put to it. It was quite confident of its ability, therefore, "I—can—help—you."

"Thank you, Mr. Robot, sir. Have you seen Robbie?"   10

"Who—is Robbie?"

"He's a robot, Mr. Robot, sir." She stretched to tiptoes. "He's about so high, Mr. Robot, sir, only higher, and he's very nice. He's got a head, you know. I mean you haven't, but he has, Mr. Robot, sir."

The Talking Robot had been left behind, "A—robot?"

"Yes, Mr. Robot, sir, A robot just like you, except he can't talk, of course, and—looks like a real person."

"A—robot—like—me?"   15

"Yes, Mr. Robot, sir."

To which the Talking Robot's only response was an erratic splutter and an occasional incoherent sound. The radical generalization offered it, i.e., its existence, not as a particular object, but as a member of a general group, was too much for it. Loyally, it tried to encompass the concept and half a dozen coils burnt out. Little warning signals were buzzing.

(The girl in her mid teens left at that point. She had enough for her Physics-1 paper on "Practical Aspects of Robotics." This paper was Susan Calvin's first of many on the subject.)

Gloria stood waiting, with carefully concealed impatience, for the machine's answer when she heard the cry behind her of "There she is," and recognized that cry as her mother's.

"What are you doing here, you bad girl?" cried Mrs. Weston, anxi-   20
ety dissolving at once into anger. "Do you know you frightened your mamma and daddy almost to death? Why did you run away?"

The robot engineer had also dashed in, tearing his hair, and demanding who of the gathering crowd had tampered with the machine. "Can't anybody read signs?" he yelled. "You're not allowed in here without an attendant."

Gloria raised her grieved voice over the din, "I only came to see the Talking Robot, Mamma. I thought he might know where Robbie was because they're both robots." And then, as the thought of Robbie was suddenly brought forcefully home to her, she burst into a sudden storm of tears, "And I *got* to find Robbie, Mamma. I *got* to."

Mrs. Weston strangled a cry, and said, "Oh, good Heavens. Come home, George. This is more than I can stand."

That evening, George Weston left for several hours, and the next morning, he approached his wife with something that looked suspiciously like smug complacence.

"I've got an idea, Grace." 25

"About what?" was the gloomy, uninterested query.

"About Gloria."

"You're not going to suggest buying back that robot?"

"No, of course not."

"Then go ahead. I might as well lis- 30 ten to you. Nothing *I've* done seems to have done any good."

> "The whole trouble with Gloria is that she thinks of Robbie as a *person* and not as a *machine*."

"All right. Here's what I've been thinking. The whole trouble with Gloria is that she thinks of Robbie as a *person* and not as a *machine*. Naturally, she can't forget him. Now if we managed to convince her that Robbie was nothing more than a mess of steel and copper in the form of sheets and wires with electricity its juice of life, how long would her longings last? It's the psychological attack, if you see my point."

"How do you plan to do it?"

"Simple. Where do you suppose I went last night? I persuaded Robertson of U.S. Robots and Mechanical Men, Inc. to arrange for a complete tour of his premises tomorrow. The three of us will go, and by the time we're through, Gloria will have it drilled into her that a robot is *not* alive."

Mrs. Weston's eyes widened gradually and something glinted in her eyes that was quite like sudden admiration, "Why, George, that's a *good* idea."

And George Weston's vest buttons strained. "Only kind I have," he 35 said.

● ● ●

Mr. Struthers was a conscientious General Manager and naturally inclined to be a bit talkative. The combination, therefore, resulted in a tour that was fully explained, perhaps even over-abundantly explained, at every step. However, Mrs. Weston was not bored. Indeed, she stopped him several times and begged him to repeat his statements in simpler language so that Gloria might understand. Under the influence of this appreciation of his narrative powers, Mr. Struthers expanded genially and became ever more communicative, if possible.

George Weston, himself, showed a gathering impatience.

"Pardon me, Struthers," he said, breaking into the middle of a lecture on the photo-electric cell, "haven't you a section of the factory where only robot labor is employed?"

"Eh? Oh, yes! Yes, indeed!" He smiled at Mrs. Weston. "A vicious circle in a way, robots creating more robots. Of course, we are not making a general practice out of it. For one thing, the unions would never let us. But we can turn out a very few robots using robot labor exclusively, merely as a sort of scientific experiment. You see," he tapped his pince-nez into one palm argumentatively, "what the labor unions don't realize—and I say this as a man who has always been very sympathetic with the labor movement in general—is that the advent of the robot, while involving some dislocation to begin with, will inevitably—"

"Yes, Struthers," said Weston, "but about that section of the factory 40 you speak of—may we see it? It would be very interesting, I'm sure."

"Yes! Yes, of course!" Mr. Struthers replaced his pince-nez in one convulsive movement and gave vent to a soft cough of discomfiture. "Follow me, please."

He was comparatively quiet while leading the three through a long corridor and down a flight of stairs. Then, when they had entered a large well-lit room that buzzed with metallic activity, the sluices opened and the flood of explanation poured forth again.

"There you are!" he said with pride in his voice. "Robots only! Five men act as overseers and they don't even stay in this room. In five years, that is, since we began this project, not a single accident has occurred. Of course, the robots here assembled are comparatively simple, but . . ."

The General Manager's voice had long died to a rather soothing murmur in Gloria's ears. The whole trip seemed rather dull and pointless to her, though there *were* many robots in sight. None were even remotely like Robbie, though, and she surveyed them with open contempt.

In this room, there weren't any people at all, she noticed. Then her 45 eyes fell upon six or seven robots busily engaged at a round table halfway across the room. They widened in incredulous surprise. It was a big room. She couldn't see for sure, but one of the robots looked like—looked like—*it was!*

"*Robbie!*" Her shriek pierced the air, and one of the robots about the table faltered and dropped the tool he was holding. Gloria went almost mad with joy. Squeezing through the railing before either parent could stop her, she dropped lightly to the floor a few feet below, and ran toward her Robbie, arms waving and hair flying.

And the three horrified adults, as they stood frozen in their tracks, saw what the excited little girl did not see,—a huge, lumbering tractor bearing blindly down upon its appointed track.

It took split-seconds for Weston to come to his senses, and those split-seconds meant everything, for Gloria could not be overtaken. Although Weston vaulted the railing in a wild attempt, it was obviously hopeless. Mr. Struthers signalled wildly to the overseers to stop the tractor, but the overseers were only human and it took time to act.

It was only Robbie that acted immediately and with precision.

With metal legs eating up the space between himself and his little 50 mistress he charged down from the opposite direction. Everything then happened at once. With one sweep of an arm, Robbie snatched up Gloria, slackening his speed not one iota, and, consequently, knocking every breath of air out of her. Weston, not quite comprehending all that was happening, felt, rather than saw, Robbie brush past him, and came to a sudden bewildered halt. The tractor intersected Gloria's path half a second after Robbie had, rolled on ten feet further and came to a grinding, long drawn-out stop.

Gloria regained her breath, submitted to a series of passionate hugs on the part of both her parents and turned eagerly toward Robbie. As far as she was concerned, nothing had happened except that she had found her friend.

But Mrs. Weston's expression had changed from one of relief to one of dark suspicion. She turned to her husband, and, despite her disheveled and undignified appearance, managed to look quite formidable, "*You* engineered this, *didn't* you?"

George Weston swabbed at a hot forehead with his handkerchief. His hand was unsteady, and his lips could curve only into a tremulous and exceedingly weak smile.

Mrs. Weston pursued the thought, "Robbie wasn't designed for engineering or construction work. He couldn't be of any use to them. You had him placed there deliberately so that Gloria would find him. You know you did."

"Well, I did," said Weston. "But, Grace, how was I to know the reunion 55 would be so violent? And Robbie has saved her life; you'll have to admit that. You *can't* send him away again."

Grace Weston considered. She turned toward Gloria and Robbie and watched them abstractedly for a moment. Gloria had a grip about the robot's neck that would have asphyxiated any creature but one of metal, and was prattling nonsense in half-hysterical frenzy. Robbie's chrome-steel arms (capable of bending a bar of steel two inches in diameter into a pretzel) wound about the little girl gently and lovingly, and his eyes glowed a deep, deep red.

"Well," said Mrs. Weston, at last, "I guess he can stay with us until he rusts."

Robbie the robot swings Gloria in the front yard of the Westons' home. Illustration by Mark Zug.

Mark Zug

Understanding the Text

1. Why is Gloria frustrated when speaking with the Talking Robot? What is the frustration for the Talking Robot?

2. During the tour, Mr. Struthers, the tour guide, mentions one problem with employing robot labor. In what ways does this problem foreshadow changes in the workplace that have come to pass in real life?

3. How is it that Robbie is present to save Gloria's life?

4. How does this work of science fiction reflect conditions in real life? Explain.

Reflection and Response

5. How does Asimov's tale, written in 1950, reflect some of the fears and anxieties of our time as well as Asimov's time? Consider what roles robots play in today's world and how close they may or may not be to being considered new life-forms.

6. How does Asimov integrate the familiar and the unfamiliar in his story? To what extent does that make it easier to accept the message of the story?

Making Connections

7. Compare attitudes toward scientific progress in Asimov's story to Bostrom's article, "Get Ready for the Dawn of Superintelligence" (p. 114). What are their similarities and differences? Which work do you find more persuasive? Does the fact that Asimov's story is a work of fiction affect its credibility?

8. Robots have long been a staple of science fiction. Find another work of science fiction that features robots and compare that portrayal of robots to Asimov's portrayal of Robbie. How are they alike, how are they different, and what do the different portrayals say about competing visions of how technology and humanity will work together in the future?

3 | How Does Gender Affect the Monster?

Few issues attract as much attention, controversy, and emotion as those connected to gender, and its role in monsters is far from clear. Some monsters have a defined gender, others seem neutral, and still others bend or push the concept of gender into entirely new realms beyond the standard binary distinctions of male and female. Issues of gender reach past the monster, involving the monster's victims and even the audience — readers or viewers whose experience of the monster story may be influenced by their own perceptions of gender. In other words, the social, cultural, and physical understanding of the monster may go well beyond the merely biological.

The experience of gender can range from the traditional and standard to the radically new and presently undefined. Amy Fuller presents the story of La Llorona, the Wailing Woman, as someone who failed to fulfill her role as a mother — she murdered her own children after learning that her lover has left her for another. As a result, she wanders forever, searching for her dead children. Her origins are found within stories from both the New and Old Worlds. The ancient Greek epic poem *The Odyssey* tells the story of Odysseus and his long journey home. In one of the oldest written depictions of female monsters, Odysseus, strapped to the mast of his ship, must hear the song of the Sirens, who entice him to their island with their knowledge of all things. These irresistible creatures embody the double characteristics of attraction and danger. Sophia Kingshill examines the half-woman, half-fish mermaid, who, while powerfully alluring, is often seen as a harbinger of danger. Even in our own times, she reappears, sometimes to save the prince, but sometimes to kill. Her connection to culturally derived definitions of femininity is undeniable. The Roman poet Ovid tells the tale of some poorly behaved wedding guests: the half-man, half-horse centaurs. Inflamed with wine and lust, the centaurs try to make off with the women at the banquet. Caeneus, a Greek hero born a woman and changed by a god into a man after she was raped, figures prominently

photo: Marco Bottigelli/Getty Images

as a warrior whom the centaurs, to their great humiliation, are unable to defeat. In an analysis of two representations of the same female monster, Karen Hollinger asserts that males — both human and monster — attempt to control female sexuality. Female monsters — in this case, a woman who turns into a panther when sexually aroused — represent a threat to male dominance and control. As such, they must be tamed and the threat of their sexuality removed. Carol J. Clover analyzes the modern slasher movie and its heroine, the Final Girl. Clover argues that this character succeeds in surviving while others fail because she has qualities that set her apart. In fact, she is more like a boy; her traits make her more masculine than other female and male victims as well as the (typically) male psycho who pursues her. Judith Halberstam picks up on Clover's analysis but carries it further. Halberstam asserts that instead of working through the binary of male-female, the slasher film doesn't just invert the categories of male and female, but moves beyond to create a new, monstrous category of gender. Thus, the meanings of male, female, and monster must be reimagined — like suturing the skin of a monster from many hides.

Monster stories enable us to reconsider issues of gender, from the traditional roles men and women are expected to play to the reinvention of the very categories of gender. No longer can we embrace the stereotypical assumption that monster stories are just for young men. The stereotype runs something like this: a young man may bring his (female) date to the theater to watch the latest horror flick, but she will avert her eyes when the scene on the screen becomes too awful. What happens if this stereotype is not true? What if, as Halberstam asks, she looks instead?

The Evolving Legend of La Llorona

Amy Fuller

The character of La Llorona, the Wailing Woman, is prominent in Mexican culture, particularly making appearances at Day of the Dead festivals held at the start of each November. She is a tragic figure: a woman who has killed her own children, after their father leaves her for another woman, typically one of higher status. She is now doomed to wander, looking for them, crying out, "¡Mis hijos!" ("My children!"). This folk tale has ancient predecessors such as Ciuacoatl and Coatlicue in ancient Aztec mythology as well as Medea in Greek mythology. However, the tale of La Llorona can also be seen as symbolic of the creation of Mexico — the Spanish conquistadors conquered the Aztecs, married or cohabited with indigenous women, but later left them (and their children) when more Spanish women arrived in the New World. Amy Fuller is a lecturer at Nottingham Trent University who teaches the History of the Americas, 1400–1700. She specializes in the history of early modern Mexico and is the author of *Between Two Worlds: The Autos Sacramentales of Sor Inés de la Cruz* (2015). This article (excerpted here) originally appeared in the November 2015 issue of *History Today*.

A Mexican woman, Juana Léija, attempted to kill her seven children by throwing them into the Buffalo Bayou in Houston, Texas in 1986. A victim of domestic violence, she was apparently trying to end her suffering and that of her children, two of whom died. During an interview Léija declared that she was La Llorona.

La Llorona is a legendary figure with various incarnations. Usually translated into English as "the wailing woman," she is often presented as a banshee-type: an apparition of a woman dressed in white, often found by lakes or rivers, sometimes at crossroads, who cries into the night for her lost children, whom she has killed. The infanticide is sometimes carried out with a knife or dagger, but very often the children have been drowned. Her crime is usually committed in a fit of madness after having found out about an unfaithful lover or husband who leaves her to marry a woman of higher status. After realizing what she has done, she usually kills herself. She is often described as a lost soul, doomed to wander the earth forever. To some she is a bogeywoman, used by parents to scare children into good behavior.

This folk story has been represented artistically in various guises: in film, animation, art, poetry, theatre and in literature aimed at both adults and children alike. The legend is deeply ingrained in Mexican culture and among the Chicano Mexican population of the United States.

The origins of the legend are uncertain, but it has been presented as having pre-Hispanic roots. La Llorona is thought to be one of ten omens foretelling the Conquest of Mexico and has also been linked to Aztec goddesses. In the Florentine Codex, an encyclopedic work on the Nahua peoples of Mexico completed during the 16th century by the Franciscan friar Bernardino de Sahagún, we find two Aztec goddesses who could be linked to La Llorona. The first is Ciuacoatl (Snake-woman), described as "a savage beast and an evil omen" who "appeared in white" and who would walk at night "weeping and wailing." She is also described as an "omen of war." This goddess could also be linked to the sixth of ten omens that are recorded in the codex° as having foretold the Conquest: the voice of a woman heard wailing at night, crying about the fate of her children.

A later codex by a Dominican friar, Diego Durán, details the origin myths of the Aztec gods and discusses a goddess, Coatlicue, who is often linked to or thought to be the same as Ciuacoatl. Coatlicue (she of the snaky skirt) was the mother of Huitzilopochtli, the Aztec god of war. Durán describes her as "the ugliest and dirtiest that one could possibly imagine. Her face was so black and covered with filth that she looked like something straight out of Hell." She waits for her son to return to her from war and weeps and mourns for him while he is gone. Durán also provides detail of some strange occurrences ahead of the Conquest that were purported to have troubled Moctezuma. Among these is a "woman who roams the streets weeping and moaning."

Though these accounts fulfil some elements of the La Llorona legend, we need to look to another goddess in order to find the links to water and infanticide. According to the Florentine Codex, Chalchiuhtlicue (the Jade-skirted one) was goddess of the waters and the elder sister of the rain god, Tlaloc. Sahagún describes her as one who was "feared" and "caused terror." She was said to drown people and overturn boats. Ceremonies in honor of the rain gods, including Chalchiuhtlicue, involved the sacrifice of children. These sacrificial victims were bought from their mothers and the more the children cried, the more successful the sacrifice was thought to have been.

La Llorona has also been conflated with La Malinche, Cortés' translator and concubine. As such she is often portrayed as an indigenous woman jilted by a Spanish lover. However, there are many similar European and Old World motifs that she could also be linked to: the "White Woman" of the Germanic and Slavic tradition, the Lorelei and, of course, the banshee. The trope° of the barbarian girl who kills her children after

5

codex: an ancient book or manuscript; an early form of books, hand-stitched.
trope: a frequently used metaphor or motif.

being betrayed by her lover and discarded for a woman of higher status or more "appropriate" race also has roots in the Greek tradition, in the legend of Medea and Jason.

It is strange that such a pervasive myth could have such different features, but still be known by the same name. Indeed, the variations in the folk story seem to be geographical, with different regions having their own slightly different versions of the wailing woman. In addition, the legend has changed over time, seemingly to reflect the socio-political climate. Just as a source will often tell us more about the author than the subject, we can glean a lot about the story-tellers' points of view when examining the development of this particular legend. It is not until the late 19th and early 20th centuries that the folk story can be found in print. However, when we look at them, far from finding an official version, we can clearly see that many elements of the La Llorona story change over time.

La Llorona, a 1917 play by Francisco C. Neve, is set during the reign of Philip II (1556–98). The protagonist is Luisa. She has a son with her lover, Ramiro, the son of Cortés, who is of much higher social status. Though they have been together for six years, Ramiro is due to marry the very wealthy daughter of a judge. Luisa is unaware of this and Ramiro believes that he can continue his relationship with her, if he marries in secret. Luisa is told of Ramiro's impending wedding by a rival suitor and she is driven mad, not only by Ramiro's infidelity and his decision to marry someone else for honor and status, but by his desire to take their son away from her. When he comes for their child after she breaks up their wedding, Luisa eventually tells him that he can have his son's life and kills him with a dagger, offering Ramiro his body in a fit of delirium, saying that she killed him after Ramiro had killed her soul. Luisa is hanged for her crime in a public execution during which she is vilified as a witch. Ramiro is presented as very remorseful and dies of sorrow and grief when La Llorona appears to haunt him.

The play satirises the class system to an extent and especially masculine ideas of honor. Ramiro's mistress and son are an open secret among court society and whispers of gossip surrounding his love life are a prominent theme at his sham wedding. He does not garner respect from his peers and courtly society in New Spain is presented as a place of backstabbing and chaos. 10

The story would appear to reflect life in colonial Mexico. Although initially there was a shortage of Spanish women in New Spain, which meant that unions between indigenous women and Spanish men were quite common and not frowned upon, by the end of 16th century the population of European women was on the rise and the status of indigenous

A young woman dressed as La Llorona for a Day of the Dead celebration in Morelia, Mexico, in 2012.
Amy Fuller

or *mestiza* (mixed race) women fell considerably. Upon their arrival in Tenochtitlan, the imperial rulers of the Aztecs offered women, usually their female relatives, to the Spaniards and marrying an Indian heiress became a familiar path to success. Cohabiting was also common and in some cases Spanish men would take advantage of the indigenous practice of polygamy by having a number of concubines.

The fates of these indigenous and *mestiza* women were mixed. Some enjoyed stability and enhanced status and, therefore, benefited from these unions, but more often than not they were cast aside after a few years for younger women or, more often, a Spanish wife. More alarmingly, the children resulting from the union were sometimes taken away from their indigenous or *mestiza* mothers in a practice that derived from a Spanish tradition of relieving so-called "wayward" women of their children. The historian Karen Vieira Powers explains that "When this practice found its way to the New World and was applied to indigenous mothers who had borne children with Spanish men, their prescribed racial 'inferiority' was combined with the 'natural' inferiority of their gender to produce a generalized negative attitude toward their ability to socialise their children properly." This was more often the case for daughters as "doubts about native women's capacity to raise their *mestizo* daughters were especially acute, as the Spanish emphasis on sexual purity was not valued in Mexica society." Generations of children were, therefore, raised as "Spanish" despite their mixed heritage and taught to believe that their mothers' indigenous culture was inferior. [. . .]

Later versions of the wailing woman story present the villain as Spain and have created heroes in the *mestizo* and indigenous cultures. Carmen Toscano's 1959 one-act play, *La Llorona*, for example, presents a harsh critique of the Conquest and colonial period, with special attention paid to the treatment of the indigenous people by the Spanish conquistadors. The spiritual Conquest is also presented as fairly shambolic° and, overall, New Spain is shown to be a place of chaos with great tensions between clergy and secular authorities. The protagonist is Luisa, a *mestiza*, and her lover, Nuño, is a Spanish conquistador who marries Ana, a wealthy Spanish lady in secret, planning then to return to Spain. He does not appear to care for Luisa and neither are particularly interested in their children. Luisa stabs them to death and throws their bodies into the canal without much remorse. Nuño does not seem at all affected by this. Luisa is tried and hanged in the city's main plaza, though before she is executed she gives a monologue stating that all blood is the same and that as a *mestiza* she does not know where she belongs or which traditions to adopt. Purity of blood is a motif throughout the play, with the conquistadors not wishing to dirty the blades of their swords with Indian blood and Luisa exclaiming that Nuño only wishes to marry Ana as they have the same blood. Luisa is glad that her children are dead so they won't suffer like she has: having to work like a slave despite the glory of both her ancestors. She cries for her children. After her execution, Luisa takes her revenge as Nuño collapses and dies. A poet describes his sad soul and the ruins of Tenochtitlan. It would seem that the abandonment of Luisa represents the abandonment of Mexico by Spain, once its land had been exhausted of resources.

shambolic: chaotic, disorganized.

Here we find a return to many of the ideas expressed in the 1917 play, though the imagery is much more explicit and seems to be representative of the ideas of Nobel prize-winner, Octavio Paz. In his 1950 essay, *The Labyrinth of Solitude*, Paz describes La Llorona as "one of the Mexican representations of Maternity" and, as such, she is presented as a symbol of Mexican identity. This identity, according to Paz, revolves around Mexicans' view of themselves as *hijos de la Chingada*. Paz explains that: "The verb [*chingar*] denotes violence, an emergence from oneself to penetrate another by force. . . . The Chingada is the Mother forcibly opened, violated or deceived. The *hijo de la Chingada* is the offspring of violation, abduction or deceit." This violation is the Conquest, the quintessential symbol of which is La Malinche, or Doña Marina, who despite having been sold into slavery and given to the conquistadors—and therefore having limited agency of her own—has been painted as a traitor to "her people."

This anachronistic and highly misogynistic view that lays the blame for the defeat of a civilization at the feet of one (disenfranchised) woman has remained popular to this day. Indeed, Paz himself states that "the Mexican people have not forgiven La Malinche for her betrayal." This is in the face of indisputable evidence that the Aztecs were defeated by a Spanish force aided by thousands of indigenous allies, a fact often conveniently forgotten in popular culture.

> "This anachronistic and highly misogynistic view that lays the blame for the defeat of a civilization at the feet of one (disenfranchised) woman has remained popular to this day."

In Mexico's creation myth, La Malinche has become Eve. In regard 15 to her relationship with Cortés, Paz insists that "she gave herself voluntarily to the conquistador, but he forgot her as soon as her usefulness was over" and so it is easy to see how she could be merged with the legend of the wailing woman. The fact that she bore Cortés a son has also fuelled this conflation: their union symbolises the birth of Mexico as a nation of forcibly mixed-race people.

The annual performance of *La Llorona* on Mexico City's Lake Xochimilco most explicitly presents the importance of the legend as an expression of Mexican identity. For example, one advert for the production states that: "Our nation was born from the tears of La Llorona." This version of the play runs for two weeks at the end of October and beginning of November, overlapping with the Day of the Dead celebrations, and has been performed for over 20 years. [. . .]

This current version of the La Llorona story is another rehashing of the Cortés/Malinche story. La Llorona is portrayed as a traitor to her people by passing information to the Spaniards, which leads to their defeat. This has now become a common element of the legend. Along with providing a nod to Doña Marina, the play also contains another element of the folk story, as it opens with an Aztec mother goddess wailing a lament for her children as a forewarning of the Conquest.

This is the fullest version of the La Llorona story. Here we find the jilted woman trope finally united with the imagery of the Aztec goddess along with the act of warning her people about their impending doom and lamenting the birth of the modern Mexican nation through the mixing of blood. It is purported by the production company to be the "original" version of the legend, but the evidence does not stack up; the codices in which we find the supposed origins for the folk story remained unpublished until the 19th century. Furthermore, the timing of the performance is telling.

Though in essence Mexico's Day of the Dead is a version of the Roman Catholic feasts of All Saints' Day and All Souls' Days, the festival, celebrated on November 1st and 2nd, has contested origins. It is thought by some to be an indigenous tradition appropriated by the colonizers and by others as a colonial practice that has retrospectively claimed an indigenous origin in order to promote a "pure" Mexican identity. According to Paz, this identity revolves around Mexicans' distinctive, jovial attitude towards death, which is bolstered by the Day of the Dead celebrations. However, the family traditions of the Day of the Dead—decorating graves and constructing altars in homes dedicated to deceased family members—are rather different to the exuberant festivities displayed in town centers for tourists to enjoy. [. . .]

The evidence would suggest that La Llorona, as she is now known, is a fairly 20 modern myth that has evolved over time and has been used since the late 19th century to reflect and comment upon the socio-political situation of Mexico. By presenting La Llorona during the Day of the Dead celebrations, both of which have disputed origins but are thought to be "quintessentially Mexican," it can be used to present to the world a new version of Mexico's history and an official representation of Mexican identity.

Understanding the Text

1. How does Fuller relate the tale of La Llorona to ancient Aztec goddesses? How are the goddesses similar to La Llorona, and how are they different?

2. How is the 1917 play *La Llorona* a satire? Be specific.

3. What is it about the character of Luisa in the 1959 version of *La Llorona* that makes her different from other portrayals of women in the La Llorona myth? How does that affect the message of the play?

4. How is La Llorona connected to Mexico's celebration of the Day of the Dead?

5. This article first appeared in *History Today*, which describes itself as a "serious" magazine. What about the article — its language, its use of evidence, its tone — separates it from less serious publications and from peer-reviewed journals intended to be read by other historians?

Reflection and Response

6. In your opinion, is La Llorona a sympathetic figure? Why or why not?

7. How do gender and power work to construct the figure of La Llorona? Examine the roles that women and men are expected to fulfill in terms of love, marriage, and children. What does the tale tell us about those roles? Do later versions of the tale, as described by Fuller, change those dynamics? How?

Making Connections

8. The article draws many connections between the story of La Llorona and the conquest by Spain of the lands now referred to as Mexico. Research further the history of the conquest of the Aztecs by the Spanish and the subsequent treatment of the indigenous population. Argue whether or not the connections Fuller is making are valid. Be specific.

9. One of the mythological characters Fuller mentions who does not come from the Aztec tradition is Medea, a character from ancient Greek mythology (par. 7). Read the story of Medea and argue whether or not she serves as an adequate comparison to La Llorona.

10. Research contemporary, real-life stories of women who have murdered their own children. Are the circumstances behind these murders similar to or different from the story line of La Llorona? Do these real-life killings reflect historical changes in traditional gender-role dynamics or not? What do you make of that?

From The Odyssey

Homer

After the ten-year war in Troy, described in Homer's *Iliad*, Odysseus, the king of Ithaca, is thwarted in his attempt to sail home by the god Poseidon. This journey, which takes an additional ten years, is the subject of Homer's epic poem *The Odyssey*. The following passage is from Book 12, in which Odysseus resumes his journey after spending a year as the witch Circe's lover. Circe warns him about the Sirens — half-woman, half-bird creatures whose singing lures sailors to their deaths — and tells him that only he must hear their song. There is much uncertainty about the dates of Homer's life, and consequently the dates of *The Iliad* and *The Odyssey*, but he is generally thought to have lived in the eighth or ninth century BCE. [Editor's note: line numbers follow the Fagles translation.]

At those words Dawn rose on her golden throne
and lustrous Circe made her way back up the island.   155
I went straight to my ship, commanding all hands
to take to the decks and cast off cables quickly.
They swung aboard at once, they sat to the oars in ranks
and in rhythm churned the water white with stroke on stroke.
And Circe the nymph with glossy braids, the awesome one   160
who speaks with human voice, sent us a hardy shipmate,
yes, a fresh following wind ruffling up in our wake,
bellying out our sail to drive our blue prow on as we,
securing the running gear from stem to stern, sat back
while the wind and helmsman   165
    kept her true on course.
At last, and sore at heart, I told
    my shipmates,
"Friends . . . it's wrong for only
    one or two
to know the revelations that
    lovely Circe
made to me alone. I'll tell you all,
so we can die with our eyes wide open now   170
or escape our fate and certain death together.
First, she warns, we must steer clear of the Sirens,
their enchanting song, their meadow starred with flowers.
I alone was to hear their voices, so she said,
but you must bind me with tight chafing ropes   175
so I cannot move a muscle, bound to the spot,
erect at the mast-block, lashed by ropes to the mast.

> "We must steer clear of the Sirens, their enchanting song, their meadow starred with flowers."

And if I plead, commanding you to set me free,
then lash me faster,° rope on pressing rope."

So I informed my shipmates point by point,   180
all the while our trim ship was speeding toward
the Sirens' island, driven on by the brisk wind.
But then—the wind fell in an instant,
all glazed to a dead calm . . .
a mysterious power hushed the heaving swells.   185
The oarsmen leapt to their feet, struck the sail,
stowed it deep in the hold and sat to the oarlocks,
thrashing with polished oars, frothing the water white.
Now with a sharp sword I sliced an ample wheel of beeswax
down into pieces, kneaded them in my two strong hands   190
and the wax soon grew soft, worked by my strength
and Helios'° burning rays, the sun at high noon,
and I stopped the ears of my comrades one by one.
They bound me hand and foot in the tight ship —
erect at the mast-block, lashed by ropes to the mast —   195
and rowed and churned the whitecaps stroke on stroke.
We were just offshore as far as a man's shout can carry,
scudding° close, when the Sirens sensed at once a ship
was racing past and burst into their high, thrilling song:
"Come closer, famous Odysseus—Achaea's° pride and glory —   200
moor your ship on our coast so you can hear our song!
Never has any sailor passed our shores in his black craft
until he has heard the honeyed voices pouring from our lips,
and once he hears to his heart's content sails on, a wiser man.
We know all the pains that the Greeks and Trojans once endured 205
on the spreading plain of Troy when the gods willed it so —
all that comes to pass on the fertile earth, we know it all!"

So they sent their ravishing voices out across the air
and the heart inside me throbbed to listen longer.
I signaled the crew with frowns to set me free —   210
they flung themselves at the oars and rowed on harder,
Perimedes and Eurylochus springing up at once
to bind me faster with rope on chafing rope.
But once we'd left the Sirens fading in our wake,

faster: stronger, tighter.
Helios: Greek god of the sun, father of Circe.
scudding: moving rapidly.
Achaea: a region in southern Greece.

once we could hear their song no more, their urgent call —   215
my steadfast crew was quick to remove the wax I'd used
to seal their ears and loosed the bonds that lashed me.

Understanding the Text

1. Homer's poem says that Circe sent a gift, "a fresh following wind ruffling up in our wake" (l. 162). Why, then, are the men later paddling with their oars?

2. What do the Sirens say they know and will reveal to Odysseus in their song? What do they say happens to those who hear their voices?

3. How does Odysseus respond to hearing the Sirens' song?

4. This passage is part of the much longer epic poem, *The Odyssey.* Examine closely the use of language to create the world of Odysseus. In what ways is reading a story in poetry different from reading it in ordinary prose?

Reflection and Response

5. Homer does not spend any time on descriptions of the Sirens, so presumably he expected that his audience would already know that they were half-woman, half-bird creatures. What about the woman-bird combination seems particularly suited to the type of danger they represent?

6. The Sirens sing, "All that comes to pass on the fertile earth, we know it all!" (l. 207). Note that Odysseus, listening to them, wishes to be freed of his bonds and sail to them. Why is the temptation of knowledge so alluring? Can you think of other similar examples of people being tempted by knowledge? What does this say about the human condition?

Making Connections

7. How are the Sirens similar to other female monsters, especially woman-animal combinations? Do further research on the Sirens, mermaids, or some other monster that combines women's features with those of another creature. What role does the composite woman-animal monster play in relation to Karen Hollinger's argument about the need for men to control the power of female sexuality ("The Monster as Woman: Two Generations of Cat People," p. 154)? In answering the question, consider the point that Sophia Kingshill makes about how the mermaid has served as a symbol of dangerous seduction, an alluring female monster who leads men to their death ("Reclaiming the Mermaid," p. 139).

8. There are two female figures in this brief passage: Circe the nymph and the Sirens. Circe is the one who helps; the Sirens are the ones who pose a threat. In other words, female characters are divided into roles of helper and threatener. The men, however, are at the center of the story — the people being helped or threatened. Research additional stories that may conform to this model or find others that do not. What do these stories say about cultural expectations of women in hero stories?

Reclaiming the Mermaid

Sophia Kingshill

One of most common monsters in the human imagination is the mermaid. Tales of women who live in the water have been told around the world for millennia. Although there are also stories of mermen, the character of the mermaid, with her human upper body and fishtail lower body, is far more popular. She served sailors as an omen of impending doom, and the medieval church viewed her as a soulless creature, a symbol of sin and temptation. Modern interpretations of the mermaid have been influenced by Hans Christian Andersen's fairy tale "The Little Mermaid," reinterpreted by Disney in the animated film. In recent portrayals, however, the mermaid may be surfacing as a new symbol of feminist empowerment. Sophia Kingshill, a British writer interested in folklore, is the coauthor of *The Lore of Scotland* (2009) and *The Fabled Coast* (2012). Her other works include the history of mermaids in the book *Mermaids* (2015) and a young adult fiction novel, *Between the Raven and the Dove* (2017), as well as plays about the Brontës, William Morris, and Sinbad. This article was published in the October 2015 issue of *Fortean Times*.

The enduring popularity of mermaids as a cultural phenomenon means that their story spans eras, continents and art forms. The earliest surviving images date from over three thousand years ago; since then, mermaids have been carved in temples and churches, decorated fountains and palaces, and been used as inn signs, figureheads and tattoos. Sightings of fishy humanoids were reported by the first sailors in the Mediterranean and by pioneers to the New World, and are still rumoured around busy modern coasts. Mermaids can be emblems of maritime trade, of the sea's beauty and terror, or of feminine seduction, and legends of water-spirits, both romantic and frightening, are told worldwide.

A mermaid's meaning depends on who's interpreting her. To a mariner, traditionally, she's an omen of storm; poets have employed her as a symbol of fickle womanhood, her sinuous tail meaning she's slippery by nature; a showman might advertise a stuffed specimen as a marvel, to bring in the crowds. Representations change over time, too. Whereas in antiquity, a hybrid woman-fish was an image of a goddess or at least an attendant on the deities of the sea, later iconography made her signify sin and temptation, a metaphor reworked by Pre-Raphaelite artists to whom a Siren was a sexy model.

In December 2013, I saw a mermaid in Madrid. She was about four foot long from her waving curls to her tail-fin, scrawled on a wall in red spray paint. Instead of a mirror she had a heart in her hand, next to the feminist symbol of a circle and cross; beneath her was the slogan Abajo el patriarcado! — "Down with patriarchy!" Alongside, another message read: No dejes a tu vida, sea escenario! — "Don't give up on your life, take center stage!"

My Spanish Siren was neither vamp nor victim, but a self-aware female, angry and confident.

Siren Songs

In 2012, an Internet article identified mermaid novels as the "hottest new   5
trend" of Young Adult fiction, but concluded that they were unlikely to oust vampires or schoolboy magicians from the bestseller lists "because they are, to put it bluntly, girls' books." Of the authors mentioned in the article, one is a man, 16 are women.

A few of the books cited are actually about sea boys, but the article's title refers to mermaids alone. This is standard usage, in spite of the fact that mermen have as ancient a presence, in legend and in art, as mermaids. Although witnesses report seeing bearded as well as breasted creatures in the waves, and if merfolk have a gender at all (given their lack of equipment), there's nothing to say that their chromosomes should be more X than Y, the people of the sea are just about unique among creatures real or fabulous, in that the female term covers both sexes: as a collective noun, we're far likelier to talk about "mermaids" than "merfolk." Mermaids, moreover, get more publicity than their he-counterparts. A Google search for "merman" yields around 800,000 results, "mermaid" well over 20 million. Males are, for once, the second sex. That doesn't automatically empower the mermaid: quite the reverse. For most of her history, she's been depicted, described, and voiced by male artists, seafarers, theologians and storytellers, and whether as object of desire or figure of fear, a half-naked woman is, or has been, obviously intended to delight or disquiet a largely male audience.

Now the pendulum's swung the other way, and mermaids are inspiring women not just in Young Adult Fish Lit, but across the media. Artist Wangechi Mutu mounted a London exhibition of paintings, sculpture and video in 2014 under the title "Nguva na Nyoka" (Sirens and Serpents). The nguva or dugong is an aquatic mammal that is the equivalent of the Siren in Kenyan coastal legend; Mutu uses images of the nguva to explore questions of feminism, ecology and metamorphosis, and contrasts its intense and sometimes savage powers with "the sanitised mermaid of popular European culture."

Singer Mariah Carey recorded her 1999 album *Rainbow in Capri*, and in an interview she recalled her pleasure when she saw the Scoglio delle Sirene, "Sirens' Rock":

The Sirens would sit there and lure in the men. They gave them this rock because women were considered less important than men, and that's their revenge: they sexually entice men with their voices to come to this rock. I just fell in love with that.

The idea that the Sirens' magnetism helped them get even with men has obvious relevance to the career of a pop diva like Carey, whose appearance and sexuality are exploited to market her singing.

The mermaid as spokeswoman for equality, typified by the Madrid graffiti I saw in 2013, goes back at least to the 1970s when the name Siren was used for a feminist magazine in Chicago. A pattern has been established of women reclaiming the mermaid, reacting against male-dominated traditions defining her as submissive or seductive.

> "A pattern has been established of women reclaiming the mermaid, reacting against male-dominated traditions defining her as submissive or seductive."

10

There are earlier examples of the belligerent mermaid, without any particular sex bias. Warsaw's city crest, which evolved from a bird-legged, scaly monster (a classical Siren, in fact) to become, by the 18th century, a recognizable mermaid with a woman's body and a fish's tail, has remained militant throughout, carrying a shield and brandishing a sword. Between 1811 and 1915, under the Fourth Partition of Poland, the Syrenka, as she's known, was officially banned, but was displayed in many places as an assertion of the city's identity, and in the Second World War she was adopted as the badge of the Polish II Corps.

Pablo Picasso, visiting a Warsaw apartment block under construction in 1948, drew the Syrenka on an interior wall, giving her the Communist hammer to hold instead of a sword. This image survives only in photographs, since the mural wasn't universally admired. The first person offered the flat in question refused it, on the grounds that he had small children and the mermaid had bare breasts, while the next (childless) candidates were equally horrified: "It was huge, my God was it huge. Her bosom was like two balloons, the eyes were triangular, at the end of her long, oddly long arm she held a hammer; and she had a short, tapering tail at the back."

After a couple of years, the flat's tenants quietly had their private Picasso whitewashed, but the Syrena has continued to appear as a political symbol, employed by supporters of Solidarity in the 1980s, and more recently by the Warsaw Gay Movement.

Statue of the Syrenka, the warrior mermaid, on the banks of the Vistula River in Warsaw, Poland.

age fotostock/Alamy Stock Photo

Little Mermaids

The common modern perception of the mermaid, however, is of a whimsical and child-friendly fantasy. This image is based to a great extent on the ubiquitous kitsch spawned by the Disney cartoon: but the Little Mermaid herself is not so wholesome, on closer inspection.

Ariel, as she's christened in the film, is drawn with a girlish figure and a pertly pretty face. Her hair is neither seaweed-green nor princess-golden, but a vibrant red, and she hides her breasts in a bikini top, modest for the family market. Ariel's inquisitive nature leads her to take an interest in the human world, and while people-watching, she falls in love with the young Prince Eric. When his ship sinks in a storm she saves his life, but swims away before he can see her. She bargains with the sea-witch Ursula for a spell allowing her to exchange her tail temporarily for a pair of legs, in return giving up her voice, which Ursula magically traps in a shell.

Unless she receives a kiss of true love, the mermaid is told, she must 15 remain in the witch's power forever. The wicked Ursula then transforms herself into an attractive woman, and sings in Ariel's voice to bewitch Eric. True identities are eventually discovered, the witch is killed, and Ariel, having regained her voice and become fully human with the help of her father the sea-king, marries her prince.

The Danish original is an altogether darker affair, with a stern message about redemption through suffering. Early in Andersen's "Little Mermaid," as in the film, its teenage heroine (here nameless) rescues the prince from a shipwreck.

Then, however, it is not love alone that impels her to beg for a human shape, but the desire for an immortal afterlife. Her grandmother tells her that this can be achieved if a man marries her: at the moment the priest joins their hands, she will be granted a share of her husband's soul.

In order to win her prince and thus her chance of eternal life, the mermaid visits a witch. She is warned that having her tail split into two legs will mean continuous agony—every step she takes will feel as if she is treading on a blade sharp enough to make her bleed—and, moreover, that becoming human is a one-way journey. She will never be a mermaid again.

In payment for her spell, the witch demands the mermaid's voice, which she takes not with a reversible charm, but by cutting out her tongue. Dumb, and in terrible pain, the mermaid reaches the palace, where she is kept as a kind of pet, allowed to sleep on a cushion outside her prince's door. The prince is fond of her, but his love is bestowed on a princess he believes to be the girl who saved him from drowning. He marries the princess, and the mermaid acts as bridesmaid at the wedding.

Her sisters, meanwhile, longing to bring her back to them, have 20 acquired a magic knife from the witch. This, they tell the mermaid, must be plunged into the prince's heart, and his blood will turn her feet back into a fish-tail. She can't bring herself to kill him. Instead she throws the knife into the sea, then dives in herself, and feels her body melt into foam, a mermaid's death.

Nevertheless she does not die, but is transformed into a spirit of the air, who can gain a soul by three centuries of good deeds. One of her ethereal companions tells her that for every good child she visits, the 300 years will be shortened by one year, but at the sight of a naughty child she will cry, and every tear shed will add a day to her probation.

The religious trappings do have a certain authority behind them. Medieval theologians had speculated as to whether mermaids and other "monsters" possessed souls, and some concluded that a mermaid did not, but wished she did. The idea that she could gain one by marrying a human being was proposed by authors earlier than Andersen, and the Little Mermaid's metamorphosis into an airy form is based on philosophical concepts of the four elements—earth, air, fire and water.

The physical and emotional torments that the mermaid undergoes are Andersen's own invention, and however unpleasant to read, they are what gives the story its power both as tragic romance and as parable of a female rite of passage. Writing for children in the early 19th century, Andersen could not say straight out that in order to be a man's wife, the mermaid would have to be able to have sex, and therefore must have sex organs. Instead, he has the wise grandmother point out that humans consider tails ugly, hence the need for legs. Then, whether intentionally or not, he invests the splitting of the mermaid's tail with all the pain and secret mess of puberty and loss of virginity, her feet standing in for what in a woman is hidden and below. Wordless, in pain, though no one sees you bleeding, unrequitedly in love, longing for a better world than this one: what adolescent can't identify?

Sadistic and didactic, the tale makes uneasy reading, and one can readily understand Disney's changes to make the plot palatable, but it was widely loved long before the studio got their hands on it. Operas and ballets have been based on it, Shirley Temple starred in it on television, and comic-book, manga and anime versions have been produced. Illustrations have tended to emphasize the mermaid's virginal purity and wistful charm, although one sketch by Lorenz Frølich hides her breasts but gives her a suggestively cleft bum above her fishtail.

Most famous of all visual interpretations must be the statue which 25 has become a national symbol of Copenhagen. After seeing a ballet based on Andersen's tale, Carl Jacobsen, head of Carlsberg Breweries and a great patron of the arts, commissioned Edvard Eriksen's sculpture, which was unveiled in 1913. Eriksen wanted to give his Little Mermaid legs, but Jacobsen held out for a tail, and a compromise was reached:

the Copenhagen mermaid has clearly defined thighs, knees and calves, terminating in two large graceful fins. The sculptor may have realized how vital it was for Andersen's heroine to be a forked animal—although locals have explained the legs as allowing their Mermaid to ride a bicycle, like the rest of the Danes. In fact the double-tailed mermaid is not a novelty, but a very old motif.

Despite being visited and admired by countless tourists, the Copenhagen Little Mermaid, like her fairytale original, has suffered. In 1964, her head was sawn off, although it was quickly replaced using a cast from the original model. An arm was removed in 1984, she was decapitated again in 1998, and in 2003 she was blown right off her base by an explosive charge, while more superficial damage has been achieved with paint.

At least some of this vandalism has been motivated by protest. In one of the latest episodes, March 8—the date of International Women's Day—was painted on the Mermaid, and she was given a dildo to hold. You could say she's an obvious target for feminist reinterpretation. Andersen's Little Mermaid is a willing sacrifice, both to the insensitive prince, and more importantly to the Church, which denies her a soul except at the cost of anguish.

Mermaids of the Caribbean

Older than either the radical or the meek mermaid is the rapacious variety, of which the fearsome creatures who appear in Pirates of the Caribbean are recent avatars. The film does feature one "good" mermaid who falls in love with a human being, but the rest of the breed are carnivorous and merciless. At their first appearance, a couple of nymphs raise heads and arms from the sea to beguile a boatful of sailors with their sweet voices and youthful faces; then the picture pulls back, to reveal more and more converging on the boat like minnows to bait, and finally we see shoals of them leaping around their terrified prey.

On dry land they appear as luscious women, legs and all (what's between is never on display, and their breasts are obscured by long hair), but underwater they are seen to have tails, and fanged mouths like vampires. Although they use their sex to entice, they only want men as food.

Much of this, including their appetite to consume men in the literal 30 sense, is longstanding legend. Homer's Sirens—who are not mermaids at all, but who significantly inform the tradition—strew their surroundings with human bones. Themes of homicide and lust intertwine from an early date: a work of the third or second century BC, purporting to record the adventures of Alexander the Great in India, mentions women living immersed in a river, who were beautiful—"Their complexion was snow-white, like nymphs their hair spread over their backs"—but who suffocated Alexander's soldiers during or after the act of love.

A 13th-century encyclopedia (in 16th-century translation from Latin) describes the Siren as temptress and cannibal:

A beast of the sea wonderfully shapen as a maid from the navell upward, and a fish from the navell downeward, and this wonderfull beast is gladde and merrie in tempest, and sadde and heavie in fayre weather. With sweetnesse of song this beast maketh shipmen to sleepe, and when shee seeth that they be asleepe, she goeth into the ship, and ravisheth which she may take with her, and bringeth him into a drye place, and maketh him first lye by her, and doe the deede of lechery, and if he will not or may not, then she slaieth him and eateth his flesh.

Pirates of the Caribbean presents an authentic characterization and an unusually forthright one for the cinema. More commonly, films have expressed a mermaid's predatory nature in terms of seduction: in *Miranda* (1948), Glynis Johns's character creates emotional havoc among her string of suitors before returning to the sea, and in *Splash!* (1984), Madison (Daryl Hannah) ultimately takes her lover (Tom Hanks) under the waves with her. Although this is presented as a happy ending, it's made clear that he can never come back to the world of humans.

It's always a risk to meet a mermaid.

Understanding the Text

1. What is the point of the graffiti image of the mermaid Kingshill saw in Madrid? How is that a redefinition of the traditional mermaid? What are some other examples of this redefinition that Kingshill presents?

2. In what key ways does the Disney presentation of Ariel in *The Little Mermaid* differ from the original story by Hans Christian Andersen? How are those differences significant?

3. How and why has the statue of the Little Mermaid in Copenhagen been a target of protestors?

4. How has Kingshill balanced pop culture with academic research in creating this article? Cite specific examples of both.

Reflection and Response

5. Kingshill points out that throughout history, the mermaid has reflected social and religious teachings about women's role in society, the question of the soul, and the importance of control of female sexuality. How has this been expressed, and how might the mermaid also been seen to subvert those teachings? Be specific.

6. How can the mermaid be a symbol of female empowerment? Explain.

Making Connections

7. Kingshill states, "Mutu uses images of the nguva to explore questions of feminism, ecology and metamorphosis" (par. 7). Research the nguva and contrast its symbolic use with that of the traditional European mermaid.

8. Research other mermaid stories from different cultures and times. Argue how these stories reinforce or challenge the views of women held by the societies that created them.

9. Largely absent in Kingshill's discussion is the male counterpart, the merman. Research historical representations of the merman and what he may symbolize or represent. Argue why the merman has been a lesser regarded figure and what important insights may be gleaned from the study of him.

The Battle of the Lapiths and Centaurs

Ovid

The legendary Greek hero Nestor tells Achilles the story of a wedding banquet gone terribly wrong. Invited to the wedding of Pirithous and Hippodamía are the centaurs — half-man, half-horse creatures. When the centaurs get drunk, they attempt to abduct the women at the banquet. A pitched battle ensues, in which many humans and centaurs are killed. The story is told by Ovid in Book 12 of *Metamorphoses*, one of the most important works of mythology. Along with Virgil and Horace, Ovid is considered one of the most important writers of the Roman era. [Editor's note: line numbers follow the Raeburn translation.]

"Piríthoüs, son of Ixíon and king of the Lapiths,   210
had married Hippodamía. He invited the cloud-born centaurs
to join the banquet at tables arranged in a leafy glen.
The chieftains of Thessaly came; I, Nestor, also attended.
The palace was filled with the festive hubbub of thronging guests.
Now hark to the wedding-hymn! Torches and rising smoke in the
    great hall!   215
Enter the bride, escorted by matrons and younger women,
and looking a picture. We all declared how blessed Piríthoüs
was in his beautiful wife. But our praise's effect as a lucky
omen was almost undone, when the wildest of all the wild centaurs,
Eúrytus, drunk already, was further inflamed by the sight   220
of the bride, and the power of wine reinforced by desire took over.
Tables were upside down in a flash, the feast was reduced
to a shambles, as Eúrytus seized Piríthoüs' newly-wed bride
by the hair and forced her away, while each of the other centaurs
grabbed any woman he fancied or found. The chaos resembled   225
a captured city, and women were screaming all over the palace.
We quickly rose from our couches. 'Eúrytus!' shouted Théseus,
taking the lead, 'you must be crazy! How dare you provoke
Piríthoüs while *I* live and foolishly injure us both?'
The centaur said nothing—he couldn't defend his outrageous
    behavior   230
by words—but used his unruly fists to punch the prince
on the jaw and to pummel his chest. On a table nearby there chanced
to be lying an antique wine-bowl, richly embossed with figures
in high relief. The bowl was huge, but Theseus was huger;
he lifted it up and hurled it directly in Eúrytus' face.   235

As globules of blood and fragments of brain poured out of the wound,
the centaur, vomiting wine from his mouth, fell backwards and
    drummed
with his heels on the sodden sand. His brothers, enraged by the
    carnage,
vied with each other in
    shouting as one, 'To
    arms, to arms!'
Inspired by the wine with
    courage, they started the
    battle by sending
their goblets flying, then
    breakable jars and round-lipped vessels,
objects intended for feasts, now used for war and for slaughter.
    "Amycus, son of Ophíon, was first among the rampaging
centaurs to raid the inner rooms of the palace and plunder
an iron stand which supported a cluster of burning candles.   245
He lifted the whole thing high, like a priest at a sacrifice straining
to raise the axe which will cleave the neck of a pure white bull,
then dashed it down on the forehead of Céladon, one of the Lapiths.
This fractured his skull and mangled his face past all recognition.
His eyes burst out of their sockets, the bones of his cheeks were
    shattered,   250
the nose smashed inwards and jammed beneath the roof of his
    mouth.
But another Lapith called Pélates wrenched the leg from a
    maplewood
table and used it to hammer Amycus down to the ground,
with his chin forced into his chest. As the centaur sputtered his
    teeth out
mingled with gore, a second blow dispatched him to Hades.   255
    "Next to the fore came Grýneus, who'd stood there, grimly inspecting
the smoking altar and said, 'Why don't we make use of this?'
With a frightening glare in his eyes, he lifted the hefty structure,
fires and all, and hurled it into a group of the Lapiths.
Two were crushed by the mountainous weight, Bróteas and Oríos   260
(Oríos' mother was Mýcale, said to have often succeeded
in drawing down the horns of the moon with her incantations).
'You won't get away with this, if I can get hold of a weapon!'
Exádius said, and then caught sight of some antlers nailed
to a tall pine tree as a votive offering. There was his weapon!   265

> "Eúrytus, drunk already, was further inflamed by the sight of the bride, and the power of wine reinforced by desire took over."   240

Armed with the horns of a stag, Exádius aimed for the centaur's
eyeballs and gouged them out. One eye stuck fast on the antlers,
and one rolled down on to Gryneus' beard, blood-coated, and clung
    there.

                              • • •

"How about Caeneus? He killed five centaurs: Antímachus, Stýphelus,
Élymus, Bromus and lastly Pyrácmus, who fought with an axe.   460
(I can't remember their wounds, but only their names and the
    number.)
Then Látreus, a centaur of massive physique, rushed forward to
    face him,
armed with the spoils of Halésus, a Macedonian he'd slaughtered.
In age he was past his youth and his temples were flecked with gray,
but his strength was still a young man's. His helmet, shield and exotic 465
pike attracted all eyes as he proudly turned to each army,
brandished his weapons and pranced around in a well-traced circle,
flinging a torrent of insolent taunts in the empty air:
'Caenis,° you bitch! Must I tolerate *you*? You will always be female
and Caenis to *me*. Perhaps you forget your original sex.   470
Do you ever recall what you did to deserve your reward? Do you
    think
of the price which you paid to achieve this specious masculine body?
Look at the girl you were born and the shame that she suffered.
    Then go,
return to your distaff and basket of wool. Go back to your spinning,
and leave the fighting to *men*!' As Látreus was galloping past him, 475
shouting these insults, Caeneus let fly with his spear, which made
    a great
gash in the mocker's side where man and horse are united.
Maddened by pain, the centaur cast at the hero's uncovered
head with his pike. The weapon rebounded like hail off a rooftop
or pebbles dropped on a drum. Then Látreus attacked at close quarters 480
and struggled to bury his sword in the young man's side, but the side
was too hard; there was no way in. 'You won't escape me,' he shouted.
'You'll die on the edge of my sword, since the point's been blunted!'
        So turning

Caenis: the female form of Caeneus. Caeneus was originally born as a woman and was
raped by Neptune, who then fulfilled her request to be transformed into a man so he
could never be raped again.

A marble tablet with a sculpture relief from the Parthenon in Athens, depicting the battle between the Lapiths and centaurs.

World History Archive/Alamy Stock Photo

his weapon sideways, he reached to slash him around his thighs,
but the blow produced no more than a thud—the flesh might well   485
    have been
marble. The metal was broken to splinters on striking such tough
    skin.
Caeneus was tired of exposing his still unwounded limbs
to the stupefied centaur. 'Come on!' he said to him, 'now let's see
how your body responds to *my* steel'; and he plunged his death-
    dealing sword
right up to the hilt in his enemy's trunk and compounded the   490
    damage
by turning and twisting the sunken blade right into his vitals.
On came the centaurs, shouting and yelling, rushing in frenzy,
everyone hurling or thrusting their weapons against one foe.
Those weapons were blunted and fell to the ground, while Caeneus
    remained
unscathed by all of their blows; not a drop of his blood had been   495
    spilt.
"This turn of events left the centaurs dumbfounded. 'Shameful,
    disgraceful!'

Mónychus cried. 'Our whole tribe worsted by one man, hardly
a man at that! No, *he* is a man and we are behaving
as feebly as women. What use is this massive girth of our bodies?
What of our double strength? Has nature combined in ourselves   500
the courage and force of the world's two mightiest creatures for
    nothing?
Our mother a goddess? I don't believe it. Our father cannot
have been Ixíon, a mortal with pride enough to aspire
to sleep with Juno on high, when *we* are defeated by someone
whose sex is in doubt! Let us roll the boulders, the trees, whole   505
    mountains
on top of this upstart. Let's hurl the forests and crush the life
from his living body. His throat will be choked by the bulk of it all,
and the weight will prove as good as a wound.' So saying, he seized
a trunk knocked down, as it chanced, by the south wind's fury, and
    threw it
against his unwoundable foe. The rest did the same; in a short while   510
Othrys° was stripped of its trees and Pelion° empty of shade.
Crushed beneath that enormous layer, the hero sweltered
under the weight of the trees, and heaved with his sturdy shoulders
to raise the pile, but after the load grew greater and greater
over his head and he couldn't breathe through his mouth any longer, 515
consciousness left him. But then he recovered and vainly attempted
to roll the trees off his body and lift himself up to obtain
some air. For a while he succeeded in moving the surface, as if
Mount Ida, which look! we can see over there, was disturbed by an
    earthquake.
No one is certain what happened next. Some said that his body   520
was thrust right down by the mass of the trees to the shadows of Hades.
Mopsus the seer said no. He'd noticed a rust-winged bird
emerging out of the pile and soaring into the air.
I also sighted the bird that day for the first and the last time.
Mopsus watched it gently circling the camp and he heard it   525
loudly clapping its wings. As he thoughtfully followed it round
with his eyes, he exclaimed, 'All hail! Hail Caeneus, pride of the
    Lapiths,
once unique among men, and now sole bird of your kind.'
The prophet said it and we believed it. Grief made our anger

Othrys: a mountain in Greece that in Greek mythology was the home of the Titans,
who were later overthrown by Zeus.
Pelion: a mountain in Greece that in Greek mythology was the home of the centaurs.

all the more bitter. That one man's life should be crushed by so many! 530
To vent our sorrow, we turned on the centaurs and didn't cease
    fighting
till most had been killed and the rest were in rout or were rescued by
    night."

Understanding the Text

1. What is special about a wedding celebration, from a public or social standpoint?

2. How do Theseus and the other Greeks respond to the centaurs' disruption of the wedding banquet?

3. What makes Caeneus a unique person? What is behind the special rage the centaurs feel toward him? How do they eventually kill him?

4. Ovid's story is told as a memory. An old man, Nestor, is telling the story to Achilles, a great warrior and hero. How might that affect the storytelling?

Reflection and Response

5. The fight escalates quickly into a battle to the death. It is human action — Theseus kills Eúrytus with a wine bowl — that turns the disruption into a mortal fight. As Ovid writes, "Objects intended for feasts [were] now used for war and slaughter" (l. 242). What does this quick turn of events say about the combination (or overlap) of human and animal traits?

6. Even though the story begins with a wedding celebration, women are conspicuously absent from most of the tale, except to be spoken of as victims. Indeed, only one woman is even named, the bride Hippodamia, even though many are abducted. What does this reveal about the role of gender? How does the passage about Caeneus support those concepts of gender roles?

Making Connections

7. Although the story is told by Nestor, a Greek, and features Greek characters, it is recorded by Ovid, a Roman author. Research the story of the rape of the Sabine women, an event that allegedly occurred several hundred years before Ovid in which Roman men, lacking wives, kidnapped Sabine women to take as their own. You might also analyze visual depictions of that event by looking at the famous sculpture by Giambologna or paintings by Pietro da Cortona, Jacques-Louis David, and Pablo Picasso. Compare the behavior of the Romans in that event with the behavior of the centaurs in this selection. What does this comparison suggest about monsters?

8. Research the history of the character Caeneus. Can Caeneus be regarded as a type of monster? Why or why not? Note the spelling change to "Caenis" in line 469. In your research, consider issues of sexual violation and how they are handled in mythology. What does this say about male and female sexuality as viewed in those times — and in our own?

The Monster as Woman: Two Generations of Cat People

Karen Hollinger

Most monsters are male, or at least seem to represent a male incarnation. Frequently, the monster's victim — or at least the attempted victim — is female. Thus, when the monster is female, there is an opportunity to explore the social messages behind the female monster. Karen Hollinger examines two versions of the movie *Cat People* — the first made in 1942 and the second in 1982. Hollinger is a professor of English at Georgia Southern University–Armstrong Campus who focuses on film studies and gender studies. She is the author of numerous books, including *The Actress: Hollywood Acting and the Female Star* (2006) and *Feminist Film Studies* (2012). This article originally appeared in the scholarly journal *Film Criticism* in 1989.

> [I]t could well be maintained that it is women's sexuality, that which renders them desirable — but also threatening — to men, which constitutes the real problem that the horror cinema exists to explore, and which constitutes also and ultimately that which is really monstrous.
>
> — STEPHEN NEALE, *Genre*

As Stephen Neale suggests, an intimate relationship seems to exist among the filmic presentation of the horror monster, the castration anxiety it evokes, and the cinematic representation of the female form. The complexity of this relationship has been suggested by several critics, but its theoretical articulation, how it works in specific horror films, and the social and historical implications it has for the positioning of women in patriarchal society still remain to be more fully examined. A possible step in this direction involves an inquiry into the filmic presentation of the monster as woman.

Critics have been slow to investigate the connection between the representation of the horror monster and that of the female image because the horror monster traditionally has been presented as male. From classic monster films like *The Cabinet of Dr. Calgari* through *Nosferatu*, *Frankenstein*, *Dracula*, *The Wolf Man*, *King Kong*, and *The Mummy* to the contemporary psychopath-as-monster films like *Texas Chainsaw Massacre* and *Halloween* or the monstrous creature-as-phallic-symbol films like *Jaws* the monster is overtly, even excessively, masculine. A closer look at theoretical approaches to the iconography of the horror monster and that of the female cinematic form, however, reveals striking similarities. The traditional maleness of the horror monster can be explained in Freudian terms as an expression of the connection between the image of the monster and the filmic representation of castration anxieties. It has been proposed that the essential nature of narrative is Oedipal,° that it involves the reactivation and eventual management of the castration anxieties for the male subject. If so, the monster film can be said to combine in the figure of its monster the fascination, fear, and anxiety that this reenactment of the Oedipal trauma evokes. Stephen Neale, for instance, argues that the traditional male horror monster mobilizes castration anxieties by his portrayal of the lack that represents castration to the male subject (*Genre* 43–44). It is this reenactment of the male Oedipal trauma in the figure of the horror monster that accounts for the male spectator's simultaneous attraction to and repulsion from the monster film and its monstrous central character.

Thus, the monster film is centrally concerned with problems of sexual difference. This concern, according to Neale, acts not to undermine the male spectator's filmic pleasure by using the monster merely to expose the lack upon which castration anxieties are founded, but rather to entertain the spectator by filling this lack (*Genre* 43–44). The monster not only represents castration, but also disavows it and provides filmic pleasure for the male viewer by soothing castration fears. The avenues of this disavowal fall into two categories: fetishistic scopophilia° and sadistic-investigative voyeurism. The horror monster by his very presence and by the spectacular nature of this presence serves fetishistically to reassure the spectator by masking the castration fear that is the real concern of the film. As Neale suggests, the positioning of the monster as a fetishistic figure of disavowal explains both why so much is made of the details of the monster's construction and why so many of the resources of costume and make-up are expended to make his appearance both spectacular and believable (*Genre* 45). He must not only frighten but also convince the spectator of the credibility of his existence and appearance if he is to disavow castration as well as symbolize it.

The rhythm of presence and absence that the horror film sets up in regard to the monster's appearance also represents an aspect of this

---

Oedipal: relating to Sigmund Freud's Oedipus complex and castration anxiety, in which the young boy fears that his father may castrate him as punishment for his attraction to his mother.
fetishistic scopophilia: the displacement of erotic interest and satisfaction to the act of looking, such as at naked bodies or pornography.

fetishistic avenue of disavowal. The random appearances of the monster throughout the horror film work, as Neale points out, to create a reassuring rhythm of presence and lack that serves to regulate and contain the irrevocable lack, castration (*Genre* 44). Thus, for the monster to ward off castration anxiety effectively, he must be shown, and if possible even unmasked, in the course of his filmic appearances so that he can visually enact his fetishistic role.

The monster's evocation of castration anxieties can be controlled not only visually by his fetishization, as Neale suggests, but also narratively by plots that involve fetishistic and sadistic-investigative aspects. In fact, the overreacher and discovery plots, two classic forms of monster film narrative, parallel these twin forms of disavowal. The overreacher plot enacts narratively the monster's positioning as a fetishistic figure by setting him up as the embodiment of his creator's lofty and unattainable dreams of reaching a god-like relationship to nature and of creating a perfect human being. Thus, we see inscribed even in the narratives of these monster films disavowal, overvaluation, and fetishistic substitution. An exemplary text in this regard is James Whale's *Frankenstein* (1931), in which Henry Frankenstein's creation of a violent and destructive monster is explained as the result of his desire to assemble a magnificent creature with a superior human brain.

The discovery plot, on the other hand, works to manage the monster and the castration anxieties that he evokes in a slightly different way. Rather than completely disavowing castration through fetishistic substitution and overvaluation, the discovery plot seeks to control the monster by a process of demystification. This narrative movement culminates in the devaluation and/or punishment of the monster or at least in the acquisition of sufficient knowledge of his mysterious behavior to find a way to deal with his threatening presence.

A comparison of this Freudian description of the filmic presentation of the horror monster and Laura Mulvey's analysis of the iconography of the female form in narrative cinema shows them to be quite similar. According to Mulvey, the figure of the woman, like that of the monster, also mobilizes castration fears in the male subject. She is "the bearer of the bleeding wound," the signifier of the male Other, and the symbol of the castration threat by her real absence of a penis (7). For Mulvey, the project of narrative cinema as a whole is both to represent this lack and to disavow it in its presentation of the female form, just as the monster film works both to represent and to disavow the threat of the castrated and castrating monster. The two avenues of disavowal for the threat of castration embodied in the filmic image of woman are also sadistic-investigative voyeurism (the investigation of the woman's mystery) and fetishistic scopophilia (the substitution of the fetish object or the turning of the represented figure itself into a fetish through overvaluation).

While a relationship thus seems to exist between the image of woman in cinema and that of the monster in the horror film, the nature of this relationship is obscured by classic monster films, which position women as victims of the monster's aggression. Just as the classic horror monster is commonly defined as male, so the primary object of his desire is almost exclusively female. As Neale points out, patriarchy positions women as subject to men and to their power, and the horror film simply "rehearses and restates this ideology" ("*Halloween*" 28), but, as Linda Williams suggests, beneath this assertion of male power that positions women only as victims there lies a sympathetic affinity and identification between woman and monster. Williams argues that the look of the female victim at the monster in the horror film reveals not only an acknowledgment of her punishment for usurping the male power of the look but also a recognition of her similar status to the monster "in patriarchal structures of seeing" (85).

The positioning of woman as victim in the classic monster film, therefore, functions as a method of masking what is really presented as monstrous and threatening in these works. The fear that lurks behind castration anxieties and the fetishized horror monster can be seen as a fear not of the lack represented by the horror monster but of the potency of female sexuality and the power of woman's sexual difference. Both Neale and Mulvey perceive the threat of the horror monster and of female sexuality to the male in terms of its evocation of a weak, castrated female form. For them, the image of the woman and of the monster recalls for the male spectator his childhood Oedipal trauma during which he came to regard his mother as rendered weak and helpless by castration. It also reactivates the Oedipal fear that he too could be reduced through castration to her situation of powerless deformity and mutilation.

This conception of female sexuality as threatening to the male in   10
terms of its representation of the castrated female's weak and helpless state is called into question by the affinity between woman and monster. If the woman is related to the monster in that they both are seen by patriarchy as representing sexual difference and castration fears, then she is allied not to a representation of weakness but to one of power in sexual difference. For the classic male horror monster, as symbol of the male Other, is not only a castrated victim of male society, but also a powerful, potentially castrating nemesis to the male hero, and he gets his power from the very fact of his dangerous difference from the normal male, from his positioning as "a biological freak with the impossible and threatening appetites that suggest a frightening potency precisely where the normal male would perceive a lack" (Williams 87).

The inadequacy of the Freudian rendering of woman as a symbol only of the lack that is castration and nothing more has led revisionist psychoanalytic theorists like Susan Lurie to challenge traditional Freudian notions of the nature of the male Oedipal experience. According to Lurie, the male child's trauma involves not his fear of being castrated and thus reduced to his mother's state of helpless mutilation, but rather a recognition that his mother, although she lacks a penis, is not, in fact, powerless or helpless. The whole notion then of woman as representing castration can be read, according to Lurie, as really a disavowal of this unsettling discovery, as a lie that covers up the male child's recognition of his mother's power in difference. Applying this theory to the monster film suggests that an interpretation with greater explanatory power than those of Neale and Mulvey in assessing the socio-historical implications of the monster as woman in patriarchal society involves a recognition that the underlying fear that informs these texts and that lies behind the fear of castration is the threat of the potency of non-phallic sexuality. As Williams, building on Lurie's theories, suggests, it is not a recognition of the weakness but of the power in difference that woman, as sexual Other and as a potentially castrating force to the male, represents (89–90).

This fear of female sexuality is carefully masked, disavowed, and displaced in the classic monster film with its male monster, fetishistic and investigative plots, and positioning of woman as victims. With the introduction of the female monster, however, this careful cover-up is destroyed because the twin avenues of disavowal no longer disavow. Castration anxieties, the underlying threat of non-phallic female sexuality, and the power in sexual difference explode from the text. Extraordinary means, therefore, must be taken to control and diminish the resulting effects on the traumatized male spectator.

A consideration of the filmic presentation of the female monster demonstrates that her existence threatens to destroy the tight control that the classic monster film imposes on the evocation of castration fears and on the portrayal of the female sexual threat that lies behind castration. From the very beginning of her cinematic career, the female monster's threatening nature was evoked only to be forcefully suppressed. James Whale's *Bride of Frankenstein* (1935) provides an early example of this suppression. The major portion of the film is devoted to a sympathetic rendering of the male Frankenstein monster. He is shown to be a pitiful creature in search of friendship and kindness who kills only when attacked and endures brutally cruel treatment, even visual crucifixion, by his captors. Much is also made in the film of the creation of the female monster, but when she does finally appear, it is only to be quickly disposed of. Despite her wild hairdo and the hissing sound she makes when approached, she is, in fact, not at all a very threatening creature: she clings submissively to Henry Frankenstein, is terrified of the male monster, and is incapable even of protesting when her rejected would-be mate sets out to destroy them both. She seems created only to act as the ultimate victim for the male monster's final demonstration of power. Clearly, however, the female sexual threat in this film, symbolized in the female monster's capacity to reject her mate, is perceived as too dangerous to allow her more than a few moments of screen time.[1]

If the female threat is forcefully controlled in *Bride of Frankenstein* by quick and total destruction, it is allowed to demonstrate its overwhelming power in Jacques Tourneur's *Cat People* (1942). Tourneur, a director noted for his subtle visual suggestion of horror, allows his female monster to triumph over all male efforts to control her. Attempts are made to utilize the traditional monster film's methods of disavowing the female sexual threat, but they are exposed here as pitifully inadequate to control the horror of the female monster. Irena (Simone Simon), the cat woman, is pursued by two men, each of whom represents one avenue of disavowal. Oliver Reed (Kent Smith) is a non-threatening male presence who tries to control Irena's sexual threat by converting her into a fetishistic figure, placing her in the cult of the beautiful and sexually provocative, but unknowable and untouchable woman. Oliver describes their relationship as involving his being drawn to Irena by the force of her sexual attraction, which holds him against his will. He confesses:

I'm drawn to her. There's a warmth from her that pulls at me. I have to watch her when she's in the room. I have to touch her when she's near, but I don't really know her. In many ways we're strangers.

In direct contrast to Oliver's passive fetishism and embodying the sadistic-investigative avenue of disavowal is the aggressive sexual threat represented by the psychiatrist Dr. Judd (Tom Conway). He sets out actively to counter Irena's dangerous sexuality with the force of his phallic presence. His aggressive sexuality is symbolized in his walking-stick, which contains within it a hidden sword. The sword connects him visually to another phallic power in the film, King John of Serbia, whose statue Irena keeps in her apartment. As she tells Oliver, the legendary

15

---

[1]Elsa Lancaster plays two roles in the film: as Mary Shelley in the prologue and later as the female monster. Shelley is presented in the prologue as an angelic Victorian woman who has demonstrated her suppressed wickedness by writing a naughty book. This positioning of the woman anticipates Tourneur's *Cat People*, in which it is suggested that the female monster is finally controlled by her own internalization of patriarchal standards.

King John rescued her village by driving out evil invaders who had led the villagers to witchcraft and devil worship. Since Irena's statue portrays King John with a panther impaled on his sword, a connection is made between the devil worshipers, whom Irena describes as having escaped King John's invasion by fleeing to the mountains, and the cat women, whom she later mentions to Dr. Judd under hypnosis. The image of a primitive, evil matriarchy threatening to male power is thus suggested. As Dr. Judd relates Irena's description of the cat women, they are:

women who in jealousy or passion or out of their own corrupt passions can turn into great cat-like panthers. And if one of these women were to fall in love and if her lover were to kiss her, take her into his embrace, she would be driven by her own evil to kill.

Irena believes herself related to these evil creatures, and Dr. Judd sets out to disprove this belief. The conflict between Irena's determination to cling to her conviction that she is, in fact, a cat woman and Dr. Judd's attempts to "cure" her becomes a struggle for power and domination.

Irena Reed (Simone Simon) in *Cat People* (1942), a horror film about a race of women who transform into panthers when sexually aroused.
Sunset Boulevard/Contributor/Getty Images

Judd initially attempts to gain control over Irena by mastering her secrets, investigating her while she is under hypnosis. After their first session together, he taps his little black notebook and tells her that although she remembers nothing of what she has revealed to him, he has it all at his command. Later, when they meet again at the zoo, she asks how he knew where to find her, and he answers with a look of mastery that makes her visibly uncomfortable, "You told me many things." Judd's attempts to control Irena do not stop with his investigation of her psyche. They culminate in his sexual advances, their kiss, and her transformation into a panther. In the resulting battle, the shadowy forms of the panther and the phallic walking-stick/sword are seen in violent conflict. The panther, although wounded, is still victorious: Judd is killed, and the walking-stick/sword is later discovered to have been broken in the battle, half of it left embedded in Irena's body.

If Judd's active attempts to exert male control result only in his death, Oliver's passive reaction to Irena's sexual threat leads him to a different fate. He turns to a seemingly asexual union with his female friend and co-worker, Alice (Jane Randolph), who describes their relationship in this way:

I know what love is. It's understanding. It's you and me and let the rest of the world go by. It's just the two of us living our lives together happily and proudly, no self-torture and no doubt. It's enduring and it's everlasting. Nothing can change it. Nothing can change us, Ollie. That's what I think love is.

There is no sexuality here. Alice offers Oliver a safe, secure, and non-threatening affection, but it is also presented as an asexual one. As they stand over Irena's dead body in the film's concluding scene, Oliver comments to Alice, "She never lied to us," reconfirming the horrible reality of Irena's sexual threat. It is a real threat to Oliver, and one that must never touch his ideal relationship with Alice, a relationship that is safe in its asexuality.

Although Irena's threatening sexuality is managed at the film's conclusion through her violent destruction, it is never brought under the sway of male dominance. Both Oliver and Dr. Judd fail to control her, and she is left to destroy herself by deliberately opening the gate to the panther's cage in the zoo and exposing herself to its attack. Acting in accord with the patriarchal standards that she has internalized, Irena punishes herself for a sexual nature that she has come to see as evil. This self-induced punishment, however, does not diminish the power of her sexual difference, and Tourneur's film remains a strong statement of female power in difference, which is controlled only by the woman's internalization of patriarchal standards.

Tourneur's version of *Cat People* thus illustrates the forceful expres- 20
sion of the female threat to the male in the character of a female monster. A consideration of this film makes it tempting to see the female
monster as defying the usual filmic avenues of disavowal and expressing a threat beyond narrative control. A comparison of Tourneur's film
with Paul Schrader's 1982 remake, however, demonstrates clearly that
the female monster, in fact, can be controlled by a strong, even brutal
evocation of phallic power. Schrader's film, in its crudely explicit narrative presentation of horror, acts as a reassertion of the phallic control
that Tourneur's subtle, visually and thematically suggestive style intentionally eschews.

The project of Schrader's *Cat People* is much like that of the male child
who finally has come to see his mother's non-phallic power and wants
desperately to disavow it. Schrader's film works to represent the female
as a weak, castrated figure and to reaffirm her submission to the phallic
dominance of the male. This reaffirmation involves the transformation
of the original film's representative of failed phallic power, Dr. Judd, into
a much more threatening male monster who can assert the force of the
male sexual threat even in death. This figure is Irena's brother Paul (Malcolm
McDowell), another cat person who in his panther form is responsible
for many brutal murders. He brings Irena (Nastassia Kinski) to live with
him, hoping that an incestuous relationship with her, another cat person,
will prevent his transformation into a panther.

Thus, Irena is introduced in this film not as a powerful sexual threat,
but as a potential victim to Paul's threatening sexuality. This portrayal
is immediately established in the film's opening scenes depicting primitive tribal ceremonies in which young women are offered as sexual
partners to male panthers. A comparison of this representation of the
origin of the cat people legend to that presented in the Tourneur version is informative. Whereas in the original, the cat women are seen
as powerful witches and devil worshipers who escape King John's male
domination by fleeing to the mountains, in Schrader's version, they
become ritual sacrifices to the lust of male panthers. Irena's connection to these primitive female victims is made visually by the transition
from these opening scenes to her arrival in New Orleans to meet Paul. A
dissolve superimposes a close-up of Irena's face as she searches through
the airport for her brother over the face of one of these female sacrificial victims.

Throughout the film, in scenes depicting his post-coital attacks on his
sexual partners, Paul's strength is contrasted to Irena's weakness. Even
in death, Paul maintains significant power. He is killed while in his panther form not by Irena or Oliver (John Heard), her zookeeper lover, but

by Alice (Annette O'Toole), Oliver's female co-worker, who represents the asexual non-threatening femininity characteristic of her counterpart in the original version. Male power in Schrader's as in Tourneur's film thus is at least partially subdued by a voluntary female renunciation of sexuality, but Paul is not really completely subdued. After his death, his corpse in its panther form is subjected to an autopsy by Oliver. When the carcass is opened up, a noxious gas is released that affects Oliver so strongly that he is sent to a hospital to recover, and the panther's body disintegrates, leaving behind only a green slime associated earlier in the film with Paul's transformations from one physical form into another. The suggestion is made that even after his death Paul remains a threatening creature capable of inflicting bodily harm on others and of escaping any attempts to understand and thus to control him. Irena, on the other hand, does not demonstrate a very powerful or threatening nature. She is shown only once with blood on her mouth after an apparent attack on a rabbit. While the phallicly potent Paul rips off a zookeeper's arm and devours unsuspecting female sexual partners, Irena can only stalk rabbits. A castrated cat, she is reduced to small acts of viciousness.

When she does finally accept her sexual power and have sex with Oliver, she takes on her panther form but then refuses to attack him; instead, she goes off into the night to find another victim. Even though Irena is shown in her panther state, the details of her animal brutality are not presented. She does kill in order to return to her human form, but she murders the custodian of Oliver's cabin; he is, significantly, an old man well past the age of sexual potency. Thus, the force of her threat to the sexually active male is reduced. The actual attack itself is not shown. In contrast to the graphic portrayals of Paul's victims' mutilations, Irena's victim is simply shown in what appears to be a non-mutilated state. He could as easily have died from fear as from Irena's attack. Irena is not seen again until she has returned to her human form and awaits Oliver in his cabin. The visual presentation of this scene is significant. The shadows from the cabin window screens cast a cage-like pattern on Irena. She seems to have willingly sought out her own imprisonment. Her lover has sought her out as well, and she begs him to kill her. When he refuses, she asks that he use his phallic power to return her to her animal state so that she can be freed from the torment of her sexual potency. He agrees, ties her to the bed in his cabin, and performs his rites of transformation.

Extraordinary means are here taken to reaffirm the power of male sex- 25 uality and to minimize the female sexual threat. In order to accomplish this reaffirmation, the non-threatening male in the film is converted into a benevolent sexual despot. He provides for the weak female a way out of the horror of her sexual potency; she can find salvation if she submits to his mastery. The final scene in the film recapitulates this theme as Oliver stands outside a panther's cage and allows the cat (by implication, Irena in her animal form) to eat from his hands through the bars. The zoo-keeper shows kindness and concern but remains completely in control. The panther growls but finally can only submit to his dominance. It is a scene that shows the threat of female power effectively subdued and the final triumph of the male complete.

A comparison of Tourneur's film to Schrader's indicates that the filmic evocation of the female sexual threat through the figure of the female horror monster involves a complex formulation related not only to the psychic needs of its male spectators and to the internal requirements of the textual systems of the films themselves, but also to the social conditions under which the films were made. Tourneur's 1942 film speaks to a patriarchy secure in its control of female power yet on the brink of the wartime initiation of women's challenges to that control. It, therefore, rehearses and restates in symbolic form a reassuring confidence in women's internalization of patriarchal standards and of images of female power as evil. This symbolic restatement of the patriarchically correct positioning of women in 1942 also involves a strong expression of women's potential power in difference and the threat it poses to a male-defined hegemony.° This expression could be tolerated by a society that still felt sure of male social dominance.

By 1982, however, when Schrader became attracted to the notion of redoing *Cat People*, women had made so many threatening advances against male power that the patriarchal assumption of women's internalization of its cultural standards and codes no longer could be confidently entertained. It became necessary to reassert male dominance in the only other way possible, through the use of force. Thus, in a period of growing assertion of female power against patriarchal hegemony, Schrader's film acts as a historically conditioned response to Tourneur's version. It attempts to master through generic variation the evocation of the female sexual threat in the original film and to reassert crudely, but effectively, the phallic control that is only subtly suggested in Tourneur's work. In both films, however, the presence of the female monster brings to the surface of the text the underlying threat of female sexuality and of the power of sexual difference that shapes it.

"The presence of the female monster brings to the surface . . . the underlying threat of female sexuality and of the power of sexual difference that shapes it."

hegemony: domination; the exercise of control and influence over others.

Works Cited

Lurie, Susan. "Pornography and the Dread of Women." *Take Back the Night*. Ed. Laura Lederer. New York: Morrow, 1980. 159–73.

Mulvey, Laura. "Visual Pleasure and Narrative Cinema." *Screen* 16 (Autumn 1975): 6–18.

Neale, Stephen. *Genre*. London: British Film Institute, 1980.

——. "*Halloween*: Suspense, Aggression, and the Look." *Framework* 14 (Spring 1981): 25–29.

Williams, Linda. "When the Woman Looks." *Revision: Essays in Feminist Criticism*. Edited by Mary Ann Doane, Patricia Mellancamp, and Linda Williams. Frederick, MD: U Pub. of America and American Film Institute, 1984. 83–99.

Understanding the Text

1. What does Hollinger mean when she says that the horror monster evokes "castration anxiety" (par. 1)? How does the female monster evoke this anxiety differently than the male monster?

2. Explain what Susan Lurie means when she challenges the traditional Freudian interpretation of the male Oedipal experience. What is the "lie" she refers to (par. 11)?

3. What are "two classic forms of monster film narrative," and how do they parallel the "twin forms of disavowal" (par. 5)?

4. How are the two main male characters in the 1982 version of *Cat People* different from those in the 1942 version? According to Hollinger, what is the significance of those differences, given the forty years that separate the two films?

Reflection and Response

5. Do you find male or female monsters more frightening? More sexual? How might your gender affect your answer?

6. Hollinger states, "It is this reenactment of the male Oedipal trauma in the figure of the horror monster that accounts for the male spectator's simultaneous attraction to and repulsion from the monster film and its monstrous central character" (par. 2). How do male monsters embody this attraction/repulsion for a male spectator? Do female monsters change how the attraction/repulsion works? If so, how?

7. In addition to the *Cat People* movies, Hollinger also examines *The Bride of Frankenstein* (1935), in which the female monster, or the Bride, is almost immediately killed by the male monster when she rejects his advances. Hollinger argues that the female monster represents the power of female sexuality (even the power to reject) that must be brought under male control, reflecting society's larger demand that female sexuality be kept within acceptable confines. Do you agree with her argument? Cite representations of monsters and other characters in specific films to support your answer.

Making Connections

8. Do representations of other female monsters, particularly those in movies, confirm Hollinger's central thesis about the desire to control female sexuality? Cite specific examples to support your answer.

9. Investigate the theories of Sigmund Freud, particularly those related to the Oedipus complex and castration anxiety and the threat posed by female sexuality. Also investigate critics of Freud, particularly feminist critics, regarding these issues. Is the use of these theories in the interpretation of film fair and appropriate? Why or why not?

Final Girl

Carol J. Clover

The slasher film has been a popular subgenre of horror since at least the mid-1970s with the release of *The Texas Chain Saw Massacre* (1974). Its basic pattern is deceptively simple: some misfit bent on murder wreaks destruction in various creative and terrifying forms of violence on a group of unlucky victims — except for one person, the Final Girl. The Final Girl shows enough courage, strength, assertiveness, and plain luck either to escape from the psycho or kill him herself. Carol J. Clover examines the psychosexual relations behind the killer and the Final Girl to reveal the complicated dynamic not only happening on the screen but with the viewer as well. Clover is a professor emerita at the University of California, Berkeley, where she specializes in film studies, rhetoric, and Scandinavian mythology. She is also the author of *The Medieval Saga* (1982). This passage is from Clover's seminal book on the slasher film genre, *Men, Women, and Chain Saws* (1992).

The image of the distressed female most likely to linger in memory is the image of the one who did not die: the survivor, or Final Girl. She is the one who encounters the mutilated bodies of her friends and perceives the full extent of the preceding horror and of her own peril; who is chased, cornered, wounded; whom we see scream, stagger, fall, rise, and scream again. She is abject terror personified. If her friends knew they were about to die only seconds before the event, the Final Girl lives with the knowledge for long minutes or hours. She alone looks death in the face, but she alone also finds the strength either to stay the killer long enough to be rescued (ending A) or to kill him herself (ending B). But in either case, from 1974 on, the survivor figure has been female. In Schoell's words: "The vast majority of contemporary shockers, whether in the sexist mold or not, feature climaxes in which the women fight back against their attackers—the wandering, humorless psychos who populate these films. They often show more courage and levelheadedness than their cringing male counterparts." Her scene occupies the last ten to twenty minutes (thirty in the case of *Texas Chain Saw I*) and contains the film's emphatic climax.

The sequence first appears in full-blown form (ending A) in *Texas Chain Saw I* with Sally's spirited self-defense and eventual rescue. Her brother and companions were dispatched suddenly and uncomprehending, one by one, but Sally survives the ninth round: long enough to see what has become of her fellows and is in store for her, long enough to meet and even dine with the whole slaughterhouse family, long enough to undergo all manner of torture (including the ancient grandfather's feeble efforts to strike a fatal hammer blow on the temple as they bend her over a washtub), and long enough to bolt and rebolt, be caught and recaught, plead and replead for her life, and eventually escape to the highway. For nearly thirty minutes of screen time—a third of the film—we watch her shriek, run, flinch, jump or fall through windows, sustain injury and mutilation. Her will to survive is astonishing; in the end, bloody and staggering, she finds the highway, Leatherface and Hitchhiker in pursuit. Just as they bear down on her, a truck comes by and crushes Hitchhiker. Minutes later a pickup driver plucks Sally up and saves her from Leatherface. The final shots show us a receding Leatherface from her point of view (the bed of the pickup): standing on the highway, wounded (having gashed open his abdomen during the truck episode) but upright, waving the chain saw crazily over his head.

Halloween's Final Girl is Laurie. Her desperate defense is shorter in duration than Sally's but no less fraught with horror. Limping from a leg wound, she flees to a garden shed and breaks in through the window with a rake. Neighbors hear her screams for help but suspect a Halloween prank and shut the blinds. She gets into her own babysitting house—by throwing a potted plant at a second-story window to rouse the children—just as the killer descends. Minutes later he comes through the window and they grapple; she manages to fell him with a knitting needle and seizes his butcher knife—but drops it when he seems dead. As she goes upstairs to the children, the killer rises, takes the knife, and goes after her. She takes refuge in a closet, lashing the two doorknobs together from the inside. As the killer slashes and stabs at the closet door—we see this from her inside perspective—she bends a hanger into a weapon and, when he breaks the door down, stabs him in the eye. Again thinking him vanquished, she sends the children for the police and sinks down in pain and exhaustion. The killer rises again, but just as he is about to stab her, Dr. Loomis, alerted by the children, rushes in and shoots the killer.

Given the drift in just the four years between *Texas Chain Saw* and *Halloween*—from passive to active defense—it is no surprise that the films following *Halloween* present Final Girls who not only fight back but do so with ferocity and even kill the killer on their own, without help from the outside.[1] Valerie in *Slumber Party Massacre* (a film directed by

---

[1]There are exceptions, some of them disturbing. In *Splatter University*, Professor Julie Parker is clearly established as a Final Girl from the outset and then killed right at the beginning of what we are led to believe will be the Final Girl sequence (she kicks the killer, a psychotic priest-scholar who keeps his knife sheathed in a crucifix, in the groin and runs for the elevator—only to be cornered and stabbed to death). So meticulously are the conventions observed, and then so grossly violated, that we can only assume sadistic intentionality. This is a film in which (with the exception of an asylum orderly in the preface) only females are killed, and in highly sexual circumstances.

Amy Jones and scripted by Rita Mae Brown) takes a machete-like weapon to the killer, striking off the bit from his power drill, severing his hand, and finally impaling him. Alice assaults and decapitates the killer of *Friday the Thirteenth*. Pursued by the killer in *Hell Night*, Marti pries the gate key from the stiff fingers of a corpse to let herself out of the mansion grounds to safety; when the car will not start, she repairs it on the spot; when the car gets stuck in the roadway, she inside and the killer on top, she frees it in such a way as to cast the killer on the gate's upper spikes. The grittiest of the Final Girls is Nancy of *A Nightmare on Elm Street I*. Aware in advance that the killer will be paying her a visit, she plans an elaborate defense. When he enters the house, she dares him to come at her, then charges him in direct attack. As they struggle, he springs the contraptions she has set so that he is stunned by a swinging sledge hammer, jolted and half-incinerated by an electrical charge, and so on. When he rises yet again, she chases him around the house, bashing him with a chair.[2] In *Texas Chain Saw II*, from 1986, the Final Girl sequence takes mythic measure. Trapped in the underground slaughterhouse, Stretch repeatedly flees, hides, is caught, tortured (at one point forced to don the flayed face of her murdered technician companion), and nearly killed. She escapes with her life chiefly because Leatherface, having developed an affection for her after the crotch episode, is reluctant to ply his chain saw as his father commands. Finally Stretch finds her way out, leaving the Texas Ranger to face certain death below, and clambers up a nearby pinnacle, Chop Top in pursuit. In a crevice near the summit she finds the mummified grandmother, ceremoniously enthroned in an open-air chamber, and on her lap, a functional chain saw. She turns the saw on Chop Top, gashing open his abdomen and tossing him off the precipice. The final scene shows her in extreme long shot, in brilliant sunshine, waving the buzzing chain saw triumphantly overhead. (It is a scene we are invited to compare to the final scene of *Texas Chain Saw I*, in which the wounded Leatherface is shown staggering after the pickup on the highway and waving his chain saw crazily over *his* head.) In Part One the Final Girl, for all her survivor pluck, is, like Red Riding Hood, saved through male agency. In Part Two, however, there is no male agency; the figure so designated, the Texas Ranger, proves so utterly ineffectual that he cannot save himself, much less the girl. The comic ineptitude and failure of would-be "woodsmen" is a repeated theme in the later slasher films. In *Slumber Party Massacre*, the role is played by a woman — though a butch one (the girls' basketball coach). She comes to the slumber party's rescue only to fall victim to the drill herself. But to focus on just who brings

---

[2]This film is complicated by the fact that the action is envisaged as a living dream. Nancy finally kills the killer by killing her part of the collective nightmare.

the killer down, the Final Girl or a male rescuer, is—as the easy alternation between the two patterns would seem to suggest—to miss the point. The last moment of the Final Girl sequence is finally a footnote to what went before—to the quality of the Final Girl's fight, and more generally to the qualities of character that enable her, of all the characters, to survive what has come to seem unsurvivable.

The Final Girl sequence too is prefigured, if only rudimentarily, in *Psycho*'s final scenes, in which Lila (Marion's sister) is caught reconnoitering in the Bates mansion and nearly killed. Sam (Marion's boyfriend) detains Norman at the motel while Lila snoops about (taking note of Norman's toys). When she perceives Norman's approach, she flees to the basement. Here she encounters the treated corpse of Mrs. Bates and begins screaming in horror. Norman bursts in and is about to strike when Sam enters and grabs him from behind. Like her generic sisters, then, Lila is the spunky inquirer into the Terrible Place: the one who first grasps, however dimly, the past and present danger, the one who looks death in the face, and the one who survives the murderer's last stab.

There the correspondences end, however. The *Psycho* scene turns, after all, on the revelation of Norman's psychotic identity, not on Lila as a character—she enters the film midway and is sketchily drawn—and still less on her self-defense. The Final Girl of the slasher film is presented from the outset as the main character. The practiced viewer distinguishes her from her friends minutes into the film. She is the Girl Scout, the bookworm, the mechanic. Unlike her girlfriends (and Marion Crane) she is not sexually active. Laurie (*Halloween*) is teased because of her fears about dating, and Marti (*Hell Night*) explains to the boy with whom she finds herself sharing a room that they will be using separate beds. Although Stretch (*Texas Chain Saw II*) is hardly virginal, she is not available, either; early in the film she pointedly turns down a date, and we are given to understand that she is, for the present, unattached and even lonely. So too Stevie of Carpenter's *The Fog*, like Stretch a disk jockey; divorced mother and newcomer in town, she is unattached and lonely but declines male attention. The Final Girl is also watchful to the point of paranoia; small signs of danger that her friends ignore, she registers. Above all she is intelligent and resourceful in a pinch. Thus Laurie even at her most desperate, cornered in a closet, has the wit to grab a hanger from the rack and bend it into a weapon; Marti can hot-wire her get-away car, the killer in pursuit; and the psych major of *Friday the Thirteenth II*, on seeing the enshrined head of Mrs. Voorhees, can stop Jason in his tracks by assuming a stridently maternal voice. Finally, although she is always smaller and weaker than the killer, she grapples with him energetically and convincingly.

The Final Girl is boyish, in a word. | *"The Final Girl is boyish."*
Just as the killer is not fully masculine,
she is not fully feminine—not, in any case, feminine in the ways of her friends. Her smartness, gravity, competence in mechanical and other practical matters, and sexual reluctance set her apart from the other girls and ally her, ironically, with the very boys she fears or rejects, not to speak of the killer himself. Lest we miss the point, it is spelled out in her name: Stevie, Marti, Terry, Laurie, Stretch, Will, Joey, Max. Not only the conception of the hero in *Alien* and *Aliens* but also the surname by which she is called, Ripley, owes a clear debt to slasher tradition.

With the introduction of the Final Girl, then, the *Psycho* formula is radically altered. It is not merely a question of enlarging the figure of Lila but of absorbing into her role, in varying degrees, the functions of Arbogast (investigator) and Sam (rescuer) and restructuring the narrative action from beginning to end around her progress in relation to the killer. In other words, *Psycho*'s detective plot, revolving around a revelation, yields in the modern slasher film to a hero plot, revolving around the main character's struggle with and eventual triumph over evil. But for the femaleness, however qualified, of that main character, the story is a standard one of tale and epic.

Works Cited

Schoell, William. *Stay Out of the Shower: Twenty-Five Years of Shocker Films Beginning with Psycho.* New York: December, 1985.

Films Cited

Alien	1979 Ridley Scott
Aliens	1986 James Cameron
Fog, The	1979 John Carpenter
Friday the Thirteenth	1980 Sean S. Cunningham
Halloween	1978 John Carpenter
Hell Night	1981 Tom DeSimone
Nightmare on Elm Street, A	1984 Wes Craven
Psycho	1960 Alfred Hitchcock
Slumber Party Massacre	1982 Amy Jones
Splatter University	1984 Richard W. Harris
Texas Chain Saw Massacre, The	1974 Tobe Hooper
Texas Chain Saw Massacre II, The	1986 Tobe Hooper

Understanding the Text

1. What point does Clover make about the difference in the endings of *The Texas Chain Saw Massacre* (1974) and *Halloween* (1978)?

2. How does the ending of Alfred Hitchcock's *Psycho* (1960) prefigure the endings of slasher films that came later? How is *Psycho* substantially different in its ending?

3. What point does Clover make about the character names of many of the Final Girl?

4. Clover states, "But to focus on just who brings the killer down, the Final Girl or a male rescuer, . . . is to miss the point" (par. 4). What is the point?

5. How does Clover use specific details from movies to support her arguments? Are there limits to using this sort of evidence, and if so, what are those limits?

Reflection and Response

6. Is the Final Girl a hero? Why or why not? Your response will depend on how you define the word *hero*.

7. What is the relevance of the comparison of the different endings of *The Texas Chain Saw Massacre I* and *II*? In your opinion, does this difference make Stretch more of a feminist character than her predecessor, Sally? What are the two movies saying about female power?

8. Clover writes, "The Final Girl is boyish, in a word" (par. 7). Do you agree or disagree with her assessment? Explain.

Making Connections

9. Are there qualities in the Final Girl that compare to qualities in female monster characters from other stories, such as La Llorona (Fuller, p. 128), mermaids (Kingshill, p. 139), or Irena from *Cat People* (Hollinger, p. 154)? What does this say about the presentation of the female in monster stories? Support your answer.

10. Clover's work was initially published in 1992. In your opinion, has her analysis of the Final Girl held true over time? To support your answer, refer to more recent films in the slasher genre.

Bodies That Splatter: Queers and Chain Saws

Judith Halberstam

The slasher horror film has typically been seen as a genre that focuses on male aggression and female victimhood. The slasher film may, however, actually scramble categories of gender as well as race, class, and sexuality. Indeed, analyzing the slasher film through the lens of queer theory may require the creation of entirely new categories to describe the monstrous. Judith Halberstam, who now uses the name Jack Halberstam, is a professor of Gender Studies and English at Columbia University. Other publications by Halberstam include *Gaga Feminism: Sex, Gender, and the End of Normal* (2012) and *The Queer Art of Failure* (2011). This essay is an excerpt from *Skin Shows: Gothic Horror and the Technology of Monsters* (1995).

The horror film has typically been theorized as a misogynist genre that provides a showcase for masculine aggression and provokes a sexual response to the spectacle of female mutilation. Such a view of horror film seems borne out by audience surveys which suggest that young males make up the primary group that watches horror films. This chapter pressures the formulation of horror as masculine pleasure and, following on from my last chapter on the productive nature of female or feminist paranoia, we will see if, when, and how the horror film can be recuperated for feminine, feminist, and queer forms of pleasure. Furthermore, in keeping with the themes of this book, I want to examine the Gothic technologies of subject production as they operate through the apparatus of the contemporary horror film. In a film like *The Texas Chainsaw Massacre 2* (1986), gender, race, class, and sexuality are thoroughly scrambled as categories and what emerges are queer identity formations literally sutured together from the scraps of flesh that survive the chain saw.

The category "horror film" at this point covers a vast range of cinema; included in this genre are slasher/splatter films (e.g., *Halloween, Friday the 13th, A Nightmare on Elm Street, The Texas Chainsaw Massacre*), Gothic psychothrillers (*Psycho, The Birds, The Silence of the Lambs*), sci-fi horror (*Alien*), rape revenge (*The Accused, Ms. 45*), supernatural horror (*The Exorcist*). In this chapter I pay careful attention to a few examples of the slasher/splatter film as precisely the location of the dismantling and reconstruction of bodily identities and also of spectatorial positions, gazes, and desires. John McCarty, in *Splatter Movies*, defines splatter films as "offshoots of the horror film genre" which "aim not to scare their audiences, nor to drive them to the edge of their seats in suspense, but to mortify them with explicit gore." He sums up: "In splatter movies, mutilation is the message."[1] In keeping with the transitions that I have been charting from the horror associated with landscapes and houses in the eighteenth-century Gothic Romance to the horror of Gothic monstrous bodies in the nineteenth century, the splatter film occupies a key place in terms of the preoccupation in the twentieth century with not simply the external monstrosities of the body but the increasingly voyeuristic quest to show what lies below the skin.

One recent book on horror has radically altered the conditions of horror film theory. *Men, Women and Chain Saws* by Carol Clover proposes that the radical potential of the horror film lies in the identification it forces between the male viewer and the female victim (a masochistic viewer position). Clover writes: "Cinefantastic horror, in short, succeeds in incorporating its spectators as 'feminine' and then violating that body — which recoils, shudders, cries out collectively — in ways otherwise imaginable for males only in nightmare."[2] Clover is less clear about the potential identification that horror allows between the female viewer and the male or female aggressor. She also has a tendency to restabilize gendered positions in relation to horror. The queer tendency of horror film, in my opinion, lies in its ability to reconfigure gender nor simply through inversion but by literally creating new categories. For example, the relations between femininity and chain saws in *The Texas Chainsaw Massacre 2* significantly alter the terrain and bodily space of the "girl" in these films. Similarly, the relations between men and a splattered masculinity significantly affects the meanings of maleness. [. . .]

The final girl is, according to Clover, the survivor; "the one who encounters the mutilated bodies of her friends and perceives the full extent of the preceding horror and of her own peril; who is chased, cornered, wounded; whom we see scream, stagger, fall, rise, and scream again" (35). As the character who lives to tell the tale of horror, the final girl, Clover argues, must be accessible as a point of identification to male viewers. For this reason the final girl's gender is ambiguous. "The final girl is boyish" (40), says Clover and she adds, "what filmmakers seem to know better than film critics is that gender is less a wall than a permeable membrane" (46). Gender, we might add, drawing from earlier formulations of identity in this project, is often a very specific "permeable

---

[1] John McCarty, *Splatter Movies: Breaking the Last Taboo of the Screen* (New York: St. Martin's, 1984), 1.
[2] Carol Clover, *Men, Women, and Chain Saws: Gender in the Modern Horror Film* (Princeton, N.J.: Princeton University Press, 1992), 53.

membrane" — the skin. Someone's skin, their hide (Hyde), precisely forms the surface through which inner identities emerge and upon which external readings of identity leave their impression. *The Texas Chainsaw Massacre 2*, in fact, provides its viewers with a virtual skinfest and constantly focuses upon skin and the shredding, ripping, or tearing of skin as a spectacle of identity performance and its breakdown.

The spectacle of skin in *Dr. Jekyll and Mr. Hyde*, as we saw, simultaneously   5 signified the hiding of sex *and* race; in *The Texas Chainsaw Massacre 2*, the dominance of the narrative action by the female protagonist makes race virtually unreadable. However, as Clover again has pointed out, in its generic affinities to the western, the horror film does have a way of coding monstrosity in ethnic terms as white trash, rednecks, or redskins. Clover writes: "If 'redneck' once denoted a real and particular group, it has achieved the status of a kind of universal blame figure, the 'someone else' held responsible for all manner of American social ills. The great success of the redneck in that capacity suggests that anxieties no longer expressible in ethnic or racial terms have become projected onto a safe target" (135). This is an extremely important account of what happens to the whole category of racial monstrosity in American horror film. As I noted in chapter I, the expression of racial fear in a contemporary context has become inseparable from racism. This does not mean, however, that racial coding disappears from the horror film; rather it becomes, as I have already suggested and as Clover eloquently elaborates, part of the class or regional makeup of the monster. In *The Texas Chainsaw Massacre 2*, the Sawyer family certainly plays the part of the rednecks living beyond the purview of urban civilization and they also bear the trappings of cinematic "redskins" with their skins, hides, and fetish feather objects.

The Texas Chainsaw Massacre 2 signifies, within my project, as a paradigmatic example of skin horror. While the postmodern horror film does not tend to produce what we have been calling, [. . .] "totalizing" monsters, the Sawyer family is perhaps as close as we get. As we will see in *The Silence of the Lambs*, monstrosity finally fades out of the picture when the monstrous becomes coextensive with the normal and indeed the dominant. Buffalo Bill and Hannibal Lecter represent an inverted couple who embody monstrosity as an effect of dominant rather than subversive notions of taste, fashion, domesticity, and identity. In *The Texas Chainsaw Massacre 2*, Tobe Hooper lingers upon skin and its shredding with a sado-pornographic eye for detail and a finely tuned sense of the metonymic° uses and abuses of skin. Human interaction, in this

---

metonymic: the use of one thing to name another that it is associated with or related to.

Gothic orgy, is literalized as skin trade, and shedding and wearing, flaying and tanning, ripping and sewing become the practices, the specifically sexual practices, of a subterranean group of skin jobs.

Furthermore, *The Texas Chainsaw Massacre 2* confronts the viewer with possibly the most virile, certainly the most heroic, and definitely the most triumphant final girl in splatter film. Stretch is a screamer alright, but her screaming is a Diamanda Galas°-like soundtrack to her own blood opera. If the empowerment of women in *The Birds*, as we saw in the last chapter, occurs subtly and stealthily through the image of the gathering of the masses, female power in *The Texas Chainsaw Massacre 2* is channeled through the perfect antidote to the hapless, aristocratic, lethargic Gothic heroine—a white trash bitch with a chain saw. Stretch not only saves the day in this film, she saves herself and learns how to be a monster. In *The Texas Chainsaw Massacre 2*, then, by contrast to the action in the previous film, *The Texas Chainsaw Massacre*, as we shall see, we witness the becoming-monstrous of a woman which does not automatically mean that she must compromise herself, sacrifice her voice, or give up her hard-won gains to a man. The chain saw massacre in *The Texas Chainsaw Massacre 2*, as opposed to the gorefest at the female's expense in *The Texas Chainsaw Massacre*, is a massacre of Stretch's making.

I intend to read Stretch as a Gothic heroine who transforms the function of woman within the Gothic text to, finally, a function that is part of the technology of monsters and that transforms the category of monster itself into an orgiastic celebration of the queer and the dangerous. Usually within Gothic technologies of monstrosity, as we have seen, the monster works as a kind of trash heap for the discarded scraps of abject humanity. Monster-making, I have argued throughout, is a suspect activity because it relies upon and shores up conventional humanist binaries. The technology of monsters when channeled through a dangerous woman with a chain saw becomes a powerful and queer strategy for enabling and activating monstrosity as opposed to stamping it out.

Gender works quite differently through Stretch than through other final girls. While Clover's formulation of the final girl and her function as a channel for the male gaze is compelling, there is a way in which she remains caught in a gender lock. The world of female victims and male monsters remains intact in Clover's reading and only lines of identification or gazes shift focus. What I want to argue is that the final girl, particularly as embodied by Stretch, represents not boyishness or girlishness

Diamanda Galas: an American singer whose style is highly original, political, and controversial. She is also associated with Gothic horror; indeed, her first album is titled *Litanies of Satan* (1982).

but monstrous gender, a gender that splatters, rips at the seams, and then is sutured together again as something much messier than male or female. Linda Williams has argued exactly this in "When the Woman Looks" and she claims that while "the male look expresses conventional fear at that which differs from itself," the female look "shares the male's fear of the monster's freakishness, but also recognizes the sense in which this freakishness is similar to her own difference."[3] Williams goes on to suggest that the woman's look and her monstrosity have subversive potential but are too often soundly punished within the horror film. Perhaps what is lacking from Williams's analysis is a sense that the woman's monstrosity and her relation to violence in the horror film changes profoundly the form of her gender itself. Gender is monstrous in the horror film and it exceeds even the category of human. The genders that emerge triumphant at the gory conclusion of a splatter film are literally posthuman, they punish the limits of the human body and

> "Gender is monstrous in the horror film and it exceeds even the category of human."

they mark identities as always stitched, sutured, bloody at the seams, and completely beyond the limits and the reaches of an impotent humanism.

If, traditionally, splatter films have not been watched by women and girls because female bodies were precisely the ones most likely to splatter, then a space of viewership has to be reopened in order to reconstitute potential gazes. As we have seen throughout this study, Gothic contains great potential for a kind of interactive dynamic between text and viewers. The suppleness of monstrosity allows for numerous interventions in the business of interpretations. It is precisely on account of the interactive potential of the horror text that female viewership and readership becomes essential to the production of meaning. In her study of spectatorship, Clover carried out impromptu and casual surveys of her local video store in order to acquire information about who watched what within the genre of the horror film. Such a survey, of course, is completely unreliable since, as she fully acknowledges, men could be renting videos for women at home, boys might be renting them for their sisters, girlfriends, or mothers. It is, however, probable that, as Linda Williams phrases it, "whenever the movie screen holds a particularly effective image of terror, little boys and grown men make it a point of honor to

---

[3]Linda Williams, "When the Woman Looks," in *Re-Visions: Essays in Feminist Film Criticism*, ed. Linda Williams, Mary Ann Doane, and Patrick Mellancamp (Frederick, MD.: University Publications of America, 1984), 88.

look, while little girls and grown women cover their eyes or hide behind the shoulders of their dates" (88). Ignoring, for a moment, the heterosexist presumption of this formulation (grown women are with male dates at the movies), it is worth asking with Williams what happens "when the woman looks." In order to begin to answer this question, we must produce reevaluations of the horror film in terms of potential feminist or woman-positive readings which make horror available to the female viewer. Furthermore, we might examine Williams's heterosexist faux pas° long enough to note that homophobia tends to run alongside misogyny within the horror film and both are often expressed as a violence against gender instability. In what follows I will try to explain the particular potential of the queer or antihomophobic look while also attending to what happens when the woman looks.

Another reason that it is often difficult for a horrorphobic female or viewer to watch a splatter film is because, as we have noted, horror works hard at dismantling the stable relations between representation and reality. And feminists in particular have not always been very attuned to the nuances that structure the relationship between representation and reality. The pornography debates of the 1980s repeatedly staged the hypothesis that representations of the violation of female bodies produce the actual rape and battery of women.[4] Similarly, feminist responses to the horror film have tended to question whether representations of violence against women would produce actual violence.

Obviously, the relationship between representation and reality is always vexed and unclear and certainly any feminist consideration of horror must take this into consideration. But in fact, it is very useful to begin by acknowledging that there is a difference between violence and its representation and that the task of interpretation is not to pinpoint what this difference is but rather to ask how the confusion between representation and reality works to produce fear and horror. Horror film very often situates itself upon the slippage between representations and their material effects.

Wes Craven's *A Nightmare on Elm Street* (1984) not only exemplifies the ways in which horror film exploits the tension between representation and reality, it actually makes this tension into its primary theme. The narrative in *Nightmare* is motored by the notion that dream life is

---

faux pas: an embarrassing mistake; a social blunder.

[4]For an excellent anthology about the sex debates and pornography, see Lynn Segal and Mary McIntosh, eds., *Sex Exposed: Sexuality and the Pornography Debate* (New Brunswick, N.J.: Rutgers University Press, 1993).

contaminated by real horror and that real horror might be contaminated by dreams. The girl in this film who negotiates the difference between dreaming and waking most successfully will live to scream/dream again. In *Nightmare* a group of teenagers are all haunted in their dreams by the figure of Freddy Krueger, a child murderer who had been killed by a mob of parents. One by one the teenagers are visited and brutalized by the man with knives for fingers until only Nancy and her boyfriend, played by Johnny Depp, remain. (Depp plays a beefcake boyfriend here but in his next dramatic role he appears as a kind of castrated Freddy Krueger, the wimpy Edward Scissorhands.) Nancy wages war on Freddy by trying to sort out the tangled relation between dreamscape, real time, and actual bodily mutilation.

This film, in fact, radically advocates for an active and aggressive spectatorship which does, as Clover might argue, feminize the audience but also empowers them. Nancy is a participant/spectator who repeatedly calls attention to herself as spectator—"it's only a dream"—and pulls herself out of dream states by physically hurting herself. In other words, she attempts always to remain embodied, to be aware of what it means to have a body, and to understand how that body can be hurt by unconscious drifting. This film suggests that it is dangerous to leave your body in the theater, watching must be an alert and self-conscious process as opposed to the conventional notions of spectatorship as a kind of escape into passive inertia. It is when you cease to watch yourself watching that you become the victim.

In the final encounter between Nancy and Krueger, however, Nancy, of course, articulates an even more powerful model of spectatorship, one which can alter what will happen by trapping the monster, pulling him into reality, and then "turning one's back on him" in order to draw energy away. Several techniques of spectatorship are at work here. First, horror depends upon energy directed at the screen, not just energy directed at viewer—you are only scared if you want to be. Second, readings of monsters *can* disable them. Nancy actually sets out to interpret her dream and thus to disarm it. While her mother calls upon the dubious authority of a sleep disorder clinic to unravel the problem of dreaming, Nancy recognizes that the clinic cannot produce a solution because their theory of the relation between the body and the imagination is limited by the medical technology that sees bodies as highly manipulable and easily read. You need a more complicated theory of dreams and pleasure and bodies in order to counter Freddy Krueger. Nancy comes up with one—he is *her* dream and *her* nightmare and if she is able to collapse the real and the imagined long enough to banish him, then she will win.

Understanding the Text

1. Why does Halberstam focus on the slasher/splatter film for her analysis?

2. What assumption does Carol Clover make in her analysis of the Final Girl that Halberstam critiques in her essay?

3. What is significant about Stretch, the Final Girl in *Texas Chainsaw Massacre 2*, which makes her different from other Final Girl characters?

4. What are the key factors to how Nancy, in *Nightmare on Elm Street*, survives the threat posed by Freddy Krueger?

5. Halberstam is presenting a complex analysis of the slasher/splatter film genre. How does she "help" the reader understand? Consider the structure of the paragraphs, the use of language, and references to films and other works. Be specific.

Reflections and Response

6. In the opening paragraph, Halberstam states that her purpose (in part) is to "see if, when, and how the horror film can be recuperated for feminine, feminist, and queer forms of pleasure" (par. 1). What does she mean by this, and in your opinion, has she been successful? Why or why not?

7. How does queer theory operate to analyze the categories of the monstrous, as Halberstam has described it? What is the benefit for a reader/viewer to adopting this new way of understanding the slasher film?

Making Connections

8. Halberstam refers to Carol J. Clover's book *Men, Women, and Chain Saws* (1992) in which she discusses the role of the "Final Girl" (p. 167). How is Clover's analysis of the horror film different from Halberstam's, particularly in regard to the female heroine? You may wish to read more from Clover's book as well as Halberstam's book *Skin Shows* (1995) in constructing your analysis.

9. Halberstam's excerpt focuses on the slasher film subcategory of horror. However, she does list other horror film subcategories: Gothic psychothrillers, sci-fi, rape revenge, and supernatural horror (par. 2). Choose a work from a horror subcategory other than slasher/splatter. Analyze the role and meaning of gender in the film as it is reconfigured or reworked through the experience of the monstrous.

10. Halberstam states, "Someone's skin, their hide (Hyde), precisely forms the surface through which inner identities emerge and upon which external readings of identity leave their impression" (par. 4). How can this statement be connected to cosmetic surgery and other forms of body enhancement commonly practiced today? How might the contemporary monster film — particularly the slasher variety — serve as a model for the physical remaking of the body, and hence, of identity?

Marco Bottigelli/Getty Images

4

What Is the Power of the Monster?

A monster is inherently dangerous and thus off-limits— the ultimate bad boy with an attractive power all its own. We are drawn to the forbidden — the desire for something outside the boundary set by society between what is acceptable and what is not. But the monster as Other isn't just dangerous and powerful; it's also exciting. After all, who wants to be normal — that is to say, boring? There is always an excitement on the edge of acceptability: never to venture past the edge is to cheapen life experience, while venturing too far could mean getting lost beyond all hope of return.

Part of what we envy in monsters is their ability to do what we cannot. Jeffrey Jerome Cohen analyzes why we are attracted to creatures that break the rules and represent an escape from our ordinary lives, which are bound by convention. In a passage from Bram Stoker's novel *Dracula*, written in the nineteenth century near the end of the Victorian era, Jonathan Harker, a young man engaged to be married, is sexually stimulated by three young female vampires who dance around him. He is excited by their presence, ignoring his sense of danger. The groundwork for changing the emphasis from the danger of vampires to their attraction was clearly being laid even before Stephenie Meyer penned her *Twilight* series, a phenomenon examined by Karen Backstein. Analyzing the new generation of vampires that *Twilight*'s Edward Cullen and his family represent, as well as why Bella Swan is attracted to him and to life as a vampire, Backstein argues that Cullen is an update of the romantic hero. Elizabeth A. Lawrence, a cultural anthropologist, investigates the power of the werewolf, which has been a monster in the human imagination for at least two thousand years. The werewolf dissolves the boundaries between human and animal, a ferocious and powerful hybrid. Lawrence asks us to consider why we might find ourselves taking on the characteristics of the wolf. In the nineteenth-century tale of *The Secret Case of Dr. Jekyll and Mr. Hyde*, Robert Louis Stevenson creates the story of a man who attempts to sever from himself all that is corrupt and wicked — only to create a more powerful and animalistic version of himself that cannot be controlled. The depraved Mr. Hyde delights in cruelty, and ultimately, he refuses to relinquish his freedom and resists returning to the form of Dr. Jekyll. Erica McCrystal further examines Hyde as a monster. She points out that Stevenson wrote his story at a time when debate about Charles Darwin's theory of evolution was beginning to stir up controversy. The question of Hyde is not whether he is evil, but what the nature of that evil may be — is he an animal, lacking morality and concern for others and looking only for its own gratifications? The freedom Hyde experiences is freedom from the bonds of human civility and norms. Christian Jarrett examines the monster from the perspective of an evolutionary psychologist. He investigates why people like to be scared. Indeed, perhaps a healthy dose of fear helped keep us alive in our far-distant past, long before modern-day monsters made their appearance. Humans used to be prey more often than predator, and the monster reminds us to stay vigilant for danger.

Whether we long to be the monster, liberated from the constraints that come with being a civilized person, or whether that monster serves as a warning signal that awakens us to real-life dangers, the monster certainly does have a purpose. We might want to see the world as Edward Cullen sees it, or maybe we long to run through the woods with the freedom of a werewolf. Maybe, like Dr. Jekyll, we would like to take a walk on the wild side, be a bit bad, and not have to pay any consequences. Whatever it may be, the monster gets to do what we do not: go beyond the limits imposed on our existence. The monster has that power.

Fear of the Monster Is Really a Kind of Desire

Jeffrey Jerome Cohen

How can something as horrible and terrifying as a monster be considered the object of desire? In this selection, Jeffrey Jerome Cohen, as part of his larger work "Monster Culture (Seven Theses)," examines the issue of desire. He considers the various ways in which we desire to be with the monster and — better yet — to be the monster ourselves. The Other that the monster represents is not bound by the same rules and conventions that ordinary people are, and thus the monster promises a freedom from convention that we can only imagine. Cohen is an English professor and director of medieval and early modern studies at George Washington University. His books include *Monster Theory: Reading Culture* (1996), *Of Giants: Sex, Monsters, and the Middle Ages* (1999), and *Hybridity, Identity, and Monstrosity in Medieval Britain: On Difficult Middles* (2006).

The monster is continually linked to forbidden practices, in order to normalize and to enforce. The monster also attracts. The same creatures who terrify and interdict can evoke potent escapist fantasies; the linking of monstrosity with the forbidden makes the monster all the more appealing as a temporary egress° from constraint. This simultaneous repulsion and attraction at the core of the monster's composition accounts greatly for its continued cultural popularity, for the fact that the monster seldom can be contained in a simple, binary dialectic° (thesis, antithesis . . . no synthesis). We distrust and loathe the monster at the same time we envy its freedom, and perhaps its sublime despair.

Through the body of the monster fantasies of aggression, domination, and inversion are allowed safe expression in a clearly delimited and permanently liminal space. Escapist delight gives way to horror only when the monster threatens to overstep these boundaries, to destroy or deconstruct the thin walls of category and culture. When contained by geographic, generic, or epistemic° marginalization, the monster can function as an alter ego, as an alluring projection of (an Other) self. The monster awakens one to the pleasures of the body, to the simple and fleeting joys of being frightened, or frightening—to the experience of mortality and corporality. We watch the monstrous spectacle of the horror film because

---

egress: an exit; an act of going out.
dialectic: the juxtaposition of conflicting opposites; logical argumentation.
epistemic: relating to knowing; cognitive.

we know that the cinema is a temporary place, that the jolting sensuousness of the celluloid images will be followed by reentry into the world of comfort and light. Likewise, the story on the page before us may horrify (whether it appears in the *New York Times* news section or Stephen King's latest novel matters little), so long as we are safe in the knowledge of its nearing end (the number of pages in our right hand is dwindling) and our liberation from it. Aurally received narratives work no differently; no matter how unsettling the description of the giant, no matter how many unbaptized children and hapless knights he devours, King Arthur will ultimately destroy him. The audience knows how the genre works.

> "The monster awakens one to the pleasures of the body, to the simple and fleeting joys of being frightened, or frightening — to the experience of mortality and corporality."

Times of carnival temporally marginalize the monstrous, but at the same time allow it a safe realm of expression and play: on Halloween everyone is a demon for a night. The same impulse to ataractic° fantasy is behind much lavishly bizarre manuscript marginalia, from abstract scribblings at the edges of an ordered page to preposterous animals and vaguely humanoid creatures of strange anatomy that crowd a biblical text. Gargoyles and ornately sculpted grotesques, lurking at the crossbeams or upon the roof of the cathedral, likewise record the liberating fantasies of a bored or repressed hand suddenly freed to populate the margins. Maps and travel accounts inherited from antiquity invented whole geographies of the mind and peopled them with exotic and fantastic creatures; Ultima Thule, Ethiopia, and the Antipodes were the medieval equivalents of outer space and virtual reality, imaginary (wholly verbal) geographies accessible from anywhere, never meant to be discovered but always waiting to be explored. Jacques Le Goff has written that the Indian Ocean (a "mental horizon" imagined, in the Middle Ages, to be completely enclosed by land) was a cultural space

where taboos were eliminated or exchanged for others. The weirdness of this world produced an impression of liberation and freedom. The strict morality imposed by the Church was contrasted with the discomfiting attractiveness of a world of bizarre tastes, which practiced coprophagy° and cannibalism; of bodily innocence, where man, freed of the modesty of clothing, rediscovered

---

ataractic: tending to tranquilize.
coprophagy: feeding on dung; the use of feces for sexual excitement.

nudism and sexual freedom; and where, once rid of restrictive monogamy and family barriers, he could give himself over to polygamy, incest, and eroticism.

The habitations of the monsters (Africa, Scandinavia, America, Venus, the Delta Quadrant—whatever land is sufficiently distant to be exoticized) are more than dark regions of uncertain danger: they are also realms of happy fantasy, horizons of liberation. Their monsters serve as secondary bodies through which the possibilities of other genders, other sexual practices, and other social customs can be explored. Hermaphrodites, Amazons, and lascivious cannibals beckon from the edges of the world, the most distant planets of the galaxy.

The co-optation of the monster into a symbol of the desirable is often accomplished through the neutralization of potentially threatening aspects with a liberal dose of comedy: the thundering giant becomes the bumbling giant.[1] Monsters may still function, however, as the vehicles of causative fantasies even without their valences° reversed. What Bakhtin calls "official culture" can transfer all that is viewed as undesirable in itself into the body of the monster, performing a wish-fulfillment drama of its own; the scapegoated monster is perhaps ritually destroyed in the course of some official narrative, purging the community by eliminating its sins. The monster's eradication functions as an exorcism and, when retold and promulgated, as a catechism.° The monastically manufactured *Queste del Saint Graal°* serves as an ecclesiastically sanctioned antidote to the looser morality of the secular romances; when Sir Bors comes across a castle where "ladies of high descent and rank" tempt him to sexual indulgence, these ladies are, of course, demons in lascivious disguise. When Bors refuses to sleep with one of these transcorporal devils (described as "so lovely and so fair that it seemed all earthly beauty was embodied in her"), his steadfast assertion of control banishes them all shrieking back

---

valences: the degrees of attractiveness an individual, activity, or object possesses.
catechism: a form of religious doctrine often put in the form of questions and answers.
Queste del Saint Graal: *The Quest for the Holy Grail.*

---

[1]For Mikhail Bakhtin, famously, this is the transformative power of laughter: "Laughter liberates not only from external censorship but first of all from the great internal censor; it liberates from the fear that developed in man during thousands of years: fear of the sacred, fear of the prohibitions, of the past, of power." *Rabelais and His World,* trans. Hélène Iswolsky (Indianapolis: Indiana University Press, 1984), 94. Bakhtin traces the moment of escape to the point at which laughter became a part of the "higher levels of literature," when Rabelais wrote *Gargantua et Pantagruel.*

to hell. The episode valorizes the celibacy so central to the authors' belief system (and so difficult to enforce) while inculcating a lesson in morality for the work's intended secular audience, the knights and courtly women fond of romances.

Seldom, however, are monsters as uncomplicated in their use and 5 manufacture as the demons that haunt Sir Bors. Allegory may flatten a monster rather thin, as when the vivacious demon of the Anglo-Saxon hagiographic° poem *Juliana* becomes the one-sided complainer of Cynewulf's *Elene*. More often, however, the monster retains a haunting complexity. The dense symbolism that makes a thick description of the monsters in Spenser, Milton, and even *Beowulf* so challenging reminds us how permeable the monstrous body can be, how difficult to dissect.

This corporal fluidity, this simultaneity of anxiety and desire, ensures that the monster will always dangerously entice. A certain intrigue is allowed even Vincent of Beauvais's well-endowed cynocephalus,° for he occupies a textual space of allure before his necessary dismissal, during which he is granted an undeniable charm. The monstrous lurks somewhere in that ambiguous, primal space between fear and attraction, close to the heart of what Kristeva calls "abjection":

There looms, within abjection, one of those violent, dark revolts of being, directed against a threat that seems to emanate from an exorbitant outside or inside, ejected beyond the scope of the possible, the tolerable, the thinkable. It lies there, quite close, but it cannot be assimilated. It beseeches, worries, fascinates desire, which, nonetheless, does not let itself be seduced. Apprehensive, desire turns aside; sickened, it rejects. . . . But simultaneously, just the same, that impetus, that spasm, that leap is drawn toward an elsewhere as tempting as it is condemned. Unflaggingly, like an inescapable boomerang, a vortex of summons and repulsion places the one haunted by it literally beside himself.

And the self that one stands so suddenly and so nervously beside is the monster.

The monster is the abjected fragment that enables the formation of all kinds of identities — personal, national, cultural, economic, sexual, psychological, universal, particular (even if that "particular" identity is an embrace of the power/status/knowledge of abjection itself); as such it reveals their partiality, their contiguity. A product of a multitude of

hagiographic: relating to the lives of saints or other highly esteemed persons.
cynocephalus: a dog-headed being.

morphogeneses° (ranging from somatic° to ethnic) that align themselves to imbue meaning to the Us and Them behind every cultural mode of seeing, the monster of abjection resides in that marginal geography of the Exterior, beyond the limits of the Thinkable, a place that is doubly dangerous: simultaneously "exorbitant" and "quite close." Judith Butler calls this conceptual locus "a domain of unlivability and unintelligibility that bounds the domain of intelligible effects," but points out that even when discursively closed off, it offers a base for critique, a margin from which to reread dominant paradigms. Like Grendel thundering from the mere° or Dracula creeping from the grave, like Kristeva's "boomerang, a vortex of summons" or the uncanny Freudian-Lacanian° return of the repressed, the monster is always coming back, always at the verge of irruption.°

Perhaps it is time to ask the question that always arises when the monster is discussed seriously (the inevitability of the question a symptom of the deep anxiety about what is and what should be thinkable, an anxiety that the process of monster theory is destined to raise): Do monsters really exist?

Surely they must, for if they did not, how could we?

References

Judith Butler, *Bodies That Matter: On the Discursive Limits of "Sex"* (New York: Routledge, 1993), 22.

Julia Kristeva, *The Powers of Horror: An Essay on Abjection*, trans. Leon S. Roudiez (New York: Columbia University Press, 1982), 1.

Jacques Le Goff, "The Medieval West and the Indian Ocean," in *Time, Work and Culture in the Middle Ages*, trans. Arthur Goldhammer (Chicago: University of Chicago Press, 1980), 197.

The Quest for the Holy Grail, trans. Pauline Matarasso (London: Penguin Books, 1969), 194.

morphogeneses: formations and differentiations of tissues and organs.
somatic: relating to the body.
mere: an expanse of standing water.
Freudian-Lacanian: based on the writings of Sigmund Freud (1856–1939) and Jacques Lacan (1901–1981). Freud posited that the human mind repressed unacceptable wishes that were fulfilled symbolically in dreams; Lacan argued that the human sciences were inherently unstable because of humans' own complexity and limitations.
irruption: a rushing in, forcibly or violently.

Understanding the Text

1. According to Cohen, why is it important that our exposure to monsters, whether in books, in movies, or on television, be temporary?

2. How do monsters represent the "margins" (par. 3)? Explain at least one of the specific examples Cohen uses in his essay.

3. What does Cohen mean by the phrase "beyond the limits of the Thinkable" (par. 7)?

4. Reading this text may be challenging because of its vocabulary and frequent use of allusions. What parts of the text did you find most difficult to understand, and what approach(es) did you use to improve your comprehension?

Reflection and Response

5. After running through a description of a typical horror narrative, Cohen states, "The audience knows how the genre works" (par. 2). How much does genre affect the expectations of the audience? In particular regarding monsters, what are those expectations? To what extent does genre limit monsters, and why might this be a good thing?

6. According to Cohen, the monster in some ways represents the expression of the repressed. In other words, it does what we cannot. In your opinion, to what extent do monsters incorporate the forbidden? Cite specific examples.

7. Cohen says that the "simultaneity of anxiety and desire . . . ensures that the monster will always dangerously entice" (par. 6). To what extent are desire and anxiety intertwined in monsters? Aside from monsters, are there other beings or phenomena that make people both desirous and fearful?

Making Connections

8. Cohen states, "The co-optation of the monster into a symbol of the desirable is often accomplished through the neutralization of potentially threatening aspects with a liberal dose of comedy" (par. 4). How do movies in popular culture reflect this tendency? Think, for example, of the *Shrek* movies (2001, 2004, 2007, 2010), the *Teen Wolf* movies (1985, 1987), and *Young Frankenstein* (1974), among others, that use humor to deflect the power of the monster.

9. Cohen cites an example from *Queste del Saint Graal* (*The Quest for the Holy Grail*) in which Sir Bors resists sexual temptation by "demons in lascivious disguise" (par. 4). To what extent is sexual desire a part of the allure of monsters, and how is that connected to the power they may have over their victims? Refer to other monster stories either in this book or from outside research to include specific details in your answer.

From Dracula

Bram Stoker

Bram Stoker was educated at Trinity College in Dublin, where he earned a degree in mathematics in 1870. His work as a theater manager at the Lyceum Theatre in the West End of London, however, initiated a second career in writing, and in 1897 Stoker published *Dracula*. Since then, Count Dracula has been the subject of innumerable film, stage, and literary renditions. In this excerpt, young Jonathan Harker is in Transylvania on legal matters. Against the advice of the count, of whom he is already suspicious, Harker wanders the castle and falls asleep in a room that is not his bedroom. He awakens to find himself the interest of three young ladies, and their attention is simultaneously sexually stimulating and horrifying.

15 May.—Once more have I seen the Count go out in his lizard fashion. He moved downwards in a sidelong way, some hundred feet down, and a good deal to the left. He vanished into some hole or window. When his head had disappeared, I leaned out to try and see more, but without avail—the distance was too great to allow a proper angle of sight. I knew he had left the castle now, and thought to use the opportunity to explore more than I had dared to do as yet. I went back to the room, and taking a lamp, tried all the doors. They were all locked, as I had expected, and the locks were comparatively new; but I went down the stone stairs to the hall where I had entered originally. I found I could pull back the bolts easily enough and unhook the great chains; but the door was locked, and the key was gone! That key must be in the Count's room; I must watch should his door be unlocked, so that I may get it and escape. I went on to make a thorough examination of the various stairs and passages, and to try the doors that opened from them. One or two small rooms near the hall were open, but there was nothing to see in them except old furniture, dusty with age and moth-eaten. At last, however, I found one door at the top of the stairway which, though it seemed to be locked, gave a little under pressure. I tried it harder, and found that it was not really locked, but that the resistance came from the fact that the hinges had fallen somewhat, and the heavy door rested on the floor. Here was an opportunity which I might not have again, so I exerted myself, and with many efforts forced it back so that I could enter. I was now in a wing of the castle further to the right than the rooms I knew and a story lower down. From the windows I could see that the suite of rooms lay along to the south of the castle, the windows of the end room looking out both west and south. On the latter side, as well as to the former, there was a great precipice. The castle was built on the corner of a great rock, so that on three sides it was quite impregnable,° and great windows were placed here where sling, or bow, or culverin° could not reach, and consequently light and comfort, impossible to a position which had to be guarded, were secured. To the west was a great valley, and then, rising far away, great jagged mountain fastnesses, rising peak on peak, the sheer rock studded with mountain ash and thorn, whose roots clung in cracks and crevices and crannies of the stone. This was evidently the portion of the castle occupied by the ladies in bygone days, for the furniture had more air of comfort than any I had seen. The windows were curtainless, and the yellow moonlight, flooding in through the diamond panes, enabled one to see even colors, whilst it softened the wealth of dust which lay over all and disguised in some measure the ravages of time and the moth. My lamp seemed to be of little effect in the brilliant moonlight, but I was glad to have it with me, for there was a dread loneliness in the place which chilled my heart and made my nerves tremble. Still, it was better than living alone in the rooms which I had come to hate from the presence of the Count, and after trying a little to school my nerves, I found a soft quietude come over me. Here I am, sitting at a little oak table where in old times possibly some fair lady sat to pen, with much thought and many blushes, her ill-spelled love-letter, and writing in my diary in shorthand all that has happened since I closed it last. It is nineteenth century up-to-date with a vengeance. And yet, unless my senses deceive me, the old centuries had, and have, powers of their own which mere "modernity" cannot kill.

* * *

Later: the Morning of 16 May. — God preserve my sanity, or to this I am reduced. Safety and the assurance of safety are things of the past. Whilst I live on here there is but one thing to hope for, that I may not go mad, if, indeed, I be not mad already. If I be sane, then surely it is maddening to think that of all the foul things that lurk in this hateful place the Count is the least dreadful to me; that to him alone I can look for safety, even though this be only whilst I can serve his purpose. Great God! merciful God! Let me be calm, for out of that way lies madness indeed. I begin

---

impregnable: very strong; not likely to be captured by attack.
culverin: a rude musket or long cannon.

to get new lights on certain things which have puzzled me. Up to now I never quite knew what Shakespeare meant when he made Hamlet say:—

"My tablets! quick, my tablets!
'Tis meet that I put it down," etc.,

for now, feeling as though my own brain were unhinged or as if the shock had come which must end in its undoing, I turn to my diary for repose. The habit of entering accurately must help to soothe me.

The Count's mysterious warning frightened me at the time; it frightens me more now when I think of it, for in future he has a fearful hold upon me. I shall fear to doubt what he may say!

When I had written in my diary and had fortunately replaced the book and pen in my pocket I felt sleepy. The Count's warning came into my mind, but I took a pleasure in disobeying it. The sense of sleep was upon me, and with it the obstinacy which sleep brings as outrider.° The soft moonlight soothed, and the wide expanse without gave a sense of freedom which refreshed me. I determined not to return tonight to the gloom-haunted rooms, but to sleep here, where, of old, ladies had sat and sung and lived sweet lives whilst their gentle breasts were sad for their menfolk away in the midst of remorseless wars. I drew a great couch out of its place near the corner, so that as I lay, I could look at the lovely view to east and south, and unthinking of and uncaring for the dust, composed myself for sleep. I suppose have fallen asleep; I hope so, but I fear, for all that followed was startlingly real—so real that now sitting here in the broad, full sunlight of the morning, I cannot in the least believe that it was all sleep.

I was not alone. The room was the same, unchanged in any way since   5
I came into it; I could see along the floor, in the brilliant moonlight, my own footsteps marked where I had disturbed the long accumulation of dust. In the moonlight opposite me were three young women, ladies by their dress and manner. I thought at the time that I must be dreaming when I saw them, for, though the moonlight was behind them, they threw no shadow on the floor. They came close to me, and looked at me for some time, and then whispered together. Two were dark, and had high aquiline° noses, like the Count, and great dark, piercing eyes that seemed to be almost red when contrasted with the pale yellow moon. The other was fair, as fair as can be, with great wavy masses of golden hair and eyes like pale sapphires. I seemed somehow to know her face, and to

---

outrider: one who clears the way for another; a forerunner.
aquiline: curving like an eagle's beak.

know it in connection with some dreamy fear, but I could not recollect at the moment how or where. All three had brilliant white teeth that shone like pearls against the ruby of their voluptuous lips. There was something about them that made me uneasy, some longing and at the same time some deadly fear. I felt in my heart a wicked, burning desire that they would kiss me with those red lips. It is not good to note this down, lest some day it should meet Mina's° eyes and cause her pain; but it is the truth. They whispered together, and then they all three laughed—such a silvery, musical laugh, but as hard as though the sound never could have come through the softness of human lips. It was like the intolerable, tingling sweetness of water-glasses when played on by a cunning hand. The fair girl shook her head coquettishly, and the other two urged her on. One said:—

> "I felt in my heart a wicked, burning desire that they would kiss me with those red lips."

"Go on! You are first, and we shall follow; yours is the right to begin." The other added:—

"He is young and strong; there are kisses for us all." I lay quiet, looking out under my eyelashes in an agony of delightful anticipation. The fair girl advanced and bent over me till I could feel the movement of her breath upon me. Sweet it was in one sense, honey-sweet, and sent the same tingling through the nerves as her voice, but with a bitter underlying the sweet, a bitter offensiveness, as one smells in blood.

I was afraid to raise my eyelids, but looked out and saw perfectly under the lashes. The girl went on her knees, and bent over me, simply gloating. There was a deliberate voluptuousness which was both thrilling and repulsive, and as she arched her neck she actually licked her lips like an animal, till I could see in the moonlight the moisture shining on the scarlet lips and on the red tongue as it lapped the white sharp teeth. Lower and lower went her head as the lips went below the range of my mouth and chin and seemed about to fasten on my throat. Then she paused, and I could hear the churning sound of her tongue as it licked her teeth and lips, and could feel the hot breath on my neck. Then the skin of my throat began to tingle as one's flesh does when the hand that is to tickle it approaches nearer—nearer. I could feel the soft, shivering touch of the lips on the super-sensitive skin of my throat, and the hard dents of two sharp teeth, just touching and pausing there. I closed my eyes in a languorous° ecstasy and waited—waited with beating heart.

Mina: Jonathan Harker's fiancée.
languorous: with weakness or weariness.

But at that instant, another sensation swept through me as quick as lightning. I was conscious of the presence of the Count, and of his being as if lapped in a storm of fury. As my eyes opened involuntarily I saw his strong hand grasp the slender neck of the fair woman and with giant's power draw it back, the blue eyes transformed with fury, the white teeth champing with rage, and the fair cheeks blazing red with passion. But the Count! Never did I imagine such wrath and fury, even to the demons of the pit. His eyes were positively blazing. The red light in them was lurid, as if the flames of hell-fire blazed behind them. His face was deathly pale, and the lines of it were hard like drawn wires; the thick eyebrows that met over the nose now seemed like a heaving bar of white-hot metal. With a fierce sweep of his arm, he hurled the woman from him, and then motioned to the others, as though he were beating them back; it was the same imperious gesture that I had seen used to the wolves. In a voice which, though low and almost in a whisper seemed to cut through the air and then ring round the room he said:—

"How dare you touch him, any of you? How dare you cast eyes on   10 him when I had forbidden it? Back, I tell you all! This man belongs to me! Beware how you meddle with him, or you'll have to deal with me." The fair girl, with a laugh of ribald coquetry,° turned to answer him:—

"You yourself never loved; you never love!" On this the other women joined, and such a mirthless, hard, soulless laughter rang through the room that it almost made me faint to hear; it seemed like the pleasure of fiends. Then the Count turned, after looking at my face attentively, and said in a soft whisper:—

"Yes, I too can love; you yourselves can tell it from the past. Is it not so? Well, now I promise you that when I am done with him you shall kiss him at your will. Now go! go! I must awaken him, for there is work to be done."

"Are we to have nothing tonight?" said one of them, with a low laugh, as she pointed to the bag which he had thrown upon the floor, and which moved as though there were some living thing within it. For answer he nodded his head. One of the women jumped forward and opened it. If my ears did not deceive me there was a gasp and a low wail, as of a half-smothered child. The women closed round, whilst I was aghast with horror; but as I looked they disappeared, and with them the dreadful bag. There was no door near them, and they could not have passed me without my noticing. They simply seemed to fade into the rays of the

coquetry: a flirtatious act or attitude.

moonlight and pass out through the window, for I could see outside the dim, shadowy forms for a moment before they entirely faded away.

Then the horror overcame me, and I sank down unconscious.

Understanding the Text

1. What observation does Harker make as he passes through the rooms in Count Dracula's castle? What does this say about his character?

2. On the morning of May 16, Harker observes in his diary, "Whilst I live on here there is but one thing to hope for, that I may not go mad, if, indeed, I be not mad already" (par. 2). Why is Harker afraid that he is going insane?

3. Count Dracula, in pushing away the three sisters, says, "This man belongs to me!" (par. 10). In response, they say that he never loved. What do they mean by this?

4. Bram Stoker's *Dracula* is a novel written near the end of the nineteenth century. Analyze Stoker's use of language — diction, sentence structures, punctuation — and describe how his use of language is different from contemporary usage. Provide examples.

Reflection and Response

5. Why does Jonathan Harker make so many comments about possible past inhabitants of Count Dracula's castle? How does alluding to the past instead of finding comfort in "modernity" (par. 1) provide him with a sense of normalcy in a place that seems anything but normal?

6. Harker comments that writing in his diary "must help to soothe me" (par. 2). How can the act of writing be therapeutic, especially given the horrific events he encounters?

7. When Harker becomes aware of the sisters, his feelings are conflicted. At one point, he comments, "There was something about them that made me uneasy, some longing and at the same time some deadly fear" (par. 5). How are sexual desire and danger intermingled in this passage? What is the basis of his contradictory feelings?

Making Connections

8. How does this selection compare with movie or television versions of *Dracula* you have seen? Be specific in your answer.

9. Read John Polidori's *Vampyre* (free reproductions are available online). How is Polidori's version of the vampire different from Stoker's, and what do these differences reveal?

10. Compare Stoker's female vampires with more recent representations of female monsters, such as those discussed in Chapter 3. How do their differences reflect changes in attitudes toward the role of women in society from the nineteenth century to today?

(Un)safe Sex: Romancing the Vampire

Karen Backstein

With a PhD in cinematic studies from New York University, Karen Backstein has written on film and dance in both academic journals and popular magazines. Her book credits include several children's books, including *The Blind Men and the Elephant* (1992) and *Little Chick's Easter Surprise* (1993). This article initially appeared in *Cineaste*, a magazine that covers the art and politics of the cinema. Backstein argues that newer vampire stories, such as the *Twilight* series and *True Blood*, have altered the traditional sexual dynamic of the vampire narrative. In the past, the vampire combined sexual allure and evil, emphasizing that the woman who is the target of the vampire's desires needs to remain chaste. Now the vampire is a romantic hero who protects the female protagonist from evil humans as well as other vampires, and sexual energy between vampire and human abounds. The woman is no longer the passive, chaste object of desire, but an active, sexually aware force of her own.

In the horror universe, the popularity of vampires never seems to die. This makes sense: forever young and beautiful, they are, as *Twilight*'s Edward Cullen points out to his inamorata,° Bella, specifically designed to be irresistible to humans. But if the greatest (and most filmed) of literary bloodsuckers, Count Dracula, served as a warning about what would happen to the pure Victorian woman who succumbed to the lure of the mercurial° and seductive man, the contemporary vampire often is a very different figure altogether. Just as the eternally living creature within the narrative must adapt to the passing centuries in dress and manner, the fictional construction of the protagonist has had to shift in order to survive as a meaningful symbol for audiences with modern sensibilities.

Across every medium, from books to films to television, today's vampire—at least, that particular type of vampire who serves as the narrative's male lead and the heroine's love interest—has transformed into an alluring combination of danger and sensitivity, a handsome romantic hero haunted by his lust for blood and his guilt for the humans he killed in the past. No bats, no capes, and perhaps just a touch of white pallor to provide a whiff of the grave (the black vampire remains a

---

inamorata: a woman whom one loves.
mercurial: unpredictable; changing.

rarity in mainstream texts)—and so much the better if he shimmers in the manner of *Twilight*'s Edward and resembles an Armani model. He's often courtly, too, in the fashion of another age—the age, in fact, when he was born and lived as a human before "being made." At the same time, the vampire's power can never be underestimated: the very notion of "devouring" and "eating" someone is redolent° of sex (and, in some cases, rape), and he could have what he wants for the taking. "When we taste human blood," Edward hesitatingly says, "a sort of frenzy begins."

But he has now become too evolved and moral to engage in that frenzy: "I don't want to be a monster." In part, the modern vampire story is one about self-control, about man struggling to master his worst impulses—perhaps even his essential nature—through whatever means necessary, be it with synthetic substances (*True Blood*) or by finding other sources of food (*Twilight*). In an almost Victorian ethos, this "civilizing impulse" is strengthened by the arrival of the heroine, who cements the vampire's determination not to succumb to his bloodthirst. To further stress the point, a "bad vampire" usually throws the hero's chivalrousness into relief: *Twilight*'s vicious and murderous tracker James contrasts with Edward, while *True Blood* juxtaposes the gentlemanly Bill Compton with the imperious and manipulative (but equally sexy) Eric Northman, *The Vampire Diaries* has two divergent brothers, and Buffy had Angel and Spike.

But the complex qualities of the hero—his mix of sex and sensibility—is not the only reason women seem to have such an insatiable appetite for vampires today; another attraction may be the point of view these texts adopt. They are female-centered narratives that strive for audience identification with the heroine—with her strength, her extraordinary capabilities, her status as an object of desire, or a combination of all these traits. She is the focus of the story, whether she's narrating it (*Twilight*) or the active visual center of the screen image (*Buffy the Vampire Slayer, True Blood*).

Apart from the pioneering works of Anne Rice (who a while ago set   5 aside Lestat and company in favor of Jesus, anyway), many of these modern vampire narratives have been directed primarily to teen females and spotlight young heroines—perhaps all the better to stand out against their centuries-old paramours. *Twilight, True Blood,* and *The Vampire Diaries,* to name but a few, all have their origins in young adult novels aimed specifically at girls. They then crossed over to capture a huge audience of older women, who lapped up their Gothic atmosphere, dreamy heroes, and romantic focus. *True Blood,* in particular, is pure Southern Gothic that moved into adult mode in its TV incarnation, with its graphic sex scenes and its use of the vampire to signify "the Other." Imagining a world where

redolent: suggestive.

an artificial blood allows vampires to live among us without feeding, the series plays with the idea of "interspecies mixing" as miscegenation—a metaphor that encompasses sexual fear and potency, as well as a social critique. Vampire Bill Compton is literally a refugee from the Civil War, when he was brought over, and the credits feature assorted images from the Old South, including a Klansman.

Despite their dissimilarities, and varied approaches to the construction of vampire life and rules, all these supernatural stories are driven largely by female desire and the female voice. The virginal Victorian ladies of *Dracula* may have needed Jonathan Harker to tell their tale; no longer. Ever since *Buffy the Vampire Slayer* came on the scene, the ladies have spoken for themselves. This is not to say that vampire narratives are necessarily feminist. Their degree of girl power varies, with Buffy perhaps the strongest, rarely in need of rescue and able to slay multiple neck biters with a single kick and knife thrust—and master them romantically, too. (A point wittily made in a fan-created viral video that juxtaposed shots of Buffy at her fiercest with images of a dreamy, clearly smitten, and physically passive Edward from *Twilight*. Rolling her eyes at his persistent advances, the Buffster resisted his charms and killed.) Like Buffy, singled out among all girls as the one in her generation to be the Slayer, Sookie in *True Blood* is not quite human; possessing extra-normal skills (including the ability to read minds and a strange kind of electrical energy that sometimes flows from her hands), she sidesteps the many lures that drag down her fellow townsfolk, family, and friends.

But no heroine, and no relationship, seems to have enthralled female readers and spectators like that of Bella and Edward in the *Twilight* saga. Unlike much in the horror genre, *Twilight*—both the book and the film—is the product of women: novelist Stephenie Meyer, screenwriter Melissa Rosenberg, and director Catherine Hardwicke. (Hardwicke was replaced by Chris Weitz for the sequel, *New Moon*, a more male-focused and presumably more action-centered narrative in which Bella cedes some of the spotlight to the Native American character Jacob, a were-wolf. The removal of Hardwicke is particularly fascinating for Hollywood watchers given the box-office success of *Twilight*—over $70 million the first weekend—as compared to the critical and financial disaster that was Weitz's *Golden Compass*.) It would be impossible to overestimate the popularity of the novels. At a time when the publishing industry is collapsing, sales of Meyer's books played a huge role in ensuring the financial health of Little, Brown, *Twilight*'s publishing house. As was the case when the final *Harry Potter* tome came out, bookstores stayed open at midnight on its release day, hosting parties to draw in readers eager to get their hands

In *Twilight* (2008), Bella Swan (Kristen Stewart) falls for fellow student Edward Cullen (Robert Pattinson), who, since he's a vampire, is truly a boyfriend to die for.
AF Archive/Alamy Stock Photo

on the next installment as soon as possible. When casting for the movie adaptation was announced, its unknown leads became instant celebrities, and the film not unexpectedly was a blockbuster, too. Despite the fact that *Twilight* is remarkably poorly written and astonishingly repetitive, clearly Meyer has her finger on the pulse of young female America.

Twilight tells the story of Bella Swan, a teenager who reluctantly leaves her home in sunny Phoenix to come to the gray and rainy climes of Forks, Washington, where her father is sheriff. The move is nothing less than a sacrifice, prompted by her mother's remarriage; Bella generously gives her mom the space, time, and freedom to travel with her new husband as he pursues his career. Almost immediately upon her arrival, however, Bella, formerly an outsider, finds herself the center of attention at school, with a group of friends and plenty of male interest. But her eye is drawn irresistibly to Edward Cullen and his four sisters and brothers, all startlingly beautiful and supremely standoffish. Bella is shocked when Edward initially reacts to her presence with pure, overt hostility. The truth will out, however, when she discovers that his coldness was just a ploy: he is so deeply drawn to her, and so scared he might harm her in the throes of passion, that he tried to resist his feelings. For Edward and his entire family are vampires—albeit vampires who wish to live peacefully with humans—and this love appears to be star-crossed. Bella and Edward's relationship grows ever more passionate, but always with Edward attempting to make Bella feel a healthy sense of fear at what he is. The true danger, however, comes in the form of a different group of neck biters, including a "tracker" who hunts down humans forever until he catches the prey he wants. And he wants Bella.

Why have female audiences of all ages so embraced the series, both on the page and on screen? Why, like the character of Edward Cullen himself, has it proven so irresistible? And how do both hero and heroine differ from their vampire/human counterparts—and what do those differences mean? First, although vampire stories generally fall within horror—and *Twilight* has its share of blood and violence—in many ways it has just as much in common with the romance novel, except with a paranormal twist. Other than his fondness for the taste of blood, Edward is the perfect dark, brooding, romantic hero; tormented by his past and so protective of the woman he loves that he willingly pushes her away for her own good. Only, he happens to have extra vampire powers to help him safeguard the woman better—and to make him even more compelling to viewers.

As with any romantic hero, Edward's worth has to be established 10 within the narrative, which measures him against both vampire and man (and eventually werewolf) in order to validate him as a singular figure and force in any world. On the human side are Bella's male schoolmates, almost all with a crush on her, and all boyish and immature in contrast to Edward (who of course is many years older than them). Sweet and welcoming, into sports and the prom, they represent a normalcy Edward can never have; they also are roundly rejected as boyfriend material by Bella, who gently guides them instead to more appropriate girls.

Also human are the men who try to rape Bella one evening in town; in the book, which is actually scarier than the film's depiction of it, they slyly "herd" a lost Bella to an abandoned cul-de-sac where she has no hope of escape. In the movie, Bella first glimpses two young men at the end of an alleyway after she emerges from a bookstore at night; apprehensively, she heads in the opposite direction, but the pair chase her to a clearing. There, they and a group of drunken friends surround and menace her; as the camera turns slowly around the leering circle of men, a series of nervous jump cuts follows the tormentors' movements as they close in on Bella. Just as she finally tries to defend herself, Edward zooms up in his car, wheels squealing, to act as her savior. The implication is clear: not all dangers come from the paranormal. That the scene is lit to have the same gray-green mistiness as ones featuring several vampire-caused murders further links the human and the undead.

Additionally, this almost-rape by flesh-and-blood males acts as a mirror image to James's even more sadistic abduction of Bella, both in its elaborate entrapment and Edward's rescue operation. Both these sequences stand out in this otherwise romantic movie for their terror, explicit threat to Bella's body, and dependence on male physical violence. After luring Bella in, James presses up against her stroking her hair, adding a sexual element to the kidnapping. Unlike the earlier sequence, a long time elapses before Edward arrives and the brutalization is visualized. When Bella tries to escape, James flies to intercept her, using techniques familiar to fans of martial arts films. The surface grace of his airborne trajectory contrasts with

> "While the vampire, in almost every artistic incarnation, symbolizes impossible desire and transgressed boundaries — the romantic idea that sex = death — . . . *Twilight*'s operative equation is love = death."

Bella's body, which goes into flight in a different way: by being thrown. The crack of her "fragile little human" bones is audible. And James films it all to torment Edward, in what is one of *Twilight*'s several interesting and negative references to still and movie cameras in relation to women.

While the vampire, in almost every artistic incarnation, symbolizes impossible desire and transgressed boundaries—the romantic idea that sex = death—*Twilight* shifts the paradigm in interesting ways. *Twilight*'s operative equation is love = death, which Bella reaffirms in a voice-over at the start, a ghostly reference to a later point in the story when she expects to die. The gentlemanly Edward not only refuses sex because of the danger to Bella, he also swoops in to pluck her out of sexually threatening situations. In fact, as we've seen, whenever someone in *Twilight* does want sex, or cannot control his desires, he is evil. *Twilight* makes an argument for abstemious love, no surprise given that the story sprung from the pen of a Mormon writer. In a day when the romance novel is packed with explicit semipornographic depictions of bedroom activities far beyond the old-fashioned bodice ripper, *Twilight* harks back to a time when sexual attraction was implied, not acted upon. In this regard, Bella stands apart from such heroines as Buffy and Sookie who consummate both human and vampire relationships. There is perhaps a touch of Heath-cliff and Catherine° in Edward and Bella, an affirmation of a powerful love that transcends the limits of human life. For young readers especially, there may be a kind of safety in a story that steers clear of perilous sexual territory and that suggests gazing into one another's eyes and holding hands are the most sublime joys.

Heathcliff and Catherine: the tormented lovers in Emily Brontë's *Wuthering Heights* (1847).

At the same time, however, the narrative is packed with sexual substitutes, so the vampire retains his potency even if he pulls back. It is always clear that when the time comes (and it does, in later novels) that sex is permissible, he will be the perfect lover. Perhaps the book, a little more than the film, overtly emphasizes the power of Edward's vampiric touch and kiss, which induces an almost orgasmic reaction in Bella (who faints). Nonetheless, the film finds its stand-in for Meyer's intricately physical descriptions in a soaringly romantic cinematic style. Manipulation of motion becomes one of the movie's hallmarks, a slowing down or hastening of time, most notably to capture Edward's vampire superspeed, but also to indicate perceptual awareness, self-consciousness, and even grace. In lengthy wordless and lushly scored sequences, cameras circle the Pacific Northwest landscape from up high, flying with Bella and Edward as he carries her up trees and cliffs, or looking down upon them lying in the grass. His near-magical powers, and his speed, his ability to bring her into a different world, imply sexuality, skill, and thrill, enhanced by the vertiginous° patterns traced by the cinematography. And a large percentage of the audience comes armed with a knowledge of the written text, which will influence their reading of the cinematic images.

Twilight the novel is told almost exclusively from Bella's perspective,   15
which the film to some extent replicates, through her voice-overs placed throughout, as well as through the use of point of view. It is Bella who first sees the Cullens, through the slats of the school windows, moving in graceful slow motion, outdoor light falling on them. "Who is that?" she asks. Edward's glance only later meets her originating gaze; with him, she is rarely the "looked at," but the one doing the looking or an equal in an exchange of glances—except at night, when Edward sneaks in simply to watch her sleep. (But we only see that when she wakes suddenly and catches him, so we never share his point of view of her vulnerable body.) And not only does the camerawork emphasize Edward as visual object through lingering shots, but actor Robert Pattinson, a former model, assumes the photographic poses and runway walks of a self-aware performer. Even when we know he is looking at her because of an eyeline match, he stays the visual object for the audience. The usual paradigm of female viewed/male viewer has shifted thoroughly, especially as Bella makes clear how much she despises being the center of attention when under the curious stares of her fellow students.

In one of the most telling scenes, students mill about in front of the school and Angela, a photographer and Bella's friend, aims her camera at something we cannot see; "Oh my God," she exclaims, lowering it, and we

vertiginous: causing or likely to cause a feeling of dizziness.

cut to a classy sports car from which Bella and Edward emerge. Pattinson plays it with the enigmatic smile of a model or movie star on the red carpet who knows all eyes are on him. "Well, everyone's staring," [actress Kristen] Stewart's unsmiling Bella points out, and we cut to her point of view. As the camera moves forward into the crowd, the scene alternates between normal and slow motion as if emphasizing the sense of unreality Bella feels.

In fact, Bella is defined through scent more than look, a more difficult quality to convey visually, hence the constant verbal allusions to her smell. But when she walks into her science classroom—where she will be seated next to Edward—she steps in front of a fan, again as slowly as the Cullens strode into the lunchroom where Bella first glimpsed them. The wind ruffles her hair, and the film cuts to Edward as the paper on the desk in front of him sharply blows as her *bella aroma* reaches his nose. His body quivers and his hand reaches up to cover his nose and face. When the scene cuts back to Bella, still standing in front of the room, her smile fades. This scene repeats, to more ominous effect, when the wind blows through her hair when James and his more vicious vampires meet Bella; hiding among Edward's family, the breeze alerts him to a human presence.

The vampire's effect on his victim has always been one of transformation, but a negative one: the draining of blood, the draining of energy, the draining of life. *Twilight*, unlike its predecessors, tells a story of transformation in a more positive sense. While it has elements of horror, particularly near the end with James's attack, it more closely resembles a fairy tale—Bella and the Beast, if you will, with elements of Cinderella. At the start of the story, Bella comes to the town of Forks without ever having had a boyfriend, and indeed having had few friends at all. But in this new territory, she turns into the central object of desire for every man, and finds her "beast" who is really a prince in disguise. Like a fairy-tale heroine, her qualities are innate, not just the beauty that's de rigueur,° but even her smell, which shocks Edward into submission and draws the deadly attention of James. And, as in a fairy tale, all females are secondary to her: helpmates whose own interior lives remain obscure.

Given this generic shift, it is logical that the vampire hero is moved out of the night and into the light, not just able to see the sun but also to sparkle brilliantly in it. *Twilight*, as a film, rejects Expressionist or neo-*noir* style: it is not a film of jagged angles or darkness, but of fog and the mossy, hazy green of the Northwestern forest. Water, mountains, and majestic trees form the backdrop for Bella and Edward's intimate talks, substituting for the moors that Heathcliff and Cathy wandered. The vampires have homes, not coffins, and because they are not limited to sundown, the

---

de rigueur: required by fashion, etiquette, or custom; proper.

night is no more threatening than the day. Bella, though a figure who can articulate her desire, becomes an object in need of protection, this time by the vampire rather than from him. Edward rescues his princess from careening cars, a roving band of human rapists, and a vampire who hunts his prey without cease. Ultimately, what Edward would most like to save her from is himself, the one task where he cannot succeed.

Understanding the Text

1. How does the character of Edward Cullen from the *Twilight* series differ from more traditional portrayals of vampires, particularly Count Dracula?

2. Backstein argues that the new vampire stories are "driven largely by female desire and the female voice" (par. 6). What evidence does she give to support this statement?

3. In discussing *Twilight*, Backstein focuses on Bella's scent. How does scent work in terms of making Bella an object of desire for Edward, as well as the prey hunted by James?

4. Read Backstein's article with an eye toward her use of topic sentences. How does her use of topic sentences help develop her arguments?

Reflection and Response

5. Backstein argues that the vampire story has always been a story of "transformation" (par. 18). How and why has the transformation changed from the days of Bram Stoker and older movie versions of *Dracula* to contemporary images of vampires as presented in *Twilight*, *Buffy the Vampire Slayer*, *True Blood*, and other stories?

6. In analyzing the scene where Edward saves Bella from the gang of potential rapists, Backstein writes, "The implication is clear: not all dangers come from the paranormal" (par. 11). What do you make of this statement? What does this scene say about humanity?

Making Connections

7. Compare the *Twilight* movies with *Interview with the Vampire*, a movie based on the books by Anne Rice. The movie features Brad Pitt, Tom Cruise, and Antonio Banderas at the peak of their physical attractiveness. Contrast that with Pattinson's portrayal of Edward Cullen. How is physical attractiveness used in these stories to wield power?

8. In the nineteenth century, when Bram Stoker was writing *Dracula* (p. 190), repression of sexuality was the norm. How are modern changes in morality and sexual expression in other aspects of life — including the entertainment world — reflected in the newer portrayals of "bad boys" and vampires, as seen in *Twilight*, *Buffy the Vampire Slayer*, *True Blood*, *The Vampire Diaries*, and other stories? How might these changes reflect how sexual expression is connected to power, such as the power to define one's own identity?

Werewolves in Psyche and Cinema: Man-Beast Transformation and Paradox

Elizabeth A. Lawrence

In this article originally published in the *Journal of American Culture*, former veterinarian and cultural anthropologist Elizabeth A. Lawrence analyzes the relationship between werewolves and humans throughout history and film. The werewolf has existed in the human imagination for thousands of years, with at least one recorded story of human transformation, *The Epic of Gilgamesh*, occurring as early as 2700 BCE. It combines the animal and the human in a different way than do creatures such as the centaur and Minotaur: the human loses his or her humanity in a complete transformation, albeit only briefly. Perhaps in our past — even longer ago than recorded history — wolves were seen more as friendly competition in the hunt for food than as predators to be feared. As people grew more civilized and began to cultivate crops and animals for food, wolves became their enemies.

The phenomenon of human beings undergoing transformations into other species has been a prevalent notion since the dawn of consciousness. It occurs readily when boundaries between humans and animals are perceived as indistinct or when the presence of those boundaries is being tested or established. Such changes may be voluntary—brought about in an effort to obtain certain desirable characteristics possessed by an animal—or they may be involuntary—inflicted wantonly by an outside force upon an innocent person or intentionally upon a guilty individual as a punishment. Over the course of history, this so called "shape-changing" has involved many animals, with the wolf being one of the most frequent and persistent. From the Anglo-Saxon *wer*, meaning man and *wulf* meaning wolf comes the term werewolf, defined as a man temporarily or permanently transformed into a wolf (Spence 426). Lycanthropy is the magical ability to assume the form and characteristics of a wolf, and is also used to denote a mental disorder in which a person believes himself to be a wolf.

Our contemporary technological world is imbued with positivism that leaves little room for human-animal forms like werewolves to prowl the night. For industrialized society, belief in the actuality of werewolves has all but vanished; yet the creatures still exist in the human psyche, lying in wait to disturb our dreams. They remain "alive and well in the twentieth century," according to recent psychiatric case studies (Keck 113; Kulick 134). They survive in popular culture through fantasy fiction, Gothic horror novels, tabloids, and even in a 1978 song about werewolves in London. No single classic gave rise to the werewolf image in the way that Mary Shelley's work established Frankenstein and Bram Stoker's novel created Dracula. Rather the contemporary human-wolf has been inspired largely by cinematic representations. The werewolf is the subject of films which have recurred quite regularly over the last six decades and in which the idea of becoming a werewolf is a real possibility, depicted with creativity and enthusiasm, encoding many symbolic meanings.

The 1994 Hollywood hit, *Wolf,* described as "the thinking man's were-wolf movie" (Janusonis D5), stars Jack Nicholson, whose "normal feral intensity and lupine features" including "demonically" arched eyebrows are said to fit him for the role ("Wolf" 13; James 13). He plays Will Randall, book editor of a New York publishing house who, when the story begins, is a polite, intelligent individual described as the "last civilized man." He is known as "a good man," but as someone remarks, "the worst things happen to the best people." His character changes after being bitten by a wolf while traveling in the wilds of Vermont. Not only does this event occur during a full moon, but also on the very night the moon was closer to the earth than it had been in 100 years. The first sign that anything unusual had happened to him is the reaction of extreme fear that he inspires in a horse. Later, birds fly in panic out of the trees when he approaches. Soon, dense hair grows around the bite wound on his hand. Then he develops an extraordinarily keen sense of smell, allowing him to detect the odor of another man on his wife's clothes, betraying her infidelity. He no longer needs glasses, hears conversations through closed doors, and can move each ear separately. Hair grows on his face. He twitches his nose and sniffs the air. His habits change to sleeping by day and being active at night. He makes love to his wife after a long abstinence, first pulling off her bathrobe belt with his teeth. She responds by calling him "You animal!" He feels 20 years younger and suddenly has courage to decide to start his own company. He beats up three thugs who attempt to rob him and leaps over a wall when policemen chase him out of a zoo where he has gone to feed. He gives up his former vegetarian lifestyle and craves meat—the bloodier the better.

Randall's conversion is complete when at the next full moon he jumps out of a window, growls revealing fangs instead of teeth, chases a deer through the woods and brings it down. His face is transformed to that of a wolf as he bites the animal's throat, and consumes its flesh. His face and hands are covered with blood. He develops paws with talons and runs on all fours. His eyes glow green. At one point he urinates to mark his territory, and later manages to urinate on the shoes of a fellow-worker who schemed to get his job. Ultimately, he attacks humans, and after

Jack Nicholson transforms into a werewolf in the 1994 Columbia Pictures film, *Wolf.*
TCD/Prod.DB/Alamy Stock Photo

his first experience, spits out the fingers of a child. He kills his wife. His arch-enemy and his lover are turned into werewolves after he bites them.

Randall describes his rejuvenation: "I feel as if the wolf passed some- 5 thing along to me, a scrap of its spirit in my blood." A Hindu expert on animal possession tells him that his wolf spirit is a "gift"; not everyone who is bitten has the talent for such transformation. "There must be something wild within, an analogue of the wolf." Through his lupine identity, Randall can experience "power without guilt and love without doubt." This contemporary depiction of the legend has been called "the male version of the heroines in *Women Who Run with the Wolves*," with Randall's "analogue of the wolf" resembling the "Wild Woman Soul" (James 13). *Wolf* is an allegory depicting the viciousness of modern life as represented in the corporate business world. And, following the werewolf tradition, the film reinforces the concept of social and sexual restraint, with loss of control having disastrous consequences. Because wolves are sexual symbols, it has also been suggested that "wolves infecting other people and turning them into other werewolves could be seen as symbolizing the spread of AIDS" (Weinraub 1, 22).

A more innocent film with some of the same motifs, *Teen Wolf* (1985), stars Michael J. Fox as Scott, a frail but handsome schoolboy who is failing both at basketball and at winning the class beauty for his girlfriend.

He is bored with working at his dad's hardware store and is "sick of being average." The first sign of his transformation comes when the sounds from a "silent" dog whistle being blown hurt his ears. His ears soon become pointed, his teeth change to fangs, his face and hands become hairy and his nails grow long. Like other werewolves before him, he howls at the full moon. When he participates in a party kissing game, his partner hits him and emerges from the closet with her dress ripped down the back as though by claws. The boy's changing into a wolf is a genetic trait inherited from his father, who explains that, "being what we are is not all bad. There are some advantages. We have great power, and with power goes responsibility. You can do things other people can't do."

Scott has a problem in that he sometimes turns into a wolf when he does not want it to happen. But at first he uses his new strength to great advantage. He becomes an extremely skillful basketball player, making his team victorious and winning popularity with the cheerleaders. He is able to seduce the glamorous girl who once spurned him. And he is suddenly assertive toward the school principal who formerly intimidated him. The whole town goes "wolf crazy" in its adulation for his new achievements, making him a hero and wearing tee-shirts marked "wolf buddy" in his honor. But ultimately his role as wolf fails to bring happiness. He realizes that he loves the quiet girl who has always been his friend, and asks her to the prom. She will only accept, however, if he goes as Scott, not as the wolf. She says she has missed the real Scott. He decides then to be himself, even though the championship game is coming up and he will be letting the team down. In spite of his friends' pleas and his teammates' chant of "wolf, wolf, wolf," he tells the coach "no wolf. I want to play and be myself." The team wins anyway, and Scott is a hero. The experience of being a wolf gave him residual power to excel by instilling confidence.

A more sinister 1981 film, *An American Werewolf in London*, also involves a teen-age boy, David, who travels to northern England accompanied by his friend Jack. The movie opens with the song, "Blue Moon," but soon becomes more ominous as the pair of hikers tries to take refuge from a stormy night at a pub called "The Slaughtered Lamb"—a portent of events to come. The boys notice a five-pointed star on the wall of the pub, a "pentangle" which is associated with witchcraft. The hostile occupants do not allow the boys to stay, driving them away into the dark with the warning, "beware of the moon, avoid the moors, and stick to the roads." But the moon rises, howls are heard, and before they have traveled far a wolf attacks, killing Jack and rendering David unconscious. He wakes up in the hospital with nail scratches on his chest and a bloody mouth after dreaming of killing and eating a deer. Jack appears as a ghost and tells David that the attack by a werewolf made him a lycanthrope. He will remain in limbo, he says, until the last werewolf is destroyed.

Conforming to the familiar pattern, David makes love to his nurse, who has fallen for him. He is shown urinating. A frightened cat spits at him. On the next full moon, he tears off his clothes, revealing a hairy body; he develops fangs and paws with long nails. He feels invigorated and his body seems very strong. He howls while "Blue Moon" plays, and heads for the zoo, where he climbs into the cage with wolves, who accept him, then jumps out and runs through the park. The next morning, six people are found murdered and mutilated. David considers suicide and wonders whether he needs a silver bullet. After a harrowing chase in which he is pursued like a mad dog through Piccadilly Circus, the werewolf is shot and changes back into the boy, David, as soon as he is dead.

The Howling, a 1981 film, also features the full moon, yellow, shining eyes, howling, and the idea that werewolves can be killed only with fire or silver bullets. It begins with comments that humankind has lost something valuable in evolution; man is still part savage and we should not deny the animal in us. The plot involves Marcia, a TV reporter who had been kidnapped by a maniac and rescued and who goes on a country retreat with her husband in order to regain her composure. But instead, she encounters werewolves, among them her abductor and her trusted psychiatrist. A graphic scene that is the delight of film makers shows a human transformation into wolf in minute detail. When the heroine is attacked by a werewolf, she fights back with a hatchet and manages to cut off one of the beast's front paws. Upon returning home, she finds her husband with a bandage covering his missing hand.

Eventually, she is caught by a pack of werewolves, who tell her that they once raised cattle for prey but they now feed on people. They explain, "You can't tame what's meant to be wild. . . . From the day we're born, there is a struggle between what is peaceful and what is violent." Finally, the police surround the pack and shut the wolves into an enclosure that is set on fire. But one werewolf gets away and succeeds in biting Marcia. She cries out, "We have to warn people, we have to make them believe." Her inevitable transformation into a werewolf is televised as proof of the reality of the phenomenon. The most striking symbolic element of this movie is an avowedly evil woman in a restaurant ordering a rare hamburger. The final scene consists of a close-up of a raw, red hamburger on a grill, with a spatula patting the meat causing the blood to drip down into the fire. The meat is turned over for cooking on the other side and again pressed, emitting bloody juice, and is served up rare.

Although the noble character of wolves is occasionally portrayed in the films just described, that aspect receives more emphasis in a

10

fascinating movie entitled *Wolfen*, also dated 1981. The plot stresses the likeness between American Indians and wolves: they evolved together and both are superb hunters that do not overpopulate the earth. Unlike most werewolves, who live in remote surroundings, the ones in this story live in New York City. The reason for this becomes clear when a native elder explains to a white man that the creatures he has seen are not wolves, but "wolfen." "For twenty thousand years—ten times your Christian era—the great hunting nations lived together in balance with nature," he points out. "Then came the slaughter" of wolves as well as Indians and buffalo by the white man. "The smartest went underground into the new wilderness." The great hunters became scavengers of garbage in urban areas. "They might be gods. They can see two looks away and they can hear a cloud pass overhead. In their world there are no lies, and no crime. In their eyes, you are the savage. You got technology but lost your senses." They are "other nations, their world is older, more complete, finished. They kill to survive, to protect their families. Man does less." Because of human arrogance, he warns, there will be "life that will prey on us as we prey upon the earth." He tells the white man, "You don't have the eyes of the hunter, you have the eyes of the dead."

Flashback films of wolves being mercilessly gunned down from helicopters drive home the history of human cruelty perpetrated upon the species. Yet the people violently killed by the wolfen are restricted to those who directly threaten their survival, individuals involved in urban renewal projects that destroy the old buildings where the creatures live in order to build luxury condos. The wolfen must protect their hunting ground. Mutilation and cannibalism represent their retribution against the humans who wrong them. Otherwise, they thoughtfully prey only upon victims who will not be missed—the sick, the old, and drug addicts. Abandoned people have become their new sources of meat.

In this film, scenes of shape-shifting take place, like other werewolf transformations, under a full moon. Belief holds that the soul can transfer the body into a different form. The shape-shifter goes to the water's edge, takes off his clothes, and with his hand makes paw prints on the shore. He goes down on all fours and laps water containing the moon's reflection and blows water out of his mouth, illustrating the ancient notion of water as a facilitator of transformation. He dashes about in a frenzy and then runs into the water and howls. His teeth grow huge. The moon turns red.

The 1941 definitive cinematic version, *The Wolf Man*, became the "key   15
generating text for the modern figure of the werewolf" (Douglas 244). Set in Wales, this film contrasts in many ways with the recent *Wolf*, demonstrating the evolution of the werewolf image over the past five decades.

The titles indicate the emphasis on the human side of the man-beast in the earlier film, with more focus on the animal in the later. In *The Wolf Man*, Lon Chaney, Jr. plays the doomed hero, Larry Talbot, a huge, hulking figure, who is at home with tools, not philosophy. He has no special "gift" like the editor in *Wolf,* and does not resemble a wolf at all, except in the slang sense of chasing a pretty girl and telling her "What big eyes you have, Grandma!" From the very beginning, the script makes clear that

> Even a man who is pure in heart,
> And says his prayers by night
> May become a wolf when the wolfbane blooms
> And the autumn moon is bright.

Larry's innocence cannot save him from his fate when the pentagram, the sign of the werewolf, appears on his hand as a warning he is the next victim of the creature's bite. A simple man, he is a passive victim who cannot be blamed for the hideous murders he commits as a savage wolf, representing the evil side of man. The gypsy woman chants over Larry's body, "The way you walked was thorny through no fault of your own, but as the rain enters the soil, the river enters the sea, so tears run to a predestined end." Her blessing ensures death will release the werewolf from further suffering.

In the recent Jack Nicholson film, despite bloody killings, there is the message, however ambivalent, that wolves can be wholesome, even noble. A new theme enters the old legend: the werewolf can be good or bad according to the character of the transformed human. In *The Wolf Man*, the "everyday world is benign, well-ordered," and Christian, whereas in the 1994 version [*Wolf*], "everyday life is a wolf pack, with rivals contending for power, sex and dominance" and with definite pagan elements (Rutherford 55).

The werewolves' vulnerability to silver, mentioned in subsequent films, is a prominent theme in *The Wolf Man*, in which a silver cane, rather than a silver bullet, is used to kill the creatures. Other patterns set in 1941 for future films are the influence of the moon, the vividly detailed transformation of man to wolf, terrified dogs that bark furiously in recognition of the human form of the werewolf, a frightened horse that rears and whinnies when such a person appears, and a charm provided by a soothsayer to protect the werewolf, who gives it to his sweetheart to protect her from himself. Eerie scenes in a misty forest, wolfbane flowers that wilt when the werewolf is about to strike, a bite wound that heals overnight and then turns into a pentagram, and gypsies with a werewolf among them who return every autumn are noteworthy elements.

The important contribution of this film is articulation of the tension between the physical aspects of the werewolf as an actual entity and the idea that the phenomenon is a mental illness. For Larry, the pragmatist who understands only what can be touched, his transformation is real. For his father, a brooding theorist, the werewolf is more complex. He explains that the werewolf legend, like all legends, has some truth; it is an "ancient explanation of the dual personality in all of us." For him, lycanthropy is a variety of schizophrenia, expressing "the good and evil in every man's soul. In this case, evil takes the shape of an animal." For some people, he says, "life is simple, black and white, with no shades of gray." For others, good and bad are complex and not so easily distinguished. Although he does not believe in the physical form of the werewolf, he feels that "anything can happen to a man in his own mind." He thinks his son has conjured up an evil thing and wants to help him "get out of this mental quagmire." The doctor who is consulted agrees that "a man lost in the mazes of his mind may imagine he is anything." He argues that lycanthropy is "mind over matter," mental suggestion, a kind of self-hyp-notism like the stigmata. Larry, he says, is a sick man with a psychic mal-adjustment who could be cured if he cooperated. But therapy does not intervene. The savage wolf who, while attacking his next victim, is killed by strokes with the silver-tipped cane, turns into the dead body of Larry.

Tales of human-wolf transformations date to the remote past and occur 20 in many cultures. The earliest known description of such a change is found in the Akkadian *Epic of Gilgamesh*, dating from the early second millen-nium BC, in which the goddess Ishtar turns a shepherd into a wolf who is then devoured by his own dogs. Ovid's *Metamorphoses* describes Jupi-ter's punishment of Arcadian king Lycaon for giving him a banquet of human flesh: Instantly Lycaon howled, "his clothes changed into bristling hairs, his arms to legs, and he became a wolf." His "savage nature showed in his rabid jaws, and he now directed against the flocks his innate lust for killing" and his mania for shedding blood. "Though he was a wolf, he retained some traces of his original shape" and "presented the same picture of ferocity" (35). Virgil's *Eighth Eclogue* mentions a werewolf as a magician who voluntarily undergoes transformation through use of herbs.

Although these epics gave brief sketches of the phenomenon, the first substantial literary description of a werewolf that became the progenitor of all later versions is included in a Roman work, *Trimalchio's Banquet*, written by Petronius in the first century AD. The tale is narrated by a for-mer slave, Niceros, who was going to visit his mistress and asked a soldier to accompany him. The two men set out under a full moon and after a time stopped to rest among some tombstones that lined the road. During that sojourn, the soldier began stripping off his clothes, putting them down by the roadside. Then he urinated in a circle around his clothes and suddenly turned into a wolf who began to howl and ran away into the woods. His clothes turned into stone. When Niceros reached his mistress's house, she informed him that a wolf had just been there and had butchered many of her herd. The wolf had escaped, but a slave had managed to stab the animal in the neck with a spear. On returning to his master's house at dawn, Niceros notices that the clothes have been removed from the roadside, leaving a pool of blood in their place. Back at home, he finds the soldier lying in bed with a doctor treating his wounded neck. Niceros realized then that the man was a werewolf—using the Latin word *versipellem*, meaning literally "turn skin" (Otten 231–233; Douglas 39, 41–42).

With this story the major elements that recur in werewolf traditions over the ages, including the Hollywood versions, were established. The transition from man to wolf must take place under the full moon. On a practical level, the moonlight enabled Niceros to see an event that had transpired at night and thus make his story believable to his listeners. But the moon also has deep associations with lycanthropy. Symbolically, the moon is associated with the hunt in almost all cultures. This may relate to the fact that for hunter-gatherers the collection of plant food was a daily chore whereas hunting was a periodic activity that may have been stimulated by the phase of the moon acting as a signal to begin the chase. This sign would be reinforced by the howling of the wolves—the predators that hunters most closely imitated. In prehistoric times the lunar cycle was a recognizable unit of time, a natural clock. In many traditions there is an association between the moon and a female deity concerned with hunting. The classic example of this association is the Graeco-Roman figure of Artemis, or Diana, called "the mistress of animals," who is known for changing a man into a stag when he saw her bathing (Douglas 38–40). The moon, of course, as the archetypal symbol of change, has a logical connection with the profound alteration inherent in the man–to–wild beast transformation.

Petronius' story also established the feature that a person must remove his clothes in order to become a werewolf, discarding the things that make him human before changing into an animal. Also initiated was the tradition that some form of magic is used to bring about the transformation, as in the case of the soldier urinating in a circle around his clothes. The urination theme became part of many versions of the werewolf, and relates to the lupine habit of territory marking. In order for the werewolf to become human again, he must return to the same spot where he left his clothes to retrieve them. The conversion of the clothes into stone would prevent anyone from taking or moving them while the owner was in wolf form. Another important motif that persists to the present day is the sympathetic wound—an injury inflicted on the werewolf that will still appear after he returns to human form. In Petronius' tale, as in others to follow, this wound is proof that the phenomenon of changing into a werewolf actually happened and confirms the shared identity of man and wolf. In cinematic versions of the werewolf, as just described, many of these motifs have been retained and others have been added. Water has been an important element in effecting human-to-wolf transformation, and its power could be imparted by drinking from a wolf's paw print, rolling in the dewy grass, bathing in a fountain or spring, or plunging into and swimming across a body of water. Charms or secret ointments rubbed on the body were also used to cause the transition, and wolf pelts or magic belts or girdles provided by a supernatural being and donned by a human could bring about the change to beast.

In order to understand the werewolf and the emotions it evokes, one must take a close look at the extraordinary history of human relationships with the wolf and the crusade of annihilation. The species was long ago extirpated in the British Isles and Scandinavia and wolf populations were decimated in its former range throughout the world (Lopez 13–14). As one wolf researcher points out, the destruction of that animal represents "the first time in the history of the planet [that] one species made a deliberate organized attempt to exterminate a fellow species." Ingrained hatred of the wolf was brought with the colonists to the New World. The American war against the species was "one of the most successful programs ever carried out by the federal government." The original wolf population in what is now the lower forty-eight states before the arrival of European settlers is estimated to have been two million. "By the 1950s, except for isolated populations of a few hundred wolves in the Upper Midwest, the gray wolf had been exterminated in those areas" (McIntyre 69, 77).

• • •

W. M. S. Russell and Clare Russell, two scholars who would be expected   25
to know better, wrote on the social biology of werewolves in 1978, giving a diatribe against wolves that more properly belongs in the Dark Ages: "To propose conserving [wolves] in the wild" is "analogous to suggesting the conservation of desert locusts or malarial mosquitoes. . . . It can only be explained by something like totemic survivals." Referring to Australian *totemism*,° they present the misleading argument that "so long as totems

---

totemism: the belief in the connection between an animal or bird that serves as an emblem of a tribe, clan, or family.

were valuable food species, the totemic system was ecologically sound."
But when it spread to embrace objects of "no actual service to the natives,"
this was no longer true. "The conservation of a pest species is, therefore,
intelligible in totemic terms, though obviously not in terms of rational
ecology" (178–179). What an unfortunate discussion to be published
during this time of ecological crisis, when modern science has demonstrated the vital role predators, particularly wolves, play in the integrity of
the natural environment and even in the health of the entire planet!

The Russells argue against the validity of what they call the "sentimen-
tal attitude" to wolves, citing the adverse opinions of stock-tenders who
must deal with predators in real life, such as the reindeer-herding Lapps.
In that society, the Boy Scout movement was resisted by the children,
who "objected strongly to being called Wolf-cubs" (179). The authors
trace the origin of the Boy Scout wolf cubs to Akela, the wolf in Kipling's
Jungle Book, and argue that through that figure "generations of urban
children have been familiarized with the wolf totem." They assert that
this may help to explain the appearance in recent years of movements
to conserve wild wolf populations, and even reintroduce them into
regions where they have been exterminated, a practice that is deplorable
because of wolves' "depredations on livestock" and their being "dangerous carriers of rabies" (178). To advocate a cultural materialist view which
excludes psychological and cultural motivations denies the preeminent
influence of human symbolic capacities.

Admittedly, the utilitarian concerns associated with the rise of
stock-tending have been strong factors in evoking hatred for the wolf. In
that regard it is relevant that a human-wolf phenomenon exists among
the Navajo, a tribe that is deeply involved with sheep-raising. However,
the anthropologist who studied Navajo human-wolves, which are a type
of witch, did not find that they have any direct relationship to the killing
of sheep, but did note that they may steal sheep, motivated by "the jealousy and envy which accrues to the owner of much jewelry and many
sheep" (Morgan 11, 40).

Navajo shape-shifters or human-wolves represent belief in fluidity
between the human and animal worlds. Human-wolves possess great
speed and the ability to cover a lot of territory without effort and then to
disappear, demonstrating their supernatural power. As recently as 1992, a
Navajo driving a truck at 75 miles an hour reported that the figure of a man
ran alongside him and then veered off, changing into a wolf just before
disappearing into the bush (Burbank 1994, 1, 5, 6). A Navajo human-
wolf can be distinguished from a real wolf because his tail hangs straight
down, in contrast to an actual wolf, who puts his tail out behind him as
he runs. The morning after shooting a wolf, a Navajo may follow its tracks

for miles, only to discover a man bleeding from a suspicious wound. Or, if a suspected werewolf is shot, the next morning a Navajo miles away may fall from his horse, wounded in exactly the same place where the werewolf had been shot. Human-wolves, also called skin walkers, are believed to climb to the top of a family's hogan° and look through the smoke hole. Occupants see a pair of pointed ears and a wolfish face with glowing eyes. The wolf then drops some powder made from the skin of a dead person, called corpse poison, into the fire below, which flares and causes the people to breathe the deadly fumes. Or the wolf may sprinkle the poison on the victim's nose or mouth or blow it at him, causing bad luck, illness or death (Burbank 1994, 7, 8; Burbank 1990, 49; Morgan 18).

William Morgan argues that the psychological and cultural meanings of Navajo werewolves lie in the fear of the "ravenous cannibalism" they represent and their association with tribal belief in "night wandering" that allows a person to be in two places at the same time (11). Also prominent is the idea that a human-wolf will dig up and eat bodies or take the jewelry that has been buried with the deceased for use in the afterlife. Navajo have "an excessive fear of the dead," shunning contact with a corpse, for the spirit is still in the physical body and must be avoided. The main defining characteristic of a Navajo witch is "trifling with the dead or the possessions of the dead." While in wolf skin, witches break powerful taboos by engaging in necrophilia, sexual excess, incest, bestiality, and cannibalism. Thus they negate world order and bring chaos, destroying the tenets of social propriety not only by obliterating the demarcation between humans and animals but also by transgressing the boundary between life and death (Morgan 11, 25–26; Burbank 1994, 6; Burbank 1990, 49, 51).

The most vivid archetypes of fearful werewolves, however, are those 30 of the Old World, still remembered with dread by each generation who shudders anew at the retelling of their history. During the fifteenth to seventeenth centuries, when belief in werewolves was most prevalent, countless hundreds of people accused of undergoing transformation to wolves were punished, usually by death, often with confessions obtained through torture. Many were burned alive. Details of these cases were carefully recorded. One of the most notorious was the German, Stubbe Peeter, who, over a twenty-five year period allegedly committed many crimes including rape, incest, murder, eating the raw flesh of people as well as animals, and adultery. He confessed to having made a pact with the devil, who had given him a girdle to transform him into a wolf. Above the instrument of torture used in his 1589 execution in Cologne

---

hogan: a house constructed of dirt and branches and then covered with mud or sod, used by the Navajo Indians.

was hung the likeness of a wolf "to show unto all men the shape wherein he executed those cruelties" (Otten 9, 53, 76).

Another self-confessed werewolf, Jean Grenier, tried in France in 1603, revealed that he had become a werewolf by applying a salve and wearing a wolf skin provided by "The Man of the Forest," an affiliate of the devil. The young lycanthrope admitted he had clawed and bitten several girls and had killed and eaten babies and children. The court, unusual for its time, took into account his mental derangement and low intelligence that made him "incapable of rational thought," and sentenced him to life in a monastery for moral and religious instruction. There a visitor noted that he had nails like claws and ran on all fours, eating rotten meat. He died at age twenty, considered to be "scarcely human" (Otten 9, 51; Lopez 244).

During the height of the werewolf craze, a person who was antisocial or marginal, living apart from others, might be accused of being a werewolf. Anyone who was conceived at the full moon, born feet first or with a caul, had a hairy body, scabbed legs, or lupine features, or whose eyebrows met in the middle might be suspect. Lack of visible fur was not a protection as one accused werewolf found when he told his tormentors his hair was on the inside and they gashed his arms and legs to verify his claim (Summers 160–161). Werewolves never had the long, bushy tails of ordinary wolves, and were distinguished from them by being tailless or having truncated tails. Werewolves might also have smaller heads or appear different in color. Many theories involving disease as the cause of belief in werewolves have been advanced. Foremost among these proposed etiologies is porphyria, a rare blood disorder whose symptoms include excessive hair growth on face, hands, arms, and legs, reddish teeth, and claw-shaped fingernails and toenails, as well as facial scarring and disfigurement from lesions resulting from a toxic reaction to sunlight that might make the sufferer prefer to travel at night ("Porphyrias" 7). Other diseases implicated are rabies and ergot poisoning, which could account for the victims' irrational actions; hypertrichosis giving a bestial appearance; malnutrition stimulating an appetite for flesh; demonic possession; melancholia, autism, schizophrenia, and various psychoses; or the ingestion of pharmacological hallucinogens leading to delusions of lupine identity. Though provocative, probably none of these factors played a substantial role in the werewolf phenomenon.

Far more significant is the cultural context in which fear and implacable hatred of predators became nearly universal at a certain stage of human history. Many indigenous predator species take human-beast form in various areas of the world, such as were-jaguars in South America, were-bears in northern Europe and Asia, were-leopards in Africa, were-tigers in China, and were-foxes in Japan. But the concept of werewolves is by far the most widespread and deeply-entrenched image of violence and aggression, occurring throughout the whole range of the wolf's former habitat: from the northern tundra of Europe and Asia down to the shores of the Mediterranean, east to India and China, and to western North America (Douglas 21).

Thousands of years ago the wolf was celebrated as a protector; thus a spiritual leader who acquired its powers to become a wolf-man was regarded with awe. But as human societies became sedentary and adopted the agricultural way of life, attitudes toward wolves, and hence werewolves, changed. They became identified with hostile forces, outcasts who lived in the woods and preyed upon humans, and were perceived as dangerous misfits or deviates with savage qualities that made them uncivilized and untamable. Originally, primitive societies had generally viewed the werewolf positively because it represented integration of the cultural and wild elements of humans. "To learn to howl with the wolves" meant "opening oneself up to the essence of nature," a process through which it was possible to achieve self-awareness. To live in a social order, a person must have spent time in the wilderness, for only by going outside the self could one's inner nature be made clear. By the Middle Ages, however, the werewolf had lost its benign ritual meaning and was considered destructive, bloodthirsty, and cunning. In the late Middle Ages, it became associated with the devil. At the end of the fifteenth century, the official Catholic position switched from considering belief in werewolves nonsensical and sinful to full belief in their existence as accomplices of Satan who, according to the 1484 Papal Bull,° must be annihilated. This change was "connected to the holy dictum to believe in witches. Along with cats, werewolves were allegedly the favorite cohorts of witches, and in many werewolf trials of the sixteenth and seventeenth centuries there was no real distinction made between werewolf and witch." The greatest fear in both Catholic and Protestant minds was chaos, which was associated with sensuality and an uncontrollable nature, and that fear was projected upon human-wolves (Zipes 68–69, 71).

Preeminently, the werewolf phenomenon articulates humankind's overwhelming penchant for symbolizing with animal images, making sense of life with metaphors from nature. The wolf is an extraordinarily rich vehicle of expression, carrying a complex web of

"Preeminently, the werewolf phenomenon articulates humankind's overwhelming penchant for symbolizing with animal images, making sense of life with metaphors from nature."

35

Papal Bull: a letter or announcement by which the pope addresses all Catholics.

embedded codes, some of which stand in paradoxical relationship to the actual animal but most of which are rooted in emphasis on its predation and meat-eating. The wolf bears projected guilt for the human predatory past and a present replete not only with consumption of animal flesh but with all manner of exploitation of and barbarity toward our own species and others. In Christian symbolism, Jesus is the lamb of God and the Good Shepherd for whom the wolf is enemy. Thus, Satan acquired lupine imagery. Christ warns his followers to "beware of false prophets, who come to you in sheep's clothing, but inwardly are ravenous wolves" (Matthew 7:15). Evil wolves became embedded in literary masterpieces. Chaucer's *Parson's Tale* includes the devil's wolves that strangle the sheep of Jesus Christ. Dante's *Inferno* depicts the wolf as a symbol of greed and fraud, for those who are condemned to hell for the sins of the wolf are seducers, hypocrites, thieves, and liars. Rude eating is described as "wolfing" one's food, and hunger is the "wolf at the door." A "discordant note on the violin is still called a wolf." An aggressive sexual signal is a "wolf whistle," and immoral acts are epitomized by the use of the French idiom "she's seen the wolf" meaning "she's lost her virginity" as well as by calling prostitutes "wolves" because they are viewed as "consuming the souls" of men (Lopez 219, 221, 239). Not only human evil, but even that emanating from nature itself is foisted upon the wolf. Lupus is the word for a dread disease that may eat away the flesh.

The uprooting of graves for devouring corpses gave wolves an association with death and their attraction to body-strewn battlefields linked them to war and desolation. Human savagery is couched in lupine terms. The fifteenth century French nobleman known as Bluebeard, who tortured, killed, and ate hundreds of children and bathed in their blood, was categorized as a werewolf by folklorist Sabine Baring-Gould (181–237), even though no man-beast transformation was reported. A Nazi terrorist organization called "Operation Werewolf" carried out a regime of murders in 1920 and in World War II one of Hitler's headquarters was named Werewolf (Douglas 26; Russell and Russell 165). Robert Eisler, following his imprisonment at Buchenwald and Dachau, argued for an evolutionist derivation of human violence, titling his study of sadism and masochism *Man into Wolf* (1951). American World War II propaganda was interwoven with opposition to Aldo Leopold's wolf preservation program. An advocate of the bounty for wolf killers wrote, "The wolf is the Nazi of the forest. He takes the deer and some small fry. . . . Can Professor Leopold justify their existence because deer meant for human consumption should be fed to the Nazi because we must have that protection for the trees? Can he justify the Jap or Nazi because he eats a rabbit or a grouse which are meant for human food, or the songbird on its nest, which are meant by the Lord for our pleasure?" A poster promoting the sale of US Savings Bonds depicts a snarling wolf, and states "There's one 100-proof way to guard your door against this fellow's visit. There's wolf poison in every US Savings Bond you buy" (Thiel 107–108).

A werewolf, according to one account, had "eyes glaring like marsh-fires" (Baring-Gould 3). A recent Broadway musical production of *Beauty and the Beast* featured snarling wolves with crimson eyes lit up like burning coals. But where many observers described a hideous red or orange glow in the werewolf's eyes, Aldo Leopold saw in the last wolf he had shot "a fierce green fire dying in her eyes." The experience made him think "like a mountain" with an ecological perspective that changed his role from wolf-killer to wolf-preserver (Flader 1). Since that day in 1944, attitudes about wolves have been gradually shifting to becoming more sympathetic, though with many fluctuations. Now, fifty years later, the principal cellist in a California symphony orchestra quit her job in protest against performing Prokofiev's 1936 work, *Peter and the Wolf.* She urged the public to boycott the performance of the work that teaches children "to hate and fear wolves and to applaud a hunter who kills a wolf" ("Wolf Pact" D1). Presently, wolves are being reintroduced to various regions of the United States where stockmen, hunters, and those who fear the wild can be out-voted. School children may visit wolf education centers and are encouraged to adopt a wolf through donations of money.

But the evil werewolf still prowls. Two 1990 British sex criminals were called the "werewolf rapist" and the "Wolfman." Yet strangely the recent multiple murders and cannibalism of Jeffrey Dahmer which resemble deeds recounted at the old European werewolf trials did not elicit those titles (Douglas 262–263). A currently popular song tells about the "Werewolf of London" with "a Chinese menu in his hand. . . . Going to get himself a big dish of beef chow mein." The lyrics warn "If you hear him howling around your kitchen door/Better not let him in. Little old lady got mutilated late last night. . . . He's the hair-handed gent who ran amuk in Kent. . . . Better stay away from him/He'll rip your lungs out. . . . I saw a werewolf drinking a piña colada at Trader Vic's/His hair was perfect/Werewolves of London draw blood" (Zevon). The human-wolf form continues to represent our species' carnivorous nature and our staggering propensity for violence. Likely, werewolves will continue to be important in the future, representing as they do the paradox of our projection into animals of traits unacceptable in humans and the assignment of human behavior patterns to animals. Both processes are deeply entrenched in human cognition and are becoming more, not less, prevalent in modern times. As the wild domain becomes ever more engulfed by the tame and we are concerned with measuring one against the other, the man-beast figure that combines them both holds renewed fascination.

Werewolves embody the conflict between instinctual urges and rational behavior—a source of ongoing controversy regarding the question of establishing valid distinctions between people and animals. The were-wolf concept represents the need to deal with animality, wildness, and otherness—urgent issues in modern life—and bridges the man-beast gulf, challenging the ingrained Cartesian dualism° that divides human-kind from animals in Western society. The sense of identification we feel with wolves horrifies us, but at the same time captivates us as we acquire deeper appreciation for the wild realm and our place within it.

Works Cited

An American Werewolf in London. Polygram Pictures, 1981.

Baring-Gould, Sabine. *The Book of Were-Wolves*. New York: Causeway Books, 1973.

Burbank, James C. *Vanishing Lobo: The Mexican Wolf and the Southwest*. Boulder: Johnson Books. 1990.

Burbank, James C. "Yenaldloosh: The Shape-Shifter Beliefs of the Navajos." *The Indian Trader* 25.6 (June 1994): 1, 5–8, 10.

Douglas, Adam. *The Beast Within*. London: Chapmans, 1992.

Eisler, Robert. *Man into Wolf: An Anthropological Interpretation of Sadism, Masochism and Lycanthropy*. London: Routledge and Kegan Paul, 1951.

Flader, Susan L. *Thinking Like a Mountain*. Lincoln: U of Nebraska P, 1974.

The Howling. Avco Embassy Pictures Corporation, 1981.

James, Caryn. "The Werewolf Within Dances with Abandon." *New York Times* 19 June 1994: 13, 18.

Janusonis, Michael. "A Ponderous Wolf Could Use More Howling." *Providence Journal-Bulletin* 17 June 1994: D5.

Keck, Paul E., et al. "Lycanthropy: Alive and Well in the Twentieth Century." *Psychological Medicine* 18 (1988): 113–120.

Kulick, Aaron R., Harrison G. Pope, Jr., and Paul E. Keck, Jr. "Lycanthropy and Self-Identification." *Journal of Nervous and Mental Disease* 178.2 (1990): 134–137.

Lopez, Barry Holstun. *Of Wolves and Men*. New York: Charles Scribner's Sons, 1978.

McIntyre, Rick. *A Society of Wolves: National Parks and the Battle over the Wolf*. Stillwater, MN: Voyageur Press, 1993.

Matthew 7:15.

Morgan, William. "Human Wolves among the Navajo." Yale University Publications in Anthropology no. 11, 1936.

Otten, Charlotte F., ed. *A Lycanthropy Reader: Werewolves in Western Culture*. Syracuse: Syracuse UP, 1986.

Ovid. *Metamorphoses*. New York: Penguin, 1955.

"Porphyrias." *Mayo Clinic Health Letter* 7.10 (1986): 7.

Cartesian dualism: the belief that the mind and body are separate, as described by the French philosopher René Descartes.

Russell, W. M. S., and Claire Russell. "The Social Biology of Werewolves." *Animals in Folklore*. Ed. J. R. Porter and W. M. S. Russell. Totowa, NJ: Rowman and Littlefield, 1978.

Rutherford, Brett. "*Wolf* and Other Wolves—An Appreciation." *Haunts* 28 Summer/Fall 1994: 55–56.

Spence, Lewis. *The Encyclopedia of the Occult*. London: Bracken Books, 1988.

Summers, Montague. *The Werewolf*. New York: E. P. Dutton, 1934.

Teen Wolf. Wolfkill Productions, 1985.

Thiel, Richard P. *The Timber Wolf in Wisconsin: The Death and Life of a Majestic Predator*. Madison: U of Wisconsin P, 1993.

Trotti, Hugh. *Beasts and Battles: Fact in Legend and History?* New York: Rivercross, 1989.

Weinraub, Bernard. "Who's Afraid of the Big Bad Book Editor?" *New York Times* 12 June 1994: Section 2: 1, 22–23.

Wolf. Columbia Pictures, 1994.

"Wolf." *People* 41.24 (27 June 1994): 13.

The Wolf Man. Universal City Studio, 1941.

"Wolf Pact." *USA Today* 6 October 1994: D1.

Wolfen. Orion Pictures, 1981.

Zevon, Warren. "Werewolves of London." *A Quiet Normal Life*. Audiotape. New York: Elektra/Asylum Records, 1986.

Zipes, Jack, ed. *The Trials and Tribulations of Little Red Riding Hood*. New York: Routledge, 1993.

Understanding the Text

1. Lawrence begins her article by recounting the plots from a number of movies from the 1980s and 1990s, including such hits as *Wolf* (1994), with Jack Nicholson; *Teen Wolf* (1985), with Michael J. Fox; and *An American Werewolf in London* (1981). What specific points does she make about the portrayals of werewolves in these movies in terms of how they either reinforce or contradict traditional werewolf mythology?

2. Examine the story told by Petronius about the Roman soldier who turned into a wolf. In what ways does this story encapsulate a number of key elements of werewolf lore?

3. How do the Navajo shape-shifters differ in their actions from European werewolves? What do the shape-shifters represent, especially in respect to those differences?

4. Why are accounts of human savagery described in wolf-related terms? Cite specific examples from this selection. Can you think of other wolf-related examples that are not in the text?

5. Lawrence's work is a scholarly article written for other scholars. Compare her writing style to the style of other challenging works, such as Judith Halberstam (p. 173) and Jeffrey Jerome Cohen (p. 184). Is Lawrence's work more difficult or less difficult for you to comprehend? Why?

Reflection and Response

6. The werewolf is an embodiment of both the animal and the human simultaneously. In what ways does it serve as a symbol of the conflict between the "instinctual urges and rational behavior" that all humans experience (par. 37)? Be specific in your answer.

7. Much is made of the role the wolf plays as a predator, hunting livestock and game that humans want to reserve for themselves. Lawrence argues that the wolf — and by extension the werewolf — is also connected to disease and human death. In your opinion, is the wolf an adequate symbol to express the power of disease and death — and our attempts to overcome them? Explain your answer.

Making Connections

8. Research the history of human attitudes and interactions with predatory animals, not only the wolf but also others, such as lions, bears, and tigers. How do these animals come to be an expression of the human desire for freedom, to break free of the bondage of social norms and expectations?

9. Apply the werewolf (or another human-animal transformation) to the argument that Jeffrey Jerome Cohen makes in "Fear of the Monster Is Really a Kind of Desire" (p. 184)? Why might we desire to be like an animal? Support your response.

Dr. Jekyll and Mr. Hyde

Robert Louis Stevenson

The binary dynamic of good and evil is a staple of much art and literature, but seldom has one been more neatly cut into two than in the characters of Dr. Jekyll and Mr. Hyde. Dr. Jekyll bears all the traits of the respectable, upper-middle-class Englishman — well bred, well educated, and well behaved. However, disrupting Dr. Jekyll's world is Mr. Hyde, a loathsome creature given to corrupt and degrading behavior, culminating in the murder of an innocent man. Yet, as the reader comes to discover in Robert Louis Stevenson's famous novella, the two are in fact one and the same. Stevenson's story forces the reader to examine whether the lines that divide good from evil are as solid as some believe. Stevenson was a nineteenth-century Scottish writer whose stories of adventure and danger, including *Kidnapped* (1886) and *Treasure Island* (1883), are still popular today. The following excerpt is taken from the final chapter of *The Strange Case of Dr. Jekyll and Mr. Hyde* (1886). After Mr. Hyde has been killed, a letter in Dr. Jekyll's handwriting has been found, describing a most horrifying experiment.

Henry Jekyll's Full Statement of the Case

I was born in the year 18 — to a large fortune, endowed besides with excellent parts, inclined by nature to industry, fond of the respect of the wise and good among my fellow-men, and thus, as might have been supposed, with every guarantee of an honourable and distinguished future. And indeed the worst of my faults was a certain impatient gaiety of disposition, such as has made the happiness of many, but such as I found it hard to reconcile with my imperious° desire to carry my head high, and wear a more than commonly grave countenance before the public. Hence it came about that I concealed my pleasures; and that when I reached years of reflection, and began to look round me and take stock of my progress and position in the world, I stood already committed to a profound duplicity° of life. Many a man would have even blazoned° such irregularities as I was guilty of; but from the high views that I had set before me, I regarded and hid them with an almost morbid sense of shame. It was thus rather the exacting nature of my aspirations than any particular degradation in my faults, that made me what I was and,

imperious: arrogant and domineering.
duplicity: lying; deception.
blazoned: displayed prominently.

with even a deeper trench than in the majority of men, severed in me those provinces of good and ill which divide and compound man's dual nature. In this case, I was driven to reflect deeply and inveterately° on that hard law of life, which lies at the root of religion and is one of the most plentiful springs of distress. Though so profound a double-dealer, I was in no sense a hypocrite; both sides of me were in dead earnest; I was no more myself when I laid aside restraint and plunged in shame, than when I laboured, in the eye of day, at the furtherance of knowledge or the relief of sorrow and suffering. And it chanced that the direction of my scientific studies, which led wholly towards the mystic and the transcendental,° reacted and shed a strong light on this consciousness of the perennial war among my members. With every day, and from both sides of my intelligence, the moral and the intellectual, I thus drew steadily nearer to that truth, by whose partial discovery I have been doomed to such a dreadful shipwreck: that man is not truly one, but truly two. I say two, because the state of my own knowledge does not pass beyond that point. Others will follow, others will outstrip me on the same lines; and I hazard the guess that man will be ultimately known for a mere polity° of multifarious, incongruous and independent denizens.° I for my part, from the nature of my life, advanced infallibly in one direction and in one direction only. It was on the moral side, and in my own person, that I learned to recognize the thorough and primitive duality of man; I saw that, of the two natures that contended in the field of my consciousness, even if I could rightly be said to be either, it was only because I was radically both; and from an early date, even before the course of my scientific discoveries had begun to suggest the most naked possibility of such a miracle, I had learned to dwell with pleasure, as a beloved daydream, on the thought of the separation of these elements. If each, I told myself, could but be housed in separate identities, life would be relieved of all that was unbearable; the unjust might go his way, delivered from the aspirations and remorse of his more upright twin; and the just could walk steadfastly and securely on his upward path, doing the good things in which he found his pleasure, and no longer exposed to disgrace and penitence by the hands of this extraneous evil. It was the curse of mankind that these incongruous faggots° were thus bound together—that in

---

inveterately: habitually; without likelihood of change.
transcendental: relating to the world of the spiritual.
polity: civil government; an organized society.
denizens: residents.
faggots: bundles of sticks of firewood.

the agonized womb of consciousness, these polar twins should be contin-
uously struggling. How, then, were they dissociated?

I was so far in my reflections when, as I have said, a side light began
to shine upon the subject from the laboratory table. I began to perceive
more deeply than it has ever yet been stated, the trembling immaterial-
ity, the mist-like transience, of this seemingly so solid body in which we
walk attired. Certain agents I found to have the power to shake and to
pluck back that fleshly vestment, even as a wind might toss the curtains
of a pavilion. For two good reasons, I will not enter deeply into this scientific branch of my confession. First, because I have been made to learn
that the doom and burden of our life is bound forever on man's shoulders, and when the attempt is made to cast it off, it but returns upon us
with more unfamiliar and more awful pressure. Second, because as my
narrative will make, alas! too evident, my discoveries were incomplete.
Enough, then, that I not only recognized my natural body for the mere
aura and effulgence° of certain of the powers that made up my spirit,
but managed to compound a drug by which these powers should be
dethroned from their supremacy, and a second form and countenance
substituted, none the less natural to me because they were the expression, and bore the stamp, of lower elements in my soul.

I hesitated long before I put this theory to the test of practice. I knew
well that I risked death; for any drug that so potently controlled and
shook the very fortress of identity, might by the least scruple of an over-
dose or at the least inopportunity in the moment of exhibition, utterly
blot out that immaterial tabernacle which I looked to it to change. But
the temptation of a discovery so singular and profound, at last overcame the suggestions of alarm. I had long since prepared my tincture°;
I purchased at once, from a firm of wholesale chemists, a large quantity
of a particular salt which I knew, from my experiments, to be the last
ingredient required; and late one accursed night, I compounded the elements, watched them boil and smoke together in the glass, and when
the ebullition° had subsided, with a strong glow of courage, drank off
the potion.

The most racking pangs succeeded: a grinding in the bones, deadly
nausea, and a horror of the spirit that cannot be exceeded at the hour of
birth or death. Then these agonies began swiftly to subside, and I came
to myself as if out of a great sickness. There was something strange in
my sensations, something indescribably new and, from its very novelty,

---

effulgence: brilliant radiance.
tincture: a chemical solution containing alcohol.
ebullition: boiling or bubbling of a liquid.

incredibly sweet. I felt younger, lighter, happier in body; within I was conscious of a heady recklessness, a current of disordered sensual images running like a mill race in my fancy, a solution of the bonds of obligation, an unknown but not an innocent freedom of the soul. I knew myself, at the first breath of this new life, to be more wicked, tenfold more wicked, sold a slave to my original evil; and the thought, in that moment, braced and delighted me like wine. I stretched out my hands, exulting in the freshness of these sensations; and in the act, I was suddenly aware that I had lost in stature.

There was no mirror, at that date, in my room; that which stands 5 beside me as I write, was brought there later on and for the very purpose

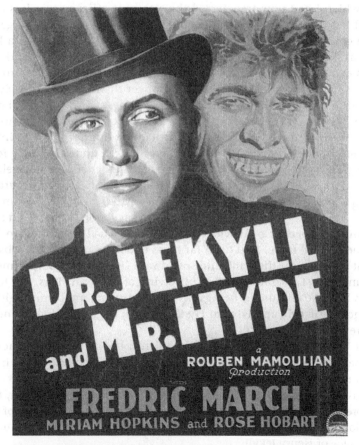

Movie poster for the 1931 film, *Dr. Jekyll and Mr. Hyde*, starring Fredric March.

Pictorial Press Ltd/Alamy Stock Photo

of these transformations. The night, however, was far gone into the morning—the morning, black as it was, was nearly ripe for the conception of the day—the inmates of my house were locked in the most rigorous hours of slumber; and I determined, flushed as I was with hope and triumph, to venture in my new shape as far as to my bedroom. I crossed the yard, wherein the constellations looked down upon me, I could have thought, with wonder, the first creature of that sort that their unsleeping vigilance had yet disclosed to them; I stole through the corridors, a stranger in my own house; and coming to my room, I saw for the first time the appearance of Edward Hyde.

I must here speak by theory alone, saying not that which I know, but that which I suppose to be most probable. The evil side of my nature, to which I had now transferred the stamping efficacy, was less robust and less developed than the good which I had just deposed. Again, in the course of my life, which had been, after all, nine tenths a life of effort, virtue and control, it had been much less exercised and much less exhausted. And hence, as I think, it came about that Edward Hyde was so much smaller, slighter and younger than Henry Jekyll. Even as good shone upon the countenance of the one, evil was written broadly and plainly on the face of the other. Evil besides (which I must still believe to be the lethal side of man) had left on that body an imprint of deformity and decay. And yet when I looked upon that ugly idol in the glass, I was conscious of no repugnance, rather of a leap of welcome. This, too, was myself. It seemed natural and human. In my eyes it bore a livelier image of

"This too was myself." | the spirit, it seemed more express and single, than the imperfect and divided countenance, I had been hitherto accustomed to call mine. And in so far I was doubtless right. I have observed that when I wore the semblance of Edward Hyde, none could come near to me at first without a visible misgiving of the flesh. This, as I take it, was because all human beings, as we meet them, are commingled out of good and evil: and Edward Hyde, alone in the ranks of mankind, was pure evil.

I lingered but a moment at the mirror: the second and conclusive experiment had yet to be attempted; it yet remained to be seen if I had lost my identity beyond redemption and must flee before daylight from a house that was no longer mine; and hurrying back to my cabinet, I once more prepared and drank the cup, once more suffered the pangs of dissolution, and came to myself once more with the character, the stature and the face of Henry Jekyll.

That night I had come to the fatal cross roads. Had I approached my discovery in a more noble spirit, had I risked the experiment while under

the empire of generous or pious aspirations, all must have been otherwise, and from these agonies of death and birth, I had come forth an
angel instead of a fiend. The drug had no discriminating action; it was
neither diabolical nor divine; it but shook the doors of the prisonhouse
of my disposition; and like the captives of Philippi, that which stood
within ran forth. At that time my virtue slumbered; my evil, kept awake
by ambition, was alert and swift to seize the occasion; and the thing that
was projected was Edward Hyde. Hence, although I had now two characters as well as two appearances, one was wholly evil, and the other was
still the old Henry Jekyll, that incongruous compound of whose reformation and improvement I had already learned to despair. The movement
was thus wholly toward the worse.

Even at that time, I had not yet conquered my aversion to the dry-
ness of a life of study. I would still be merrily disposed at times; and as
my pleasures were (to say the least) undignified, and I was not only well
known and highly considered, but growing towards the elderly man, this
incoherency of my life was daily growing more unwelcome. It was on
this side that my new power tempted me until I fell in slavery. I had but
to drink the cup, to doff at once the body of the noted professor, and to
assume, like a thick cloak, that of Edward Hyde. I smiled at the notion; it
seemed to me at the time to be humorous; and I made my preparations
with the most studious care. I took and furnished that house in Soho,
to which Hyde was tracked by the police; and engaged as housekeeper a
creature whom I well knew to be silent and unscrupulous. On the other
side, I announced to my servants that a Mr. Hyde (whom I described) was
to have full liberty and power about my house in the square; and to parry
mishaps, I even called and made myself a familiar object, in my second
character. I next drew up that will to which you[1] so much objected; so
that if anything befell me in the person of Doctor Jekyll, I could enter
on that of Edward Hyde without pecuniary loss. And thus fortified, as I
supposed, on ever side, I began to profit by the strange immunities of my
position.

Men have before hired bravos° to transact their crimes, while their own   10
person and reputation sat under shelter. I was the first that ever did so for
his pleasures. I was the first that could thus plod in the public eye with a
load of genial respectability, and in a moment, like a schoolboy, strip off
these lendings and spring headlong into the sea of liberty. But for me,
in my impenetrable mantle, the safety was complete. Think of it—I did

---

bravos: a robber or assassin for hire.

[1]"You" refers to Gabriel John Utterson, a friend of Dr. Jekyll.

not even exist! Let me but escape into my laboratory door, give me but a second or two to mix and swallow the draught that I had always standing ready; and whatever he had done, Edward Hyde would pass away like the stain of breath upon a mirror; and there in his stead, quietly at home, trimming the midnight lamp in his study, a man who could afford to laugh at suspicion, would be Henry Jekyll.

The pleasures which I made haste to seek in my disguise were, as I have said, undignified; I would scarce use a harder term. But in the hands of Edward Hyde, they soon began to turn towards the monstrous. When I would come back from these excursions, I was often plunged into a kind of wonder at my vicarious depravity. This familiar that I called out of my own soul, and sent forth alone to do his good pleasure, was a being inherently malign and villainous; his every act and thought centered on self; drinking pleasure with bestial avidity from any degree of torture to another; relentless like a man of stone. Henry Jekyll stood at times aghast before the acts of Edward Hyde; but the situation was apart from ordinary laws, and insidiously relaxed the grasp of conscience. It was Hyde, after all, and Hyde alone, that was guilty. Jekyll was no worse; he woke again to his good qualities seemingly unimpaired; he would even make haste, where it was possible, to undo the evil done by Hyde. And thus his conscience slumbered.

Into the details of the infamy at which I thus connived (for even now I can scarce grant that I committed it) I have no design of entering; I mean but to point out the warnings and the successive steps with which my chastisement approached. I met with one accident which, as it brought on no consequence, I shall no more than mention. An act of cruelty to a child aroused against me the anger of a passer by, whom I recognized the other day in the person of your kinsman; the doctor and the child's family joined him; there were moments when I feared for my life; and at last, in order to pacify their too just resentment, Edward Hyde had to bring them to the door, and pay them in a cheque drawn in the name of Henry Jekyll. But this danger was easily eliminated from the future, by opening an account at another bank in the name of Edward Hyde himself; and when, by sloping my own hand backward, I had supplied my double with a signature, I thought I sat beyond the reach of fate.

Understanding the Text

1. What does Dr. Jekyll mean when he says that "man is not truly one, but truly two" (par. 1)? What is it about Dr. Jekyll himself that leads him to this conclusion?

2. Dr. Jekyll observes that he feels "younger, lighter, happier in body" (par. 4) when he becomes Edward Hyde. Later, he observes that Hyde is "smaller, slighter and younger" (par. 6). What does Dr. Jekyll surmise accounts for these differences? How might they also be connected to his feeling of experiencing an "unknown but not an innocent freedom of the soul" (par. 4) when being Hyde?

3. Does Dr. Jekyll feel remorse for the actions taken by Mr. Hyde? Why or why not?

4. Stevenson's text contains many words that have been defined in glossary notes because they are no longer commonly used. What sort of tone or atmosphere is created by using these terms? If the text were rewritten in more contemporary vocabulary, what might be gained? What might be lost?

Reflection and Response

5. How is *The Strange Case of Dr. Jekyll and Mr. Hyde* a cautionary tale about human overreach? You should consider the roles of science and religion in the story when formulating your response.

6. Stevenson writes that when Dr. Jekyll transforms into Mr. Hyde, he experiences feelings of freedom (par. 4). How is evil connected to freedom? Explain.

Making Connections

7. In Jeffrey Jerome Cohen's essay "Fear of the Monster Is Really a Kind of Desire" (p. 184), he argues that "we envy [the monster's] freedom, and perhaps its sublime despair" (par. 1). How is Cohen's observation true for Stevenson's story? You may need to read the full text of *The Strange Case of Dr. Jekyll and Mr. Hyde* in formulating your response.

8. Find other monster stories that feature two characters who are doubles, similar to Dr. Jekyll/Mr. Hyde (such a double is also referred to as a "doppelganger"). Consider the ways in which the use of the double is similar or different from Stevenson's double. Argue how the use of the double serves as an adequate or inadequate means of exploring human nature. Be specific.

Hyde as a Monster Villain

Erica McCrystal

Robert Louis Stevenson wrote *The Strange Case of Dr. Jekyll and Mr. Hyde* during the late nineteenth century, a time when the theory of evolution started to compete with religious teachings about the origins of humanity. The notion that people had the capacity to be both good and evil was a long-held belief, but now the concept conflated Satan with the animal world. Add the growing interest in physiognomy — a pseudoscience that held that a person's moral character was revealed by his or her facial features — and you have the fertile ground for Stevenson's character of Edward Hyde. The fear that Hyde represents goes beyond the mere criminal: there is something about Hyde that is deeply disturbing to the existing social structure. Thus, he must be controlled. Erica McCrystal teaches English and writing at Montclair University, Berkeley College, and St. John's University. She is also the host of the Villains 101 podcast. This excerpt is part of "Hyde as Hero: The Changing Role of the Modern-Day Monster," which appeared in the Winter 2018 issue of the *Toronto Quarterly*.

In Stevenson's novella, Hyde is a villainous creature—the pure embodiment of *fin de siècle*° Gothic monstrosity. His barbarism is visible through both his aberrations from respectable society's code of conduct and his physical appearance. Hyde exists as a Gothic villain who embodies the abject living conditions of the working class and the threat of degeneration and biologically inherited criminality. The novella draws awareness to psychological conditions, the dangerous uncertainties of science, and class disparities. As Peter Conolly-Smith argues, the novella employs a "strategy of confronting its Victorian readers with their own inner demons," suggesting the ease with which the monster within can emerge (n. pag.). Certainly, the novella grapples with the psychological capacity for an individual to unleash repressed monstrosity. But the text also exacerbates the terrifying biological possibilities of human degeneration, which could instigate a widespread decline of humanity. Theories of degeneration, popularized by Max Nordau, and criminal anthropologist Cesare Lombroso's theories on atavism and anatomical signifiers of criminality raised anxieties within the *fin de siècle* populace. Hyde is the physical embodiment of such concerns; thus, his character as a Victorian monster represents the horrific possibilities for human degeneration and retrogression to a primitive, bestial state.

novella: a short novel.
fin de siècle: the end of the century, particularly the nineteenth century.

During the nineteenth century, Charles Darwin, Thomas Henry Huxley, Herbert Spencer, and others presented their theories on evolution. In response, degeneration theorists suggested that the degenerate figure is one who is unhealthy, abnormal, and deformed and who can pass such traits to offspring. Nordau draws parallels between the physical appearance of a degenerated human face and corrupt morality. He further finds:

That which nearly all degenerates lack is the sense of morality and of right and wrong. For them there exists no law, no decency, no modesty. In order to satisfy any momentary impulse, or inclination, or caprice, they commit crimes and trespasses with the greatest calmness and self-complacency, and do not comprehend that other persons take offence thereat. (17–18)

Degenerates are abnormal because they do not have a moral code. They are misaligned with society and the expectations of proper human behavior. The deviation from normalcy and lack of morality reveals degenerates as monstrous figures (found in both real-world criminals and Gothic fiction). Degeneration theory thus instigated fears in the people of Victorian England of the threat of human retrogression to such a state. Although now proven inaccurate, Lombroso's theories on criminology present traceable physiognomical° abnormalities in criminals. Atavism, which Lombroso defines as the reversion to a savage, animalistic race, is a major component of his studies on criminality: "Born criminals, programmed to do harm, are atavistic reproductions of not only savage men but also the most ferocious carnivores and rodents . . . these beings are members of not our species but the species of bloodthirsty beasts" (348).[1] Lombroso dehumanizes criminals, envisioning them, essentially, as animalistic monsters.

Linking Mr. Hyde to a feared degenerate, Stevenson frequently uses bestial and animalistic rhetoric in describing his Gothic villain. Hyde attacks Danvers Carew "with ape-like fury" (Stevenson 46). Jekyll later describes Hyde's actions: "Hence the apelike tricks that he would play me, scrawling in my own hand blasphemies on the pages of my books, burning the letters and destroying the portrait of my father; and indeed, had it not been for his fear of death, he would long ago have ruined himself in order to involve me in the ruin" (92). Jekyll finds more animal

---

physiognomical: related to the practice of judging character from one's facial appearance.

[1]Lombroso compares the atavistic criminal to the primitive man, noting the similarities in bone structure and other physical qualities as well as "waywardness among women, low sensitivity to pain, complete absence of moral and affective sensibility, laziness, absence of remorse and foresight, great vanity, and fleeting, violent passions" (222).

than human in Hyde because of his destructive and unrestrained tendencies. He does note that fear of death provides mild restraint, but this is instinctual; Hyde's behavior cannot be controlled by morality. He does not care for consequence and, instead, engages in destructive behavior simply because he is a simian beast, not a human.

As Hyde's monstrosity is clearly animalistic, the novella also links monstrosity to the inhuman, essentially creating a hierarchy in which humans are superior beings to Others. Jekyll writes about Hyde: "That child of Hell had nothing human; nothing lived in him but fear and hatred" (Stevenson 90). Emotions and passions may be present within Hyde, but his existence as a being with only "fear and hatred" makes him a spawn of Satan, an inhuman monster. Mr. Utterson exclaims that Hyde

seems hardly human! Something troglodytic, shall we say? or can it be the old story of Dr. Fell? or is it the mere radiance of a foul soul that thus transpires through, and transfigures, its clay continent? The last, I think; for, O my poor old Harry Jekyll, if ever I read Satan's signature upon a face, it is on that of your new friend. (42)

Describing Hyde as "troglodytic"° suggests a reversion to a primitive state, which embodies the fear of how far degeneration can go, transforming humans into something Other, unknown, and lost centuries ago. But, after contemplating the possibilities of what Hyde actually is, Utterson concludes that he must be a creation of Satan. Utterson refers to this being visible on Hyde's face, suggesting that the sign of monstrosity, in contrast to being human, is a physical aberration.

Stevenson's Hyde is a monstrous being that lacks organic humanity. 5 His barbaric tendencies mark him as more than a degenerate man or a criminal; he is an inhuman monster. Jekyll "thought of Hyde, for all his energy of life, as of something not only hellish but inorganic. This was the shocking thing; that the slime of the pit seemed to utter cries and voices; that the amorphous dust gesticulated and sinned; that what was dead, and had no shape, should usurp the offices of life" (Stevenson 91). Here, he describes Hyde as "slime," "amorphous dust," and "dead" and, in doing so, defines characteristics of a monster as ones that completely contrast with those of a living human being. Even though they share a human body, Hyde emanates something inhuman — the "radiance of a foul soul" — that Utterson describes (42) and that is physically noted here by tangible monstrous features.

---

troglodytic: behaving in a primitive manner; like a caveman or a person deliberately ignorant and backwards.

Hyde's animalistic and unnatural qualities contribute to his rejection from society. Hyde does not fit "normal" society, as Mr. Enfield remarks: "He must be deformed somewhere; he gives a strong feeling of deformity" (Stevenson 35). Jekyll, too, describes the image of Hyde as evil having left "an imprint of deformity and decay" (81). The visual impression of deformity suggests a deviation from normalcy that is based on societal expectations. In his statement, Jekyll notices that "when I wore the semblance of Edward Hyde, none could come near to me at first without a visible misgiving of the flesh" (81). Hyde does not meet the image of acceptable society. With such a perspective, Dr. Lanyon notes that "there was something abnormal and misbegotten in the very essence of the creature . . . there was added a curiosity as to his origin, his life, his fortune and status in the world" (74–75). Hyde's animalistic and often indescribable body puts him in opposition to a more traditional, standardized image of man, one who cannot be placed or truly known. In this way, Mr. Hyde is assumed to be Other, and the disgust that the other characters feel upon seeing him amounts to judgment and rejection from acceptable society.

Hyde's monstrosity is physical, behavioral (found in his cruel actions toward others and in committing murder), and moral. Robert Mighall finds that "moral monsters" include "the criminal, the degenerate, and the pervert" and were studied by the sciences of "mental pathology, criminology, and sexology" (173). Hyde's

> "Mr. Hyde is assumed to be Other, and the disgust that the other characters feel upon seeing him amounts to judgment and rejections from acceptable society."

moral monstrosity emerges in his lack of concern for others and his ease in hurting others. Enfield details the incident on the street where Hyde "trampled calmly over the child's body and left her screaming on the ground" (Stevenson 33). Hyde clearly has no care or concern for others. He has a degenerated morality or perhaps none at all. Hyde's moral monstrosity sets him apart from Jekyll, who, in his statement, says that he grew unable to handle "the horror of being Hyde" (90). Jekyll characterizes Hyde as having "moral insensibility and insensate readiness to evil" (86). Such monstrosity is characteristic of a Gothic villain, a degenerate whose mere existence threatens the social fabric of humanity for fear of widespread degenerative morality.

Truly embracing the Gothic, *The Strange Case of Dr. Jekyll and Mr. Hyde* exacerbates *fin de siècle* anxieties and raises social awareness to psychological, biological, and societal threats to humanity. Sarah D. Harris claims that "monsters are simultaneously universal and particular: they emerge from universal societal needs, including the need to exteriorize fears and build an 'us' in contrast to a 'them,' but the particular form that monsters take speaks to the specificity of a time and place" (116). Harris's reference to "us" versus "them" positions Manichean dualities of good and evil in contrast to one another. Stevenson's novel excels in establishing such oppositional forces but complicates them by putting "us" and "them" into one Jekyll/Hyde body that destabilizes notions of both human identity and social infrastructures. The monster figure is, first, timely in its ability to embody and incite *fin de siècle* anxieties and, second, timeless through its adaptations and their arousal of twentieth- and twenty-first-century concerns.

Hyde is certainly an outsider due to his monstrosity. The root of the monstrosity may affirm fears of degeneration or the effects of scientific experimentation. But Jekyll finds that Hyde originates from a bifurcated interiority—a "dual nature"—and he laments his existence because of this. He wishes, instead, that he could separate the two selves, even calling it "the curse of mankind that these incongruous faggots were thus bound together" (Stevenson 78–79). Jekyll rationalizes Hyde's social rejection by suggesting that he is the embodiment of one aspect of mankind. He claims: "[A]ll human beings, as we meet them, are commingled out of good and evil: and Edward Hyde, alone in the ranks of mankind, was pure evil" (81). Jekyll assumes he is the "good" in contrast to Hyde's "evil," presuming a superior understanding of the composition of man. Linda Dryden finds that Hyde's monstrosity is a testament to the complexity of mankind in which man can be both moral and monstrous: "Hyde is an expression of a bestiality that is part of the human condition, and the human dilemma is that the Hyde in each of us must be suppressed" (32). In this case, all humans have the capacity to be a monster—to appear as atavistic reversions of an uncontrollable version of man. Such a possibility instigates terror in the novella, as anyone could potentially turn into an inhuman beast.

Works Cited

Conolly-Smith, Peter. "The Outsider Within: *The Strange Case of Dr. Jekyll and Mr. Hyde.*" *The Image of the Outsider.* Ed. Will Wright and Steve Kaplan. Pueblo: Society for the Interdisciplinary Study of Social Imagery, 2008. 79–83. *Literature Resource Center.* 15 Jan. 2015.

Dryden, Linda. *The Modern Gothic and Literary Doubles: Stevenson, Wilde, and Wells.* New York: Palgrave Macmillan, 2003. https://doi.org/10.1057/9780230006126.

Harris, Sarah D. "The Monster Within and Without: Spanish Comics, Monstrosity, Religion, and Alterity." *Representing Multiculturalism in Comics and Graphic Novels.* Ed. Carolene Ayaka and Ian Hague. New York: Routledge, 2015. 113–29.

Lombroso, Cesare. *Criminal Man.* 1876. Trans. and Introd. Mary Gibson and Nicole Hahn Rafter. Durham: Duke UP, 2006.

Mighall, Robert. *A Geography of Victorian Gothic Fiction: Mapping History's Nightmares.* Oxford: Oxford UP, 1999.

Nordau, Max. *Degeneration.* 1895. New York: Fertig, 1968.

Stevenson, Robert Louis. *The Strange Case of Dr. Jekyll and Mr. Hyde.* 1886. Toronto: Broadview, 2005.

Understanding the Text

1. McCrystal states that *The Strange Case of Dr. Jekyll and Mr. Hyde* is horrifying because it shows the "psychological capacity for an individual to unleash repressed monstrosity" (par. 1). How does this happen within Stevenson's story?

2. What is important about Stevenson's comparison of Hyde to animal behavior? Does it advance an understanding or a misunderstanding of Hyde?

3. Why is Hyde unable to fit into normal human society? Be specific.

4. McCrystal's essay relies on multiple research sources. How does she integrate her research into her argument? That is, how does she retain control of her own analysis while still supplying evidence from others? Examine her use of quotations and paraphrases in formulating your response as it can be a model for your own academic writing.

Reflection and Response

5. McCrystal states, "Degenerates are abnormal because they do not have a moral code" (par. 2). What implications does that have for the understanding of the monster, especially as it relates to religious or ethical boundaries that often limit human action?

6. McCrystal argues, "Hyde exists as a Gothic villain who embodies the abject living conditions of the working class and the threat of degeneration and biologically inherited criminality" (par. 1). How is the story of *Jekyll and Hyde* connected to questions of social and economic class?

Making Connections

7. McCrystal quotes Linda Dryden: "Hyde is an expression of a bestiality that is part of the human condition, and the human dilemma is that the Hyde in each of us must be suppressed" (par. 9). In other words, everyone is capable of evil because we still have an animalistic side. How is this reflected in other monster stories, such as Elizabeth A. Lawrence's discussion of the werewolf (p. 205) in which the human is overwhelmed by the animalistic? How is the issue of freedom (as discussed in Cohen, p. 184) connected to this animalistic behavior?

8. Research the practice of physiognomy, which was a popular practice in the nineteenth century. Show how this practice has been used not only by Stevenson in *Jekyll and Hyde* but in other monster stories as well. Cite examples from contemporary works as well as older ones.

The Lure of Horror

Christian Jarrett

Taken from the view of evolutionary psychology, fear of monsters may well have kept us alive over time. Although monsters such as vampires and werewolves may seem to have distinct cultural origins, perhaps our fears predate any culture — they may come from a time when humans were more likely to be prey than predator. The strangeness of monsters makes them remarkable and memorable so that we might better recognize and escape them. Thus, the true power of the monster might be that it helps us survive in the real world. Among his many writing credits, Christian Jarrett is the author of *30-Second Psychology: The 50 Most Thought-Provoking Psychology Theories, Each Explained in Half a Minute* (2011), *The Rough Guide to Psychology: An Introduction to Human Behaviour and the Mind* (2011), and *Great Myths of the Brain* (2014). He is also a staff writer for the *Psychologist*, which published this article in its November 2011 issue.

Fear coils in your stomach and clutches at your heart. It's an unpleasant emotion we usually do our best to avoid. Yet across the world and through time people have been drawn irresistibly to stories designed to scare them. Writers like Edgar Allen Poe, H.P. Lovecraft, Stephen King, and Clive Barker continue to haunt the popular consciousness. Far longer ago, listeners sat mesmerized by violent, terrifying tales like *Beowulf* and Homer's *Odyssey*.

"If you go to your video store and rent a comedy from Korea, it's not going to make any sense to you at all," says literature scholar Mathias Clasen based at Aarhus University, "whereas if you rent a local horror movie from Korea you'll instantly know not just that it's a horror movie, but you'll have a physiological reaction to it, indicative of the genre."

Why Is Horror the Way It Is?

Fresh from a study visit to the Center for Evolutionary Psychology at the University of California, Santa Barbara, Clasen believes the timeless, cross-cultural appeal of horror fiction says something important about humans, and in turn, insights from evolutionary psychology can make sense of why horror takes the form it does. "You can use horror fiction and its lack of historical and cultural variance as an indication that there is such a thing as human nature," he says.

This nature of ours is one that has been shaped over millennia to be afraid, but not just of anything. Possibly our ancestors' greatest fear was that they might become a feast for a carnivorous predator. As science writer David Quammen has put it, "among the earliest forms of human self-awareness was the awareness of being meat." There's certainly fossil evidence to back this up, suggesting that early hominids were preyed on by carnivores and that they scavenged from the kill sites of large felines, and vice versa. Modern-day hunter-gatherers, such as the Aché foragers in Paraguay, still suffer high mortality rates from snakes and feline attacks.

Such threats have left their marks on our cognitive development. 5 Research by Nobuo Masataka and others shows that children as young as three are especially fast at spotting snakes, as opposed to flowers, on a computer screen, and all the more so when those snakes are poised to strike. Modern-day threats, such as cars and guns, do not grab the attention in this way. That we're innately fearful of atavistic° threats is known as "prepared learning." Another study published just this year by Christof Koch and his team has shown how the right amygdala, a brain region involved in fear learning, responds more vigorously to the sight of animals than to other pictures such as of people, landmarks or objects.

Viewing the content of horror fiction through the prism of evolutionary evidence and theory, it's no surprise that the overriding theme of many tales is that the characters are at risk of being eaten. "Do we have many snakes or snake-like creatures or giant serpents in horror fiction?" Clasen asks. "Yes we do: look at *Tremors* — they were really just very big snakes with giant fangs." In fact, many horror books and movie classics feature oversized carnivorous predators, including James Herbert's *The Rats*, Shaun Hutson's *Slugs*, *Cat People*, *King Kong*, and the *Jaws* franchise, to name but a few. Where the main threat is a humanoid predator, he or she will often be armed with over-sized claws (Freddy Krueger in *Nightmare on Elm Street*) or an insatiable taste for human flesh (e.g. Hannibal Lecter in the 1981 novel *Red Dragon*).

Vampires and Other Mythical Monsters

And yet, arguably, the most iconic horror monsters are not the furry or slimy toothed beasts of the natural world, but the unreal, mythical fiends that we call vampires, werewolves, zombies and ghosts. Can a psychological approach explain their enduring appeal too? On the face of it, the answer is straightforward: with the exception of ghosts, these mythical monsters are exaggerated, souped-up versions of the more realistic threats faced by our ancestors. They're strong, they're unstoppable and very, very hungry.

---

atavistic: reverting to the ancient or ancestral past.

But digging deeper, these monsters may also endure culturally because they press the right cognitive buttons. For example, just as Pascal Boyer (cited in Barrett, 2000) has argued that many religious entities thrive by being "minimally counter-intuitive"—that is, they fulfill nearly all the criteria for a given category, but violate that category in one particularly memorable, attention-grabbing fashion (a random example would be Moses and the bush that's in flames but doesn't burn)—a similar account could explain the enduring appeal of horror monsters. In this vein (ahem), vampires fit the human category in most respects, except they are undead. Ghosts are similarly person-like but have no body.

Another cognitive button pressed by horror would be our tendency to see agency where there is none, a kind of over-active theory of mind that facilitates a belief in wraiths and specters. Similarly, perhaps clowns (e.g. as in Stephen King's 1986 novel *It*) have the capacity to provoke fear because their make-up conceals their true facial emotions, thus thwarting our instinctual desire to read other people's minds through their faces (it's notable that many other horror baddies conceal their faces with masks).

There are other overlaps with religion based around the disgust-reaction   10
and the far-reaching effects of our deep-seated fear of infection. The term "psychological immune system" is used to describe findings such as that people are more prone to racial prejudice when primed with reminders of infection. In the same way that many religious practices are thought to have evolved to deal with corpses and the infectious health risks they present, the cultural origin and persistence of some mythical monsters can similarly be understood in terms of our fixation with death and infection. For example, one theory has it that the vampire myth emerged from a prescientific misinterpretation of the appearance of corpses—bloated and apparently full of fresh blood. A 16th century skeleton with a brick jammed posthumously in its jaw was uncovered recently from a mass grave near Venice. Archaeologists at the University of Florence believe the brick was intended to prevent the corpse feasting after death.

The horror creature whose popularity feeds most obviously from our fear of contagion is the unstoppable, flesh-eating automaton known as a zombie. One possible source of the zombie myth is Haiti where deceased relatives are sometimes believed to be living with their families in an undead state. Research suggests these "zombies" in reality are brain-damaged or mentally ill relatives, but a controversial suggestion made by anthropologist Wade Davis is that victims are enslaved by witch doctors using a "zombie powder" containing tetrodotoxin, a compound found in puffer fish, which can cause zombie-like symptoms such as lassitude and loss of will.

Besides its disgustingness, another feature of the zombie movie monster that exploits our cognitive machinery is known as the uncanny valley

[. . .]—that is, there's something particularly unnerving about an entity that moves jerkily in a way that's nearly human, but not quite. "Zombies also drastically reduce the moral complexity of life," says Clasen. "Zombies are unequivocally bad, they need to be killed, they need to be shot in the head. There is no moral shade of grey and that can be a pleasurable fantasy—a way to relax your mind." No wonder, in the competition to scare audiences, zombies are staggering towards dominance at the box office (recent hits including *Zombieland*, *I am Legend* and *28 Days Later*).

Does this idea, that fictional monsters tap into our evolved mental habits and fears, amount to anything other than speculation? In a 2004 paper, Hank Davis and Andrea Javor at the University of Guelph provided a simple test. They took three of the evolutionary-cognitive themes we've discussed so far—predation, contagion and violations of the person category—and had 182 participants rate 40 horror films on their successful portrayal of these features. Films that scored higher tended to have performed better at the box office. *The Exorcist*, often described as the ultimate horror film, scored highest and came out joint fifth in terms of box office revenue. "Successful horror films are those that do the best job of tapping into our evolved cognitive machinery—they exploit topics and images we already fear," says Davis.

If monsters succeed by playing on our primal fears and flicking our cognitive switches, this begs the question: which monster does it most successfully? The zombie may be clawing its way ever deeper into pop culture, but vampires probably remain the quintessential movie monster, at least according to a 2005 survey by Stuart Fischoff at California State University's Media Psychology Lab.

Fischoff's team asked 1166 people aged 6 to 91 to name their favorite 15 movie monster and the reasons for their choice. Vampires, and in particular Count Dracula, came out on top overall. The youngest age group (aged 6–25) preferred Freddy Krueger, but vampires still came in at number two. In general, younger viewers were more partial to slasher film baddies than older participants. Popular reasons for participants' choice of monster included superhuman strength, intelligence and luxuriating in evil. "Movie monsters tap into our archetypal fears that never entirely disappear no matter how mature, smart, informed and rational we think we've become," says Fischoff. "As the American cartoonist of Pogo, Walt Kelly, might have said, 'We've met the monster and he is us.'"

"We've met the monster and he is us."

But why the particular appeal of vampires? Fischoff thinks it may have to do with their sexiness. Since at least Bram Stoker's *Dracula* (but with the exception of F.W. Murnau's Nosferatu) and continuing to modern incarnations in the *True Blood* and *Twilight* series, they are, Fischoff says, ". . . inherently sexy . . . Even their act of monstrousness, neck biting and blood sucking, with or without killing, is intimate and sensuous." Other factors, according to Fischoff, include: their immortality; their fascinating, tormented characters (most of them are not simple killing machines); and the fact they often have a vestige of humanity, and can fight their impulses. "They can be 'us,'" Fischoff says, "epitomising our flirtation with our dark side, our Id, our selfish, impulse-ridden, tantruming child who battles with our adult-parent side."

Who Wants to Be Afraid?

Psychology can help explain why horror takes the persistent form that it does, but that still leaves the question of why we should want to scare ourselves through fiction in the first place. One suggestion is that, like play, it allows us to rehearse possible threatening scenarios from a position of relative safety. "Movie monsters provide us with the opportunity to see and learn strategies of coping with real-life monsters should we run into them, despite all probabilities to the contrary," says Fischoff. "A sort of covert rehearsal for . . . who knows what." Despite its fantastical elements, Clasen explains that successful horror fiction is usually realistic in its portrayals of human psychology and relationships. "That's where horror matters," Clasen says; "that's where horror can teach us something truly valuable."

Further clues come from a line of inquiry, most of it conducted in the 80s and 90s (coinciding with the rising popularity of slasher films), that looked at individual differences in horror film consumption. After all, although many people enjoy horror, most of us don't. Who are these people who pay out money to be scared? A meta-analysis of 35 relevant articles, by Cynthia Hoffner and Kenneth Levine published in 2005 in *Media Psychology*, highlights the principal relevant traits: affective response; empathy; sensation seeking; aggressiveness; gender; and age.

The more negative affect° a person reports experiencing during horror, the more likely they are to say that they enjoy the genre. Media experts like Dolf Zillmann make sense of this apparent contradiction as a kind of conversion process, whereby the pleasure comes from the relief that follows once characters escape danger. This explanation struggles to account for the appeal of slasher films, in which most characters are killed. Part of the answer must lie with meta-emotion—the way we interpret the emotional feelings we're experiencing, with some people finding pleasure in fright. Another possibility is that, for some, pleasure is derived from the sense that film victims are being punished for what the viewer considers

affect: an emotion or desire, especially influencing behavior.

to be their immoral behavior. Consistent with this, a 1993 study by Mary Oliver found that male high school viewers who endorsed traditional views on female sexuality (e.g. "it's okay for men to have sex before marriage, but not women"), were more likely to enjoy horror movie clips, especially if they involved a female victim portrayed with her lover.

Other researchers have examined related claims that female charac- 20 ters are more likely to be killed than male characters, especially if they're portrayed as sexually promiscuous. A 2009 study by Andrew Walsh and Laurier Brantford analyzed 50 slasher films released between 1960 and 2007, including the *Texas Chainsaw Massacre* and *Hatchet*. The researchers found that male characters were more likely to be victims of rapid, serious violence, whereas females were more likely to be victims of less serious, but more drawn-out violence, including confinement and stalking. Female characters were also more likely to be seen partially or fully naked, and when scenes involved a mix of sex and violence, the victim was more likely to be female. "Frequent depictions of women in prolonged states of terror may reinforce traditional gender schemas of women as helpless and, as a result, may serve to normalise aggression or hostile attitudes toward women," Walsh and Brantford said.

Unsurprisingly perhaps, people with lower self-reported empathy levels are also more likely to say they enjoy horror films. However, this literature is hampered by conflicting findings depending on whether one includes or omits films that include scenes of graphic torture and violence. People who seek out intense thrills and experiences (as measured by Marvin Zuckerman's Sensation-Seeking Scale), and those who are more aggressive, are also more likely to report enjoying horror films, as are men, probably in part because they tend on average to be more aggressive and have lower empathy. [. . .]

With regard to age, there's a suggestion that enjoyment rises through childhood, peaks in adolescence and then gradually fades with age. Related to this is the "snuggle theory"—the idea that viewing horror films may be a rite of passage for young people, providing them with an opportunity to fulfill their traditional gender roles. A paper from the late 1980s by Dolf Zillmann, Norbert Mundorf and others found that male undergrads paired with a female partner (unbeknown to them, a research assistant), enjoyed a 14-minute clip from *Friday the 13th Part III* almost twice as much if she showed distress during the film. Female undergrads, by contrast, said they enjoyed the film more if their male companion appeared calm and unmoved. Moreover, men who were initially considered unattractive were later judged more appealing if they displayed courage during the film viewing. "Scary movies and monsters are just the ticket for girls to scream and hold on to a date for dear life and for the date (male or female) to be there to reassure, protect, defend and, if need be, destroy the monster," says Fischoff. "Both are playing gender roles prescribed by a culture."

Conclusion

The horror genre, as popular as ever, offers intriguing insights into our psyches and is surely ripe for further investigation. Brain-imaging technology is only just starting to be deployed to study the neural correlates of the horror experience. The notion of meta-emotion, or how some people are able to interpret negative affect as a positive experience, is another intriguing area for study. Norbert Mundorf at the University of Rhode Island, one of the scholars who studied individual differences in horror appreciation back in the 80s and 90s, admits that he and colleagues perhaps focused too much on the enjoyment of slasher films, neglecting the psychology of more subtle horror experiences, which would have been trickier to study. Looking ahead he believes that changes to the way we consume media—especially the ability to access niche material online in limitless supply—also poses new questions about our enjoyment of horror. "We need to understand how this media-rich environment affects consumption of extremely violent and disturbing content," he says. "In particular, one would expect that it provides unlimited material for those high in sensation-seeking. New research approaches would benefit from analysing media consumption in this virtually unlimited virtual environment."

Another intriguing angle for the future is whether insights from psychology could help guide horror writers and producers to develop even scarier material. Clasen believes most successful horror writers have an intuitive insight into human psychology—"H.P. Lovecraft, for example, had a solid grasp of human biology and psychology and used that in stories to creep people out"—but he agrees the ultimate horror story has yet to be told. It's when the day comes that there is no horror fiction, if it ever does, that we should probably worry. As Arthur Conan Doyle wrote, "Where there is no imagination there is no horror."

Bibliography

Barrett, J.L. (2000). Exploring the natural foundations of religion. *Trends in Cognitive Sciences, 4*, 29–34.

Clasen, M. (2010). The horror! The horror! *The Evolutionary Review, 1*, 112–119.

Clasen, M. (in press). Monsters evolve: A bio-cultural theory of horror stories. *Review of General Psychology.*

Clasen, M. (2012). "Can't sleep, clowns will eat me": Telling scary stories. In C. Gansel & D. Vanderbeke (Eds.) *Telling stories: Literature and evolution.* Berlin: de Gruyter.

Davis, H. & Javor, A. (2004). Religion, death and horror movies. Some striking evolutionary parallels. *Evolution and Cognition, 10*, 11–18.

Fischoff, S., Dimopoulus, A., Nguyen, F. & Gordon, R. (2005). The psychological appeal of movie monsters. *Journal of Media Psychology, 10,* 1–33.

Freud, S. (1919/1955). The uncanny. In J. Strachey (Ed.) *Standard edition of the complete psychological works of Sigmund Freud* (pp. 219–256). London: Hogarth Press.

Hoffner, C.A. & Levine, K.J. (2005). Enjoyment of mediated fright and violence: A meta-analysis. *Media Psychology, 7,* 207–237.

Ketelaar, T. (2004). Lions, tigers, and bears, oh God! How the ancient problem of predator detection may lie beneath the modern link between religion and horror. *Behavioral and Brain Sciences, 27,* 740–741.

Masataka, N., Hayakawa, S. & Kawai, N. (2010). Human young children as well as adults demonstrate "superior" rapid snake detection when typical striking posture is displayed by the snake. *PLoS ONE, 5,* e15122.

Mori, M. (1970). The uncanny valley. *Energy, 7,* 33–35.

Mormann, F., Dubois, J., Kornblith, S. et al. (in press). A category-specific response to animals in the right human amygdala. *Nature Neuroscience.*

Oliver, M.B. (1993). Adolescents' enjoyment of graphic horror. Effects of viewers' attitudes and portrayals of victim. *Communication Research, 20,* 30–50.

Quammen, D. (2004). *Monster of God.* New York: W.W. Norton.

Steckenfinger, S.A. & Ghazanfar, A.A. (2009). Monkey visual behaviour falls into the uncanny valley. *PNAS, 106,* 18362–18366.

Straube, T., Preissler, S., Lipka, J. et al. (2010). Neural representation of anxiety and personality during exposure to anxiety-provoking and neutral scenes from scary movies. *Human Brain Mapping, 31,* 36–47.

Tudor, A. (1997). Why horror? The peculiar pleasures of a popular genre. *Cultural Studies, 11,* 443–463.

Welsh, A. & Brantford, L. (2009). Sex and violence in the slasher horror film: A content analysis of gender differences in the depiction of violence. *Journal of Criminal Justice and Popular Culture, 16,* 1–25.

Zillmann, D., Weaver, J.B., Mundorf, N. & Aust, C.F. (1986). Effects of an opposite-gender companion's affect to horror on distress, delight, and attraction. *Journal of Personality and Social Psychology, 51,* 586–594.

Understanding the Text

1. What does Jarrett mean when he says, "Another cognitive button pressed by horror would be our tendency to see agency where there is none" (par. 9)?

2. How does religion overlap with our fear of monsters, according to Jarrett? Explain.

3. What is the "uncanny valley" (par. 12)? Where does this idea come from, and what are its implications?

4. How does the experience of viewing horror films encourage traditional gender roles by the spectators?

5. Although this article is not from a peer-reviewed journal and does not contain extensive in-text citations, it does nevertheless have a list of sources labeled "Bibliography." What is the value of such a list, especially since it includes works that are not specifically referred to in the article?

Reflection and Response

6. As quoted by Jarrett, Fischoff argues, "Movie monsters provide us with the opportunity to see and learn strategies of coping with real-life monsters should we run into them, despite all probabilities to the contrary" (par. 17). Argue how exposure to fictional monsters may have real-life value. Give examples.

7. One observation that Jarrett makes is that although horror films are popular, they are not the most popular, and indeed many people dislike them. Why do some people enjoy being afraid and others do not? Consider the psychology behind fear in your response.

Making Connections

8. One argument Jarrett makes for the lure of horror is that it connects to the horror of being prey, not predator. Research the far past of the human species. How might our early human experiences have shaped our psychology to give us the power to survive today's real-world monsters?

9. Jarrett refers to Wade Davis's argument that in Haiti, people were turned into "zombies" through poisonous substances taken from puffer fish. This argument supports Matt Kaplan's "Cursed by a Bite" (p. 91), in which he presents a similar argument. Research the use of chemicals to induce a trance-like state by which people can be enslaved. Based on your research, do you find these arguments to be credible or not?

10. Jarrett reports on a study that showed that people with traditional values were more likely to be fans of horror than people with nontraditional values. Recall that Stephen King also argued in "Why We Crave Horror Films" (p. 16) that conservatives were more drawn to horror than liberals. Do you agree with these observations? Support your response.

Marco Bottigelli/Getty Images

5 | Is the Monster within Us?

T here is a certain comfort in the concept of the Other, that indescribable thing that commits such horrible atrocities and is so very different from us. But nowhere in literature are there vampires, werewolves, aliens, or other monsters that can destroy and kill with the ferocity — and senselessness — of real-life humans. Indeed, at times we are the monsters. How can we account for the actions of human monsters such as serial killers, cannibals, murderous autocrats, and others who do things that go far beyond the realm of what is typically termed "human"? The psychology of a serial killer, the rationalizations of a cannibal, the bloodlust of a tyrant — these are characteristics of monsters that might make even Count Dracula return to his coffin in revulsion.

Within the memory of many people still living today was one of the most horrific examples of the savage human monster. Adolf Hitler, writing in jail after a failed attempt to overthrow the German government in 1925, outlined his belief in racial superiority in his book *Mein Kampf* ("my struggle"). In the selection included in this chapter, he explains how the race he deemed superior must not only reject association with lower races but should eliminate them as well. His ravings were ignored by many at the time, but he would eventually put his words into action during the Holocaust leading up to and lasting throughout World War II. Turning to the monsters of today, the Christian ethicist Patrick McCormick bemoans the tendency to create nonhuman monsters — aliens, dragons, and beasts — that people revel in killing. As he points out, on some level we identify and sympathize with monsters possessing human qualities, such as Frankenstein's creature, werewolves, and vampires, but we don't think twice about blasting aliens and other nonhuman monsters to smithereens. These attitudes can carry over into real life, as people become less tolerant and accepting of marginalized people and their struggles. Thomas Fahy recounts how the murder of a family in tiny Holcomb, Kansas, caught the interest of Truman Capote, who turned the story into the shocking true-crime novel

photo: Marco Bottigelli/Getty Images

In Cold Blood. Capote's interest, however, was not in the suspense of the detectives tracking down the killers, but in the effects the crime had on the people of that small town, whose lives were radically changed by the realization that there was a monster in their midst. Crime reporter Anne E. Schwartz looks at another killer wearing the mask of normalcy. Living in Milwaukee, Wisconsin, Jeffrey Dahmer did not look the part of a serial killer and cannibal, but that's exactly what he was. Schwartz gives an exciting, detailed account of Dahmer's arrest, as well as a look into the mind of this most unusual monster. Richard Tithecott continues the theme of Dahmer being an "Average Joe" on the surface and explores how masks — such as the blank white mask of Michael Myers, the hockey mask of Jason in *Friday the 13th*, and the placid face of Dahmer — hide the truth. Dahmer was as much a zombie as a serial killer, going through the same mechanical motions with the bodies of all his victims. Philosophy professor William Andrew Myers examines the challenge presented by what he calls "extreme perpetrators" — people whose actions are beyond the pale of normal bad behavior. Looking at the murderous dictator, serial killer, and ideological killer, Myers analyzes how they represent a moral challenge for us. He argues that we do a disservice to ourselves if we see them as the Other, pushing them aside as being barely human. When we dismiss such people, we fail to see the origins of evil in the world. Finally, Kevin Berger conducts an interview with Stephen T. Asma (see also Asma, p. 59) about the role that monsters — both real and fictional — play in our world today. Asma, a professor of philosophy, talks about the meanings of monsters, their origins, and the purpose they still serve in our (supposedly) more rational, scientific times.

Human monsters are the greatest monsters of them all, for they are real and therefore the most dangerous. We can attribute evil qualities to a Siren or Slender Man, wonder at mermaids or supersmart robots, fear Dr. Frankenstein's creature or a werewolf in the woods, or be awed or disgusted by vampires or zombies, but in the end, the greatest challenge is to confront the human monster, to explore what it means to be human in all its various forms.

Nation and Race

Adolf Hitler

Few human beings have ever had as immense an impact on the human race as Adolf Hitler. After Germany's humiliating defeat in World War I and the passage of the economically ruinous Treaty of Versailles, Hitler was able to take advantage of national resentment to come to power, rebuild the German war machine, and launch a new war largely targeted at those he considered weaker than his own race. By the end of the war, nearly fifty million people had died in the European theater. Among the casualties were nine million people who had died in concentration camps, including six million Jews and three million Communists, Gypsies, homosexuals, disabled persons, and others. What sort of monster would do these things? In this excerpt from Hitler's book *Mein Kampf* (1925), which he began writing in jail after a failed coup attempt against the German government, he explains his brutal philosophy by which the strong must by necessity conquer the weak.

There are some truths which are so obvious that for this very reason they are not seen or at least not recognized by ordinary people. They sometimes pass by such truisms as though blind and are most astonished when someone suddenly discovers what everyone really ought to know. Columbus's eggs° lie around by the hundreds of thousands, but Columbuses are met with less frequently.

Thus men without exception wander about in the garden of Nature; they imagine that they know practically everything and yet with few exceptions pass blindly by one of the most patent principles of Nature's rule: the inner segregation of the species of all living beings on this earth.

Even the most superficial observation shows that Nature's restricted form of propagation and increase is an almost rigid basic law of all the innumerable forms of expression of her vital urge. Every animal mates only with a member of the same species. The titmouse seeks the titmouse, the finch the finch, the stork the stork, the field mouse the field mouse, the dormouse the dormouse, the wolf the she-wolf, etc.

Only unusual circumstances can change this, primarily the compulsion of captivity or any other cause that makes it impossible to mate within the same species. But then Nature begins to resist this with all possible means, and her most visible protest consists either in refusing further capacity for propagation to bastards or in limiting the fertility of later offspring; in most cases, however, she takes away the power of resistance to disease or hostile attacks.

Columbus's eggs: brilliant ideas or discoveries that seem obvious afterward.

This is only too natural. ⁵

Any crossing of two beings not at exactly the same level produces a medium between the level of the two parents. This means: the offspring will probably stand higher than the racially lower parent, but not as high as the higher one. Consequently, it will later succumb° in the struggle against the higher level. Such mating is contrary to the will of Nature for a higher breeding of all life. The precondition for this does not lie in associating

> "The stronger must dominate and not blend with the weaker, thus sacrificing his own greatness."

superior and inferior, but in the total victory of the former. The stronger must dominate and not blend with the weaker, thus sacrificing his own greatness. Only the born weakling can view this as cruel, but he after all is only a weak and limited man; for if this law did not prevail, any conceivable higher development of organic living beings would be unthinkable.

The consequence of this racial purity, universally valid in Nature, is not only the sharp outward delimitation of the various races, but their uniform character in themselves. The fox is always a fox, the goose a goose, the tiger a tiger, etc., and the difference can lie at most in the varying measure of force, strength, intelligence, dexterity, endurance, etc., of the individual specimens. But you will never find a fox who in his inner attitude might, for example, show humanitarian tendencies toward geese, as similarly there is no cat with a friendly inclination toward mice.

Therefore, here, too, the struggle among themselves arises less from inner aversion than from hunger and love. In both cases, Nature looks on calmly, with satisfaction, in fact. In the struggle for daily bread all those who are weak and sickly or less determined succumb, while the struggle of the males for the female grants the right or opportunity to propagate only to the healthiest. And struggle is always a means for improving a species' health and power of resistance and, therefore, a cause of its higher development.

If the process were different, all further and higher development would cease and the opposite would occur. For, since the inferior always predominates numerically over the best, if both had the same possibility of preserving life and propagating, the inferior would multiply so much more rapidly that in the end the best would inevitably be driven into the background, unless a correction of this state of affairs were undertaken. Nature does just this by subjecting the weaker part of such severe living conditions that by them alone the number is limited, and by not

---

succumb: to yield to a superior power; to die as a result of destructive forces.

permitting the remainder to increase promiscuously,° but making a new and ruthless choice according to strength and health.

No more than Nature desires the mating of weaker with stronger indi- 10
viduals, even less does she desire the blending of a higher with a lower race, since, if she did, her whole work of higher breeding, over perhaps hundreds of thousands of years, might be ruined with one blow.

Historical experience offers countless proofs of this. It shows with terrifying clarity that in every mingling of Aryan° blood with that of lower peoples the result was the end of the cultured people. North America, whose population consists in by far the largest part of Germanic elements who mixed but little with the lower colored peoples, shows a different humanity and culture from Central and South America, where the predominantly Latin immigrants often mixed with the aborigines on a large scale. By this one example, we can clearly and distinctly recognize the effect of racial mixture. The Germanic inhabitant of the American continent, who has remained racially pure and unmixed, rose to be master of the continent; he will remain the master as long as he does not fall a victim to defilement of the blood.

The result of all racial crossing is therefore in brief always the following:

(a) Lowering of the level of the higher race;

(b) Physical and intellectual regression and hence the beginning of a slowly but surely progressing sickness.

To bring about such a development is, then, nothing else but to sin against the will of the eternal creator.

And as a sin this act is rewarded.

When man attempts to rebel against the iron logic of Nature, he comes 15
into struggle with the principles to which he himself owes his existence as a man. And this attack must lead to his own doom.

Here, of course, we encounter the objection of the modern pacifist, as truly Jewish in its effrontery as it is stupid! "Man's rôle is to overcome Nature!"

Millions thoughtlessly parrot this Jewish nonsense and end up by really imagining that they themselves represent a kind of conqueror of Nature; though in this they dispose of no other weapon than an idea, and at that such a miserable one, that if it were true no world at all would be conceivable.

But quite aside from the fact that man has never yet conquered Nature in anything, but at most has caught hold of and tried to lift one or

---

promiscuously: indiscriminately; not restricted to one class or sort of person.
Aryan: a word used by the Nazis to indicate non-Jewish Caucasians, especially those having Nordic features.

another corner of her immense gigantic veil of eternal riddles and secrets, that in reality he invents nothing but only discovers everything, that he does not dominate Nature, but has only risen on the basis of his knowledge of various laws and secrets of Nature to be lord over those other living creatures who lack this knowledge—quite aside from all this, an idea cannot overcome the preconditions for the development and being of humanity, since the idea itself depends only on man. Without human beings there is no human idea in this world, therefore, the idea as such is always conditioned by the presence of human beings and hence of all the laws which created the precondition for their existence.

And not only that! Certain ideas are even tied up with certain men. This applies most of all to those ideas whose content originates, not in an exact scientific truth, but in the world of emotion, or, as it is so beautifully and clearly expressed today, reflects an "inner experience." All these ideas, which have nothing to do with cold logic as such, but represent only pure expressions of feeling, ethical conceptions, etc., are chained to the existence of men, to whose intellectual imagination and creative power they owe their existence. Precisely in this case the preservation of these definite races and men is the precondition for the existence of these ideas. Anyone, for example, who really desired the victory of the pacifistic idea in this world with all his heart would have to fight with all the means at his disposal for the conquest of the world by the Germans; for, if the opposite should occur, the last pacifist would die out with the last German, since the rest of the world has never fallen so deeply as our own people, unfortunately, has for this nonsense so contrary to Nature and reason. Then, if we were serious, whether we liked it or not, we would have to wage wars in order to arrive at pacifism. This and nothing else was what Wilson, the American world savior, intended, or so at least our German visionaries believed—and thereby his purpose was fulfilled.

In actual fact the pacifistic-humane idea is perfectly all right perhaps 20 when the highest type of man has previously conquered and subjected the world to an extent that makes him the sole ruler of this earth. Then this idea lacks the power of producing evil effects in exact proportion as its practical application becomes rare and finally impossible. Therefore, first struggle and then we shall see what can be done. Otherwise mankind has passed the high point of its development and the end is not the domination of any ethical idea but barbarism and consequently chaos. At this point someone or other may laugh, but this planet once moved through the ether for millions of years without human beings and it can do so again some day if men forget that they owe their higher existence, not to the ideas of a few crazy ideologists, but to the knowledge and ruthless application of Nature's stern and rigid laws.

Everything we admire on this earth today—science and art, technology and inventions—is only the creative product of a few peoples and originally perhaps of *one* race. On them depends the existence of this whole culture. If they perish, the beauty of this earth will sink into the grave with them.

However much the soil, for example, can influence men, the result of the influence will always be different depending on the races in question. The low fertility of a living space may spur the one race to the highest achievements; in others it will only be the cause of bitterest poverty and final undernourishment with all its consequences. The inner nature of peoples is always determining for the manner in which outward influences will be effective. What leads the one to starvation trains the other to hard work.

All great cultures of the past perished only because the originally creative race died out from blood poisoning.

The ultimate cause of such a decline was their forgetting that all culture depends on men and not conversely; hence that to preserve a certain culture the man who creates it must be preserved. This preservation is bound up with the rigid law of necessity and the right to victory of the best and stronger in this world.

Those who want to live, let them fight, and those who do not want to fight in this world of eternal struggle do not deserve to live.   25

Even if this were hard—that is how it is! Assuredly, however, by far the harder fate is that which strikes the man who thinks he can overcome Nature, but in the last analysis only mocks her. Distress, misfortune, and diseases are her answer.

The man who misjudges and disregards the racial laws actually forfeits the happiness that seems destined to be his. He thwarts the triumphal march of the best race and hence also the precondition for all human progress, and remains, in consequence, burdened with all the sensibility of man, in the animal realm of helpless misery.

Understanding the Text

1. What does Hitler mean by using the analogy that animals mate only with animals of their own species? How does he jump from species to race?

2. What does Hitler say happens when a higher-level race mates with a lower-level race? Why, in his view, is this bad for the higher race?

3. What does Hitler mean when he argues that man has not conquered nature?

4. Hitler relies heavily on the use of analogy in this excerpt. What are the advantages of using analogies in arguments? What are some of the drawbacks?

Reflection and Response

5. What is the logical fallacy that occurs when Hitler compares the segregation of animals by species and the segregation of humans by ethnicity? How does that affect the rest of his argument? To what extent does the idea that different races of humans represent different species underlie his entire philosophy?

6. A key part of Hitler's argument rests on observations of nature. In fact, he argues that humans are subject to nature and cannot escape it. Yet much of the Judeo-Christian tradition calls on humans to rise above their animalistic tendencies. How does Hitler's philosophy serve as a justification for his later, monstrous actions, such as the Holocaust?

7. Many of the readings in this book broadly define a monster as something "unnatural" or "different," yet Hitler's entire argument is based on his view of nature and sameness. What do you make of this contradiction?

Making Connections

8. Research the Holocaust, which involved the systematic execution of more than nine million people, including more than six million Jews. How did the philosophy described in this passage justify the extermination of so many? What is the difference between the destruction wrought by Hitler and that caused by many of the monsters described in previous chapters of this book?

9. Hitler states, "All great cultures of the past perished only because the originally creative race died out from blood poisoning" (par. 23). Research some of the great civilizations of the past and argue whether this statement is true or not.

Why Modern Monsters Have Become Alien to Us

Patrick McCormick

A professor of religious studies at Gonzaga University, Patrick McCormick teaches and speaks regularly on issues of social justice. Since 1994, he has written a regular column on Christianity and character for *U.S. Catholic*, the magazine in which this selection originally appeared. His other publications include *Sin as Addiction* (1989) and *A Banqueter's Guide to the All-Night Soup Kitchen of the Kingdom of God* (2004). In this article, McCormick argues that, traditionally, monsters have been warped manifestations of ourselves. Creatures such as Count Dracula, Frankenstein's monster, and the Hunchback of Notre Dame have an element of humanity with which we identify. We can, in fact, even find ourselves sympathizing with them. McCormick points out that today's monsters — often aliens — have no trace of humanity, which allows us to cheer unabashedly as they are destroyed. The effect of this disconnection may be to lessen our own sensitivity to people in the real world who are in need of comfort and understanding.

Late autumn has arrived and with it comes the dark magic of Halloween — and, of course, the murky thrill of monsters. Yet our appetite for a good monster knows no season. Ever since ancient times we have been fascinated with all sorts of tales about monsters and intrigued by myths and legends about those wild half-human beasts who haunt the edges of our forests and lurk in the recesses of our oceans. The sphinxes, Minotaurs, and Sirens of early mythology gave way to Beowulf's Grendel and Saint George's dragon, then to the mermaids, trolls, and one-eyed giants of our fairy and folk tales, and finally to those 19th-century Gothic classics. Nor are these stories on the wane, for the monster tales that made Lon Chaney, Boris Karloff, and Bela Lugosi stars of the silver screen continue to draw megacrowds six and seven decades later.

In 1994 Kenneth Branagh and Robert De Niro brought us [a] reincarnation of Shelley's story of Frankenstein's tortured creature, and Tom Cruise and Brad Pitt starred in *Interview with the Vampire*, the first installment of Anne Rice's homage to Stoker's *Dracula*. Meanwhile, Andrew Lloyd Webber's musical production of Gaston Leroux's *Phantom of the Opera* continues to pack in audiences from London to L.A.

Much of the initial appeal of monster stories comes from the fact that they, like their twisted siblings, "creature features" and "slashers," both terrify and fascinate us with their ghoulish brand of horror. It's the rattling-the-tiger's-cage kind of thrill that Scout and Jem Finch got from sneaking onto Boo Radley's° porch under a pale moon. Reading or watching great monster stories, we get to accompany the frightened heroes or heroines as they descend into the dragon's lair; crane our necks over the tops of books or movie seats and peek into the dank recesses of the giant cyclops' cave; stretch out our trembling hands and actually touch the monster's reptilian scales, hairy paws, or cloven hoofs; and then run screaming like a banshee the instant it wakes from its slumber. What a rush!

> "[In] classic monster stories we are also haunted by an underlying sense of sympathy — and, yes, responsibility — for these misshapen men."

As frightening as these creatures are, in monster stories it is always the beast that ends up taking the fall, which means that this is a place where we not only get to tangle with evil's most daunting and dangerous minions but to vanquish them with regularity. Pretty heady stuff. No wonder we never seem to tire of these tales.

And yet the truth is that the best of these stories are much more than 5 simple-minded creature features. In the original versions of *Frankenstein, The Hunchback of Notre Dame, Phantom of the Opera, Jekyll & Hyde,* and even *Dracula* we aren't simply terrified and enraged by these ghouls trolling about in our dungeons, sewers, or bell towers. Instead, in such classic monster stories we are also haunted by an underlying sense of sympathy—and, yes, responsibility—for these misshapen men. In their deaths and destruction we experience some pathos, some tragedy, perhaps even some shred of regret for the ways they have been abused, goaded, and abandoned.

Nowhere is this so clear as in *Frankenstein.* When, at the end of Shelley's novel, her narrator, Walton, finally sets eyes on Victor Frankenstein's dreaded creature, he describes him as having "a form I cannot find words to describe; gigantic in stature, yet uncouth and distorted in its proportions. . . . Never did I behold a vision so horrible as his face, of such loathsome yet appalling hideousness. . . . I dared not again raise my eyes to his face, there was something so scaring and unearthly in his ugliness."

Still, Walton, like the reader, feels "a mixture of curiosity and compassion" toward this disfigured beast. The very monster who has murdered all of Frankenstein's loved ones is himself a tortured soul, and the strange, misshapen creature—who has studied Plutarch and read Milton— cries out to his human maker in such eloquent anguish that we cannot help being moved.

Scout and Jem Finch, and Boo Radley: characters in Harper Lee's novel *To Kill a Mockingbird* (1960).

Then, must I be hated, who am miserable beyond all living things. . . . Oh Frankenstein, be not equitable to every other, and trample upon me alone, to whom thy justice, and even thy clemency and affection, is most due. . . . Accursed creator! Why did you form a monster so hideous that even you turned from me in disgust? God, in pity, made man beautiful and alluring, after his own image; but my form is a filthy type of yours, more horrid even from the very resemblance.

At first glance, Stevenson's story of *Dr. Jekyll & Mr. Hyde* doesn't seem to invite much pity for the villain Edward Hyde, the murderous dwarf whom the character Dr. Lanyon describes as "something seizing, surprising and revolting" and who, according to Henry Jekyll, "alone in the ranks of mankind, was pure evil." Still, when Jekyll's manservant Poole hears the poor creature "weeping like a woman or a lost soul," he admits to having come "away with that upon my heart" and comments "that I could have wept too." The truth is that for all his physical and moral deformities, Hyde, too, is but "a filthy type" of his maker, a doppelgänger of Henry Jekyll, "knit to him closer than a wife, closer than an eye," and the physical manifestation of all his vile and unruly passion. And though he is not as eloquent as Frankenstein's beast, Hyde could well have quoted Milton's *Paradise Lost* to his all-too-human creator.

"Did I request thee, Maker, from my clay to mold me man? Did I solicit thee from darkness to promote me?"

And even in *Dracula* there is a trace of compassion for the monstrous   10
Prince of the Undead, the viper who takes a dozen repulsive forms. In Stoker's original narrative the vampire hunter Van Helsing, unlike so many modern action heroes, is not out simply to avenge himself against Dracula and his minions; he actually wants to redeem their lost and tortured souls. Even in visages that do not show up in mirrors, Van Helsing is capable of recognizing a shared humanity and, indeed, of feeling some pity for their frightful plight. And at the end of Stoker's novel, Mina Harker, who has more than enough reason to despise this foul creature of the underworld and to savor his destruction, describes Dracula's death with a note of unrestrained sympathy. "I shall be glad as long as I live that even in that moment of final dissolution, there was in the face a look of peace, such as I never could have imagined rested there." Stoker's vampire is not so much murdered as forgiven.

These stories, again and again, remind us that in biology and myth monsters are disfigured versions of ourselves, fun-house mirrors of our own frail and sometimes monstrous humanity. Monster stories, then, by confronting us with these disfigured embodiments of ourselves, invite us to reflect on our own humanity, and, indeed, our inhumanity. In a way that is not so very different from Luke's parable of the Good Samaritan, these Gothic tales challenge us to recognize the humanity of the beast and to acknowledge the beastliness of our own inhumanity. Indeed, the best of them are reminders and warnings about the ways in which we make and become such beasts.

Victor Hugo's 1831 classic *The Hunchback of Notre Dame* (so pathetically sanitized in Disney's [1996] animated version) may be one of the best modern monster stories we have. Even the name of the misshapen bell ringer, Quasimodo, tells us that this brutish creature is but "half-formed," and, like Frankenstein's beast, Hugo's disfigured monster seems cruelly fashioned of mismatched parts, his body a tortured terrain, his face a terrifying visage. As one critic writes:

Nowhere on earth was there a more grotesque creature. One of his eyes was buried under an enormous cyst. His teeth hung over his protruding lower lips like tusks. His eyebrows were red bristles, and his gigantic nose curved over his upper lip like a snout. His long arms protruded from his shoulders, dangling like an ape's.

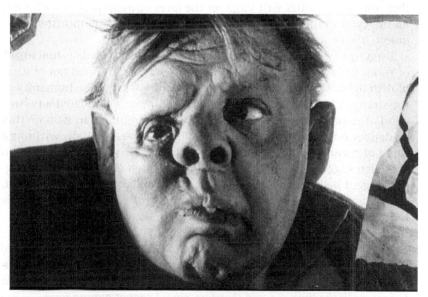

Quasimodo, as portrayed by Charles Laughton in the 1939 film, *The Hunchback of Notre Dame*.
Photo 12/Alamy Stock Photo

Further, not unlike Stevenson's brutal Hyde, Quasimodo is a henchman of the night, a stalker of darkened alleys, and a hunter of women,
finding cover by day deep within the bowels of Notre Dame. Here, it
seems, is a fiend to haunt the nightmares of children and whip mobs
into a fury.

Still, as Hugo's narrative unfolds, it is not Quasimodo but the cathedral's
archdeacon, Claude Frollo, who is revealed as the novel's real monster.
Like Frankenstein and Jekyll, the ascetic scholar and priest Frollo is a man
who cannot abide the limits of his own mortality or acknowledge the
all-too-human passions that burn within him. But Frollo's attempts to
fly above this mortal flesh, or to bury it within the cathedral's shadowy
vaults and Gothic spires, are all in vain. And in the end, it is he who
dispatches Quasimodo — his own Mr. Hyde — to stalk and kidnap the
Gypsy Esmeralda; it is he who will destroy her; and it is he who — like the
thoughtless Victor Frankenstein — cruelly abandons the tortured beast he
was sworn to protect.

The real fiends, then, in so many classic monster stories, are the   15
Frankensteins, Jekylls, and Frollos who cannot abide their own humanity
and cannot or will not show any compassion for those whose disfigured
humanity has made them outcasts. It is the men who cannot recognize
their own deformities writ large on the faces of these brutes — who feel
no mercy, no responsibility, no pity — who are the true monsters, and
indeed, the creators of monsters.

Even in *Richard III*, Shakespeare's tale of the sociopathic "Hunchback
of York," there is some reminder that monsters are fashioned not of some
brutish ugliness but of our own failure to acknowledge the humanity of
the stranger. In Richard of Gloucester Shakespeare has created a twisted
fiend of unparalleled malice, a misshapen stump of a man who neither
evidences nor invites pity. Here is a Shakespearean villain without a
shred of conscience, a Renaissance Ted Bundy, Gary Gilmore, or, as Ian
McKellen suggests in his [1989] production, Adolf Hitler. But this disfigured regent believes that he has the same complaint against the world,
the same cause for rancor,° as Frankenstein's creature — which is that he
is not, and indeed cannot be, loved.

I, that am rudely stamped, and want love's majesty . . . that am curtailed of
this fair proportion, cheated of feature by dissembling nature, deformed, unfin-
ished, and sent before my time into this breathing world . . . have no delight
to pass away the time . . . and therefore, since I cannot prove a lover . . . am
determined to prove a villain." (act I, scene i)

rancor: deep-seated ill will.

Indeed, Ken Magid and Carole McKelvey argue in *High Risk: Children without a Conscience* (M & M Publishers, 1987), sociopaths are all too often the products of emotional abandonment, children who have never been able to form an attachment or bond with a loved one.

Such insights are, of course, not really so different from the central argument of monster stories like *Frankenstein.* As the creature says to his maker/parent:

I am thy creature, and I will be even mild and docile to my natural lord and king, if thou wilt also perform thy part, that which thou owest me. . . . I ought to be thy Adam, but I am rather the fallen angel, whom thou drivest from joy for no misdeed. . . . I was benevolent and good, misery made me a fiend. Make me happy, and I shall again be virtuous.

The underlying message of these stories is that monsters are made, not born, and that they are fashioned out of our inability to accept our own limits and care for others. We don't make monsters by playing God or fooling with Mother Nature. We make monsters by failing to be human and recognize and respect the humanity of others.

Maybe that's why it bothers me that monster stories seem to be being replaced by a kind of tale that has no sense of our own responsibility for evil and no compassion for the disfigured creatures who serve as the stories' foils or foes. In the '50s and '60s the monsters in most creature features were often the result of some nuclear explosion or radiation experiment gone awry and so reflected some consciousness of our guilt or anxiety about the cold war and arms race. Today, however, we seem to be facing a new breed of monstrous creatures, for whom we are invited to feel neither responsibility nor sympathy. Instead, we're just to blast those little suckers out of the sky.

In a number of films the monster in question has been a beast from 20 outer space, an alien creature to whom we are not related and who we can hunt and destroy with all the heat-seeking missiles and nuclear arsenals at our command. Meanwhile, in Michael Crichton's *Jurassic Park* (1993) we're confronted with a brood of dinosaurs from 65 million years in the past and given permission to blast and fry these reptilian sociopaths with nothing short of glee.

Nowhere, however, is this trend so evident as in [1996's] biggest blockbuster *Independence Day* — one of Bob Dole's° recommended family

---

Bob Dole, Pat Buchanan: candidates for the 1996 Republican nomination for president.

films and a feel-good movie that lets us blow the living daylights out of the meanest pack of really illegal aliens that ever came to town. What a thrill to be able to mount a nuclear Armageddon without the slightest concern about political or radioactive fallout of any sort, to finally find an enemy who it's not politically incorrect to hate, and to live in a world of such stark moral clarity and simplicity, where good and evil are so sharply polarized and where we are the absolutely innocent good guys. (Watching the movie, I thought I was at a Pat Buchanan rally.)

I confess to liking action films. Still, I am concerned about the presence of what seem to me to be some very dangerous trends leading to the production of more and more movies where evil is being projected onto an enemy so foreign and alien that it can be destroyed without any trace of regret. My concern is not just that such stories keep us unconscious of our own responsibility for evil and that movies like *Independence Day* help us forget that "the problem, dear Brutus, lies not in the stars, but in ourselves,"° but that they may well be tapping into some very unhealthy rage and bias in our culture.

When you start designing movies to be theme park rides and video games, they stop being stories. It's not that stories don't or shouldn't entertain, and it's not that stories can't have thrills and chills. But real stories, at least good stories, have depth and character and plot. They wrestle with ambiguity, conflict, even paradox; pose questions—often very unsettling ones; and are open to interpretation on various levels.

Stories inspire, upset, disturb, and haunt us. They engage, not replace, our imagination, challenge our moral sensitivities, and invite us to wrestle with the mystery of being human. They're about suffering, guilt, remorse, passion, anguish, even redemption.

Video games and theme parks, on the other hand, are about adrena- 25 line. They are engineered to stimulate the fight or flight response, and, as a rule, they're geared for 12- to 14-year-olds. Like pornography, they have the thinnest of plot lines—hunt down and kill or flee from danger—and their "characters" are strictly cartoon stuff. In the midst of an adrenaline rush you don't have the time or inclination to wonder about the moral ambiguity of this situation, or the humanity of the foe. You just duck and shoot.

The problem, dear Brutus, lies not in the stars, but in ourselves: a misquote of William Shakespeare's *Julius Caesar*, act 1, scene 2, lines 140–41: "The fault, dear Brutus, lies not in our stars, but in ourselves. . . ."

A second problem with these features is that their monsters turn out to be not so foreign after all, but rather poorly disguised surrogates of our rage against women and immigrants. You'd think [conservative radio host] Rush Limbaugh had written the scripts. In the Alien trilogy° Sigourney Weaver finds herself battling against a matriarchal colony of insect-like beasts, whose eggs she is always destroying. Indeed, in the second film *Aliens,* Weaver's major confrontation is with the queen bee of this monstrous breed, while the advertisements for *Alien 3* excitedly proclaim that "The Bitch is Back!"

Likewise, [British novelist] Marina Warner points out that the dinosaurs in *Jurassic Park* are dangerous females who outflank their keepers by figuring out how to propagate without males. In *Species* the alien is a Jackie the Ripper from outer space, a praying mantis who is looking for a good mate. The most dangerous monster in the universe, according to these films, is a woman having a child without permission. It's hard to miss the underlying rage against welfare moms and pregnant teens in these movies.

Meanwhile, in *Predator,* Arnold Schwarzenegger faces off against a murderous extraterrestrial who inhabits the jungles of Central America, and when Danny Glover confronts the alien's replacement in *Predator 2,* the monster has decided to visit Los Angeles, of all places. One wonders just which aliens these movies are talking about. In a time when so much political rage is directed at illegal aliens, it can't be all that surprising that films like *Independence Day* would be such a hit.

Finally, there is the little matter of the bomb, or bombs. Explosives are, by far and away, the most popular special effect in these video-arcade movies. It would be impossible to imagine a contemporary action film or creature feature that isn't littered with the detritus of demolitions, preferably nuclear. Not only do these toys give us the biggest bang for the buck, they are also the perfect tool for obliterating an enemy for whom we feel nothing but rage. Bombs are macho and impersonal, how perfect.

Until, of course, they start going off in the World Trade Center, in 30
front of a government building in Oklahoma, aboard a TWA flight out of New York, or at a disco outside the Olympic Village. Then bombs are murderous, insane, cowardly, craven, and—yes—monstrous.

We need to pay attention to the kinds of monster stories we tell. They could come back to haunt us.

Alien trilogy: the movies *Alien* (1979), *Aliens* (1986), and *Aliens 3* (1992), starring Sigourney Weaver as Warrant Officer Ellen Ripley.

Understanding the Text

1. What reason(s) does McCormick give for the enduring popularity of monster stories?

2. McCormick argues that in the best monster tales, we are "haunted by an underlying sense of sympathy — and, yes, responsibility — for these misshapen men" (par. 5). What specific examples of this does he provide, and how are we responsible for them?

3. Who does McCormick believe are the real villains in *Doctor Jekyll and Mr. Hyde*, *Frankenstein*, and *The Hunchback of Notre Dame*? Why?

4. McCormick says that contemporary monster movies lack a story. What does he mean? What does he think is necessary to have a story?

5. McCormick's argument can be described as an ethical argument, an argument about morality. Given that people's understanding of right and wrong can vary so widely, how does McCormick attempt to sway the reader to agree with his values?

Reflection and Response

6. McCormick states, "The underlying message of these [monster] stories is that monsters are made, not born, and that they are fashioned out of our inability to accept our own limits and care for others" (par. 18). Do you agree or disagree? Support your answer with specific examples.

7. McCormick cites aliens and dinosaurs as examples of contemporary monsters that lack humanity. Do you agree with his statement that such monsters are "rather poorly disguised surrogates of our rage against women and immigrants" (par. 26)? Include specific examples in your response.

Making Connections

8. In discussing Shakespeare's characterization of Richard III, McCormick makes a connection to real-life people he sees as monstrous: Ted Bundy, Gary Gilmore, and Adolf Hitler. What is it about these people — or others like them — that connects them to monsters? Explain your answer.

9. Update McCormick's 1996 argument about nonhuman monsters using some of today's creatures. What political messages are being sent by current representations of nonhuman monsters — zombies, aliens, dinosaurs, dragons, and the like?

Hobbes, Human Nature, and the Culture of American Violence in Truman Capote's *In Cold Blood*

Thomas Fahy

In a sleepy town in the heartland of America at the end of the 1950s, a family of four was brutally murdered for no apparent reason. When Truman Capote read about this crime in the *New York Times*, he decided to travel to Holcomb, Kansas, to investigate not only the crime, but its effects on the residents of Holcomb whose sense of peace and safety had been brutally shattered. Thomas Fahy examines how Capote wrote about the crime, not as a suspense-filled detective saga — he gave away the ending at the start of the book — but as an examination of what happens when the monstrous looks just like the normal. Thomas Fahy is the director of the English graduate program at Long Island University. He has written extensively about horror. Among his many publications are *Dining with Madmen: Fat, Food, and the Environment in 1980s Horror* (2019) and two young adult novels, *The Unspoken* (2008) and *Sleepless* (2009). This excerpt was taken from *The Philosophy of Horror* (2010), a collection of scholarly essays on horror.

The life of man [is] solitary, poor, nasty, brutish, and short.

—THOMAS HOBBES, *Leviathan*

[Men are] creatures among whose instinctual endowments is to be reckoned a powerful share of aggressiveness. As a result, their neighbor is for them not only a potential helper or sexual object, but also someone who tempts them to satisfy their aggressiveness on him, to exploit his capacity for work without compensation, to use him sexually without his consent, to seize his possessions, to humiliate him, to cause him pain, to torture and to kill him.

—SIGMUND FREUD, *Civilization and its Discontents*

My epigraphs are taken from Thomas Hobbes, *Leviathan*, ed. J. C. A. Gaskin (Oxford: Oxford University Press, 1998); and Sigmund Freud, *Civilization and Its Discontents*, trans. and ed. James Strachey (New York: Norton, 1961). [Author's Note.]

On November 15, 1959, Dick Hickock and Perry Smith drove several hundred miles to the small town of Holcomb, Kansas, and brutally murdered four members of the Clutter family. Armed with a hunting knife and a twelve-gauge shotgun, the two men entered the house through an unlocked door just after midnight. They had been hoping to find a safe with thousands of dollars, but when Herb Clutter denied having one, they tied him up and gagged him. They did the same to his wife, Bonnie, his fifteen-year-old son, Kenyon, and his sixteen-year-old daughter, Nancy. Afterward, they placed each of them in separate rooms and searched the house for themselves. When they found no more than forty dollars, Smith slit Herb Clutter's throat and shot him in the face. He then proceeded to execute the rest of the family. Each one died from a point-blank shotgun wound to the head.

One month later, Truman Capote, who had first read about these crimes in the *New York Times,* arrived in Holcomb with his longtime friend, the author Nelle Harper Lee.[1] Both the horrifying details of the murders and the strangeness of the place appealed to Capote. Everything about Kansas—the landscape, dialect, social milieu, and customs—was completely alien to him, and he was energized by the prospect of trying to capture this world in prose. He recognized that the case might never be solved, since the police had no clues about the identity of Hickock and Smith at the time, but that didn't concern him. He primarily wanted to write about the impact of these horrific killings on the town. As biographer Gerald Clarke explains, Capote was less interested in the murders than in their potential "effect on that small and isolated community."[2] Six years later, after the execution of Hickock and Smith, he completed his "nonfiction novel" *In Cold Blood: A True Account of a Multiple Murder and Its Consequences*—a work that offers a chilling portrait of violence and fear in American culture.

But why is this book so terrifying? Before reading the first page, we know the outcome. Even if we haven't heard of the Clutter family, the description on the back of the book tells us that there is no mystery here. Capote even announces as much at the end of the first short chapter: "four shotgun blasts that, all told, ended six human lives." We know the Clutters will die and that the killers will be caught and executed. So what makes Capote's narrative so frightening and unsettling? The author gives some clue in the next sentence: "But afterward the townspeople, theretofore sufficiently unfearful of each other to seldom trouble to lock their

---

[1]Harper Lee's novel, *To Kill a Mockingbird,* was finished at the time but not yet published.
[2]Gerald Clarke, *Capote: A Biography* (New York: Carroll & Graff, 2005), 319.

doors, found fantasy re-creating them over and again—those somber explosions that stimulated fires of mistrust in the glare of which many old neighbors viewed each other strangely, and as strangers."[3] In Capote's rendering of this event, we, too, re-create "those somber explosions" and share in the fearful mistrust of others. We try to grapple with what these killings suggest about human nature, and in the process our neighbors become strangers, too. They become potential threats, undermining our own sense of safety and security.

Capote's book raises several disturbing questions for the reader as well: How and why were Hickock and Smith capable of such brutality? Could you or I do such things? These questions resonate with Thomas Hobbes's philosophy about the innate aggression and brutality of human beings. His pessimistic outlook can provide some insight into the source of terror in Capote's work—that such violence, resentment, and anger are in all of us. Before discussing this connection, I will situate *In Cold Blood* in the horror genre by focusing on its use of a horrific event and the imagined encounter with the monstrous. I will then discuss Hobbes's notion of human nature and the sovereign—a figure that promises to provide moral justice and prevent mankind from being in a perpetual state of war. But what happens if this source of moral authority (the sovereign) is absent? If the veneer of civilization is removed? Capote's answer, like the one offered by Hobbes, is clear: we will all act in cold blood.

The Horror of *In Cold Blood*

The horror of *In Cold Blood* operates on several levels: its realism, the brutality of the crime, the random selection of victims (Smith and Hickock had never met the Clutters before the night of the killing), the incongruity between the primary motive (theft) and the ultimate outcome (multiple murders), the fear that swept through the state in its aftermath, and the callous indifference and lack of remorse on the part of Hickock and Smith. So can *In Cold Blood,* which promises a journalistic account of actual events, be understood in terms of the horror genre as well?

By making this connection I'm not trying to minimize the real tragedy of these crimes. I'm merely suggesting that Capote uses some of the conventions of horror, as well as the suspense/thriller genres, to craft his rendering of these events. Capote himself labeled the work a nonfiction novel, and this invites us to think about the literary devices shaping *In Cold Blood.*

5

---

[3]Truman Capote, *In Cold Blood: A True Account of a Multiple Murder and Its Consequences* (1965; reprint, New York: Vintage, 1994), 5. Subsequent page references to this work will be given parenthetically in the text.

"Journalism," he said, "always moves along a horizontal plane, telling a story, while fiction—good fiction—moves vertically, taking you deeper and deeper into character and events. By treating a real event with fictional techniques . . . it's possible to make this kind of synthesis."[4] Capote's fusion of reporting and fiction here enabled him to present Hickock and Smith's crime and its subsequent investigation as a novelist. He could make choices to create a certain effect and to manipulate the reader's response.

As suggested above, part of the momentum of *In Cold Blood* comes from the details that resonate with suspense/thriller fiction. A crime has been committed that launches a nationwide manhunt. Lead detectives work around the clock, piecing together clues and interviewing suspects in hopes of a lucky break. At one point, the special agent in charge learns that the men are back in Kansas, and the chase intensifies. But the facts of the case undermine these familiar-sounding conventions at every turn. The crime has been "solved" for the reader before the first page. The identity of the criminals is discovered by accident when Hickock's former cellmate, who told him about the Clutters in the first place, hears a radio broadcast about the murders and reveals Hickock's identity to the authorities. Smith and Hickock are caught not because of Special Agent Dewey's hard work and ingenuity; they are apprehended because of their own incompetence and arrogance. The book also suggests that Smith's abuse as a child, his family's neglect, his inability to pursue an education, and his association with people like Hickock helped shape him into a killer. Such revelations often occur in the suspense/thriller genres as well, but Capote is using them here to create sympathy for the killer—a response that complicates our response to his execution. When the people of Holcomb first see Smith and Hickock after they have been apprehended, for example, Capote notes that they all respond with stunned silence. "But when the crowd caught sight of the murderers, with their escort of blue-coated highway patrolmen, it fell silent, as though amazed to find them humanly shaped" (248). When faced with such horrible crimes, we expect the monstrous, the inhuman. Yet Capote's sympathetic characterization of Smith, in particular, makes it difficult for the reader to view him as a monster.

This is where *In Cold Blood* intersects with the horror genre as well—an encounter with the monstrous. Noël Carroll, in his influential work *The Philosophy of Horror; or, Paradoxes of the Heart,* argues that monsters are the central feature of horror. Vampires, werewolves, and zombies, for example, are recognizable threats, and the danger they pose must be destroyed/defeated to restore harmony. Monsters also elicit the emotional effect that the genre seeks—horror—because they literally embody the abnormal.

---

[4]Quoted in Clarke, *Capote,* 357.

As Carroll explains, "The objects of art-horror are essentially threatening and impure."[5] They inspire revulsion, disgust, and nausea.

A number of scholars have criticized this narrow definition, arguing that serial killers and more realistic monsters must be accounted for as well. David Russell, for example, offers a broader taxonomy for the horror genre, arguing that "some types of monsters may be explained as *'real'* . . . [in that they] are not remarkable in any physical sense. Their threat to normality is manifested solely through abnormal behavior challenging the rules of social regulation through 'monstrous' and transgressive behavior."[6] He labels these monsters "deviant"—a category that includes stalkers, slashers, and psychokillers. Critic Matt Hills also responds to Carroll's limited framework by suggesting an event-based definition of the genre (as opposed to Carroll's entity-based definition) so that "we can take in the widest possible range of texts that have been discussed as 'horror' by audiences and labeled as such by filmmakers and marketers."[7] Both of these characteristics are evident in Capote's book. As a ruthless killer, Smith is certainly a realistic monster, and the Clutter murders qualify as horrific events.

But let's return to Carroll's emphasis on monsters for a moment. Even 10 though *In Cold Blood* doesn't fit the supernatural requirements of his definition of horror, Capote does present Hickock and Smith as monstrous on physical and psychological levels. His descriptions of their anomalous, damaged bodies attempt to ascribe some physical difference to their aberrant behavior. Smith is first depicted as a man with "stunted legs that seemed grotesquely inadequate to the grown-up bulk they supported" (15), and Special Agent Dewey takes note of Smith's disproportionate body at his execution: "He remembered his first meeting with Perry in the interrogation room at Police Headquarters in Las Vegas—the dwarfish boy-man seated in the metal chair, his small booted feet not quite brushing the floor" (341). Likewise, Hickock has a tattooed body, serpentine eyes "with a venomous, sickly-blue squint," and a face "composed of mismatched parts . . . as though his head had been halved like an apple, then put together a fraction off center" (31). As a boy-man (dwarf/adult) and serpent-man (with a divided face), Smith and Hickock are hybrid figures like the monsters that typically appear in horror fiction. Their

---

[5]Noël Carroll, *The Philosophy of Horror; or, Paradoxes of the Heart* (New York: Routledge, 1990), 42.
[6]David J. Russell, "Monster Roundup: Reintegrating the Horror Genre," in *Refiguring American Film Genres: History and Theory,* ed. Nick Browne (Berkeley: University of California Press, 1998), 241.
[7]Matt Hills, "An Event-Based Definition of Art-Horror," in *Dark Thoughts: Philosophic Reflections on Cinematic Horror,* ed. Steven Jay Schneider and Daniel Shaw (Lanham, MD: Scarecrow, 2003), 138.

bodies, like their actions, violate social norms and categories (moral/ immoral, good/evil, human/inhuman), and this element resonates with Carroll's argument about monsters as repelling and compelling "because they violate standing categories."[8]

At the same time, these physical aberrations are not so pronounced that the townspeople of Holcomb can comfortably "Other" Hickock and Smith. Their bodies do not live up to the monsters whom they imagined responsible for the killings. As noted above, they initially responded to these men with stunned silence, "as though amazed to find them humanly shaped," but in many horror stories unreal monsters come in human form. The horror, in other words, resides within. Just like a serial killer who seems like a nice guy to his neighbors, werewolves "hide" inside human beings until a full moon; vampires can "pass" as human until they reveal their fangs. The notion of a threat from within is integral to the terror of *In Cold Blood*.[9] Smith isn't a werewolf or a vampire. He is a person just like us, but a killer lurks inside. Like these supernatural counterparts, he can transform at any moment from charming loner to ruthless murderer, which is evident in his confession: "I thought [Herb Clutter] was a very nice gentleman. Soft-spoken. I thought so right up to the moment I cut his throat" (244). What makes Smith so terrifying is not simply the suddenness of his transformation here, but the fact that he doesn't physically turn into a monster. At some level, the town of Holcomb, as well as the reader, fears this lack of visual otherness because it implies that *anyone* can be like Smith.

This implication also fuels fears in the community that the killer lives among them. On hearing the news of the murders, one townsperson responds: "If it wasn't him, maybe it was you. Or somebody across the street" (69). Another remarks: "What a terrible thing when neighbors can't look at each other without a kind of wondering!" (70) And even when the killers are apprehended, their suspicions don't vanish. "For the majority of Holcomb's population, having lived for seven weeks amid

---

[8]Carroll, *Philosophy of Horror*, 188.

[9]I'm using the terms *horror* and *terror* somewhat interchangeably here. Carroll argues that the presence of a literal monster distinguishes horror from works of terror, such as Edgar Allan Poe's "The Pit and the Pendulum" and "The Telltale Heart," which explore a psychological state or phenomenon. But I prefer seeing the terms as interconnected, which is the way Stephen King discusses them in *Danse Macabre*. He argues that horror operates on three levels: (1) *terror*, which comes not from seeing something terrible but from imagining it; (2) *horror*, or "the emotion of fear that underlies terror" and that is connected to a visible manifestation which is frightening; and (3) *revulsion*, or what King calls the "gross-out" (*Danse Macabre* [New York: Everest House, 1981], 35). In this paradigm, terror, which pulses through *In Cold Blood* as the town continues to imagine the crime and fears for its own safety, is the highest achievement of the horror genre.

unwholesome rumors, general mistrust, and suspicion, appeared to feel disappointed at being told that the murderer was not someone among themselves" (231). Once they admit that anyone has the potential to be a monster, they can't stop being afraid of one another.

Understanding the Text

1. Restate in your own words what the quotation from Thomas Hobbes is saying about human life.

2. Why did Truman Capote choose to reveal the outcome of the crime right from the very beginning of his book? What effect might this have had on the reader?

3. Fahy writes, "Monsters also elicit the emotional effect that the genre seeks — horror — because they literally embody the abnormal" (par. 8). How is this reflected in Dick Hickock and Perry Smith?

4. What does Fahy mean when he writes about "visual otherness" (par. 11)? How is that connected to Hickock and Smith?

5. *In Cold Blood* has been called a true-crime novel. How is truth (i.e., the real-life story of the murder of the Clutters) connected to fiction in this story? How can these opposites — truth and fiction — be resolved?

Reflection and Response

6. Capote observed that until Smith and Hickock were caught, the residents of Holcomb, Kansas, began to fear each other. Indeed, Fahy records that, in Capote's words, "old neighbors viewed each other strangely, and as strangers" (par. 3). What is the effect of believing that the familiar can suddenly be the unknown danger? In what ways might we see this in today's world? Give specific examples.

7. Capote concludes, echoing the idea of Thomas Hobbes, that when moral authority or rule of law has been removed, humans "will all act in cold blood" (par. 4). Do you agree or disagree? Support your answer.

Making Connections

8. Fahy writes, "When faced with such horrible crimes, we expect the monstrous, the inhuman" (par. 7). What is the relationship between physical appearance and morality in this story? Compare the real-life Hickock and Smith with the fictional character of Edward Hyde from Robert Louis Stevenson's *The Strange Case of Dr. Jekyll and Mr. Hyde* (p. 224). What does this comparison tell us about how people perceive the monstrous and the good?

9. Research other stories of horrific crimes committed by people who seem on the surface to be unlikely villains. Compare those criminals to Hickock and Smith. What characteristics do they share that make these seemingly ordinary people monsters?

Inside a Murdering Mind

Anne E. Schwartz

Two police officers were nearing the end of their beat on a blistering-hot night in Milwaukee when they encountered a short, skinny black man with a handcuff on one wrist and an incredible tale of a crazy white man. Their investigation led to the discovery of one of the most gruesome and famous human monsters of our time: Jeffrey Dahmer. Anne E. Schwartz was a reporter for the *Milwaukee Journal Sentinel* at the time. These excerpts come from her book *The Man Who Could Not Kill Enough* (1992) and details not only Dahmer's crimes and his trial but also the psychology of this unusual serial killer.

Police Officers Rolf Mueller and Robert Rauth were finishing their four p.m.–to–midnight shift in Milwaukee's Third Police District. They had been driving along the 2600 block of West Kilbourn Avenue, a grimy neighborhood on the fringes of the downtown area near Marquette University, the highest crime area in the inner city. To the north, the main thoroughfare was peppered with strip bars and small, corner grocery stores. Faded, tattered signs in the windows advertised: WE TAKE FOOD STAMPS.

The neighborhood included drug dealers, prostitutes, and the unemployed mentally ill, who collected state aid because they managed to live on their own or in one of the area's numerous halfway houses. They would carry their belongings in rusty metal grocery carts and sleep in doorways. There was evidence of the area's glory days: expansive turn-of-the-century Victorian homes, rambling apartment complexes, and stately cathedral-style dwellings. For the police, the district has the dubious distinction of being the place where more than half the city's homicides have occurred in the last five years.

That Monday, July 22, [1991,] felt oppressively hot and humid, the kind of heat that would cling to the body. For cops on the beat, the sweat would trickle down their chests and form salty pools under their steel-plated bulletproof vests. Their gun belts would hang uncomfortably from their waists, and the constant rubbing chafed their middles. The squad cars they patrolled in reeked of burning motor oil and the body odor of the last prisoner who sat in the back seat. It was on nights like this that they could not wait to go home.

Anxious to see his wife and daughter, Mueller hoped to make it to the end of the shift without stumbling into any overtime. Mueller, thirty-nine, was a ten-year veteran of the Milwaukee Police Department. Born in Germany, he had moved to America as a youngster but he spoke a little

German at home with his daughter to preserve his heritage. He sported a mass of perpetually tousled blond curls on top of his six-foot frame. Mueller enjoyed horror movies and always talked about how much he loved a good scare.

Mueller's partner, Bob Rauth, forty-one, had spent thirteen years in the department. His strawberry-blond hair had begun to thin, exposing a long scar on his forehead from a car accident that pushed his face through the windshield. His stocky build seemed more suited to a wrestler than a policeman. Like many police officers, Rauth was divorced. His fellow officers knew he consistently took as much overtime as he could get, anxious to find an assignment so he could squirrel away some extra money for a couple more hours' work, something cops call "hunting for overtime." To work with Rauth was to "work over." Other cops described Rauth as one of those guys to whom all the strange, almost unbelievable things happen on the job. Fortunately, Rauth had a self-deprecating sense of humor and would frequently keep the station in stitches about something that happened to him on an assignment or "hitch."

Sitting in their squad car waiting to take a prisoner to jail, Mueller and Rauth were approached by a short, wiry black man with a handcuff dangling from his left wrist. Another summer night that brings out the best in everybody, they thought.

"Which one of us did you escape from?" one of the officers asked through an open window in the car.

The man was thirty-two-year-old Tracy Edwards. While someone coming down the street with a handcuff dangling from his wrist would be an attention-grabber in Milwaukee's posher suburbs, on 25th and Kilbourn it's nothing out of the ordinary. Police calls in that area can range from a man with his head wrapped in aluminum foil spray-painting symbols on houses to a naked man directing traffic at a major intersection. The area is filled with "MOs," citizens brought to the Milwaukee County Mental Health Complex for "mental observation" rather than taken to jail when arrested.

Rauth and Mueller were hesitant to let Edwards go on his way in case he had escaped from another officer, so they asked whether the scuffed silver bracelets were souvenirs of a homosexual encounter. Cops practice the cover-your-ass motto with every shift they work. They don't want to stand in somebody's glass office the next day, trying to explain their way out of a situation that went bad after they left and citizens called screaming their name and badge number to the Chief.

As Edwards stood next to the squad car, he rambled on about a "weird dude" who slapped a handcuff on him during his visit to the dude's apartment. After initially rebuking Edwards, telling him to have his

5

10

"friend" remove the handcuffs, the two officers eventually listened to Edwards's story. It would not have been unusual for the two men to write the incident off as a homosexual encounter gone awry, but Rauth sniffed overtime and asked Edwards to show him where all this happened. That's how close Jeffrey Dahmer came to not getting caught that day. Criminals sometimes escape arrest because they are stopped at the end of a cop's shift or because an officer, tired from working late the night before, does not want to spend the next day tied up in court and then have to report for work.

The two officers decided to go with Edwards to apartment 213 in the Oxford Apartments at 924 North 25th Street. They were not familiar with the building, a reasonably well maintained three-story brick structure. They were rarely called there because most of its occupants held jobs and lived quietly. Once inside the building, the officers were struck by the rancid odor hanging heavy in the air as they approached the apartment.

But all these places stink around here, they thought. A variety of smells greet the police when they are sent to check on the welfare of an apartment full of children who, officers discover, have been sitting alone for several days in their own feces and who have been using the bathtub and the toilet interchangeably while their mother sits at a tavern down the street. Foul smells are as much a part of the inner city as crime.

"Milwaukee police officers," Rauth shouted for all to hear as he rapped loudly with his beefy hand on the wooden door of apartment 213.

Jeffrey Dahmer, thirty-one, an attractive but scruffy, thin man with dirty blond hair and a scar over his right eye, opened the door and allowed the officers and Edwards to enter.

Inside, Mueller and Rauth talked to Dahmer about the incident with   15
Edwards and asked him for the key to the handcuffs. This way, if they got the right answers, they could "advise" the assignment, meaning they could handle the problem and leave without writing a ticket or making an arrest.

Dahmer talked to the officers in the calm voice that, we would later learn, had manipulated so many victims and officials in the past. He told them that the key was in the bedroom. But before Dahmer left the room, Edwards piped up that they would find there a knife that Dahmer had used to threaten him.

It did not appear that Mueller would get home on time, but maybe they could still "advise" the situation if they discovered no knife. Mueller told Dahmer to stay put and went into the bedroom.

Mueller peered into an open dresser drawer and saw something he still describes with difficulty: Polaroid photographs of males in various stages of dismemberment, pictures of skulls in kitchen cabinets and freezers, and a snapshot of a skeleton dangling from a shower spigot. He stopped breathing for a time as he stood frozen, staring at the gruesome Polaroids that barely seemed to depict humans.

In a tremulous voice Mueller screamed for his partner to cuff Dahmer and place him under arrest. "Bob, I don't think we can advise this any more," he shouted, with that gallows humor cops use to keep a safe distance from the stresses of their jobs.

Realizing he was bound for jail, Dahmer turned violent. He and Offi- 20 cer Rauth tumbled around the living room floor until Dahmer was safely in handcuffs. Mueller emerged from the bedroom clutching several photos in his hand.

"You're one lucky son of a bitch, buddy," Mueller told Edwards. "This could have been you," he added, his hands shaking as he waved a photo of a severed human head at Edwards.

Edwards looked wide-eyed at Mueller and told him how Dahmer "freaked" when he went toward the refrigerator to get a beer. "Maybe he's got one of those heads in there," Edwards said uncomfortably. "Yeah, right, maybe there's a head in there." Mueller laughed at Edwards's fear.

Mueller opened the refrigerator door to taunt Edwards, then let out two screams from deep in his gut that neighbors would later recall had awakened them. Mueller slammed the door shut and shouted, "Bob, there's a fucking head in the refrigerator!"

● ● ●

An unassuming third-shift worker at the Ambrosia Chocolate Co. in Milwaukee, Jeffrey Dahmer fancied roses, his fish tank, and his laptop computer.

Until July 23, 1991, chances were that no one knew of his very secret 25 desires.

But who would have?

Many people fit the profile of a mass murderer, according to Dr. James Alan Fox, dean of the College of Criminal Justice at Northeastern University in Boston and a nationally recognized expert on mass murder. There are thousands of angry, depressed people out there, and there is no way to tell in that haystack of humanity who is going to be a killer.

Fox, co-author, along with Northeastern University sociologist Jack Levin, of *Mass Murder: America's Growing Menace*, studied serial killers for eleven years. He has testified before Congress on the subject of crime in America. I came to know him while he was working on a new book, *Overkill*, a study of different varieties of serial murder that [would] include a chapter on Jeffrey Dahmer.

A 1992 mugshot of Jeffrey Dahmer, the Milwaukee serial killer who was sentenced to fifteen life sentences.
Curt Borgwardt/Contributor/Getty

The terms *serial killing, mass murder,* and *massacre* are often used interchangeably but in fact refer to distinguishable phenomena. According to Fox, mass murderers typically target people they know and conduct the murders simultaneously. Serial killers kill over a period of time, killing one person at a time and usually using the same method each time. Family massacres are the most common type of mass murder and generally do not attract national publicity. They involve private conflicts in private places, and the victim count usually is modest compared, for example, to the large number of bystanders killed at random in a restaurant shooting.

As I delved into Dahmer's childhood, I believed I would uncover some- 30 thing sinister that would explain how a person could come to commit such acts. For my own peace of mind, I just had to have an explanation. If I discovered that he felt neglected as early as age six, that his mother had abandoned him, and that he was fascinated with dead animals, I could explain why he did it. Fox told me my effort was futile.

"There was nothing we could have done to predict this [tragedy] ahead of time, no matter how bizarre the behavior," Fox explained. "[Dahmer] had an alcohol problem in high school. So do a lot of kids, and they don't all become serial murderers. Most serial murderers do tend to have difficult childhoods, but so do lots of other people. Victims of abuse are just as likely, if not more likely, to grow up and become ruthless businessmen and victimize unsuspecting consumers for pleasure—not just for profit, but because they get pleasure out of other people's pain—as they are to grow up to become serial killers."

Fox believes that some experiences of adolescence and early adulthood are just as critical in determining the fate of someone as their youths, for example, how well he fit in in high school, whether he had lots of friends, what sort of successes he had. It was apparent that Dahmer was devastated when his mother left him and took his little brother with her. But it would take a giant leap to blame Joyce Flint Dahmer or Lionel Dahmer somehow for what happened.

"Ever since Sigmund Freud, we blame everything bad that kids do on their parents, and that's unfortunate and it doesn't make sense," Fox said. "What we do is scare lots of innocent people who are suffering in their own way for what their kids did. The culprit is Dahmer. Not his father, not his family, not the police."

Fox, who knew many parents of serial murderers, said they go through hell. "In a sense they've lost a child, too, but they don't get lots of sympathy from us," he said. "We should have lots of sympathy for the families of the victims but we obviously have no sympathy for the family of the killer. We think of them as a Dr. Frankenstein who created a monster. We blame them and we hound them."

Hillside Strangler Kenneth Bianchi's mother was hounded out of her Rochester, New York, home by the media, and she still lives in hiding. Yet she never committed the crime; her son did. 35

"You have psychiatrists who want to theorize that the reason why all these people died is because a child hated his parents and wanted to get back at them indirectly by killing these people," Fox said. "When [Florida killer] Ted Bundy was executed, there was a psychiatrist who said he hated his mother and that's why he killed all the women. We focus too much on the childhood.

"If Dahmer had grown up to become the vice president of a corporation, we would have looked at his background and said that he became a stronger individual because of it."

As I watched the Dahmer case unfold in Milwaukee, I saw our focus shift from the actual killer to a scapegoat for his deeds. As soon as people found out that cops had had contact with Dahmer and his fourteen-year-old victim, we seemed to push aside the fact that Dahmer was the one who committed the murders. Except for the days when Dahmer appeared in court, the papers and newscasts were filled with tales of police insensitivity and community outrage—but not outrage so much toward Dahmer as toward the police.

In Fox's eleven years of studying serial killers, he told me, Jeffrey Dahmer stood out. "He's different than the usual serial killer. He more fits the stereotype of someone who really is out of control and being controlled by his fantasies," Fox said. "The difference is most serial killers stop once the victim dies. Everything is leading up to that. They tie them up; they like to hear them scream and beg for their lives. It makes the killer feel great, superior, powerful, dominant. He rapes her or him while the victim is alive, and when the person is dead, they take the body somewhere and leave it where it won't be found. That's the typical pattern.

"In Dahmer's case, everything was post-mortem. In a certain way, he 40 was merciful, because he drugged his victims. They didn't have the same sort of terror and horror the victims of other serial killers have had. For Dahmer, all of his 'fun' began after the victims died."

Dahmer did not overpower his victims to get them to come to his home; they returned willingly with him to his apartment. He fed them a drugged drink and strangled them when they were unconscious. The victims probably never knew anything terrible was happening to them. Dahmer confessed that he had had sex with some of the victims before he killed them, but for the most part, his efforts were concentrated on them after they were dead. He had oral or anal sex with the corpses and took elaborate measures to pose their lifeless bodies for photographs, using the camera as a means to enhance his fantasy life. He dismembered the victims, preserved some of their body parts, and disposed of the rest.

It would have been a small comfort to share with the families that at least their loved ones did not appear to have suffered before their deaths. But the families were caught in the horror of what happened to them after they were dead.

We know that Dahmer liked to experiment on drying out animal pelts with his chemistry set as a child. Some psychiatrists believe that torturing small animals stands out as a precursor of cruelty to human beings, and that the torture of dogs and cats is more of an indicator of future violent behavior than that of flies, toads, and turtles. When Dahmer performed his experiments on the pelts of squirrels and raccoons, the majority of people I talked to in Ohio did not think he had killed the animals himself but, rather, had collected road kills.

Based on their research, Fox and Levin assembled a composite profile of a mass murderer:

He is typically a white male in his late twenties or early thirties. In the 45 case of simultaneous mass murder, he kills people he knows with a handgun or rifle; in serial crimes, he murders strangers by beating or strangulation. His specific motivation depends on the circumstances leading up to the crime, but it generally deals directly with either money, expediency, jealousy, or lust.

Rarely is the mass murderer a hardened criminal with a long criminal record, although a spotty history of property crime is common. Mass murder often follows a spell of frustration when a particular event triggers sudden rage; yet, in other cases, the killer is coolly pursuing some goal he cannot otherwise attain.

Finally, though the mass killer often may appear cold and show no remorse, even denying responsibility for his crime, serious mental illness or psychosis is rarely present. In background, in personality, and even in appearance, the mass murderer is "extraordinarily ordinary," Fox said. This may be the key to his extraordinary talent for murder. "After all, who would ever suspect him?" Fox added.

Dahmer did have something in common with other serial killers in that he led a rich fantasy life that focused on having complete control over people and was controlled by it.

Fox continued, "That fantasy life, mixed with hatred, perhaps hatred of himself which is being projected into his victims. If he at all feels uncomfortable about his own sexual orientation, it is very easy to see it projected into these victims and punishing them indirectly to punish himself."

"He hated anyone who was more gay than he. This was his method 50 of punishment. He could be attracted to these people and then feel extremely horrible about it, and he lashes out at them as opposed to himself. So it's a combination of his hatred for these victims, mixed in with some racial hatred, combined with fantasies that do involve this idea of cutting up people."

While most of Dahmer's victims were black—and a great deal was made of that fact by Milwaukee's black community—it was not clear whether he hated blacks enough to target them deliberately. Our only indication of an animosity toward blacks was the various racial slurs that former prisoners at the Milwaukee County House of Correction and his Army bunk mates remember him uttering.

"Murders instigated by racial hatred are surprisingly rare in a country that has experienced so much racial conflict and violence," Fox said. Interestingly enough, while blacks commit half the homicides in this country (in Milwaukee, 75 percent of the city's 1991 homicides were committed by blacks, who are 40 percent of the population), only one in five mass killers is black, according to Fox.

Fox characterized the serial killer as a "skillful practitioner" because he murders repeatedly without getting caught. In most cases, police do not realize that a number of homicides were the work of one person until the killer is apprehended.

In a bizarre sort of way, Jeffrey Dahmer's crimes seemed very matter-of-fact when discussed clinically with someone like James Fox. But sociology aside, there will always be those who like to bring the explanation down to basics: "He was crazy."

At the January 1992 trial, Dahmer's attorney, Gerald Boyle, used the 55
insanity defense in an unsuccessful effort to keep Dahmer out of prison and locked away in a state mental hospital. On September 10, 1991, at his pretrial hearing, Dahmer pleaded not guilty by reason of mental disease or defect. Under Wisconsin law, a person is not responsible for criminal conduct if at the time of the offense that person was suffering from a mental disease and lacked either the capacity to distinguish right from wrong or to conform his conduct to the law. Therefore, if convicted, Dahmer would be committed to a state mental hospital for no specific term but instead would be held until a judge or jury concluded that he no longer posed a danger to the community.

Criminally insane patients cannot be committed for longer than the maximum prison terms for their crimes, in this case, life. A 1988 *Milwaukee Journal* study of criminally insane patients found that the average confinement was five years for patients committed for first-degree murder. Patients such as Dahmer, who were involved in particularly brutal or highly publicized cases, usually were confined much longer, the study showed.

Although not confined to any sort of treatment facility in the past, Jeffrey Dahmer was under the care of psychiatrists during his probation for assaulting the brother of Konerak Sinthasomphone in 1988. A psychiatric treatment professional who met Dahmer observed, "For some men their only means of expressing things is through sex. Men express their feelings very poorly, according to the common lore. The crimes may reflect anger first—sex is only the medium for that." The doctor said Dahmer disclosed nothing and was very guarded about his formative childhood years.

A psychologist who worked with inmates for the Wisconsin Department of Corrections said Dahmer had an illness that was likely transmitted through heredity, if newspaper reports of Joyce Flint Dahmer's alleged mental illness were true. The psychologist noted that Lionel Dahmer's self-described strict religious leanings could indicate rigidity about other matters, such as sexual morality, and [he] probably had great difficulty accepting his son's sexual preference. "Most parents don't handle it too well when their kids diverge from the norm," the psychologist said.

The psychologist talked about Dahmer's confessions. "There may be some psychological dynamics to his confessions. There could be some relief in being caught. Whatever pain he had is finally over. Or there could be some charge for him for all of this confessing."

He described Dahmer as a formidable liar who used untruths to blan- 60
ket and protect parts of his life. "Sometimes the man has lied so often that the lie becomes the truth. He tells the lie so often, he starts to believe it himself."

After his conviction for sexual exploitation of a child in 1989, court-appointed psychiatrists prescribed at least two drugs for Dahmer, lorazepam, an antianxiety drug, and doxepin, an antidepresssant. He also had an old prescription for Halcion, a drug akin to Valium, which he gave to Konerak Sinthasomphone's brother in 1988. Psychiatrists often prescribe antianxiety drugs, similar to barbiturates, to treat what they regard as major mental disorders. The drugs are intended to chemically control anxiety, nervousness, tension, and sleep disorders. The antidepressants cause frequent effects like drowsiness, lethargy, and difficulty thinking. The drug Halcion has come under fire for allegedly causing aberrant behavior in some of its users.

Several psychiatrists probed Dahmer's mind after his pleas of not guilty and not guilty by reason of mental disease or defect on September 10, 1991. A two-part trial was scheduled: the first phase

> "I think he knew exactly what he was doing and how he was going to do it. There's nothing wrong with Jeffrey Dahmer."

would determine if Dahmer had committed the killings, and the second would determine if he was insane at the time. Despite his insanity plea and what Boyle called his client's depressed condition, Boyle had already established early on that Dahmer was mentally competent to go to trial and to assist in his own defense.

A number of the families were eager to talk to me after Dahmer made his plea in court in September 1991. They felt the not guilty plea was a disgrace.

"I was mad as hell," said Carolyn Smith, Eddie Smith's sister. "The man's just got it too good. Everywhere I turn it's just like everything's catered for Dahmer, and to have him just turn my life upside down. Well, it's just not right."

Inez Thomas, mother of David Thomas, rejected the claim of insanity. 65
"I think he knew exactly what he was doing and how he was going to do it. There's nothing wrong with Jeffrey Dahmer."

Understanding the Text

1. Why were Officers Rauth and Mueller initially reluctant to let Tracy Edwards go on his way? To what extent did that play a role in the discovery of Jeffrey Dahmer?

2. What are the differences between a mass murderer and a serial killer, as defined in "Inside a Murdering Mind"?

3. What does Dr. James Alan Fox argue are the problems with blaming childhood traumas for the formation of serial killers?

4. Schwartz was a reporter for the *Milwaukee Journal Sentinel* and was the first reporter on the scene for Dahmer's arrest. What about her writing style seems connected to the practice of journalism? Consider, by way of contrast, how a different type of writer (e.g., a creative writer, a scientist, or a lawyer) might have approached the same subject matter. Be specific.

Reflection and Response

5. After his victims were dead, Dahmer sometimes had sex with their bodies, cut them up, and even ate their flesh. Yet Dr. Fox says, "In a certain way, he was merciful, because he drugged his victims. They didn't have the same sort of terror and horror the victims of other serial killers have had" (par. 40). What is your reaction to these details? How do they differ from the pattern of the typical serial killer? Were Dahmer's crimes more monstrous or less monstrous than those of other serial killers?

6. Schwartz refers to the issue of Dahmer's need for control. How can the quest for control of self and others lead to monstrous behavior?

Making Connections

7. How does Jeffrey Dahmer compare to Dick Hickock and Perry Smith, the two killers from Thomas Fahy's article about *In Cold Blood* (p. 265)? Are they monstrous in the same way? What about them is similar, and what is different? Consider issues of motive, action, and remorse in your response.

8. Research additional information about Dahmer — his crimes, his trial, and his death. In what ways can his story be called a monster story? Consider whether there was any humanity left in Dahmer in the end.

The Horror in the Mirror: Average Joe and the Mechanical Monster

Richard Tithecott

The horror of Jeffrey Dahmer was that he was so ordinary, so unremarkable, just an "Average Joe," and yet he was capable of such horrific deeds. The question then becomes how we can reconcile the idea of normalcy with the facts of killing, necrophilia (an erotic interest in corpses), dismemberment of corpses, and cannibalism. Much rests on how we define ourselves as human and how we answer the question of what constitutes normal and natural. Richard Tithecott is the author of *Of Men and Monsters: Jeffrey Dahmer and the Construction of the Serial Killer* (1997) from which this excerpt is taken.

To Randy Jones, one of Dahmer's neighbors, Dahmer seemed "like the average Joe" (*Newsweek*, 5 August 1991: 41). Helping us to disseminate a picture of Dahmer in court, a caption in Anne E. Schwartz's book describes Dahmer as an "average-looking man." To Tracy Edwards, whose escape from Dahmer's apartment led to Dahmer's arrest, Dahmer "seemed like a normal, everyday guy," and presumably in order to justify that characterization, Edwards agrees with Geraldo Rivera's suggestion that he and Dahmer were out to "hustle some chicks" (*Geraldo*, 12 September 1991). Dahmer "is a very gentle man" according to his attorney, and "that's what makes it so absolutely intriguing and unbelievable to see how a fellow like that you saw in court today could have done all these horrific acts" (*Larry King Live*, 17 February 1992). To make it even more intriguing, as a *Washington Post* columnist notes, Dahmer is not from one of the "nation's urban areas with more of a reputation for cold-bloodedness," but from Wisconsin, "America's heartland" (1 August 1991: C3). . . . The idea that "appearances are deceptive" is repeated in article after article: "Concealed amongst all this normality lies dormant evil." Like the surrealists, in the banal we see, and perhaps like to manufacture, something extraordinary.

Average Joe often has a story to tell about himself and his friends that calls into question his claim to his name. This celebrated embodiment of middle America is often hiding something. His normality, we say, is an illusion. But when we look at our monsters and wait for the true gargoyle within to burst through that familiar shell, sometimes we experience a more horrifying or thrilling possibility: the monster that appears actually is Average Joe; what is unspeakable turns out to be impossible to put into words not because it is so extraordinary but because it is so ordinary. Thus, we have a twist on the story behind Daniel Vigne's *The Return of Martin Guerre* or Jon Amiel's *Sommersby*: not an intruder in the guise of familiarity, but familiarity in all its glory. It is a possibility that Hannah Arendt describes in *Eichmann in Jerusalem*: "[The prosecutor] wanted to try the most abnormal monster the world had ever seen. . . . [The judges] knew, of course, that it would have been very comforting indeed to believe that Eichmann° was a monster. . . . The trouble with Eichmann was precisely that so many were like him, and that the many were neither perverted nor sadistic, that they were, and still are, terribly and terrifyingly normal" (Arendt 276). The "trouble" with Eichmann is the trouble with our serial killers, both new and old. "I shall clip the lady's ears off . . . wouldn't you?" asks Jack the Ripper in a letter to his fellow man. As Martin Tropp suggests, the writer "speaks directly to his readers, implying by his words and literacy (despite the [possibly intentional] misspellings) that he is one of them" (113) and that this is why he is so difficult to catch.

Halloween director John Carpenter, commenting on the success of *The Silence of the Lambs*, remarks, "I think we're all frightened of the unknown and also of the repressed people in our society. There's a duality that touches off sparks in all of us" (*People Weekly*, 1 April 1991: 70). Those sparks are theorized by Jonathan Dollimore thus: "Since, in cultural terms, desiring the normal is inseparable from and conditional upon not desiring the abnormal, repression remains central to identity, individual and cultural" (246). We often figure the serial killer as failing to repress the desire for the abnormal. Joan Smith, for example, figuring identity in hydraulic terms, says, "The otherwise inexplicable actions of a serial killer . . . can . . . be understood as a survival mechanism, a means of coping with intolerable stress. The fact that they commit such terrible crimes enables them to function normally in the periods between their crimes" (3). Our desire for normality, our fetishization of Average Joe, inevitably means that abnormality is constructed as something that *needs* to be repressed, something that inevitably becomes desirable, mysterious, sexy. As it comes into focus, our depiction of the serial killer as "letting off steam" is also a picture of Average Joe who has given in to his deeper desires. Our monster turns out to be not something monstrous disguised as Joe but Joe who has let it all hang out.

> "Our monster turns out to be not something monstrous disguised as Joe but Joe who has let it all hang out."

Attempting to satisfy our hunger for horror, we revert sometimes to what John Carpenter says indicates fifties conservatism: the cheap scare.

Eichmann: Adolf Eichmann (1906–1962), a prime Nazi architect of the Holocaust.

Our monsters, more animal than human, spring at us from behind bushes, prey on us, return to their lairs far from everyday, familiar society. At such times we might, like Dahmer's neighbor, John Bachelor, compare Dahmer to Jason in *Friday the 13th* (*Los Angeles Times*, 24 July 1991: A14)—he who, like Lecter,° we like to conceal behind a hockey-mask—or we might, like Robert Dvorchak and Lisa Holewa, describe Dahmer's reported "wailing" and "screeching" when he is arrested as "all those forces seething inside him erupt[ing] to life" (Dvorchak and Holewa 8). But we are generally movie-literate people, and to truly scare ourselves, we want sometimes to be a little more subtle, to show that we can write and speak a little more fully, a little more *knowingly* about those "forces." At these times, we must be able to mistake our monsters for ourselves—or ourselves for them. We must build a house of mirrors.

If we are white, scaring ourselves in this way is a little easier. Aver-   5
age Joe is white, and so is Average Joe, the serial killer. Average Joe has power, the power of being average, of being a representative of middle America. And so does Average Joe, the serial killer. The sister of one of Dahmer's many black victims is curious about why her fellow guest on *The Maury Povich Show* should be so fascinated with Dahmer that she regularly attends his trial: "Did you want to read about the man [Joachim Dressler] that sat up there and cut up 11 people in Racine. Did you want to read about him? No, see, you don't even remember him. But he was—came from an insane place. But see, that's not big news. This white man that killed almost all minorities, he is big news" (*Maury Povich*, 4 February 1992). Not that the whiteness of a serial killer becomes an issue—but his "normality" does. We not only place the white Dahmer or the white Bundy or the white Gacy on the covers of magazines, we give them the power to look back at us. And that's a thrill.

Looking at our monsters is a good way of finding out who we think we are, or who we think we might be, or even who we want to be. They can be figures who have realized our frightening or fantastic potentials. The trick is to identify how subtle we are being. Take, for example, the representation of Dahmer as automaton. Seizing on classmates' memories of Dahmer's ritual walk to the school bus—four steps forward, two back, four forward, one back (Masters 1991, 267)—we deal with his lack of feeling towards his victims by constructing an image of Dahmer as boy-machine who develops into something which, when arrested, "looked so emotionless, so harmless, as if he were a robot being led away" (Norris 1992, 41). In court his face is "passionless" (*Geraldo*, 12 September

Lecter: Hannibal Lecter, cannibalistic serial killer, a fictional character in novels by Thomas Harris and film adaptations, such as *The Silence of the Lambs* (1991).

1991), his eyes "almost vacant" (*Newsweek*, 3 February 1992: 45). For the *Washington Post*, Dahmer, "his face . . . pale and impassive," "walked with the near-drop pace of a zombie" (7 August 1991: B1). *People Weekly* magazine, countering the claims of his lawyer that he was in a "state of anguish," says, "but Jeffrey Dahmer was impassive in court as he was charged with first-degree murder" (12 August 1991: 32). While defense and state attorneys differ in their assessments of Dahmer's responsibility for his actions, their portrayal of him as unfeeling, inhuman, and machinelike are indistinguishable. Dahmer's attorney, Gerald Boyle, describes him in court as a "steamrolling killing machine," "a runaway train on a track of madness, picking up steam all the time, on and on and on," while Michael McCann for the prosecution describes Dahmer as a "cool, calculating killer who cleverly covered his tracks" (*New York Times*, 16 February 1992: 24).

Such estrangement can be of the unsubtle variety, a case of "pathologizing and thus disavowing the everyday intimacies with technology in machine culture" (Seltzer 98), but it can also indicate not so much a disavowal as an expression of anxiety on our part about modern humanity or, more specifically, modern man in "machine culture." Klaus Theweleit describes the masculine self of members of the First World War German Freikorps as "mechanized through a variety of mental and physical procedures: military drill, countenance, training, operations which Foucault° identified as techniques of the self' " (Rabinbach and Benjamin in Theweleit 1989, xvii), and Mark Fasteau, among others, describes the stereotype of the contemporary male self in similar terms, a stereotype which we are still struggling to outgrow. In *The Male Machine* Fasteau describes the ideal image to which the title refers as

functional, designed mainly for work. He is programmed to tackle jobs, override obstacles, attack problems, overcome difficulties, and always seize the offensive. . . . He has armor plating which is virtually impregnable. His circuits are never scrambled or overrun by irrelevant personal signals. He dominates and outperforms his fellows, although without excessive flashing of lights or clashing of gears. His relationship with other male machines is one of respect but not intimacy; it is difficult for him to connect his internal circuits to those of others. In fact, his internal circuitry is something of a mystery to him. (Fasteau 1)

Fasteau's "male machine" is a frightening but familiar image. It corresponds with the way we often figure our monsters: "If there's anything monstrous about [Dahmer], it's the monstrous lack of connection to all

Michel Foucault (1926–1984): French philosopher and critic known for his theories on power and knowledge

things we think of as being human—guilt, remorse, worry, feelings that
would stop him from hurting, killing, torturing" (Davis Silber, quoted in
Dvorchak and Holewa 141). It corresponds with the way we represent
our mostly male psychopaths who can be diagnosed as such by demonstrating, among other things, "a shallow understanding of the meaning
of words, particularly emotional terms" and by not showing "the surge
of anxiety that normal people exhibit" when they are about "to receive
a mild electric shock" (*New York Times*, 7 July 1987: C2). And, apparently
keen to confer buddy-status on as many of society's others as possible,
Fasteau's male ideal also corresponds with necrophiles° and schizophrenics.° "According to Eric Fromm's findings," says Brian Masters,
necrophiles "often have a pallid complexion, and they speak in a mono-
tone. . . . They are fascinated with machinery, which is unfeeling and
antihuman" (quoted in Masters 1991, 266). *In Cold Blood* examiners of
Lowell Lee Andrews produce a diagnosis of "schizophrenia, simple type,"
and by "simple," Capote tells us, "the diagnosticians meant that Andrews
suffered no delusions, no fake perceptions, no hallucinations, but the primary illness of separation of thinking and feeling" (Capote 315). How
different are our killing machines from our male machines? While we are
familiar with and still sometimes valorize the male machine, how sensitive are we to the idea that it is logical for such machines also to regard
their others as mirror-reflections of themselves, as unfeeling, interesting
only as mechanical objects? While Dahmer the schoolboy explains to a
classmate his reason for cutting up the fish he catches—"I want to see
what it looks like inside, I like to see how things work" (Dvorchak and
Holewa 41)—the adult Dahmer confesses to the police "in the unin-
flected language of an affidavit" that he disassembles his human victims
"to see how they work" (*Newsweek*, 5 August 1991: 40). Our construction
of the serial killer resembles a figure of masculinity, or rather a reassem-
bled figure of masculinity, who has turned on all that frustrates masculinity either within himself or without. When we represent serial killers,
necrophiles, psychopaths, schizophrenics, and a male ideal in similar
ways, we sometimes refuse to identify links between them, but sometimes we allow the representations to merge, to form an almost conflated
image in which the other is seen through the familiar self, the familiar
self seen through the other. An uncanny effect, as Freud might say.

What Freud *does* say is that the uncanny hints at "nothing new or
foreign, but something familiar and old established in the mind that has

necrophiles: people with an erotic interest in corpses.
schizophrenics: people with a psychotic disorder characterized by the loss of contact
with the environment, a noticeable deterioration in the level of functioning in everyday life, and the disintegration of personality.

been estranged only by the process of repression" (Freud 1953, 47). In the same essay he mentions the uncanniness of mechanization: "Jentsch has taken as a very good instance [of the uncanny] 'doubts whether an apparently animate being is really alive; or conversely, whether a lifeless object might not be in fact animate'; and he refers in this connection to the impression made by wax-work figures, artificial dolls and automatons. He adds to this class the uncanny effect of epileptic seizures and the manifestations of insanity, because these excite in the spectator the feeling that automatic, mechanical processes are at work, concealed beneath the ordinary appearance of animation" (31). A *Newsweek* article on Dahmer describes serial killers as "taking their cues from some deranged script" (5 August 1991: 40) and concludes with a quotation from Park Dietz: "These people are the most controlled people you can imagine" (41). While Dahmer was found to be *in control*, not out of it, his actions perceived to be those of a man who knew what he was doing, he is also represented as someone/something being controlled. The figure of the killer as unfeeling, programmed machine—the writer of the program remaining a mystery—is one with which the Gothic and our representation of serial killers are particularly occupied. And contributing to our sense of the uncanny is the defining characteristic of the serial killer, the repetitiveness of the killing act. For Freud, "repetition-compulsion" is "based upon instinctual activity and probably inherent in the very nature of the instincts—a principle powerful enough to overrule the pleasure-principle, lending to certain aspects of the mind their daemonic character" (Freud 1953, 44). In other words, "repetition-compulsion" can signify oxymorons such as "mechanized nature" or "natural machine."

With Freud's understanding of the uncanny in mind, the mechan-   10
ically repetitive serial killer is a construction which can suggest for us the power of "natural instinct," an instinct whose naturalness we may or may not wish to question. But whether we see the power of "mechanized nature" or of a "natural machine," our particular representation of the body as machine may appear as both a powerful fantasy and a fantasy of power. Mark Seltzer, who argues that "the matter of periodizing persons, bodies, and desires is inseparable from the anxieties and *appeals of the body-machine complex*" (my italics; Seltzer 98), refers to the type of fantasy which "projects a transcendence of the natural body and the extension of human agency through the forms of technology that supplemented it" (99). And just as dreams about technology can reflect more than just our anxieties, our construction of mechanized monsters, as I mentioned earlier, can indicate more than just our worries about humanity's "naturalness" or its future in a technological age. Gilles Deleuze says, "Types of machines are easily matched with each type of society—not

that machines are determining, but because they express those social forms capable of generating and using them" (Deleuze 6). Reinventing Deleuze's comment, one might say that our constructions of automated monsters, rather than indicating what we fear machines are doing to us, indicate what kind of a culture is "capable of generating and *using them*."

In the mythology of modern America the serial killer is a character able both to scare and thrill us in unsubtle and subtle ways. He can be monstrous, but he can also demonstrate a monstrosity which is familiar. The figure of the mechanized serial killer—the serial killer as automaton, unable to stop—offers us a version of familiar, "natural," and to some extent "appealing" behavior "that has been estranged only by the process of repression."

References

Arendt, Hannah. *Eichmann in Jerusalem*. New York: Penguin, 1963.

Capote, Truman. *In Cold Blood: A True Account of Multiple Murder and Its Consequences*. London: Hamish Hamilton, 1966.

Deleuze, Gilles. "Postscript on the Societies of Control." *October* 59 (1992): 3–7.

Dollimore, Jonathan. *Sexual Dissidence*. Oxford: Clarendon Press, 1991.

Dvorchak, Robert J., and Lisa Holewa. *Milwaukee Massacre*. New York: Dell, 1991.

Fasteau, Mark Feigen. *The Male Machine*. New York: McGraw-Hill, 1974.

Freud, Sigmund. "The Uncanny," in *Standard Edition of the Complete Psychological Works*. Trans. under the general editorship of James Strachey, in collaboration with Anna Freud, assisted by Alex Strachey and Alan Tyson. Vol. 17. London: Hogarth Press, 1953.

Gerald. Investigative News Group, Inc.

Larry King Live. Cable News Network, Inc.

Masters, Brian. "Dahmer's Inferno." *Vanity Fair* (November 1991): 183–269.

The Maury Povich Show. Paramount, Inc.

Norris, Joel. *Serial Killers: The Growing Menace*. New York: Doubleday, 1988.

Schwartz, Anne E. *The Man Who Could Not Kill Enough*. New York: Birch Lane Press, 1992.

Seltzer, Mark. "Serial Killers (1)." *Differences* 5 (Spring 1993): 92–128.

Smith, Joan. "The Fear and the Fantasy." *The Guardian* (sec. 2), 18 (June 1993): 2–3.

Theweleit, Klaus. *Male Fantasies*. Vol. 1. *Women, Floods, Bodies, History*. Foreword by Barbara Ehrenreich. Trans. Stephen Conway in collaboration with Erica Carter and Chris Turner. Minneapolis: University of Minnesota Press, 1987. Vol. 2. *Male Bodies: Psychoanalyzing the White Terror*. Foreword by Jessica Benjamin and Anson Rabinbach. Trans. Erica Carter and Chris Turner in collaboration with Stephen Conway. Minneapolis: University of Minnesota Press, 1989.

Tropp, Martin. *Images of Fear: How Horror Stories Helped Shape Modern Culture, 1818–1918*. Jefferson, NC: McFarland, 1990.

Understanding the Text

1. Tithecott says, "Average Joe often has a story to tell about himself and his friends that calls into question his claim to his name" (par. 2). What does Tithecott mean by this?

2. What does *Halloween* director John Carpenter mean by the "cheap scare" in regard to horror (par. 4)? Why does Jeffrey Dahmer not represent that sort of scare?

3. According to Tithecott, how is race connected to serial killers and our perceptions of them?

4. Analyze how Tithecott builds his paragraphs in terms of rhetorical structure. For instance, where does he typically place his topic sentences? How does he use language to present his evidence? Does he analyze the evidence sufficiently? How does he end his paragraphs? Compare the paragraphs in Tithecott's writing to Anne E. Schwartz's paragraphs in "Inside a Murdering Mind" (p. 272) to get a sense of how paragraphs can differ structurally.

Reflection and Response

5. Tithecott quotes John Carpenter as saying, in reference to the movie *The Silence of the Lambs*, "I think we're all frightened of the unknown and also of the repressed people in our society. There's a duality that touches off sparks in all of us" (par. 3). Do you agree? Why or why not? Cite examples to support your argument.

6. Consider how serial killers have become celebrities: people know their names and want to learn details about their upbringing, their killings, and how they were ultimately caught. Many killers have "fans" even as they serve time in prison. There are serial killer trading cards and a serial killer trivia game. What does this suggest about our cultural values?

Making Connections

7. Tithecott cites a report from the *Washington Post* stating that Dahmer "walked with the near-drop pace of a zombie" (par. 6). How was Dahmer like a zombie? Research other texts about zombies, including Chuck Klosterman's essay "My Zombie, Myself: Why Modern Life Feels Rather Undead" (p. 39). Argue whether or not contemporary serial killers, such as Jeffrey Dahmer, are zombies.

8. Much is made of the issue of control in discussing serial killers. In fact, Tithecott states, "while Dahmer was found to be *in control*, not out of it, his actions perceived to be those of a man who knew what he was doing, he is also represented as someone/something being controlled" (par. 9). How does that observation relate to other monsters such as vampires and werewolves, or even the creation myths of creatures such as the Minotaur, and the level of control they have — or don't have — over their own actions? Use specific details to develop your answer.

Ethical Aliens: The Challenge of Extreme Perpetrators to Humanism

William Andrew Myers

There are criminals, there are murderers, and then there are what William Andrew Myers calls "extreme perpetrators" — those whose actions are so evil, so beyond our ability to understand, that they seem like a different species: aliens. Murderous dictators, serial killers, and ideological killers qualify because their actions seem to negate their own humanity. In Aristotle's terms, they act more bestial than merely wicked. In an essay originally published in 2009, Myers examines these extreme perpetrators not to salvage them, but to save us: we must recognize the human in them in order to recognize the human in all of us. Myers is professor emeritus of philosophy at College of St. Catherine.

Societies have many ways of marking off individuals and groups, both to establish social and political hierarchies and to create categories for exclusion from a normative mainstream. The specific functions of these markers vary with time, place, and application, but no society, it seems, can get along without them. And categories established within societies have pragmatic consequences: members of out-groups are treated differently, and the different treatment is sanctioned, itself as normative as the categories themselves. We create images of the poor, of ethnic and religious minorities, of the insane, of criminals, and we justify our different treatment of them by reference to their out-group status. Yet the categories and the treatment based on them may or may not stand up to scrutiny. The exclusionary marker I want to explore here is the category, perpetrator of extreme harm.

Part of our experience as humans includes awareness, if not direct experience, that some people are quite extraordinarily vicious. Some behavior seems to go beyond ordinary criminality, so far beyond that we struggle to comprehend it as human action. I call people who behave so badly extreme perpetrators. Their behavior leads us to grope for comprehension and to dismiss them as utterly alien. But should we regard such individuals as so distinct from the human community? And what does our attitude toward extreme perpetrators say about our understanding of what it means to be human? I will argue that uncritical acceptance of the social mechanisms that treat extreme perpetrators as absolute outsiders, barely or not even human, impermissibly limits our shared beliefs about what it means to be human — and hence our self-understanding — but also constricts our conception of the humane.

Extreme Perpetrators

In a brief passage in the *Nicomachean Ethics* Aristotle distinguishes between ordinary human wickedness and bestiality:° "Bestiality is less 'evil' than vice," he says, "though more horrible." He continues that in contrast to the wicked person, whose "highest part," that is, the intellect or reason, is corrupted, in the bestial individual it is not corrupt "but entirely lacking." Aristotle thought the wicked person could do much more harm than a bestial person, but that in terms of moral character the two are not comparable. "[I]t is like comparing an inanimate with an animate thing [*apsychon* versus *empsychon*: literally, an unsouled with an ensouled thing], and asking which is the more evil; for the badness of a thing which has no originating principle—and intelligence is such a principle—is always less capable of mischief." Thus Aristotle regards bestiality as something outside the range of our framework of ethical concepts. Extreme behaviors and the minds they evince cannot even count as vice—excess or deficiency—in our calculations of the mean that constitutes excellence or virtue. In the sentences just preceding the quoted passage he notes that the concepts of moderation and profligacy° do not pertain to lower animals because they "have neither the faculty of choice nor of calculation," and he adds, "they are like men who are insane." So we get here a comparison between lower animals, who lack *nous*, intellect—and therefore cannot make rational choices—and the bestial person, who likewise cannot make rational choices due to insanity.

> "Uncritical acceptance of the social mechanisms that treat extreme perpetrators as absolute outsiders . . . impermissibly limits our shared beliefs about what it means to be human."

Perhaps because this is merely an aside in Aristotle's discussion of vices, he gives us no examples here of bestial human behavior; in fact he seems to dismiss it as outside the topic. But his point seems to be that the actions of some persons are so far outside the range of ordinary human wickedness that we can safely ignore them in constructing a descriptive and normative account of human ethical life. What interests me in the distinction Aristotle makes between the wicked or vicious person and the bestial is that his dismissal of the latter conforms to modern ways of regarding some perpetrators of extreme harm as inhuman, or alien. And indeed, clearly some acts do challenge our norms of behavior that is merely criminal.

bestiality: the manifestation of the traits or desires of a lower animal.
profligacy: excessive or immoral behavior; wastefulness.

Hannah Arendt speaks of the abyss between a normal society's moral 5
and legal frames of reference and the revelations of Nazi depravity at the
end of WWII. "What meaning has the concept of murder when we are
confronted with the mass production of corpses?" she asks. Most moral
theory, not just Aristotle's and its modern descendants, addresses norms
ill-suited to comprehend, say, the creatively sadistic serial killer or the
willing participant in mass murder. And the social determinants that lead
us to dismiss the extreme perpetrator as outside the range of ethical reflection are strong. Richard Tithecott, in his analysis of the social construction
of the serial killer, which focuses on Jeffrey Dahmer, comments, "With
our condemnation of Dahmer as evil, we say, simply, *he happened*: there
is no need to explain the crime, to speculate about context, only to deal
with him, the criminal." But to show that this dismissal of the extreme
perpetrator as absolutely alien has undesirable consequences, I must now
be more specific about what counts as the extreme in this context.

A Description

To be more precise about who counts as an extreme perpetrator I must
refer to some distinctions among theories of evil. Three emphases have
emerged in the recent philosophical literature. The first looks to the
actual damage a person causes, the second to motivations, intentions, or
the will, and the third to the feelings a person has about the actions. As
Daniel M. Haybron points out, none of these emphases is sufficient on
its own to provide a "robust bad/evil distinction." But my purpose here
is not to develop a theory of evil, nor to examine in any detail Haybron's
attempt; I merely wish to use these emphases to ground a description of
extreme perpetrators.

First, we do commonly measure harm, suffering, and injury as indica-
tors of the extreme. In its crudest form, a harm-based view literally counts
the victims. Thus a planner and implementer of mass murder (Heinrich
Himmler,° say) is widely regarded as being in a different category from
that of a man who kills a store clerk during a robbery. A perverse manifestation of this kind of thinking treats serial killers as sports heroes, scoring
their total victims like game statistics. (There are, I read, even serial killer
trading cards.) Despite such aberrations, the scope of damage done does
figure importantly in our sense of the extreme.

Another harm-based marker of the extreme is sadistic cruelty. Christopher
Browning, in his study of "ordinary men" induced to commit atrocities

---

Heinrich Himmler (1900–1945): a Nazi leader of the infamous SS, a paramilitary
organization under Adolf Hitler.

during the Nazi mass murder program in Poland, reports that a few of the men ordered to shoot women, children, and elderly persons face to face, one by one, in Józefów, Poland, in July of 1942, were unable to comply; while these men were treated by their fellows as cowards, they suffered no serious reprisals for their unwillingness to carry out the orders. We may applaud such a small triumph of human decency in terrible circumstances, but there are plenty of other cases in the bloody twentieth century in which multiple murders were carried out with a maximum of cruelty and humiliation to the victims. At least some perpetrators take obscene pleasure in their work. [Lavrenty] Beria, Stalin's henchman who oversaw the murderous infighting in the dictator's inner circle, personally tortured arrested members of the leadership (some former friends) and their wives, raping the women before murdering them.

The wantonness of such actions, the depravity it reveals, seems to mark such perpetrators as Beria as fundamentally different from those who, we may say (without in any way discounting the suffering they cause), merely murder. Extent of harm caused and sadistic cruelty thus are important markers of an extreme perpetrator. Note that the cruelty of actions treated in a harm-based account reflects only measures of the perpetrator's actual actions: that victims were in fact tortured, for example. In the case of someone whose actions spring from a deformed character, the character of one who derives pleasure from inflicting suffering on others, motivations may well count in our assessment and subsequent judgment that the individual represents an extreme. A deranged form of pleasure-seeking might be behind the actions of someone who tortures victims before killing them. Nevertheless, it remains the actual harm done, including its manner, that predominates in our delimiting of the extreme.

Second, the inner life of the perpetrator does count in our assessment 10
of the ethics of ordinary actions, but at the extremes motives and intentions become far less weighty, for two reasons. For one thing, the scale of harm can overwhelm our willingness to dissect and analyze motives. Contemplating events such as the 1994 genocidal massacres in Rwanda, our ordinary moral sensibilities, including for example such attitudes as that children should be nurtured and the elderly cared for, are so completely violated that no account of individual motivations seems relevant to our ethical assessments. As Arendt says, the mass production of corpses makes ordinary concepts of murder meaningless. While we may indeed be curious to understand the linkages between what a person thought and what he did to bring about extraordinary harms, in extreme cases like those at various levels of the Nazi mass murder programs accounts of motives notoriously fail to align with the scale of the atrocity we seek to understand. (This is the paradox of the banal perpetrator as described by Arendt.)

Moreover, motives, though they may be constituted by extraordinary malice, cannot be a sufficient condition for identifying an extreme perpetrator. For instance, we can imagine an individual so consumed with malice against some group that almost her entire mental life is devoted to imagining horrors she wishes to visit upon members of that group, whereas in fact she never does anything about these fantasies. We would hardly be justified in calling her an extreme perpetrator, or a perpetrator at all. And if she revealed publicly her mental life to be what it is, we would probably counsel therapy, regarding her pathological ideation as unhealthy rather than criminal. She may have the necessary *mens rea,*° but lack the means and opportunity to act. It is actual perpetrators who seem to merit classification as the worst of the worst.

Similarly, affect pales in significance before the scale of some atrocities. Whereas in everyday contexts it matters to us whether someone took pleasure in doing harm or felt remorse later, for extreme perpetrators these aspects of their actions do not help us to describe the extremes of our moral universe. As Haybron notes, "We don't particularly care whether Hitler cried into his pillow every night. We care about the millions of lives he destroyed." That is, we assess the moral characters of ordinary perpetrators on the basis of their actions, their motives, and how they feel about themselves and their actions. For extreme perpetrators, it appears to be actions alone that we take as primary, though we might also at times reason from those actions to judgments of depraved character.

With this background now, we can distinguish extreme perpetrators from ordinary malefactors as *those who commit acts so heinous in extent or in cruelty that they stand outside the norms of mere criminality,* even when they commit acts that are prosecutable. This concept of the extreme perpetrator is based on an idea of degrees: there are many ways to be bad, even very bad, but some people create so much mayhem—including real suffering—that their actions set them apart from ordinary malefactors. The idea of the extreme perpetrator is a harm-based concept because it is the extremes of injury and suffering to which we refer in our horror at the actions of some people. Recognizing people at this extreme of evil leads to the various distancing strategies we see.

Keeping Our Distance

Societies have various mechanisms to distance themselves from the worst of the worst. Each of the three principles of exclusion I will describe here

---

mens rea: Latin for "a guilty mind"; a legal term used to mean a person's knowledge or intention to commit a crime.

(not by any means an exhaustive list) marks those it refers to as irretrievably Other, aliens in the fullest sense. That in each case there is a huge descriptive and analytical literature and a vast array of popular entertainments devoted to them reveals our fascination with the extremes; but these productions also *create* the alien as a category.

The Murderous Dictator

National leaders who carry out programs of genocide or other mass atrocity, 15 *claiming to act on behalf of the nation, are outside our normative moral framework.*

Some of the people we want to distance ourselves from include murderous dictators, like Stalin, Idi Amin, or Pol Pot. Distancing is easy in this kind of case because these figures are physically and often culturally distant to start with. Their actions seem inexplicable when we learn of them, and in many cases we do not learn of the extent of their damage until long after they have died or fled the scene. The discovery of mass graves, publications of survivor narratives, reports of truth commissions, even films such as *The Killing Fields*, may give us insight into their atrocities, but typically the perpetrators remain shadowy and their story is revealed only slowly over time as historians and biographers do their patient scholarship. In some cases, prosecutions in the International Criminal Court at The Hague will elicit testimony that reveals the nature and extent of a leader's depravity. Such knowledge can itself be an alienating factor. The mere fact that a person has had the power to act on his darkest fantasies without—for a time—reprisal separates the murderous dictator from the rest of us.

Such people need others acting with complicity, often in large numbers, to carry out their depredations, but it is the leader himself (nearly always male) who bears the full onus of the atrocities—in the public mind if not legally. For the rest of us, especially those outside the sphere of operation, the murderous dictator is an inexplicable and alien being. Distance from the worst of the worst of humanity seems built in for those of us fortunate enough to be outside the ambit° of their power to do harm.

The Serial Killer

People who commit murder repeatedly, depending on their methods and numbers of victims, are outside our normative moral framework.

The enormous industry that has developed over the last twenty-five years devoted to mythologizing the serial killer in America through novels, movies, and television programs has had the effect of creating a new

---

ambit: the range or limit that is covered by something (such as a law).

kind of outlaw (a somewhat perverse replacement for the defunct Western gunslinger); it has exaggerated in the popular mind both the number of such killers and the number of their victims; and it has made it harder for us to see through the various constructions to the people who actually commit multiple murders. As Philip Jenkins comments,

From being a person whose sickness derived from family or social circumstances, the serial killer of the 1980s was increasingly seen as a ruthless incomprehensible monster undeserving of sympathy and meriting only destruction. . . .

The monstrous is even more titillating when it involves forbidden practices, such as occult rituals or cannibalism. "In constructing the characteristics of dangerous outsiders, tales and legends usually focus on their supposed inversion of normal culture," Jenkins notes. Serial killers capture the public imagination for many reasons, but one of them is surely that, until apprehended, such people represent an atavistic° terror of the secret and secretive predator among us, able to strike at any time. The real and justified fear communities feel when, for example, young women or children are going missing, lends itself easily to the construction of the predatory monster, the Other in its most threatening form.

The Ideological Killer

People who commit atrocities for religious or ideological reasons are outside our 20 *normative moral framework.*

Finally, there are ideological killers, motivated by religious or political convictions that lead them to attack, sometimes suicidally, innocent people. We can distance ourselves from someone like Timothy McVeigh, who constructed and planted the bomb that blew up the federal building in Oklahoma City in 1995 with a loss of 168 lives, many of them children, because we see the appalling gap between his grievance against the U.S. Government and his attack on a building full of ordinary people. Similarly, the hijackers and pilots of the airliners that crashed into the World Trade Center towers and the Pentagon [in 2001] seemed to be motivated by such aberrant beliefs we find ourselves at a loss to see ourselves in them.

This construction of the Other runs somewhat counter to my claim that the primary marker of the extreme perpetrator is the harm done rather than motivation. Here the harm done is certainly primary; but part of the alienation we experience springs from contemplation of the fanaticism of the perpetrator. "How could anyone *do* that?" we ask. But then we find that the answer to that question is as confounding as the

atavistic: exhibiting behavior connected to a much earlier generation or time period.

act itself, given that most of us, though we may have passionately held beliefs, would not commit mass murder on their behalf. The very idea of the *fanatic* marks someone so labeled off from the normative mainstream.

Distancing strategies based on these principles (and others like them) portray the perpetrator as so different from us that we are empowered to regard the actual individual voyeuristically, titillated by accounts of his or her crimes (those trading cards!). And being so empowered, we are able to cancel out any sense of common humanity that might intrude on our objectification. Perhaps, I speculate, we need these distancing principles because we cannot countenance seeing ourselves in the lives and actions of extreme perpetrators. This is not a failure of empathy, but a genuine blocking of the imaginative processes by which we might see ourselves as potentially like them. Tithecott says, "How much easier it is to comprehend the serial killer as akin to a bolt of lightning than as something whose origin lies within histories we can write for ourselves." In contrast, forensic psychiatrist Dorothy Lewis comments that her attitude toward many of the severely damaged individuals on death rows all over the U.S. whom she has studied and extensively interviewed has been, "There but for the grace of God go I." I submit that hers is a highly unusual attitude (she notes that it differs even from that of her co-researcher, neurologist Jonathan Pincus). Most of us would recoil at the suggestion that we have anything important in common with sadistic serial murderers like Jeffrey Dahmer or John Wayne Gacy.

We could never ever do such things, we like to think. And for the most part, we are correct. But regarding the extreme perpetrator as being in a category utterly unlike us leads us to regard such persons as totally beyond the scope of our humane concern. I hasten to add that I am not recommending in any way that we should regard extreme perpetrators empathetically or that we should imaginatively try to see the world through their eyes. In fact that might be quite dangerous for our own psyches. I do recommend that we resist the distancing mechanisms that society imposes on us to the extent that we can recognize extreme perpetrators as individuals and as part of the human community regardless of their aberrant histories.

This point obviously runs counter to the tradition of regarding some 25 people as moral monsters, and dismissing them accordingly. But as Haybron points out, an ascription of evil character (as opposed to mere badness) carries with it considerable simplification of a person's actual biography. He says,

If I am correct about the simplifications involved in ascribing evil, then regarding individuals as evil amounts to treating them as moral write-offs, as monsters who are not fully human and certainly not fit for any kind of society.

But, one may ask, isn't such categorization exactly what such people deserve? Hasn't their evil behavior itself marked them irrevocably as beyond the pale of human society? Shouldn't the purpose of studying such monsters be the purely pragmatic one of learning how to protect ourselves from them?

The pragmatic purpose is certainly valid, and the point should be taken further: it is highly valuable for us to understand the family, social, and educational conditions in which moral monsters arise, insofar as any generalizations can be drawn about causation. But my point here is that, however we assess culpability and just deserts for extreme perpetrators, writing them off as outside the scope of moral regard damages *our* self-understanding. It is our ability to recognize our full human potential that is at stake.

The Human and the Humane

Though my topic here is not the culpability of people who commit atrocities, in the conditions of some people who do terrible things we do find factors that we should take to reduce their legal and moral responsibility for their actions. Virtually all of the large number of death row inmates, including juveniles, examined by Lewis and Pincus over twenty years were discovered to have brain damage caused by childhood abuse, injury, and accident. Commonly, the damage took the form of disconnecting the frontal lobes of the cerebral cortex, responsible for controlling or modulating impulses from the limbic system; the result of such damage is an inability to control impulses. Such damage can explain the extraordinarily rageful violence sometimes seen, such as extreme mutilation of already dead victims. These diagnostic facts about certain individuals do mark significant differences between us and them. Should this matter to us? Regardless of the organic condition of the brains of some extreme perpetrators, don't we still need to keep them incarcerated once they are caught lest they do further harm? Certainly. But part of the social dynamic of distancing described here is to keep the details out of sight; it is the harms caused by extreme perpetrators that allow us to construct them as alien. The factors that may explain their extraordinary behavior may at the same time go too far in mitigating it, and we need them to be as alien as possible to justify our treatment of them in our justice systems, particularly those we execute.

And yet, despite the vast difference between extreme perpetrators and the mainstream "us," there are common threads. People who do depraved and vicious acts, even on a large scale, remain, in some sense, part of the human family. There are basic universals that pertain to all human beings, and among these are the fact that we are born (our natality), we are dependent on others and live among others (our plurality), and we all die (our mortality). Other universals, such as embodiment, could be added to this list (derived from Hannah Arendt), but the point is that the minimum conception of humanity is that as human we are united in inescapable ways. The rhetoric that constructs the extreme perpetrator as an alien, as inhuman or bestial, contradicts that conception, with the consequence that while we may study our worst perpetrators, write books and make movies about them, regard them as objects of curiosity and even entertainment, our distancing strategies tend to narrow the scope of our understanding of what it means to be human.

And by thus constricting our self-understanding, we also cut off the 30
scope of our humanity, in the sense of the set of attitudes and beliefs which, when acted upon, constitute such traits as kindness and moral regard for others. This is a huge topic in itself; here I wish only to indicate that putting extreme perpetrators in the category of Other (particularly those in our own society and time) invites us to limit our moral regard to those we see more as peers and to respond with indifference to cruelties visited upon those outside that circle. It also blinds us to the origins of evil in our own humanity. In [Dostoyevsky's] *The Brothers Karamazov*, Ivan complains, "People speak sometimes about the 'animal' cruelty of man, but that is terribly unjust and offensive to animals, no animal could ever be so cruel as a man, so artfully, so artistically cruel." We do not have to be as cynical as Ivan to see that understanding ourselves as fully human includes paying attention to the details of the extremes, the Other in all its forms, as Us.

Bibliography

Arendt, H., *The Portable Hannah Arendt*, edited by P. Bachr. Penguin, New York, 2003.

Browning, C., *Ordinary Men: Reserve Police Battalion 101 and the Final Solution in Poland*. HarperCollins, New York, 1998.

Dostoyevsky, F., *The Brothers Karamazov*, trans. R. Pevear and L. Volokhonsky. Alfred A. Knopf, New York, 1992.

Haybron, D. M., "Moral Monsters and Saints." *The Monist* 85:2, April 2002, pp. 260–284.

Jenkins, P., *Using Murder: The Social Construction of Serial Homicide*. Aldine de Gruyter, New York, 1994.

Lewis, D. O., M.D., *Guilty by Reason of Insanity*. Ballantine, New York, 1998.

Tithecott, R., *Of Men and Monsters: Jeffrey Dahmer and the Construction of the Serial Killer*. University of Wisconsin Press, Madison, 1997.

Understanding the Text

1. What is the distinction that Aristotle makes between "ordinary human wickedness and bestiality" (par. 3)? Why is that distinction important? How does it connect to what Myers terms "extreme perpetrators"?

2. What are the three emphases in the theories of evil Myers refers to? How does he use them to describe approaches to extreme perpetrators?

3. Why does Myers want to examine only the actions of extreme perpetrators rather than take into account their motivations or emotions?

4. According to Myers, how have serial killers in particular captured the public's attention?

5. In your opinion, are there other types of extreme perpetrators that Myers has not included? If so, what are they? Why might Myers not have included them?

Reflection and Response

6. Myers quotes Richard Tithecott as saying, "With our condemnation of Dahmer as evil, we say, simply, *he happened*: there is no need to explain the crime, to speculate about context, only to deal with him, the criminal" (par. 5). What, according to Myers, are the "undesirable consequences" that might result from this attitude? Does the public put itself more at risk by ignoring the motivations of the extreme perpetrator or not? Support your response with specific details.

7. Myers calls the serial killer "the Other in its most threatening form" (par. 19). Do you think this characterization is appropriate? Why or why not?

Making Connections

8. Myers alludes to a number of people from the twentieth century, including Lavrenty Beria, Pol Pot, and Heinrich Himmler, among others. Choose one of these people and research how he is an extreme perpetrator, committing crimes beyond the norm of conventional murderers.

9. Describe the ways in which our culture has created an industry devoted to "mythologizing the serial killer" (par. 19). How is this phenomenon like or unlike our treatment of celebrities? In what ways does publicity help or hurt extreme perpetrators — and us? Use research to support your response.

10. Myers quotes Ivan from *The Brothers Karamazov*: "People speak sometimes about the 'animal' cruelty of man, but that is terribly unjust and offensive to animals, no animal could ever be so cruel as a man, so artfully, so artistically cruel" (par. 30). Research how different thinkers, writers, and artists have attempted to explain the human capacity to commit evil. Which ones seem more persuasive to you? Why?

Why We Still Need Monsters

Kevin Berger

Shots ring out, people fall, and another mass murder is in the news. Is the killer a monster? What do we mean by "monster," and is the word adequate to describe the shooter? Kevin Berger conducts an interview with Stephen T. Asma, a professor of philosophy at Columbia College Chicago. Asma remarks on the historical definition of monster, what the monster means today, the origins for our fears and understanding about people who behave monstrously, and the neuroscience behind fear. Asma is the author of *On Monsters* (2009) and "Monsters and the Moral Imagination" (p. 59). Berger is the feature editor for *Nautilus*, an online and print magazine covering the world of science and culture. This interview was published on October 19, 2017, as part of an issue that focused on the theme "Monsters: Imagination's Borders."

It doesn't seem enough to call Stephen Paddock, who killed 58 innocent people in Las Vegas this month, a monster. The term has lost its power to evoke the unimaginable. The beasts that terrorized the mental lives of our ancestors have been tamed by religion and culture, notes Stephen T. Asma this week in a *Nautilus* essay, "Why Are So Many Monsters Hybrids?" So what do we call Paddock?

Asma, a professor of philosophy at Columbia College Chicago, and author, most recently, of *On Monsters* and *The Evolution of Imagination*, says the term "monster" is not ready to be retired. The moniker suits Paddock, he says. "Monster is a term we reserve for people who cannot be negotiated with. It's almost impossible, if not impossible, to understand their behavior, their motives, their mind. Our regular theory of mind doesn't work on these people."

In a ranging interview with *Nautilus* about mythic and real monsters, Asma talked about the evolutionary origin of werewolves and the psychological fears that give rise to tyrannous leaders. Asma lived in Cambodia for a while and learned about the monstrous rule of Pol Pot. He offered his view of what appeals to Americans about Donald Trump. We delved into the roles that desire and repulsion play in our conceptions of monsters, and why he disagrees with neuroscientist Lisa Feldman Barrett about the source of emotions.

Given the strange and gruesome tales in his chosen field of study—"You definitely want to wait until you have tenure before you write a book on monsters," the philosophy professor says wryly—Asma

was invariably amiable in conversation. He is the cheerful amanuensis°
of humanity's darkest fears.

BERGER: What is a monster?   5

ASMA: It's from a Latin word, *monstrare*, to warn. If you look at
early uses of the term and concept, particularly in Greek
and Roman cultures, it was applied to something like a
baby born as a conjoined twin or missing a limb or with
extra limbs. These were thought to be monsters. The
Greeks called them *teratos*. They thought they were horrifying punishments for immoral activity—a theme the
medieval Christians jumped on and articulated. It was
a sign that things were going to be bad for the state, or
for this particular emperor, or this particular battle. It's a
mix of natural calamity and supernatural significance.

BERGER: Are monsters a manifestation of repulsion?

ASMA: Yes, there's always an emotional or affective component
to it. An interesting philosopher named Noel Carroll
argues that when you look at monsters, particularly
modern monsters of horror genres, you'll see they're
oozing slime or have extra appendages and tentacles.
There's something violating our sense of bodily barriers
or bodily limits. That tends to activate the disgust emotion. That's also why monsters are so useful politically.
When a culture is about to go to war it demonizes or
monsterizes the other group. That requires casting them
as uncivilized and disgusting. You target their sexual
hygiene, for example. You target them as objects of disgust.

BERGER: So in sociological terms, monsters are the "out group"?

ASMA: Right, you're different from us. There's a xenophobia°   10
running through the whole history of monsters. If you're
different from us, we'll have a disgust-response or will be
afraid and on guard. You see that in the ancient world.
You see it through the medieval period and all the way
up to the present, in the way we cast our enemies.

BERGER: Did religion play a role in the concept of monsters?

ASMA: Religion never just builds a pantheon of gods. It always
builds the gods as the response to a threat structure,
which is going to be a monster story of some kind. If

amanuensis: an assistant, usually for a writer or artist.
xenophobia: fear of outsiders or foreigners.

you look at the earliest stories, whether it's in Hindu, Chinese, or Mesopotamian literature, like Gilgamesh, you always confront a monster-hero or hero-monster. This must be part of an adaptive strategy for building fictive kin groups. How do you get cooperative groups among large numbers of people who aren't blood relations? You've got to have these narratives.

BERGER: Do monsters have an adaptive function?

ASMA: From the point of view of evolution, casting others as monsters would have been extremely adaptive and helpful to your own survival as a group. Nature was not a warm and fuzzy place. Some of these horror stories were helpful in getting you to be nervous about real predators—both non-human animals and human predators. The traditional werewolf story was very strong in Europe. That makes sense because wolves in northern Europe, as they evolved, were a predator for Europeans. There's a werebear tradition in the Americas because Native Americans were worried about real bears and violence through bear predation or bear attacks. If you look at the monsters of these ecologies or environments, you'll see they share a transformational function. The animal that you can become, or that you should be afraid of, is the local predator.

BERGER: You write there's another side to the story. What's that?   15

ASMA: It's an interesting thread that doesn't get a lot of attention. It's not xenophobic but xenocurious. A classic example is from St. Augustine. He knows monsters are supposed to be living in Africa and the East. This includes Cyclops; the cynocephali, the dog-headed men; and the blemmyes, which had no head, but their face appears in their chest. Everybody thinks these monsters are evil incarnate, the children of Cain, stake them in the heart, that's the end of it. But Augustine stresses the "wondrous" aspects of these creatures. He says, "These guys are scary, but if we can talk to them, and they demonstrate some kind of rationality, they might be capable of being saved, they could be part of redemption."

BERGER: How's this tradition been passed down over the years?

ASMA: It's the project of Western liberalism to increase the circles of tolerance to those who are different from you. From the modern liberal point of view, having disgust toward strangers is a terrible thing. You shouldn't monsterize or demonize others, you shouldn't feel disgust toward them. That's one way to interpret *Frankenstein*. When they teach *Frankenstein* in high schools, they teach it as a way to show that you create aggression and violence by not welcoming difference into your group. It's a liberal interpretation of the monster. The monster is not evil. What the monster needs is a hug, understanding, and rational negotiation.

BERGER: When did monster become a term for a person?

ASMA: That's a really interesting issue. There's a few threads we 20 could trace. One is from the ancient Greeks, who had a notion of monstrous desire. You could have a desire in you that was so overwhelming that it would alienate you from yourself. The reason why Medea kills her children, the reason why this person slays that person, or love drives you insane, is because Eros made you do monstrous things. It was a possession from within. It's a psychological ability that you failed to educate properly. I think that thread goes all the way to Freud and the idea of an id being who we are deep down. There's a part of us all that has to be carefully managed. Otherwise it does psychopathological actions. You see this now with the Las Vegas shooter. We want to know why he did it. Is there some part of ourselves that if we don't manage it correctly, it could, in fact, lead us to some kinds of behaviors like this?

BERGER: Would you call Stephen Paddock, the Las Vegas killer, a monster?

ASMA: Yes. And that's where the term "monster" still does good work. It applies to a category of monster we can't understand. It's like, "I can't even process this. This makes no sense to me."

BERGER: How does the term "monster" do good work?

ASMA: A lot of people think, "Well, a monster is an old word that needs to go away entirely, and what you have to do is understand people and what makes them tick." I'm of the view that monster just still does good work as a term when you get to somebody like Stephen Paddock. One of the things about a monster is that it's not someone you can negotiate with rationally. You might find common ground with an enemy. Maybe your enemy hates you. Maybe it's economically based. Monster is a term we reserve for people who cannot be negotiated with. It's almost impossible, if not impossible, to understand their behavior, their motives, their mind. Our regular theory of mind doesn't work on these people. Monster has negative connotations, and that has to be talked about. But in this case it's perfectly appropriate to use it.

BERGER: Do we simply have to be content with the fact that human beings can be monstrous? 25

ASMA: It's a hard question. I interviewed a judge who's spent the last 30 years dealing with some of the most heinous criminals that we read about in the newspaper. The same goes for my brother, who's an investigator for a public defender. Both have told me that when you're interviewing somebody who's been arrested for killing his children or some other horrible act, once you start talking with him, it becomes very hard to see them as monsters.

I remember my brother telling me about this guy who's supposed to be a monster. After a few hours, they get onto music. It turns out they have common music tastes. Maybe they share a smoke. All of a sudden you're in this human relation with them that is natural. That really modifies this tendency to see this person as just a monster.

The judge made this distinction. He said, "I think their actions are monstrous, but I don't think of the person as monstrous." I think the law makes a further distinction. There's a category in jurisprudence where they say, "OK, you got drunk or high on something, and been angry and then committed some horrible murder."

There's another category of person recognized in U.S. common law with this wonderful term, which sounds very 19th-century; they say this person has a "malignant heart." That's actually a legal term, since it is part of the common law definition of "malice" and appears in the California Penal Code. It means it's a character issue. This person intends and possibly enjoys the pain of another person. I think it's interesting the law recognizes that there's some people who are just rotten and have to be contained. They didn't just have a monstrous moment or commit a monstrous act. These are the monsters.

BERGER: But can we separate a person from his or her actions?   30
There's only one brain behind both.

ASMA: Yeah, these are folk categories, I guess. But folk categories often dominate in the law. On the other hand, if I just go the route of neuroscience, I can see myself quickly tipping toward determinism. If we went into somebody like Stephen Paddock's brain, are we going to find a tumor? The fact that no other motive is popping up might make me tilt in that direction. Perhaps there was something like this. The jury's still out. We need more information.

But you're right: Is there a sense in which a heinous activity can't be separated out from the person, or the person can't be separated out from the sum of their actions? On the other hand, we do need some distinction between somebody who does something in a state of temporary loss of self control vs. somebody who is premeditating and working out in detail some nefarious act. That's why terms like "character" still do good work in the humanities. In terms of neuroscience, yeah, there isn't going to be a separate homunculus in the brain, but there might be some story to be told about failures of the impulse control system.

BERGER: Do you think every human being is capable of being monstrous?

ASMA: I think every person is capable of committing monstrous acts, but true monsters are quite rare. Our Darwinian inheritance provides all of us with adaptive forms of aggression, but the nurture of caregivers and cultural education tempers and domesticates our predatory tendencies. Failures of parenting and cultural education, together with brain anomalies, are usually in the background of psychopathic personalities. Having said that, certain ideologies like jihadism or imperialism can re-educate an otherwise compassionate person into a monster. Bad ideas can redirect our pro-social emotions, and create a malignant heart.

> "I think every person is capable of committing monstrous acts, but true monsters are quite rare."

BERGER: Who or what's responsible for monstrous leaders?   35

ASMA: There's something about the tyrannical man that's attractive to people who feel under threat, or in a body politic that feels under threat. You see this time and again. Sociologists and anthropologists call it the "big-man phenomenon." A lot of them agree that when a group feels under threat and their basic needs are not being met, a really charismatic, tyrannical person rises to the top. You saw this with Hitler. You saw it with Stalin. I've lived in Cambodia and know a lot about the Khmer Rouge story and Pol Pot. But even Plato said the same thing in *The Republic*.

What's interesting is it's hard to critique, or counter-weight, because the tyrant, or monstrous leader, only has to be aggressive. That's his whole job. If you complain that he's irrational or not making sense, or hard to coop-erate with, it doesn't matter. Those are the "virtues" of the monstrous leader. Take Donald Trump's thing with "Little Rocket Man," as he now calls Kim Jong-un. The appeal of Trump, I think, for his supporters, is Trump now looks crazy, and so maybe other big men, big chiefs, will recog-nize and respect another crazy man. This could actually have a deterrent effect. It could also be part of the explanation of why a monstrous leader stays in power.

BERGER: What do you mean when you write monsters have a moral purpose?

ASMA: Monsters can be part of the moral imagination as a way to define what we don't want to be. An obvious case would be a jihadi, who cuts off the head of a journalist. But there's also subtle permutations like Ebenezer Scrooge. Our literature and culture creates icons of immorality, and they help shape our behavior and our thinking. A lot of people enjoy horror like *The Walking Dead* because it's a form of rehearsal. I'm not expecting a zombie apocalypse, but I do wonder what would hap-pen if the grid went down and we had no electricity and suddenly there's a food shortage. What would happen if modern society came to some screeching halt? Many of the monster scenarios would be a surrogate training for what could happen between human beings.

BERGER: What is your monster?   40

ASMA: I'm afraid of deep or murky water. It's almost a paralyzing fear because I fear sea monsters, which is an utterly irrational and ridiculous fear. It's made me wonder what's going on.

BERGER: So, what's going on?

ASMA: When you study philosophy, there's this bias in the field against irrationality. Once it works out the kinks, rationality is supposed to be the great light of the psyche. It shines in and clarifies supernaturalism and irrational fears. All you have to do is train your mind well and you'll be able to clean out the basement of the psyche using the bright light of reason. I began to realize that is just not right. Reason is not the great operating system. It is built on a much bigger and older operating system, which is the emotional operating system. There's a lot of research showing that rational or cognitive behavioral therapy does little to help people get over real, debilitating phobias. It really appears to be something else or something deeper.

BERGER: What's the seat of that paralyzing fear?

ASMA: I think the full story will not be told for another decade 45
or two, but I do think work by affective neuroscientists like the late Jaak Panksepp, Antonio Damasio, Kent Berridge, and Richard Davidson, is getting us there. These thinkers believe there's an innate emotional wiring that is flexible enough to grab onto different things and experience. I think that view is right, although it's currently under critique by people like Lisa Feldman Barrett. But I really disagree with her theory of constructed emotions. I think she's way too up in the conceptual space of the mind.

BERGER: Her view is emotions aren't readymade circuits in the brain triggered by experiences. They're constructions, the brain's way of making sense of the world.

ASMA: Yeah, and I think what she's describing makes sense for a certain domain of mental life, namely a rarefied human domain of mental life. But I'm too much of a Darwinian about the mind to think this is how most of our emotions happen. There are more subtle kinds of emotions, the sense of angst or ennui, or other language based emotions, that might fit well with Barrett's view. But I think, homologously,° we share basic affective°

---

homologously: having the same structure or relation to something else.
affective: related to mood or feeling.

systems with other mammals. She denies this and that's where I just disagree. She intellectualizes emotions so much—seeing them as concepts—that she cannot explain animal emotion or emotion in babies. Ultimately, the story of fear, phobia, and horror has to be rooted in the more ancient emotional systems.

BERGER: How did monsters lead you to writing about imagination?

ASMA: I'd been thinking a lot about images. Long before we had written language and stories, we had images in our brains as a result of perception. We must have been engaging in a kind of communication with images and with bodily gestures before we had language. This got me thinking about how old the imagination is. Is it something that comes along after language, or were we able to communicate with images long before we had language? I feel like there are many ways of having knowledge and communicating with others that's non-linguistic, that has to do with body gesture, in the form of dance, or in the course of drawing or imagery, like cave paintings at Lascaux or Chauvet. There's a whole language of the imagination and a life of the mind that preexisted propositional thinking.

BERGER: Does that ancient imaginative life still exist within us? 50

ASMA: My view is we still have it, yes. It's obscured by the dominance of propositional thinking. We're very executively organized in our brains now. That's what you're doing when you raise a kid. You're sculpting a neocortical operating system over the mishmash of much more associational motor perceptual processes. We're all taught how to discipline our minds just like we're taught to discipline our behavior. But we can, in the course of creative activities like the arts, shut off that neocortical editor and take little field trips to this earlier form of mind.

BERGER: What would you be if you weren't a philosophy professor?

ASMA: I'm torn because my allegiances are equally divided between music and visual art, but I would definitely be some kind of an artist. I still am an artist. I just don't get paid much for it anymore.

Understanding the Text

1. What is the relationship between the classical understanding of monsters and the later medieval Christian church's understanding?

2. On October 1, 2017, Stephen Paddock opened fire on a large crowd attending a country music festival on the Las Vegas Strip, killing 58 and wounding more than 850 other people. What is necessary for a person to be considered a monster, according to Asma, and does Paddock fit that definition? Why?

3. What does Asma mean by "propositional thinking" (par. 49)? Explain.

4. This work is an interview presented in a question-and-answer format. What are the benefits of such a format? What are the drawbacks?

Reflection and Response

5. Asma states that the origin of the word *monster* is from a Latin word meaning "to warn" (par. 6). How does this origin fit with your understanding of monsters? Give examples.

6. Asma states: "It's the project of Western liberalism to increase the circles of tolerance to those who are different from you. From the modern liberal point of view, having disgust toward strangers is a terrible thing. You shouldn't monsterize or demonize others, you shouldn't feel disgust toward them" (par. 18.) Do you agree or disagree with this statement? Support your answer with specific examples.

Making Connections

7. In paragraph 43, Asma states that "rationality is supposed to be the great light of the psyche." Research the relationship between irrationality — such as fear of monsters — and rationality. Argue what the role of the monster is in a world that is supposedly understood best by rational inquiry. You might begin by investigating the work of the neuroscientists cited by Asma in paragraph 45.

8. Asma argues that monsters have a moral purpose. Research a monster — either fictional or real life, contemporary or historical — and argue how it serves (or served) a moral purpose within its culture. Be sure to define what you specifically mean by "moral purpose."

9. Stephen King (p. 16) argues that we need monsters, and Asma echoes the same need. Create your own argument for why we do or do not need monsters. Use multiple examples of fictional or real-life monsters in your response.

Sentence Guides for Academic Writers

B eing a college student means being a college writer. No matter what field you are studying, your instructors will ask you to make sense of what you are learning through writing. When you work on writing assignments in college, you are, in most cases, being asked to write for an academic audience.

Writing academically means thinking academically — asking a lot of questions, digging into the ideas of others, and entering into scholarly debates and academic conversations. As a college writer, you will be asked to read different kinds of texts; understand and evaluate authors' ideas, arguments, and methods; and contribute your own ideas. In this way, you present yourself as a participant in an academic conversation.

What does it mean to be part of an *academic conversation*? Well, think of it this way: You and your friends may have an ongoing debate about the best film trilogy of all time. During your conversations with one another, you analyze the details of the films, introduce points you want your friends to consider, listen to their ideas, and perhaps cite what the critics have said about a particular trilogy. This kind of conversation is not unlike what happens among scholars in academic writing — except they could be debating the best public policy for a social problem or the most promising new theory in treating disease.

If you are uncertain about what academic writing *sounds like* or if you're not sure you're any good at it, this booklet offers guidance for you at the sentence level. It helps answer questions such as these:

> How can I present the ideas of others in a way that demonstrates my understanding of the debate?
>
> How can I agree with someone, but add a new idea?
>
> How can I disagree with a scholar without seeming rude?
>
> How can I make clear in my writing which ideas are mine and which ideas are someone else's?

The following sections offer sentence guides for you to use and adapt to your own writing situations. As in all writing that you do, you will have to think about your purpose (reason for writing) and your audience (readers) before knowing which guides will be most appropriate for a particular piece of writing or for a certain part of your essay.

The guides are organized to help you present background information, the views and claims of others, and your own views and claims — all in the context of your purpose and audience.

Academic Writers Present Information and Others' Views

When you write in academic situations, you may be asked to spend some time giving background information for or setting a context for your main idea or argument. This often requires you to present or summarize what is known or what has already been said in relation to the question you are asking in your writing.

SG1   Presenting What Is Known or Assumed

When you write, you will find that you occasionally need to present something that is known, such as a specific fact or a statistic. The following structures are useful when you are providing background information.

As we know from history, _____.

X has shown that _____.

Research by X and Y suggests that _____.

According to X, _____ percent of _____ are/favor _____.

In other situations, you may have the need to present information that is assumed or that is conventional wisdom.

People often believe that _____.

Conventional wisdom leads us to believe _____.

Many Americans share the idea that _____.

_____ is a widely held belief.

In order to challenge an assumption or a widely held belief, you have to acknowledge it first. Doing so lets your readers believe that you are placing your ideas in an appropriate context.

Although many people are led to believe X, there is significant benefit to considering the merits of Y.

College students tend to believe that _____ when, in fact, the opposite is much more likely the case.

SG2 Presenting Others' Views

As a writer, you build your own *ethos*, or credibility, by being able to fairly and accurately represent the views of others. As an academic writer, you will be expected to demonstrate your understanding of a text by summarizing the views or arguments of its author(s). To do so, you will use language such as the following.

X argues that _____.

X emphasizes the need for _____.

In this important article, X and Y claim _____.

X endorses _____ because _____.

X and Y have recently criticized the idea that _____.

_____, according to X, is the most critical cause of _____.

Although you will create your own variations of these sentences as you draft and revise, the guides can be useful tools for thinking through how best to present another writer's claim or finding clearly and concisely.

SG3   Presenting Direct Quotations

When the exact words of a source are important for accuracy, authority, emphasis, or flavor, you will want to use a direct quotation. Ordinarily, you will present direct quotations with language of your own that suggests how you are using the source.

X characterizes the problem this way: ". . ."

According to X, _____ is defined as ". . ."

". . . ," explains X.

X argues strongly in favor of the policy, pointing out that ". . ."

Note: You will generally cite direct quotations according to the documentation style your readers expect. MLA style, often used in English and in other humanities courses, recommends using the author name paired with a page number, if there is one. APA style, used in most social sciences, requires the year of publication generally after the mention of the source, with page numbers after the quoted material. In *Chicago* style, used in history and in some humanities courses, writers use superscript numbers (like this[6]) to refer readers to footnotes or endnotes. In-text citations, like the ones shown below, refer readers to entries in the works cited or reference list.

MLA	Lazarín argues that our overreliance on testing in K-12 schools "does not put students first" (20).
APA	Lazarín (2014) argues that our overreliance on testing in K-12 schools "does not put students first." (p. 20)
Chicago	Lazarín argues that our overreliance on testing in K-12 schools "does not put students first."[6]

Many writers use direct quotations to advance an argument of their own:

> Standardized testing makes it easier for administrators to measure   Student
> student performance, but it may not be the best way to measure it. Too much   writer's Idea
> testing wears students out and communicates the idea that recall is the
> most important skill we want them to develop. Even education policy advisor   Source's
> Melissa Lazarín argues that our overreliance on testing in K-12 schools "does   Idea
> not put students first" (20).

SG4   Presenting Alternative Views

Most debates, whether they are scholarly or popular, are complex — often with more than two sides to an issue. Sometimes you will have to synthesize the views of multiple participants in the debate before you introduce your own ideas.

On the one hand, X reports that _____ , but on the other hand, Y insists that _____ .

Even though X endorses the policy, Y refers to it as " . . . "

X, however, isn't convinced and instead argues _____ .

X and Y have supported the theory in the past, but new research by Z suggests that _____ .

Academic Writers Present Their Own Views

When you write for an academic audience, you will indeed have to demonstrate that you are familiar with the views of others who are asking the same kinds of questions as you are. Much writing that is done for academic purposes asks you to put your arguments in the context of existing arguments — in a way asking you to connect the known to the new.

When you are asked to write a summary or an informative text, your own views and arguments are generally not called for. However, much of the writing you will be assigned to do in college asks you to take a persuasive stance and present a reasoned argument — at times in response to a single text, and at other times in response to multiple texts.

SG5   Presenting Your Own Views: Agreement and Extension

Sometimes you agree with the author of a source.

X's argument is convincing because _____.

Because X's approach is so _____, it is the best way to _____.

X makes an important point when she says _____.

Other times you find you agree with the author of a source, but you want to extend the point or go a bit deeper in your own investigation. In a way, you acknowledge the source for getting you so far in the conversation, but then you move the conversation along with a related comment or finding.

X's proposal for _____ is indeed worth considering. Going one step further, _____.

X makes the claim that _____. By extension, isn't it also true, then, that _____?

_____ has been adequately explained by X. Now, let's move beyond that idea and ask whether _____.

SG6   Presenting Your Own Views: Queries and Skepticism

You may be intimidated when you're asked to talk back to a source, especially if the source is a well-known scholar or expert or even just a frequent voice in a particular debate. College-level writing asks you to be skeptical, however, and approach academic questions with the mind of an investigator. It is OK to doubt, to question, to challenge—because the end result is often new knowledge or new understanding about a subject.

Couldn't it also be argued that _____?

But is everyone willing to agree that this is the case?

While X insists that _____ is so, he is perhaps asking the wrong question to begin with.

The claims that X and Y have made, while intelligent and well-meaning, leave many unconvinced because they have failed to consider _____.

A Note about Using First Person "I"

Some disciplines look favorably upon the use of the first person "I" in academic writing. Others do not and instead stick to using third person. If you are given a writing assignment for a class, you are better off asking your instructor what he or she prefers or reading through any samples given than guessing what might be expected.

First person (I, me, my, we, us, our)

I question Heddinger's methods and small sample size.

Harnessing children's technology obsession in the classroom is, I believe, the key to improving learning.

Lanza's interpretation focuses on circle imagery as symbolic of the family; my analysis leads me in a different direction entirely.

We would, in fact, benefit from looser laws about farming on our personal property.

Third person (names and other nouns)

Heddinger's methods and small sample size are questionable.

Harnessing children's technology obsession in the classroom is the key to improving learning.

Lanza's interpretation focuses on circle imagery as symbolic of the family; other readers' analyses may point in a different direction entirely.

Many Americans would, in fact, benefit from looser laws about farming on personal property.

You may feel as if not being able to use "I" in an essay in which you present your ideas about a topic is unfair or will lead to weaker statements. Know that you can make a strong argument even if you write in the third person. Third person writing allows you to sound more assertive, credible, and academic.

 Presenting Your Own Views: Disagreement or Correction

You may find that at times the only response you have to a text or to an author is complete disagreement.

X's claims about _____ are completely misguided.

X presents a long metaphor comparing _____ to _____; in the end, the comparison is unconvincing because _____.

It can be tempting to disregard a source completely if you detect a piece of information that strikes you as false or that you know to be untrue.

Although X reports that _____, recent studies indicate that is not the case.

While X and Y insist that is _____ so, an examination of their figures shows that they have made an important miscalculation.

SG8   Presenting and Countering Objections to Your Argument

Effective college writers know that their arguments are stronger when they can anticipate objections that others might make.

Some will object to this proposal on the grounds that _____.

Not everyone will embrace _____; they may argue instead that _____.

Countering, or responding to, opposing voices fairly and respectfully strengthens your writing and your *ethos*, or credibility.

X and Y might contend that this interpretation is faulty; however, _____.

Most _____ believe that there is too much risk in this approach. But what they have failed to take into consideration is _____.

Academic Writers Persuade by Putting It All Together

Readers of academic writing often want to know what's at stake in a particular debate or text. Aside from crafting individual sentences, you must, of course, keep the bigger picture in mind as you attempt to persuade, inform, evaluate, or review.

SG9   Presenting Stakeholders

When you write, you may be doing so as a member of a group affected by the research conversation you have entered. For example, you may be among the thousands of students in your state whose level of debt may change as a result of new laws about financing a college education. In this case, you are a *stakeholder* in the matter. In other words, you have an interest in the matter as a person who could be impacted by the outcome of a decision. On the other hand, you may be writing as an investigator of a topic that interests you but that you aren't directly connected with. You may be persuading your audience on behalf of a group of interested stakeholders—a group of which you yourself are not a member.

You can give your writing some teeth if you make it clear who is being affected by the discussion of the issue and the decisions that have or will be made about the issue. The groups of stakeholders are highlighted in the following sentences.

Viewers of Kurosawa's films may not agree with X that _____.

The research will come as a surprise to parents of children with Type 1 diabetes.

X's claims have the power to offend potentially every low-wage earner in the state.

Marathoners might want to reconsider their training regimen if stories such as those told by X and Y are validated by the medical community.

SG10 Presenting the "So What"

For readers to be motivated to read your writing, they have to feel as if you're either addressing something that matters to them or addressing something that matters very much to you or that should matter to us all. Good academic writing often hooks readers with a sense of urgency—a serious response to a reader's "So what?"

Having a frank discussion about _____ now will put us in a far better position to deal with _____ in the future. If we are unwilling or unable to do so, we risk _____.

Such a breakthrough will affect _____ in three significant ways.

It is easy to believe that the stakes aren't high enough to be alarming; in fact, _____ will be affected by _____.

Widespread disapproval of and censorship of such fiction/films/art will mean _____ for us in the future. Culture should represent _____.

_____ could bring about unprecedented opportunities for _____ to participate in _____, something never seen before.

New experimentation in _____ could allow scientists to investigate _____ in ways they couldn't have imagined _____ years ago.

SG11 Presenting the Players and Positions in a Debate

Some disciplines ask writers to compose a review of the literature as a part of a larger project—or sometimes as a freestanding assignment. In a review of the literature, the writer sets forth a research question, summarizes the key sources that have addressed the question, puts the current research in the context of other voices in the research conversation, and identifies any gaps in the research.

Writing that presents a debate, its players, and their positions can often be lengthy. What follows, however, can give you the sense of the flow of ideas and turns in such a piece of writing.

_____ affects more than 30% of children in America, and signs point to a worsening situation in years to come because of A, B, and C. Solutions to the problem have eluded even the sharpest policy minds and brightest researchers. In an important 2003 study, W found that _____, which pointed to more problems than solutions. [. . .] Research by X and Y made strides in our understanding of _____ but still didn't offer specific strategies for children and families struggling to _____. [. . .] When Z rejected both the methods and the findings of X and Y, arguing that _____, policy makers and health-care experts were optimistic. [. . .] Too much discussion of _____, however, and too little discussion of _____, may lead us to solutions that are ultimately too expensive to sustain.

Student writer states the problem.

Student writer summarizes the views of others on the topic.

Student writer presents her view in the context of current research.

Appendix: Verbs Matter

Using a variety of verbs in your sentences can add strength and clarity as you present others' views and your own views.

When you want to present a view fairly neutrally

acknowledges	observes
adds	points out
admits	reports
comments	suggests
contends	writes
notes	

X points out that the plan had unintended outcomes.

When you want to present a stronger view

argues	emphasizes
asserts	insists
declares	

Y argues in favor of a ban on _____; but Z insists the plan is misguided.

When you want to show agreement

agrees
confirms
endorses

An endorsement of X's position is smart for a number of reasons.

When you want to show contrast or disagreement

compares	refutes
denies	rejects
disputes	

The town must come together and reject X's claims that _____ is in the best interest of the citizens.

When you want to anticipate an objection

admits
acknowledges
concedes

Y admits that closer study of _____, with a much larger sample, is necessary for _____.

Acknowledgments (continued from page iv)

Isaac Asimov, "Robbie" from *I, Robot* by Isaac Asimov, copyright © 1950 and renewed 1977 by Isaac Asimov. Used by permission of Bantam Books, an imprint of Random House, a division of Penguin Random House LLC. All rights reserved.

Stephen T. Asma, "Monsters and the Moral Imagination." Originally published in *Chronicle of Higher Education* (2009, Vol. 56, No. 10); excerpted and reprinted by permission of the author.

Karen Backstein, "(Un)safe Sex: Romancing the Vampire," *Cineaste*, Winter 2009, pp. 38–41. Copyright © 2009 by Cineaste. Used with permission.

Beowulf. Excerpt from *A Readable Beowulf* translated by Stanley B. Greenfield, published by Southern Illinois University Press, copyright 1982. Used with permission.

Kevin Berger, "Why We Still Need Monsters," *Nautilus*, October 19, 2017, Issue 53. Copyright © 2017 by Nautilus. Used with permission.

Nick Bostrom, "Get Ready for the Dawn of Superintelligence," *New Scientist*, July 2014, Vol. 223, No. 2976. Copyright © 2014 New Scientist Ltd. First published in *New Scientist* as "We Must Prepare for Superintelligent Computers." All rights reserved. Distributed by Tribune Content Agency LLC.

Peter H. Brothers, "Japan's Nuclear Nightmare: How the Bomb Became a Beast Called Godzilla," *Cineaste*, Summer 2011, Vol. 36, Issue 3, pp. 36–40. Copyright © 2011 by Cineaste. Used with permission.

Carol Clover, "Final Girl." Republished with permission of Princeton University Press, from *Men, Women, and Chain Saws: Gender in the Modern Horror Film* by Carol Clover, copyright © 1992 by Princeton University Press; permission conveyed through Copyright Clearance Center, Inc.

Daniel Cohen, "The Birth of Monsters." Excerpted from pages 11–18 in *A Modern Look at Monsters* by Daniel Cohen, copyright 1970, 1997. Reprinted by permission of Henry Morrison, Inc.

Jeffrey Jerome Cohen, "Fear of the Monster Is Really a Kind of Desire," excerpted from pages 16–20 of "Monster Culture: Seven Theses" from *Monster Theory* edited by Jeffrey Jerome Cohen, published by University of Minnesota Press, copyright 1996; originally titled "Thesis VI: Fear of the Monster Is Really a Kind of Desire." Used with permission.

Thomas Fahy, excerpted from pages 57–62 of "Hobbes, Human Nature, and the Culture of American Violence in Truman Capote's *In Cold Blood*." Originally published in the essay collection *The Philosophy of Horror* edited by Thomas Fahy, published by The University Press of Kentucky, copyright 2010. Reprinted by permission.

Amy Fuller, excerpted from "The Evolving Legend of La Llorona." *History Today*, November 2015. Reprinted by permission.

Ted Genoways, "Here Be Monsters." Originally published in *The Virginia Quarterly Review* (Winter 2005, Vol. 81, 1–3), Copyright © 2005 by The Virginia Quarterly Review. Reprinted by permission.

Judith Halberstam, "Bodies That Splatter: Queers and Chain Saws" in *Skin Shows*, pp. 138–160. Copyright © 1995 Duke University Press. All rights reserved. Republished by permission of the copyright holder. www.dukeupress.edu.

Susan Tyler Hitchcock, "Conception." Excerpted from pages 15–39 of *Frankenstein: A Cultural History* by Susan Tyler Hitchcock, copyright © 2007 by Susan Tyler Hitchcock. Used by permission of W. W. Norton & Company, Inc.

Adolf Hitler, from *Mein Kampf*, translated by Ralph Manheim. Copyright © 1943, renewed 1971 by Houghton Mifflin Company. Reprinted by permission of Houghton Mifflin Harcourt Publishing Company. All rights reserved.

Karen Hollinger, "The Monster as Woman: Two Generations of Cat People." Originally published in *Film Criticism* (Winter 1989, Vol. 13, No. 2). Reprinted by permission of the author.

Homer, from "Book 12: The Cattle of the Sun" from *The Odyssey* by Homer, translated by Robert Fagles, translation copyright © 1996 by Robert Fagles. Used by permission of Viking Books, an imprint of Penguin Publishing Group, a division of Penguin Random House LLC. All rights reserved.

Christian Jarrett, "The Lure of Horror," *Psychologist*, Vol. 24, No. 11, November 2011, pp. 812–815. Copyright © 2011 The British Psychological Society. Reproduced with permission of The British Psychological Society through PLSclear.

Matt Kaplan, "Cursed by a Bite," excerpted from pages 136–163 from *Medusa's Gaze and Vampire's Bite: The Science of Monsters* by Matt Kaplan. Copyright © 2012 by Matt Kaplan. Reprinted with the permission of Scribner, a division of Simon & Schuster, Inc. All rights reserved.

Stephen King, "Why We Crave Horror Movies." Copyright © 1982 by Stephen King. Originally appeared in *Playboy*, 1982. Reprinted with permission. All rights reserved.

Sophia Kingshill, "Reclaiming the Mermaid," *Fortean Times*, No. 332, October 2015, extracted and adapted from *Mermaids* by Sophia Kingshill (Little Toller Books, 2015). Reprinted by permission of Little Toller Books.

Chuck Klosterman, "My Zombie, Myself: Why Modern Life Feels Rather Undead," from *The New York Times*, December 5, 2010. Copyright © 2010 The New York Times. All rights reserved. Used under license.

Elizabeth A. Lawrence, "Werewolves in Psyche and Cinema: Man-Beast Transformation and Paradox." Originally published in *Journal of American Culture*, Vol. 19, Issue 3, Fall 1996, pages 103–112; copyright 2004 by John Wiley and Sons. Reprinted by permission.

Clarisse Loughrey, "Slender Man: A Myth of the Digital Age." Originally published online in *Independent* (August 26, 2018). https://www.independent.co.uk/arts -entertainment/films/features/slender-man-film-true-story-internet-stabbing-urban -legend-horror-origins-a8508716.html. Reprinted by permission of Independent Digital News & Media Ltd.

Patrick McCormick, "Why Modern Monsters Have Become Alien to Us." Originally published in *U.S. Catholic* (November 1996, pp. 37–41). Reprinted by permission of Claretian Publications.

Erica McCrystal, "Hyde as a Monster Villain," excerpted from pages 235–239 of "Hyde the Hero: The Changing Role of the Modern-Day Monster" by Erica McCrystal, published in *University of Toronto Quarterly*, Vol. 87, No. 1, Winter 2018. Reprinted by permission of the University of Toronto Press.

William Andrew Myers, "Ethical Aliens: The Challenge of Extreme Perpetrators to Humanism." Republished with permission of Brill Academic Publishers from *Something Wicked This Way Comes: Essays on Evil and Human Wickedness*, edited by Colette Balmain and Lois Drawmer. Copyright © Editions Rodopi, 2009; permission conveyed through Copyright Clearance Center, Inc.

"Naanabozho and His Father" and "Naanabozho and the Gambler." Republished with permission of the University of Oklahoma Press from *Summer in the Spring: Anishinaabe Lyric Poems and Stories* edited and interpreted by Gerald Vizenor. Copyright © 1965 University of Oklahoma Press; permission conveyed through Copyright Clearance Center, Inc.

Ovid, "The Battle of the Lapiths and Centaurs," excerpted from Book 12 (lines 210–535) of *Metamorphoses*, "Battle of the Lapiths and Centaurs" by Ovid, translated by David Raeburn, (Penguin Books, 2004). Translation copyright © David Raeburn, 2004. Reprinted by permission of Penguin Books, Ltd.

Index of Authors and Titles